Studies in Environmental History

Series Editors
J. R. McNeill, Georgetown University
Edmund P. Russell, University of Kansas

Editors Emeritus
Alfred W. Crosby, University of Texas at Austin
Donald Worster, University of Kansas

Other Books in the Series

George Colpitts, *Pemmican Empire: Food, Trade, and the Last Bison Hunts on the North American Plains, 1780–1882*
John Brooke, *Climate Change and the Course of Global History: A Rough Journey*
Emmanuel Kreike, *Environmental Infrastructure in African History: Examining the Myth of Natural Resource Management*
Gregory T. Cushman, *Guano and the Opening of the Pacific World: A Global Ecological History*
Sam White, *Climate of Rebellion in the Early Modern Ottoman Empire*
Alan Mikhail, *Nature and Empire in Ottoman Egypt: An Environmental History*
Edmund Russell, *Evolutionary History: Uniting History and Biology to Understand Life on Earth*
Richard W. Judd, *The Untilled Garden: Natural History and the Spirit of Conservation in America, 1740–1840*
James L. A. Webb, Jr., *Humanity's Burden: A Global History of Malaria*
Frank Uekoetter, *The Green and the Brown: A History of Conservation in Nazi Germany*
Myrna I. Santiago, *The Ecology of Oil: Environment, Labor, and the Mexican Revolution, 1900–1938*
Matthew D. Evenden, *Fish versus Power: An Environmental History of the Fraser River*

(*continued after the index*)

The Ecology of War in China
Henan Province, the Yellow River, and Beyond, 1938–1950

This book explores the interplay between war and the environment in Henan Province, a hotly contested frontline territory that endured massive environmental destruction and human disruption during the conflict between China and Japan that raged during World War II. In a desperate attempt to block Japan's military advance, Chinese Nationalist armies under Chiang Kai-shek broke the Yellow River's dikes in Henan in June 1938, resulting in devastating floods that persisted until after the end of the war. Greater catastrophe struck Henan in 1942–1943, when famine took some 2 million lives and displaced millions more. Focusing on these war-induced disasters and their aftermath, this book conceptualizes the ecology of war in terms of energy flows through and between militaries, societies, and environments. Ultimately, Micah S. Muscolino argues that efforts to procure and exploit nature's energy in various forms shaped the choices of generals, the fates of communities, and the trajectory of environmental change in North China.

Micah S. Muscolino is Associate Professor of History at Oxford University.

The Ecology of War in China

*Henan Province, the Yellow River,
and Beyond, 1938–1950*

MICAH S. MUSCOLINO
The University of Oxford

CAMBRIDGE
UNIVERSITY PRESS

32 Avenue of the Americas, New York NY 10013-2473, USA

Cambridge University Press is part of the University of Cambridge.

It furthers the University's mission by disseminating knowledge in the pursuit of education, learning and research at the highest international levels of excellence.

www.cambridge.org
Information on this title: www.cambridge.org/9781107417595

© Micah S. Muscolino 2015

This publication is in copyright. Subject to statutory exception and to the provisions of relevant collective licensing agreements, no reproduction of any part may take place without the written permission of Cambridge University Press.

First published 2015
First paperback edition 2016

A catalogue record for this publication is available from the British Library

Library of Congress Cataloguing in Publication data
Muscolino, Micah S., 1977–
The ecology of war in China : Henan Province, the Yellow River, and beyond, 1938–1950 / Micah S. Muscolino (Georgetown University).
pages cm. – (Studies in environment and history)
ISBN 978-1-107-07156-8 (hardback)
1. Henan Sheng (China) – History, Military – 20th century. 2. Henan Sheng (China) – Environmental conditions. 3. Yellow River (China) – History, Military – 20th century. 4. Yellow River (China) – Environmental conditions. 5. Sino-Japanese War, 1937–1945 – Environmental aspects – China – Henan Sheng. 6. Sino-Japanese War, 1937–1945 – Environmental aspects – China – Yellow River. 7. Sino-Japanese War, 1937–1945 – Refugees. 8. Environmental degradation – China – Henan Sheng – History – 20th century. 9. Nature – Effect of human beings on – China – Henan Sheng – History – 20th century. I. Title.
DS793.H5M88 2015
940.53′1–dc23   2014027966

ISBN 978-1-107-07156-8 Hardback
ISBN 978-1-107-41759-5 Paperback

Cambridge University Press has no responsibility for the persistence or accuracy of URLs for external or third-party internet websites referred to in this publication, and does not guarantee that any content on such websites is, or will remain, accurate or appropriate.

Contents

List of Figures		page viii
List of Tables		ix
Acknowledgments		xi
List of Abbreviations		xiii
	Introduction	1
1	A Militarized River: The 1938 Yellow River Flood and Its Aftermath	21
2	Stories of Survival: Refugee Migration and Ecological Adaptation	59
3	Military Metabolism and the Henan Famine of 1942–1943	87
4	Against the Flow: Hydraulic Instability and Ecological Exhaustion	120
5	The Ecology of Displacement: Social and Environmental Effects of Refugee Migration	142
6	The Land Needs the People; the People Need the Land: The Beginnings of Post-Conflict Recovery	172
7	Reconstruction and Revolution	201
	Conclusion	236
Glossary of Chinese Characters		247
Archives		255
Bibliography		263
Index		285

Figures

Cover image: Chinese Nationalist troops in Henan's Yellow River flooded area, 1938

I.1	Henan Province	*page* 14
I.2	The Yellow River flooded area	15
1.1	The Japanese military advance in North China, Spring 1938	24
1.2	Henan's Yellow River flooded area	28
1.3	Chinese Nationalist soldiers walking barefoot through Yellow River floodwaters	29
1.4	Nationalist soldier directing laborers working on Yellow River dikes	30
2.1	Henan residents evacuating the Yellow River flooded area by boat	67
2.2	Refugees in Henan's flooded area	68
2.3	Map of central Shaanxi Province (Huanglongshan at upper right)	69
4.1	Shifts in Henan's Yellow River flooded area	123
5.1	Refugee settlers and draft animals at Huanglongshan	164
6.1	Land types in Henan's Yellow River flooded area, 1946	176
6.2	Malaria distribution in Henan Province, 1946–1947	183
6.3	Soil map of Henan's Yellow River flooded area, 1947	187
6.4	Post-conflict landscape in Henan's flooded area near Fugou	198
6.5	Yellow River floodwaters and abandoned settlements	198
7.1	Displaced people returning to Henan's flooded area	209
7.2	Tent village set up by UNRRA-CNRRA for returning refugees	210
7.3	Tractor team clearing land for cultivation	211

Tables

3.1	Price indices for wholesale goods in Henan's main counties and towns (1942 average) January 1941 = 100	*page* 103
3.2	Grain prices in Henan cities, November 1941–September 1942 Units: *Guobi yuan* per *shidan*	104
3.3	Military grain loans from armies in Henan and grain obtained by abstaining from food to assist famine relief (1 *jin* = 500 grams)	111
5.1	Refugees from Henan transported on the Long-Hai railroad, August 1942–June 1943	157
7.1	Agricultural population and cultivated area in Fugou and Xihua counties	231
7.2	Agricultural productivity per unit of area in Fugou County (*jin/mu*)	231

Acknowledgments

This book has been written for readers interested in the history of modern China, as well as those seeking to better comprehend the environmental legacies of war. In the process of bringing it to completion, many friends and colleagues in the fields of Chinese history and environmental history (along with a few who straddle both) have kindly offered me their advice and assistance. To all of them I owe a debt of gratitude.

First, I would like to express my sincerest thanks to Hou Yongjian of Shaanxi Normal University, Huang Zhenglin and Wu Pengfei of Henan University, and especially Wang Xingguang of Zhengzhou University for helping me gain access to archives on which this book is based. While I was in China, Bao Maohong, Bao Mengyin, Bu Fengxian, Cao Zhihong, Li Dahai, Miao Changhong, Pan Wei, Wang Tao, Xia Mingfang, Xu Youli Zhang Li, Zhang Ping, and Zhang Yanbin took time out of their busy schedules to make my work easier and more enjoyable. Research for this project has been generously supported by a Summer Academic Grant and a Junior Faculty Research Fellowship from the Georgetown Graduate School, as well as a Junior Scholar Grant from the Chiang Ching-Kuo Foundation. Most of the book was drafted in 2010–2011 while I was a member of the School of Historical Studies at the Institute for Advanced Study in Princeton, New Jersey, with funding provided by a Mellon Fellowship for Assistant Professors and the National Endowment for the Humanities. I thank my former chairs in Georgetown's History department, John Tutino and Aviel Roshwald, for endorsing my applications for these grants and Djuana Shields for her assistance in administering the awards.

Nicola DiCosmo was a gracious and convivial host during my year at the Institute for Advanced Study, where I was also lucky enough to befriend Juhn Ahn, John Herman, and Norman Kutcher. Susan Naquin kindly attended my seminar presentation at IAS and offered incisive feedback. William Kirby invited me to spend the 2012–2013 academic year as a visiting professor at Harvard, where Lydia Chen and the staff of the Fairbank Center for Chinese Studies provided a wonderful setting for me to finish revising the manuscript.

Acknowledgments

At the many conferences where I tested out ideas contained in this book, I benefited from the thoughtful criticism of more people than I can mention. Comments from David Biggs, Lisa Brady, Philip Brown, Yan Gao, Tait Keller, Emmanuel Kreike, Ian J. Miller, David Pietz, William Storey, and Julia Adeney Thomas were instrumental in helping me develop and refine my analysis, and Richard Tucker has supported the project from start to finish. Antonio Feros of the University of Pennsylvania, Peter Perdue of Yale University, Joanna Waley-Cohen of New York University, and Wen-hsin Yeh of the University of California, Berkeley, kindly invited me to give presentations on portions of this work. For their feedback on these talks, I thank Karl Appuhn, Shana Brown, Robert Cliver, Fabian Drixler, Siyen Fei, Feng Xiaocai, Gail Hershatter, Peter Holquist, Brooks Jessup, Rebecca Karl, Elisabeth Köll, Yang Kuisong, Christopher Leighton, Stephen MacKinnon, Man Bun Kwan, Niu Dayong, Eugene Park, Brett Sheehan, Mark Swislocki, Ying Jia Tan, Di Wang, Tim Weston, Yi-li Wu, and Angela Zito. If I have left anyone out, which I undoubtedly have, I will be sure to thank them in person.

Several colleagues read and critiqued preliminary versions of chapters. For that service, I thank Parks Coble, Jonathan Schlesinger, Keith Schoppa, and Ling Zhang. Carol Benedict, Peter LaVelle, Seung-Joon Lee, Robert Marks, Edward McCord, James Millward, Steve Phillips, and Michael Szonyi were all generous enough to give the entire manuscript a thorough reading and offer insights that did much to clarify and strengthen my arguments. I would also like to thank William Tsutsui and Rana Mitter, erstwhile anonymous reviewers for Cambridge University Press, for all of their valuable comments. I am especially grateful to J. R. McNeill, who not only read and commented on the manuscript but also enlisted the graduate students in his environmental history seminar to do the same. I am likewise indebted to the students in my own courses who read portions of the draft manuscript. Special thanks go to Clark Alejandrino, John Gregory, Jason Halub, Faisal Husain, Robynne Mellor, Yubin Shen, Yue Shi, and Yongle Xue, most of whom endured the task of reading it more than once. Any errors that remain are entirely my own.

As always, I have been blessed with the constant support of my parents and my sister. My wife, Jeong-Hyun, has given her unflagging patience and enthusiastic encouragement. This book is dedicated to her.

M. S. M.
Washington, DC

Abbreviations

AH	Academia Historica
HIA	Hoover Institution Archives
HPA	Henan Provincial Archives
IMH	Institute of Modern History Archives
MHD	Huanghe shuili weiyuanhui, *Minguo Huanghe da shiji* [Chronology of the Yellow River in the Republican period]
MHS	Minguo Huanghe shi xiezuo xiaozu, *Minguo Huanghe shi* [History of the Yellow River in the Republican period]
SJZHFZ	*Shanhou jiuji zongshu Henan fenshu zhoubao* [Weekly report of CNRRA's Henan branch office]
SPA	Shaanxi Provincial Archives
UN	United Nations Archives and Records Management Section
YRCC	Yellow River Conservancy Commission Archives
ZMA	Zhengzhou Municipal Archives

Introduction

The Second Sino-Japanese War (1937–1945) began in July 1937 when a skirmish between Chinese and Japanese armies at Marco Polo Bridge (*Lugouqiao*) outside of Beiping (known today as Beijing) escalated into full-scale warfare. The incident ignited tensions that had been mounting since 1931, when the Japanese army occupied Manchuria (China's northeastern provinces) to secure Japan's economic privileges in the region. China's Nationalist government initially pursued a policy of appeasement, while preparing for a future confrontation with Japan's more formidable military. This non-resistance stance enraged many patriotic Chinese, who viewed Japanese aggression as a national humiliation. Instead, the Nationalist regime and its leader Chiang Kai-shek made exterminating the insurgent Chinese Communist Party (CCP) first priority. Only after Chiang was kidnapped by his own troops, who favored resisting Japan over fighting the CCP, did he agree to form a united front with the Communists. With the eruption of conflict in 1937, the Nationalist regime decided it could make no further concessions and the two countries entered into total war. Japan launched a full-scale invasion southward into China marked by fierce battles and horrific violence, including the Nanjing Massacre of December 1937. After less than a year of fighting, Nationalist China stood on the brink of annihilation.

In June 1938, Nationalist armies under the command of Chiang Kai-shek broke the dikes on the south bank of the Yellow River (*Huanghe*) in northern China's Henan Province in a desperate attempt to block the Japanese assault. The river's turbid waters, not yet swollen by yearly summer rains, moved slowly at first. But floodwaters rolled steadily out of the dike opening and advanced southeast, cutting off the Japanese army's path. Only people living in the immediate vicinity received any sort of warning from the Chinese authorities. Yet the flat, alluvial plain of eastern Henan was densely covered with farm villages and fields. As rains fell and the river cascaded onward, its waters spread across the landscape. The flood coincided with the peak agricultural season, when wheat stood ripe in the fields or lay newly harvested, ready for threshing. Hesitant to abandon crops and fields, rural residents left their farms only reluctantly. Some villagers tried to build or strengthen dikes to protect their land and homes, but when waters actually came, many people decided to flee. Those not caught completely by surprise stacked their possessions on wheelbarrows and ox-carts or carried them on shoulder poles, joining the long lines of refugees. People tried to rescue young children and the aged. They tried to save tools, livestock, grain, and other belongings but there was not enough time to salvage everything. Many people drowned in the flooding; far more would succumb to illness or hunger in the difficult months and years that followed. To the east, however, the river's diversion halted the invading Japanese, who abandoned their westward march. The vital railroad junction at Zhengzhou was safe for the time being. The city of Wuhan, China's provisional wartime capital after the fall of Nanjing, won a temporary breathing spell.[1]

Perhaps the most environmentally damaging act of warfare in world history, the Yellow River's strategic diversion threw long-established water control systems into disarray, leading to floods that persisted until after World War II had come to an end. In China's Henan, Anhui, and Jiangsu provinces, wartime flooding killed hundreds of thousands of people and displaced millions.[2] Even greater catastrophe struck Henan Province in 1942–1943, when war-related floods, an El Niño event, transport disruptions, and the food energy demands of Chinese and Japanese armies stationed in the province precipitated a famine of terrific magnitude. The Henan famine of 1942–1943 led to nearly as many deaths – approximately two million – as the famous Bengal famine that occurred at nearly the same time, and millions more Henan residents migrated to escape this subsistence crisis.[3] Grappling with the consequences of flood and famine, as this book shows, became a point of contention and competition among various regimes that controlled parts of Henan at different times during the war years: the Chinese Nationalists, the Chinese Communist Party, the Japanese, and their Chinese collaborators. By exploring the history of war-induced disasters and their consequences, this book adds significantly to our understanding of the interplay between military conflict and natural environment.

Studies linking war and the environment have grown into a flourishing subfield of environmental history. Examining the ecological consequences of

---

[1] Perry O. Hanson, "A History of UNRRA's Program Along the Yellow River, Chapter I. – Background" (1947), 1–2: UN S-1021 Box 55 File 3.

[2] Dutch (2009). Several works examine the 1938 Yellow River flood primarily from the perspective of military history. See especially, Lary (2001): 191–207; Qu (2003); Lary (2004). For an illuminating cultural interpretation of the disaster, see Edgerton-Tarpley (2014).

[3] The oldest and most influential account of the Henan famine is in White and Jacoby (1980). For more recent scholarship, see Lary (2004); Wou (2007). For an effort to quantify the famine's causes and consequences, see Garnaut (2013). On the Bengal famine, see Sen (1981); Greenough (1982).

military conflict as a central element in evolving human relationships with the natural world, this scholarship captures war's importance as a distinctive force shaping environmental change, as well as the environment's role in shaping warfare. Environmental factors mold the experience of war for soldiers and civilians alike, while war and militarization transform people's relationships with the environment in enduring ways.[4]

Historians have likewise highlighted the formative significance of war and militarization in modern China's politics, economy, and culture.[5] The Sino-Japanese conflict that raged during World War II, or the "Anti-Japanese War of Resistance" (*Kang Ri zhanzheng*) as it is known in Chinese, has garnered a great deal of attention.[6] But as Ruth Rogaski points out, research on the environmental impact of the Sino-Japanese War of 1937–1945 is "long overdue."[7] This observation applies even more to the Chinese Civil War (1946–1949) between the Nationalists and Communists, which historians have written far less about.

Military and political histories of wartime China invariably mention the breaching of the Yellow River's dikes in 1938 and the Henan famine of 1942–1943, if only in passing. This book offers new perspectives on these events, and the conflicts in which they occurred, by taking an in-depth look at them through the lens of environmental history. What were the effects of warfare on China's environment and people's interactions with it? What direct impacts did fighting and the dislocations that it caused have on flora, fauna, and the land? What were the environmental effects of wartime mobilization of resources? How did war's ecological consequences shape the military and political context? How enduring were the environmental effects of war? The history that follows addresses these questions.

Given China's vast geographical scale and ecological diversity, any meaningful investigation of the environmental history of World War II and its aftermath must start from the regional or even sub-regional scale. Accordingly, this book centers on the interplay between World War II and the environment in Henan Province. The war-induced ecological disasters that Henan endured from 1938 to 1945 vividly illustrate the vulnerability of human-engineered hydraulic infrastructure and agro-ecosystems to disruption during periods of

---

[4] Tucker and Russell (2004); McNeill (2004); Bennett (2009); Closmann (2009); Pearson (2009); McNeill and Unger (2010); Pearson et al. (2010); Biggs (2011); Brady (2012).
[5] Perhaps because of a tendency to see war and transformation of nature as distinct categories, little has been written about war's environmental history in China. Notable exceptions include Elvin (2004): chapters 5, 8; Perdue (2005).
[6] Lary and MacKinnon (2001); Coble (2003); van de Ven (2003); Waldron (2003); Westad (2003); MacKinnon (2008); Lary (2010); MacKinnon et al. (2007); Peattie, Drea, and van de Ven (2010); Flath and Smith (2011); Schoppa (2011); Mitter and Moore (2011). The most authoritative overview is Mitter (2013a).
[7] Rogaski (2002): 401. Yue (2008) catalogues damage caused by the Japanese invasion in Shanxi rather than presenting a coherent environmental history.

violent conflict. Examining how Henan's rural populace lived through these massive perturbations also adds to our understanding of the complex, multifaceted experiences of military conflict in twentieth-century China by demonstrating their inextricable connections to the war's ecological impact. The Yellow River and other parts of the environment, as much as Chinese and Japanese armies, shaped the wartime experiences of Henan's rural populace. The environmental history and the social history of war illuminate one another, while making it necessary for us to rethink the boundaries between them.

As a hotly contested territory in the military struggle between Chinese and Japanese forces, Henan suffered as much human disruption and environmental damage as anywhere in China during World War II. Due to the combined trauma of Japanese invasion and war-related floods and famine, Henan had a larger refugee population than any other province. From 1937 to 1945, an estimated 14,533,200 people in Henan (43 percent of the province's total prewar population) lived as refugees for a least a time.[8] This book assesses the far-reaching consequences of Henan's wartime ecological disasters, as well as the displacement that they generated.[9] Spatially, the book focuses on the localities in eastern Henan that bore the brunt of wartime floods as well as famine. While other counties are given passing attention, most of the study centers on Henan's Zheng, Zhongmu, Weishi, Yanling, Taikang, Fugou, Xihua, Huaiyang, and Luyi counties, which from 1938 until the river's re-diversion in 1947 were the heart of the province's Yellow River flooded area (*Huangfangu*). At the same time, the narrative moves with displaced people from these counties to Shaanxi Province to the west, where hundreds of thousands of flood and famine refugees from Henan migrated during the war years.

THE ENERGETICS OF MILITARIZED LANDSCAPES

To tie together warfare, flood, and famine, this analysis of Henan's wartime ecological catastrophes and their aftermath employs an approach that traces energy flows through and between societies and environments.[10] Metabolic processes transform energy and materials, enabling biological systems (whether organisms or higher-level ecosystems) to maintain life, grow, and reproduce. Socioeconomic systems also depend on throughputs of energy and

---

[8] MacKinnon (2001): 122; Zhang (2006): 128–135. Refugee migration from Anhui, another province seriously affected by the 1938 Yellow River flood, is usefully covered by Zhang (2004).
[9] Xia Mingfang (2000a: 59–78) argues that for China's rural populace, ecological disasters that emerged as second-order effects of war were an important catalyst for refugee migration. Postwar damage estimates for Henan support this point (Chen 1986: 69).
[10] This framework draws inspiration from Fiege (2004) and Laakonnen (2004).

materials to maintain their internal structures. Exploiting various energy sources, human societies modify and manipulate land, water, plants, and animals to fulfill their needs. The concept of "social metabolism" likens this dependence to the biological metabolism of a living organism. Unlike the biological notion, this socio-ecological concept links energy and material flows to social organization. The quantity of resources used, their material composition, and sources are a function of socioeconomic production and consumption systems that vary greatly across time and space. This approach analyzes socio-metabolic patterns at different spatial, functional, and temporal scales, while also tracing their environmental consequences.[11] By seeing human societies as embedded in larger organic systems, an energy-centered approach renders legible connections between phenomena that historians conventionally see as discrete. Rather than artificially separating socioeconomic and biophysical processes, this framework highlights multifaceted interrelationships and interdependencies among societies, military systems, and environments.

Like all socioeconomic systems, militaries have metabolisms. Nature's energy makes warfare possible. Fighting and preparing for war, like all work, requires appropriating and exploiting energy. Militaries consist of agglomerations of humans, animals, machines, raw materials, logistical networks, engineering works, and many other components. No military systems can survive without energy inputs from the environment. They take in food, fuel, building materials, and other resources; they emit wastes. This book analyzes the redirection of energy flows that occurred in Henan during World War II, and recounts the massive ecological disturbances that it caused. A focus on energy and its transformations allows for a better understanding of war–environment connections than any interpretation premised on a division between the "human" and "natural." Thinking in terms of energy also makes it possible to integrate the Yellow River as an actor into the history of military conflict, for the same energy that propels rivers drives all human activities – including the waging of warfare.

Most environmental histories that employ the metabolism approach try to measure and quantify flows of energy and materials for entire societies, particularly during the industrial age. By contrast, this history offers the notion of metabolism as a conceptual apparatus to help us better comprehend environmental dimensions of war and militarization. Pivoting on the notion of energy and energy flows, the study argues that the metabolism of militaries and societies shapes the choices of commanders, the fates of communities, and the course of environmental change. Hopefully, this analytical framework can be applied to environmental histories of wars fought in other times and places. Even though specific details will differ considerably, recognizing the

---

[11] Weisz (2007): 291–292. My approach has also benefited greatly from Martinez-Alier (1987); Martinez-Alier (2007); and Fischer-Kowalski and Haberl (2007).

primacy of nature's energy for all military conflicts should open up avenues for comparative inquiry.

We conventionally define energy as the capacity to do work. Work occurs when a force acts on a body, causing it to move some distance in that force's direction. Moving an object entails doing work and expending energy. The specific amount of energy depends on the object's size, how far it moves, and the resistance that it encounters. Energy assumes many forms, all of which have the potential to do work. Capturing more of that energy and using it more efficiently enables more work to be done. On this planet, the primary source of energy is the sun. Solar energy drives energy conversions at all levels. Photosynthesis, the process by which plants capture and store solar energy as chemical energy, is central to life on earth. As Edmund Burke III explains, "All complex life forms have devised methods for accessing the solar energy stored in plants. Human metabolism allows us to unlock this store of energy either directly, by consuming plants, or indirectly, by consuming animals. Alone among other complex forms of life, humans have been able to devise means of storing and using solar energy."[12]

Two laws govern the flow of energy. The first law of thermodynamics states that energy can change from one form to another, but cannot be created or destroyed. The same amount of energy exists before and after it is transformed.[13] The second law of thermodynamics dictates that whenever energy changes forms, part of the energy becomes heat. Energy conversion is never one hundred percent efficient. Some energy always becomes heat and dissipates into the environment. No energy transformations occur without some energy being degraded from a concentrated to a more dispersed form. The functioning of complex entities involves numerous energy conversions. As energy gets converted to do work, some changes into heat. Energy transferred as heat is still energy, but no longer useful for doing work. The total quantity of energy is definite, but its quality is not. As energy conversion chains progress, potential for useful work steadily declines. Entropy measures this dissipation of useful energy.

All complex structures require energy inputs from the environment to maintain their organization and keep functioning. In a closed system, energy dissipation due to entropy will lead to loss of complexity, greater homogeneity, and more disorder. In actuality, however, most energy conversions happen in open systems that interact with the surrounding environment. Complex entities temporarily defy entropy by importing and metabolizing energy. They arise in a balance between the usable free energy in the environment, which they put to work, and the entropy they throw off. Inputs of high-quality energy make it possible for complex structures to combat decay from within. In the process, they also dissipate large amounts of energy as heat,

---

[12] Burke (2009): 35. See also White (1995): 4–5.
[13] Marten (2001): 109; Pimentel and Pimentel (2007): 9; Smil (2008): 4–5.

increasing entropy overall. As complex systems, living organisms maintain continuous energy inflows and outflows. Metabolism enables organisms to avert decay and stay alive by drawing energy from their environment, but they maintain their structures at the expense of increased contribution of entropy to the surrounding environment.[14]

To better grasp the environmental dimensions of war and militarization, we should therefore consider ways in which energy is converted for military purposes. Militaries can be thought of as organic systems that continuously interact with their environments, engaging in transfers of energy and materials. Militaries must constantly find new sources of useful energy and develop more effective mechanisms for handling large energy flows. As complex organisms, military systems extract free energy to do work and maintain their internal organization, while at the same time releasing low-level energy via entropy (waste).

The forms of energy that can support the "military metabolism" are strictly limited. Other complex systems – including agrarian ecosystems and hydraulic networks – draw on these finite energy sources as well. As it is transferred across different spatial scales, energy changes forms. But because the total amount of energy remains constant, appropriating energy in forms needed to fight or prepare for war necessarily entails losing it in others. Even when war and militarization lead economies to exploit new energy forms, they nevertheless render energy unavailable for other purposes. Militaries have to struggle for strategic advantage, as well as for energy sources that drive their metabolism. The better militaries gather, store, and deploy energy, the greater their potential for organized violence, coercion, and destruction. Military systems exploit finite sources of useful energy to maintain themselves, to do work, and expand. They also release heat, pollution, and other wastes. This waste, it should be noted, occurs at the level of ecosystems, as well as in the wastage of human bodies. Building complex military structures and expanding their realm of operations adds disorganization, chaos, and degradation to environments on which they depend.

The energy-centered approach employed in this book complements other ways of thinking about the war–environment nexus. Edmund Russell, for instance, has suggested that analyzing military supply chains as food chains "will help us uncover the indirect and hidden, but absolutely essential, links between armed forces and civilian, agricultural and natural systems." Thinking in terms of food chains, as Russell notes, demonstrates "that the area of militarized landscapes extends far beyond battlefields and bases, growing ever wider as the supply chain lengthens."[15] For ecologists, trophic pyramids represent roles of different organisms within food chains. In

---

[14] Smil (2008): 6–7; Marten (2001): 109–110; Pimentel and Pimentel (2007): 9–11; Christian (2005): Appendix II; Burke (2009): 34.
[15] Russell (2010): 237.

terrestrial ecosystems plants anchor the bottom level, herbivores the next, and predators the level above them. "Species at each level depend not only on the level immediately below them, but on *all* lower levels – though their dependence becomes less apparent as the food chain lengthens."[16]

Though Russell does not dwell on the point, it is worth stressing that trophic pyramids map *energy transfers* between producers and consumers at each step in the food chain. As he explains, "The width of the pyramid represents biomass (the weight of organisms). Transforming energy from one form to another always comes at the cost of lost energy, so the biomass of each level must always be less than that of the level below it."[17] Russell usefully applies the model of a trophic pyramid to militarization's ecological effects: "Starting at the bottom, we can label the levels natural systems, agricultural systems, political, economic and technological systems, and armed forces." Armed forces depend on political, economic and technological systems for their sustenance. "Less apparently but just as much, they rely on the agricultural and natural systems that support the political and economic systems. Moreover, since each level must harvest greater biomass than itself to survive, the impact of military consumption widens as one goes down the scale. This means that militarization grows ever more pervasive as it becomes ever less visible."[18] Fully grasping the ecological impact of warfare and militarization requires investigating energy conversions at every level of the food-web pyramid.

To expand the environmental history of warfare "beyond the battlefield" to the "host of semiperipheral contexts where war etched its distant imprint on the land," Matthew Evenden analyzes commodity chains – "the linked labor and production processes involved in the making of a commodity from production to finished good."[19] As Evenden explains in his path-breaking research on aluminum production during World War II, "Far from dividing the environmental history of the Second World War into a series of national histories, commodity chains bridge the distance between places, point up the importance and irrelevance of international boundaries, and connect social and environmental change on several spatial scales. The commodity chain thus offers a useful angle of vision to help understand the dynamics of warfare and environmental change over distance."[20] Evenden's approach examines the development of new geographies of production, military efforts to defend vital commodity chains, and environmental repercussions of these strategically important processes. As Evenden shows, wartime expansion of aluminum production increased the character and the extent

---

[16] Ibid., 236. On energy transfer within food webs, see Smil (2008): 113–118.
[17] Russell (2010): 236.
[18] Ibid., 236–237.
[19] Evenden (2011): 70.
[20] Ibid.

Introduction

of environmental effects.[21] Commodity-chain analysis highlights the "unprecedented capacity of the Second World War to gather and scatter materials with untold human and environmental consequences, linking diverse locations with no necessary former connections."[22]

As a conceptual framework for investigating links between war and the environment, commodity chain analysis also melds nicely with the mode of analysis employed in this study of World War II and its aftermath in Henan, which focuses on energy transfers to understand the ecological dimensions of war and militarization. Most significantly, for our purposes, wartime expansion of aluminum commodity chains "required massive material and energy inputs" derived from multiple world regions, from extraction of tropical soils to the damming of rivers for hydroelectricity. What is more, "These critical links in the supply chain were bound together by a fossil-fueled, long-distance transportation system."[23] Commodity chain analysis, like the concept of metabolism, directs our attention to how military systems acquire the inputs of energy and materials they need to survive and function, as well as the environmental consequences of these flows. Taking a cue from the frameworks proposed by Evenden and Russell, this study explores the history of World War II through the lens of energy conversion to better understand its environmental dimensions.

TRANSLATING ENERGY AND POWER

One does not need to impose the language of thermodynamics and ecology on the historical record to engage in this type of analysis. More than anything, the specific language employed in sources from wartime Henan drew my attention to energy. Historical actors in the Sino-Japanese War of 1937–1945 engaged in constant discussion of topics that approximate what we now think of as forms of "energy." But they did so on their own terms, utilizing their own conceptual and semantic categories. None of the archival documents and other sources related to wartime Henan that I have consulted contain the Chinese word *nengyuan*, which contemporary dictionaries gloss as the translation for the English word "energy." Yet they make constant reference to *li*, a character that connotes power and capacity to do work. Wartime documents discuss *li* in a myriad of forms. They speak of *bingli* (military power), *renli* (human power), *minli* (common people's power), *caili* (financial power), *wuli* (material power), *chuli* (draft animal power), and *shengchanli* (productive power). All these terms can be understood as specific incarnations of energy and power. The documentary record presents vivid

---

[21] Ibid., 71.
[22] Ibid., 88.
[23] Ibid., 83.

accounts of how Chinese and Japanese forces maneuvered to appropriate *li*, as well as the demands that warfare placed on finite energy sources.

The entry for *li* in the dictionary *Shuo wen jie zi* (Explaining Single Component Graphs and Analyzing Compound Characters), compiled during the Han dynasty (206 BCE–220 CE), explained the character's connotations. "*Li*: Muscle. It resembles human muscle's form. Effective governance is called *li*. It is able to defend against great disaster. Everything that is subordinate to *li* all follows from *li*."[24] This definition connected *li* with muscle power and its application to carry out work and accomplish tasks. All forms of *li*, moreover, were manifestations of a single generalized capacity. A later commentary on the entry for *li* in *Shuo wen jie zi* by the Qing dynasty (1644–1911) scholar Duan Yucai elaborated on the character's implications:

> *Li*: Muscle. Muscle is called flesh's *li*. The two seals are mutually explanatory. Muscle is its substance; *li* is its function. There are not two things. Extending this meaning, everything that vitality is capable of is called *li*. It resembles human muscle's form. It resembles its ordered pattern. Humans' pattern-principle is called *li*. Therefore, wood's pattern is called its grain. Earth's pattern is called terrain. Water's pattern is called weathering.[25]

A basic unity existed between muscle and *li*, which as substance and function were intrinsically related as ontological and functional aspects of the same entity. Muscle was original substance and *li* its function. *Li* referred to muscle put to use. *Li* flowed through human beings in the same way that physical features patterned landscapes, wood was patterned by its grain, and running water carved patterns in stone. This vital impetus underlay everything vigorous action could accomplish. *Li* was the animating force that ran through humans and the environment, constantly changing its character and manifestations, with greater and lesser concentrations appearing in different places and times.

These meanings persisted into the twentieth century, even as the character acquired additional ones. Like many other Chinese words, *li* was appropriated to translate Western scientific concepts that entered China in the late nineteenth and early twentieth century. This diffusion often occurred by way of Japan, which spearheaded translation of Western terms.[26] The entry for *li* in the dictionary *Ciyuan* (Source of Words), published in the 1930s, kept definitions contained in older dictionaries, while superimposing the newly introduced concept of "force" drawn from modern physics: "1) Muscle power. The effects of animal muscle accomplished by moving the limbs. In science, any influence that causes another object to move, rest, or change direction is called *li* ... 2) Everything that vitality is capable of is called *li* ... 3)

---

[24] Xu (121CE).
[25] Duan (1815).
[26] Weller (2006): Chapters 2–3.

That which objects are capable of is also called *li*, such as powerful writing strokes (*bili*) and horsepower (*mali*). 4) Exhausting ones power is called *li*, such as fighting vigorously (*lizhan*) or working hard in the fields (*litian*). 5) Serving others is called *li*."[27] New ways of thinking about *li* did not supplant earlier ones, but supplemented them. Here, one does not see a "break in the line" of cultural transmission, but rather an accretion of meanings. The significance attached to *li* in the documents from wartime China melded the scientific concept of "force" together with earlier ways of thinking about *li* as the capacity to do work.

The emphasis on the body and its muscular exertions that runs through these understandings of *li* resonates with what J. R. McNeill has termed the "somatic energy regime," in which energy resources came primarily in the form of human and animal muscle power. Under the somatic energy regime, more people and livestock meant more productive power. Human and animal populations were a "flywheel in the society's energy system" that could be mobilized at any time regardless of the abundance or scarcity of plant crops that were the primary source of energy. Since muscle was the main energy source, attaining power required controlling and coordinating large numbers of people and livestock.[28] The only way to achieve political dominance and military success was to direct the somatic energy regime, harness its surplus, and apply it to fuel warfare. Viewed in this way, agriculture was "a solar-energy system controlled by humans, in which the energy output of selected plants is monopolized for human purposes." States and militaries thus regarded humans as "ambulatory solar-energy storage systems."[29] Animals too were energy sources that humans could use to do work or ingest as food. Differential access to these energy sources corresponded to power differentials between groups of people.

One can therefore render *li* as power, understood as stores of energy harnessed and exploited in pursuit of human ends. Throughout World War II, Chinese and Japanese armies fought to manipulate nature's energy and deploy its power against their military adversaries. During the 1930s and 1940s, the North China Plain remained overwhelmingly an "advanced organic economy" without a significant industrial sector powered by fossil fuels. Virtually no mechanisms existed to extract and transport hydrocarbon energy, or to process it into forms useful for modern militaries.[30] Waging war

---

[27] Lu et al. (1997): 205. Comparable definitions can also be found in Shu et al. (1940): 414. Routes of transmission were complex. Liu (1995: 274, 347–348) notes that the word *lixue* (mechanics) reached Japan via missionary translator W. A. P. Martin's Chinese book *Gewu rumen* (1868) and came back to China via round-trip diffusion. She also lists a number of terms with the suffix *-li* (*-ryoku* in Japanese) that came to China by way of Japan.

[28] McNeill (2001): 11–12.

[29] Burke (2009): 36.

[30] The concept originated with Wrigley (1990). Late imperial and early twentieth-century China has been characterized as an advanced organic economy by Marks (2002) and Marks (2012).

in this particular region of China required massive concentrations of people, animals, food, and fuel in battle zones. Extracting energy stores from eastern Henan's war-ravaged environment threw fragile ecological systems into disarray and yielded catastrophic results. Framing the environmental history of World War II and its aftermath in terms of struggles over incarnations of energy and power, this book recounts how rival military forces tried to exploit ecological systems, and the distortions caused by their interventions. By relating how civilian populations endeavored to obtain energy for their own survival, moreover, this study provides insight into the social history of how residents of Henan's flooded area lived through these war-related disasters.

When referring to the Yellow River's energy, our sources do not use the word *li*. They instead employ the related character *shi* (position-power), speaking of *shuishi* (the water's position-power) or *liushi* (the flow's position-power).[31] Significantly, the explanation for the character *shi* in *Shuo wen jie zi* explicitly connects it directly with *li*: "*Shi*: Full of power and authority. It follows from *li* with *shi* as its sound (*cong li shi sheng*) ..."[32] *Shi*, in other words, referred to existence of abundant power (*li*). *Li* was the root of *shi*, both literally in terms of the character's structure and in terms of its definition. Best thought of as a kind of gradient or force-field, *shi* moved matter or objects in a particular direction, flowing easily downhill and moving uphill only at great cost. In the 1930s, *Ciyuan* still linked the definition of *shi* with *li*, glossing it as, "The power of movement. All that exerts great power is all called *shi*, such as fire's position-power and water's position-power. A state of movement is also called *shi*, such as gestures (*shoushi*) and posture (*zishi*). 2) Form; the features of the land. 3) Power (*quanli*)."[33] The river's "position-power" was a manifestation of power, a generalized vital force that impelled action. The river's energy was but one of many forms that power could take.

As power flowed through society and environment, it formed areas of stronger and weaker concentration. Gaining power in one of its incarnations necessarily led to loss in others. Understood in this way, war's environmental history involved perpetual gains and losses of energy/power among various human and non-human entities. This book narrates violent competition for energy sources between Chinese and Japanese militaries, struggles between the Nationalist regime and its subordinates at the local level, and contradictions between pursuit of immediate military advantage by unleashing the Yellow River's energies and consequent loss of power embodied in human and animal labor, agricultural output, and other resources. Focusing on flows of energy and its conversions uncovers vital connections between military, agricultural, hydraulic, and natural systems.

---

[31] My translation of *shuishi* as "position-power" follows Elvin (2004).
[32] Xu (121CE).
[33] Lu et al. (1997): 213. See also, Shu et al. (1940): 431.

Introduction

One can imagine far-reaching webs woven together by transfers of energy; various actors that struggle for power occupy and move from one node to another in these webs. Energy transfers occur across vast spaces, as military and non-military actors re-negotiate their roles and possessions. By straining one of the threads in these webs of energy transfer, actors may break another thread.

GEOGRAPHY AND ENVIRONMENT

The biophysical landscape was integral to these dramas. Henan is a province in north-central China's densely populated agrarian heartland, with an area of approximately 167,000 square kilometers. Topographically, Henan can be roughly divided into two parts: the highlands in the west and far southeast, and the vast eastern plains formed by the alluvium deposited by the Yellow River and the other waterways that run through the province. Terrain is higher in the west than the east, sloping downward from the northwest to southeast. Climatically, Henan is situated between temperate and subtropical zones, midway between the cold, dry winds of the north and the warm, moist monsoons of southern China. The province has a mild climate with sharp transitions between seasons. Precipitation levels exhibit a great deal of inter-annual variation in amount and timing. This irregularity and unpredictability means Henan is subject to alternating years of heavy rains and droughts. Average annual precipitation in Henan ranges from 600 to 1200 millimeters, but steadily increases from north to south. Rainfall displays a marked summer maximum, when 45–60 percent of all annual precipitation occurs. Winters are cold and dry; summers are hot and humid. Temperatures average 13–15 degrees centigrade, but vary widely through the year. The hottest summer months average 27–28 degrees centigrade; the coldest winter months have average temperatures around zero. Henan has a long growing season, with 210–230 days over ten degrees centigrade. Accumulated temperatures afford ample solar energy for agriculture. Henan once had considerable forest cover, but it had mostly disappeared by the early centuries of the first millennium CE as growing human populations cleared land for agriculture.[34] Dry farming predominates, with wheat, sorghum, millet, cotton, legumes, sweet potatoes, sesame, and tobacco as the main crops.[35]

Although the mild climate makes it agriculturally rich, Henan has also been prone to flooding for centuries. This vulnerability derives primarily from the Yellow River, which runs through Henan for about 700 kilometers and drains over 21 percent of its land area. The Yellow River turns eastward after its confluence with the Wei River immediately west of where Henan's borders

---

[34] Henan sheng difangshizhi bianzuan weiyuanhui (1990): 1–3, 9–10, 172–174, 180–203, 210–222; Todd (1949): 44; Zhang (2000): 21.
[35] Henan sheng difangshizhi bianzuan weiyuanhui (1990): 7; Zhang (2000): 22.

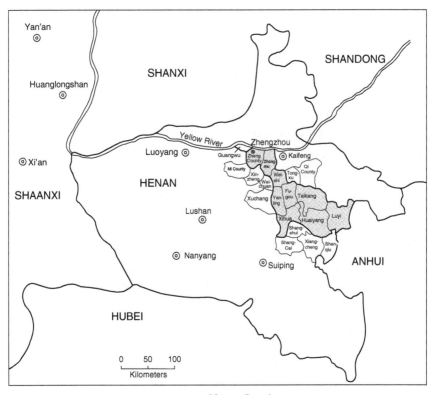

FIGURE I.I Henan Province

meet those of Shaanxi and Shanxi provinces. From there, the Yellow River enters Henan, flowing east-northeast for some 130 kilometers before issuing onto the eastern plain. Due to seasonal variations in rainfall, the Yellow River's waters swell to a torrent in summer and decrease to a mere trickle in winter. The river's discharge fluctuates widely on a seasonal basis, with floods occurring in the summer rainy season. During flood season, the river carries an enormous quantity of silt, which it gathers as it runs through the barren, deforested Loess Plateau of Shaanxi and Shanxi provinces. Every time it rains, mud streams down from eroded hillsides into the river. The river carries this sediment until it reaches Henan's eastern plain, where the river's bed widens, velocity slows, and its huge silt load settles out.[36]

In imperial times, China's state and local societies organized dike construction to contain the Yellow River and prevent it from flooding. The river deposited its silt within the dikes, causing its bed to rise above the surrounding

---

[36] Henan sheng difangshizhi bianzuan weiyuanhui (1990): 3–4, 124, 153; Todd (1949): 44; Zhang (2000): 22–24.

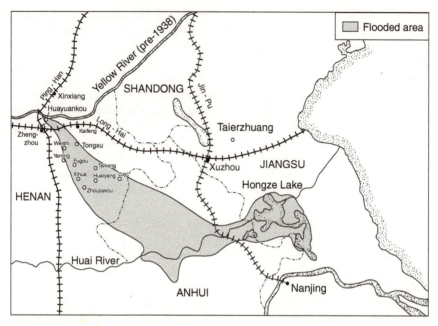

FIGURE I.2 The Yellow River flooded area

countryside. For this reason, embankments had to be built higher and higher. When the river broke through the dikes, which happened frequently, it descended onto the plain to seek a lower course and caused floods. The Yellow River has radically changed its course several times over the last three millennia, flowing to the south and then north of China's Shandong peninsula. The Yellow River moved to a lower bed each time it altered its course, usually overtaking the channels of other rivers. As the river repeatedly shifted course, its silt built up the alluvial fan that comprises Henan's eastern plain. Sediments deposited by floodwaters shaped the landscape. The plain's alluvial soils tend to be porous, granular, and poor in organic matter. Since the Yellow River's elevated bed lies above the surrounding plain, low-lying land on either side often becomes waterlogged. As a result, soil salinity and alkalinity affect many areas. Thanks to the Yellow River's sediments, moreover, from the Song dynasty (960–1279 CE) onward parts of Henan have been covered by bleak, sterile sands. During the dry and windy early-spring season, the blowing of these sands gives rise to severe dust storms.[37]

From the twelfth century onward, the Yellow River's watershed has intertwined with that of the Huai River, which originates in the Tongbai

---

[37] Henan sheng difangshizhi bianzuan weiyuanhui (1990): 4–5, 124–125, 310–327, 372–376, 397–398; Todd (1949): 44; Marks (2012): 152–156.

Mountains and flows through eastern Henan. The Huai River drains 88,310 square kilometers in Henan, or about half the province's land area, making it Henan's largest river system. The southern section of Henan's eastern plain constitutes part of the Huai River's watershed. During periods when the Yellow River's course shifted south, as it did from 1194 to 1855, it overtook tributaries of the Huai River, which flowed northwest to southeast before entering the Huai's main stream. The largest such tributary, the Shaying River, originates in western Henan's highlands and has tributaries of its own, including the Sha River, the Ying River, the Jialu River, and the Shuangji River. Northeast of the Shaying River flows yet another tributary of the Huai, the Guo River. By the time the Yellow River underwent its next great shift to the north in the mid-1850s, it caused extensive damage to the Huai River system.[38]

The arrival of railroads in Henan at the dawn of the twentieth century dramatically altered the province's socioeconomic geography. Fossil-fueled transport lines cut through the expansive agrarian landscape of the North China Plain, but they did not transform the advanced organic economy that surrounded them in terms of energy regime. Nevertheless, the railroads did much to alter production and distribution patterns. Some areas prospered and others declined. From the early 1900s, the transport of commercial products, which formerly depended on inland waterways, came to rely largely on railroads. Locales in Henan that once flourished as hubs of water transport steadily lost importance. New commercial centers such as Zhengzhou sprang up along the Ping-Han railroad, which traversed Henan from north to south, and the Long-Hai railroad, which ran east–west through the northern part of the province. Odoric Wou distinguishes between three "ecological zones" formed in Henan after the introduction of railroads: the underdeveloped west, the low-lying degenerating zone in the east, and the more developed zones located along railroads and in the northern part of the province. This study focuses primarily on the environmental history of war in the post-1938 flooded area on Henan's eastern plains.[39]

Waterways, railroads, and warfare intertwined. Henan's central geographical position has long imbued it with military significance. Strategically, armies invading from the north viewed Henan as the "gateway to central China." During the early 1900s, the Ping-Han and Long-Hai railroads crisscrossed Henan and met in Zhengzhou, which gave Henan even greater military

---

[38] Henan sheng difangshizhi bianzuan weiyuanhui (1990): 3, 255–261, 271–302; Todd (1949): 40; Pietz (2002): Chapter 1; Han (2010): 203–247; Marks (2012): 233–240. During the eighteenth century, Henan's Jialu River was an important branch in waterborne grain transport between southern and northern China. By the nineteenth century, Yellow River flooding silted up the Jialu and made it unnavigable, so shipments no longer followed the waterway. Ecological damage, combined with construction of railroads, led to the Jialu River's abandonment. Henan sheng difangshizhi bianzuan weiyuanhui (1990): 259–260; Zhang (2000): 25.
[39] Wou (1994): 15.

importance. During the Sino-Japanese War of 1937–1945, as was the case during earlier military conflicts in Chinese history, Henan's central position made it the site of pitched battles.⁴⁰ With virtually no other geographical barriers to impede armies moving across the flat North China Plain, manipulation of waterways fulfilled a vital strategic function. To slow the invading Japanese army, Chinese Nationalist armies turned to time-honored tactics in 1938 by breaching the Yellow River's dikes near Zhengzhou and diverting it south. For the next nine years, the Yellow River's waters spread to the southeast into the Huai River system via its tributaries. The starting point for this history is the counties along the Huai River's tributaries in eastern Henan, which suffered the worst effects of the resulting inundations.

In addition to the war-related ecological disasters that struck Henan, this book assesses the impact of wartime refugee flight on the landscapes where displaced people resettled. Following the path of war-induced migration from Henan's flooded area, the study's spatial scope extends west into Shaanxi's Wei River valley and the upland areas to its north, which took in hundreds of thousands of refugees from Henan during the war. The Wei River flows from west to east through Shaanxi, joining the Yellow River at the province's border with Shanxi and Henan. Since imperial times, the Wei River Valley has been part of the main transport route running from the North China Plain in the east to the Gansu (*Hexi*) corridor to the west. The city of Xi'an's geographical location – roughly in the middle of the Wei River Valley – has long made it an important transport hub. People crossed into and out of Henan during times of flood, famine, and war. Highway construction in the 1920s and 1930s, as well as the Long-Hai railroad's extension to Xi'an in 1934 and to the city of Baoji in 1938, only strengthened these ties. Given Shaanxi province's well-established connections with the North China Plain, huge numbers of flood and famine victims from Henan moved west to Shaanxi during the war, congregating in Xi'an and other parts of the Wei River Valley. North of the Wei River Valley runs a chain of mountains that includes the northwest-to-southeast Huanglongshan (Yellow Dragon Mountain) range to the east. During World War II, state-sponsored resettlement schemes brought tens of thousands of refugees into this sparsely populated upland area and thoroughly altered its landscape.⁴¹

WAR AND NORTH CHINA'S AGRICULTURAL LANDSCAPES

War and militarization exploited and disrupted Henan's human-constructed agrarian ecosystems, which also demanded huge inputs of energy. All

---

⁴⁰ Des Forges (2004); Henan sheng difangshizhi bianzuan weiyuanhui (1990): 9–10; Wou (1994): 17; Zhang (2000): 25–28.
⁴¹ Vermeer (1988): 2–5, 47–55, 70–88. See also Shaanxi sheng difangzhi bianzuan weiyuanhui (2000).

agricultural landscapes are human-made or "anthropogenic." From late imperial times, human labor sculpted China's agricultural landscapes to an unusually high degree. These hyper-anthropogenic landscapes required vigilant management, as well as constant investments of labor and resources. Without such inputs, rapid and costly deterioration followed. Given the vulnerability of human-engineered landscapes to neglect, wartime population loss brought about rapid and severe ecological decline. To put it another way, creating and maintaining agro-ecological and hydraulic systems consumed huge energy flows in the form of human labor power and materials. In the 1930s and 1940s, diversion of energy flows due to military conflict led to environmental degradation and disorder.[42] For the purposes of this history, "degradation" refers primarily to destruction of humanized, domesticated environments and their conversion into unpopulated landscapes that Chinese considered "wastelands" (*huang*).

North China's anthropogenic environments were neither purely "natural," nor entirely the product of human artifice. Rather, these human-constructed landscapes inhabited the "twilight zone between Nature and Culture" characteristic of what Emmanuel Kreike calls "environmental infrastructure." Examples of environmental infrastructure include cultivated landscapes, farms, fields, and water-management systems. Yet human agency's role in creating this infrastructure was far from absolute. Rather, as Kreike explains, "The use of the adjective 'environmental' highlights that human control, use, and agency are neither absolute nor exclusive." Humans, as environmental actors, "work *with* nature (which is at once an actor and a medium), rather than dominating nature or being dominated by nature." People have to "create, configure, maintain and remake 'environmental infrastructure' in interaction with other local, regional, and global actors, factors, and processes (for example, climate change)." Any changes in how human societies interact with and maintain their environment will have implications for the environmental infrastructure as well.[43]

During the early twentieth century, the task of maintaining North China's environmental infrastructure had come to entail mounting ecological costs. By analyzing the effects of violent conflict on these fragile landscapes, this study of Henan's flooded area stresses the importance of baselines in environmental histories of warfare. Prior to the Japanese invasion of the late 1930s, North China's environment did not exist in a pristine or "natural" condition. Centuries of intensive human exploitation and management thoroughly altered landscapes, removing forests and other vegetation to make way for farms. Ecological diversity, and hence resilience, declined. Population growth pressed resources to their limit; ecological buffers were lost. The North China Plain, according to Robert Marks, "had been heavily farmed since the Han

---

[42] Elvin (1993); Marks (2012): 336.
[43] Kreike (2006): 18–19. These ideas are refined and elaborated in Kreike (2013).

dynasty [206 BCE–220 CE] and deforested by the Song, so it is not too surprising that it would have been among the first parts of China to exhibit clear signs of environmental degradation."[44]

By the nineteenth century, North China confronted what several historians have labeled an environmental crisis. Deforestation intensified erosion and caused sediments to accumulate in the Yellow River, the Huai, and many other river systems, which necessitated higher dikes and resulted in more frequent and costly flooding. Loss of vegetation cover led to critical shortages of fuel and building materials.[45] Maintaining a balance between hydraulic and agricultural systems demanded ever greater amounts of energy. During the early twentieth century, in Lillian Li's assessment, "Environmental decline, especially the siltation of rivers, was historically unprecedented .... The cumulative effect of centuries of deforestation, intensive land use, and excessive control of rivers posed a problem of greater magnitude than had ever been experienced." The frequency and scale of flood and famine in the Republican period (1911–1949) "far exceeded anything that had occurred previously."[46] Under these conditions, the Sino-Japanese War of 1937–1945 resulted in dislocations that destabilized fragile environments and upset precarious ecological balances, triggering acute and cataclysmic shocks.

During World War II, upheavals created by the Japanese invasion and the Yellow River's strategic diversion led to large-scale population displacement that dispersed energy embodied in human labor and made intensive management of Henan's environmental infrastructure impossible. Rapid ecological damage was the result. Attaining and maintaining order in anthropogenic agro-ecological and hydraulic systems, as with militaries and other complex structures, takes energy. But energy used to maintain armies and fight wars – or energy that is dispersed due to military dislocations – cannot be utilized for other purposes. Without adequate inputs of labor and resources, Henan's agricultural and hydraulic systems quickly spiraled into disarray and recovery became nearly impossible. Military conscription drained labor power from local societies, while the army's appetite for energy took food supplies away from civilian populations. As the direction of energy flows changed, agricultural landscapes transitioned into "warscapes" transformed by destructive human action.[47] War-induced flood and famine displaced millions of people, forcing them to adapt to new environments and find ways to secure the energy they needed to stay alive. Their survival strategies had an impact on

---

[44] Marks (2012): 243.
[45] Abundant literature exists on the environmental crisis that prevailed in North China from the 1800s through the 1930s. See Pomeranz (1993); Dodgen (2001); Elvin (2004); Lillian M. Li (2007); Pomeranz (2009); Marks (2012): 235–243.
[46] Lillian M. Li (2007): 307. Su (2004) surveys flood and drought disasters in Henan during the Republican period. Oral histories and memoir literature are collected in Wen (2004).
[47] The term "warscapes" is drawn from Nordstrom (1997).

the landscape as well. Displaced people put additional pressure on scarce resources in areas of in-migration and dramatically altered environments where China's wartime state resettled refugees to reclaim wasteland for agricultural production. All these ecological changes carried deleterious consequences for the health and well-being of refugee populations.

Whether or not this history qualifies as what William Cronon has termed a "declensionist" narrative of progressive degradation and loss depends largely on the timeframe under examination.[48] Although World War II clearly did tremendous damage to China's landscape, war-induced destruction and intensified environmental decline was only one part of this history. Assessments of war's longer-term ecological legacies must also consider the capacity of societies to restore war-ravaged landscapes to productivity.[49] Repairing the ecological degradation caused by war-induced neglect came about only through active human management. After World War II ended – and even as China was embroiled in civil war – eastern Henan's flooded areas experienced resettlement, socio-environmental reconstruction, and the re-creation of humanized agricultural landscapes. This recovery demanded huge flows of energy embodied in labor and resources, as well as official agencies that could channel and coordinate them. In addition to presenting a graphic example of the immediate impact of military conflict, which has been the focus of previous environmental histories of warfare, this study also details the post-conflict restoration of war-ravaged landscapes into productive agro-ecosystems. Ending the story in 1945, one sees a narrative of unmitigated ecological destruction. Continuing a few years further to 1952, when most of eastern Henan's flooded area was again under cultivation and agricultural production had returned to prewar levels, gives the impression of a precipitous decline that gave way to reconstruction. Extending the view to the late 1950s reveals a narrative of decline and recovery, followed by the ecological catastrophes that resulted from the "war against nature" waged in China during the Mao period (1949–1976).[50]

---

[48] Cronon (1992).
[49] Tucker (2011).
[50] Shapiro (2001).

I

A Militarized River: The 1938 Yellow River Flood and Its Aftermath

No one who looked upon the Yellow River as it flowed across Henan's landscape during the high-water season in the late 1930s could have failed to appreciate its tremendous energy. Nor would they have failed to see how much human labor was expended to keep the river in check. In abstraction, as Richard White notes, river currents and human labor are both forms of energy. The labor that human actors expend trying to control rivers ties them so closely to the environment's energy that they become inseparable from it.[1] For energy to do work there has to be a gradient or some other kind of difference between two points.[2] The sun's radiant energy evaporates ocean water and drives winds that move moisture inland and uphill. As clouds cool, moisture falls to the earth as rain. Gravity propels waters from higher to lower elevations, causing rivers to flow. A river starts, as White puts it, "wherever the rain that enters it falls."[3] The Yellow River starts when weather systems move evaporated water to the high elevations of northwest China's Qinghai-Tibetan Plateau, where the river begins and most of its runoff originates.[4]

Energy and work intertwine with power. In some cases, power measures rates of energy flow and energy use. Sometimes, power means doing work and effecting change. In other instances, power refers to the ability to command the energy and work of others. All these different meanings of power, in White's words, "involve the ability to do work, to command labor. To be

---

[1] White (1995): 4–5.
[2] Christian (2005): 507.
[3] White (1995): 5.
[4] The Qinghai-Tibetan Plateau's steep rock slopes, low evaporation, high moisture retention, and relatively high precipitation levels mean that over 56 percent of the river's runoff originates in its upper reaches above Lanzhou. The river's middle reaches provide most of the remaining runoff, with the lower reaches contributing only a lesser percentage. See Pietz and Giordano (2009).

powerful is to be able to accomplish things, to be able to turn the energy and work of nature and humans to your own purposes."[5]

Energy alone is merely capacity to do work. Only when energy gets exploited according to human motives and desires does it yield power. Energy flows are one thing; the human capture or manipulation of them is another. Energy harnessed as power becomes a means of attaining human ends and pursuing human goals. Analogous meanings adhere to the Chinese character *li*, which connotes power and capacity to do work. Throughout World War II, Chinese and Japanese armies vied to harness the Yellow River's energy in their struggle for military and political power. The result for residents of Henan's flooded area was prolonged disaster.

By the twentieth century, exploiting China's rivers and waterways for military-strategic purposes had plenty of precedent. China's extensive water control systems had long been a "sword of Damocles – and almost anyone could snip the thread."[6] On more than one occasion, armies intentionally diverted rivers to gain the upper hand against their military adversaries and as a strategic barrier against external aggression.[7] Chiang Kai-shek and his subordinates perceived the Yellow River in similar strategic terms. In June 1938, Nationalist armies transformed nature's awesome energy into a weapon by breaking the river's southern dike in Henan, exploiting it to counter Japanese military power. Manipulating rivers in this fashion can be thought of as a way to alter the energy needs of the enemy. Breaching the dikes increased the energy required by the Japanese army to carry out its military advance, as well as increasing other logistical requirements. Those logistical requirements, of course, were also energy requirements.

Long after its initial diversion, the Yellow River remained a central actor in the Sino-Japanese War, frustrating human efforts to shape its behavior and thereby reshaping the military terrain. Throughout the conflict, Chinese and Japanese armies undertook hydraulic engineering projects aimed at redirecting the river to fortify their military positions and consolidate their power. Opposing Chinese and Japanese forces consumed massive quantities of energy working with, on, and against the river. Their struggles were over power – contests over who would control the river, alter its course, and exploit its energies. But the Yellow River was no passive object. It resisted and complicated human actions, generating unforeseen consequences.

Manipulating the river to attain military advantage required power in another sense – the ability to gain advantage from the labor of others. To carry out hydraulic engineering projects, military forces and water control agencies had to mobilize massive flows of labor and materials. Yet, war-

---

[5] White (1995): 14.
[6] McNeill (1998): 46. For a hodgepodge of early examples, see Sawyer (2004).
[7] See: Bi (1995): 2–5; Lamouroux (1998): 546; Qu (2003): 61–62; Elvin (2004): 139; Zhang (2011): 22, 24, 31.

induced dislocations, especially as a result of the 1938 flood, made that energy difficult to obtain. Most of the burden fell on counties in Henan's flooded area, from which higher-level state and military actors extracted labor and resources. Tensions emerged between the central authorities, who wanted to exploit limited energy sources for national defense, and the localities in the flooded area, which sought to retain them for their own needs. Competition for energy and power played out not simply between Chinese and Japanese armies – or between military forces and the river – but also between militaries and the local communities they exploited.

By the twentieth century, the Yellow River was as much a human-engineered technology as a "natural" environmental feature. Centuries of hydraulic engineering had made it into a hybrid of non-anthropogenic and anthropogenic elements. Neither natural nor artificial, the river had become a form of environmental infrastructure. Human-constructed water-control systems, as Elvin observes, are "inherently unstable, and constantly in interaction with disruptive external environmental factors." Rainfall, flooding, sediment deposition, and a host of other factors affect them. In such hydraulic networks, "society and economy meet in a relationship that is more often than not adversarial."[8] Maintaining this infrastructure greedily devoured energy. In late imperial times, Yellow River water control was characterized by "the unending battle between natural and human forces."[9] During World War II, these battles grew more intense as combatants tried to manipulate the river to wage hydraulic warfare. Adversarial relations among humans, the environment, and other humans placed massive burdens on societies and ecosystems. In this manner, military conflict between China and Japan remolded relations between human labor and the energies of nature. War-induced distortion of energy flows rearranged the environment physically, disrupted human-engineered hydraulic and agro-ecological systems, and made their repair all but impossible. The river's hydro-energy benefited the Nationalist military in the short term by slowing down the Japanese, but its diversion left them stuck in a quagmire of their own making.

WATER AS A SUBSTITUTE FOR SOLDIERS

After the Chinese and Japanese armies clashed at Marco Polo Bridge outside Beijing (then known as Beiping) in July 1937, Japan's military forces launched a full-scale offensive into the heart of China. The Japanese took Beiping and Tianjin in under a month. Larger battles raged in the Lower Yangzi delta region. The Chinese defense of Shanghai ended in a bitter and costly defeat. The Japanese army seized Nationalist China's capital of Nanjing in December 1937 and perpetrated brutal atrocities against its civilian residents. The

---

[8] Elvin (2004): 115.
[9] Ibid., 128.

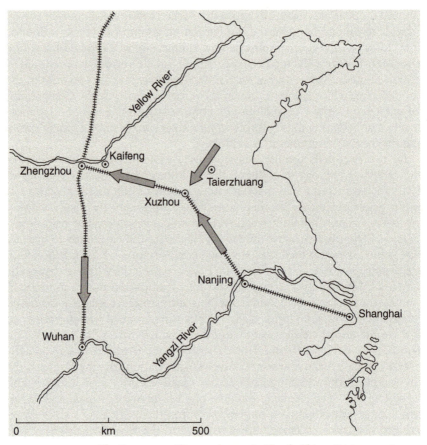

FIGURE 1.1 The Japanese military advance in North China, Spring 1938

Japanese army then set its sights on Wuhan, where the Nationalist regime had relocated its capital.

In early 1938, the Japanese army launched assaults from the Jin-Pu railway's northern end at Tianjin and from its southern terminus at Pukou near Nanjing. Once they met at the rail junction of Xuzhou, the Japanese plan was to move west toward Zhengzhou in Henan, the junction of the east–west Long-Hai and the north–south Ping-Han railways. From there, Japanese forces planned to advance south along the Ping-Han railway toward Wuhan. The Japanese army, which had eradicated China's strongest central government forces and drawn many Chinese regional armies to its side, anticipated little resistance in the Xuzhou campaign. To their surprise, however, Chinese armies held out for nearly five months. Japanese forces at Xuzhou numbered over 200,000; Chinese forces numbered 600,000. From March 24 to April 7, Chinese armies won a victory defending Taierzhuang, to the northwest of Xuzhou, but their counteroffensive failed. By May, the Japanese had nearly encircled Xuzhou and Chinese armies withdrew to the southwest.[10] Once they took Xuzhou in late May, the Japanese moved to bring the war to a decisive conclusion. They struck west along the Long-Hai railway, planning to press south along the Ping-Han railway and attack Wuhan. As the Japanese assault moved west in spring 1938, Henan was partially occupied. Most of northern Henan had fallen in the winter of 1937–1938 and the Japanese occupied towns and transport routes on the Yellow River's northern bank. Chinese armies held areas to the south, with only the river separating them from the invaders.

After Kaifeng fell in June 1938, the Japanese focused their assault on Zhengzhou. Chinese armies kept the Japanese from crossing the Yellow River by destroying the railway bridge north of the city, but they had little chance of maintaining their position for much longer. The Japanese were poised to capture Wuhan and the collapse of China's entire war effort seemed a distinct possibility. As the tide of war turned against them, Nationalist military officers raised the possibility of breaking the Yellow River dikes to impede the Japanese. After flying to Zhengzhou and realizing that Nationalist forces could not repel the Japanese, First War Zone Commander Cheng Qian contacted Chiang Kai-shek with the idea of breaking the river's southern dike west of the Japanese position. The objective was to cut the Long-Hai railway, which ran along the river's southern bank, before the Japanese could reach Zhengzhou. The strategic interdiction would halt the enemy's advance, thereby ensuring the escape of Chinese armies that had fought in the Xuzhou campaign. Otherwise, Wuhan would fall in only a matter of days, the Nationalist regime might not have time to withdraw, and China would have to surrender. Breaking the dikes was thus a product of utter desperation.[11]

In deliberating on the last-ditch strategy of diverting the Yellow River, Nationalist military commanders described the decision as a way to unleash the river to counter Japanese military power. In late May 1938, Chiang Kai-shek's military advisor He Chengpu stated, "Now is the time of the Yellow River's spring high waters. If a project is undertaken to breach the dike, the Yellow River will follow its old course and flow directly to Xuzhou. Not only will the land be flooded, which will make the enemy's mechanized units lose their effectiveness, but it will also suffice to destroy their military power (*zhanli*), making their plan to advance along the Jin-Pu railway come to

---

[10] Lary (2001): 194–196; van de Ven (2003): 217–224; Lary (2004): 146; MacKinnon (2008): 31–36; Drea and van de Ven (2010): 32–34; MacKinnon (2010): 190–196; Tobe (2010): 208–211; MHS: 171–173.

[11] Bi (1995): 26–41; Zhang (1997): 472; van de Ven (2003): 226; Lary (2004): 146–147; Cheng et al. (2007): 284; MacKinnon (2008): 35–36; Drea and van de Ven (2010): 34; MacKinnon (2010): 195; Tobe (2010): 209–210; MHS: 174–175; Mitter (2013a): 157–158. For primary sources on these campaigns see Chen (1986): 9–21.

naught, and it is hoped that it will be pursued at an early time."[12] The objective was to utilize floodwaters to disrupt the Japanese army's mechanized transport system, making it difficult to transfer troops and materials along North China's railway networks.

Several days later, on June 3, the Western Henan Divisional Command wired Chiang Kai-shek stating that "Xuzhou has fallen and the enemy's main force (*zhuli*) has gone deep into eastern Henan and western Shandong. Unless we break the cauldrons and sink the ships in order to show our determination, the Central Plain cannot be defended. We intend to divert the Yellow River's waters to submerge the enemy's main force. It is clearly known that the sacrifice will be heavy, but with the urgent need to save the nation the pain must be endured."[13] Once unleashed, the waters would counter the Japanese army's fighting power. Nationalist leaders accepted this stratagem as a military necessity. For them, national survival outweighed the damage that they knew the floods would cause. Chiang gave orders to breach the dikes and none of his subordinates voiced disagreement.

Nationalist military leaders decided to make the breach in Zhongmu County, west of Zhengzhou. That the Yellow River dikes in Zhongmu had burst in 1868 and 1887 may have influenced their decision. Zhongmu already had a large military garrison. Nationalist armies fortified the Yellow River's southern bank in 1937, constructing blockhouses every 50–100 meters, and troops stood ready to repel Japanese encroachments across the river. But they had no defenses against the impending Japanese attack from the east other than the river itself.[14] On June 3, 1938, Chiang Kai-shek jotted a pressing question in his diary: "What has been the result of breaching the dike and creating a flood to Zhoujiakou?" Chiang at this point had clearly made up his mind to hasten the Nationalist withdrawal while using the river as an obstacle against the Japanese to prevent them from pressing onward.[15]

Chinese troops worked to destroy hydraulic infrastructure that laborers had in the past expended so much energy to construct. But breaking the dikes proved more difficult than anticipated. On June 4–6, Nationalist armies made two failed attempts to hollow out and blast open the dike at Zhaokou in Zhongmu. Only minimal public warning was given, lest the Japanese find out and accelerate their advance. From Wuhan, Chiang telephoned military commanders in Henan to ensure his orders were carried out. A second attempt to break the dike by excavating it was made at Huayuankou, north of Zhengzhou, a few days later. On June 9 the river's waters spilled through the

---

[12] "He Chengpu jianyi chen taoxun juedi" (May 5, 1938): 4. See also Bi (1995): 37; Zhang (1997): 472.
[13] "Liu Zhongyuan deng jiang dian" (June 3, 1938): 4.
[14] Todd (1949): 40; Lary (2001): 198–199.
[15] Chiang Kai-shek Diary (June 3, 1938): HIA.

opening. The breach occurred at a critical juncture, with the Japanese less than 50 kilometers away. During the annual dry season, when the river's waters were low, a strategic flood would have been impossible. But the Japanese advance came in early summer, when the river was at its highest point. Gradually, its waters scoured open the breach at Huayuankou and expanded it to 200 meters in width. Over the next few days, the river rose and weakened defenses at Zhaokou as well. From this point, the Yellow River flowed southeast across Henan's flat eastern plain.[16] As Nationalist military officer Xiong Xianyu, who oversaw the breaking of the dike, wrote in his diary, "This action has been taken to impede the enemy and to redeem the overall situation. For this reason, [we] did not hesitate to make this great sacrifice in pursuit of final victory."[17]

Strategically, breaking the dike prevented the Japanese from immediately capitalizing on their victory at Xuzhou, buying the Nationalist army time to withdraw and regroup, bogging down Japanese tanks and mobile artillery in fields of mud. Chinese forces were able to secure their defenses around Zhengzhou. By preventing the Japanese from taking the railway junction, the river's diversion postponed the seizure of Wuhan by several months, giving the Nationalist government time to relocate its capital southwest in the city of Chongqing. Having consolidated their positions in Henan, Chinese armies launched counterattacks in Zhongmu, Weishi, Fugou, Yanling, and Taikang, retaking sections of each of these counties. In Weishi, armies under First War Zone Commander Cheng Qian annihilated Japanese forces that had been isolated by the flood and recovered the county seat. However, the flood gave the Nationalists only temporary breathing space and did not afford Wuhan permanent protection. The Japanese redirected their advance from a north–south land attack along the railways to an amphibious assault along the Yangzi River that combined naval and infantry forces. Wuhan fell in October 1938, after the Nationalist central government had withdrawn into the southwestern interior.[18]

Once Wuhan fell, the Sino-Japanese War settled into a stalemate. The major battles were over, though guerilla warfare continued. With its advance halted, the Japanese army occupied most rail lines and urban centers in northern and eastern China. The Chinese Nationalist regime consolidated its control over the northwest and southwest parts of the country. Frontlines were defined largely by topographical features. The Japanese army could not fight a mechanized war in the mountains and hills that divided China's

---

[16] Zhang (1997): 472–473; Lary (2001): 198–199; Lary (2004): 148; MHD: 130–131; MHS: 176; Cheng et al. (2007): 284; Mitter (2013a): 158–160.
[17] Selection from Xiong Xianyu's diary (June 9, 1938), in "1938 nian Huanghe juedi shiliao yi zu" (1997): 11.
[18] Zhang (1997): 474–475; Lary (2001): 201–202; Qu (2003): 140; van de Ven (2003): 226; Lary (2004): 144; MHS: 176–177.

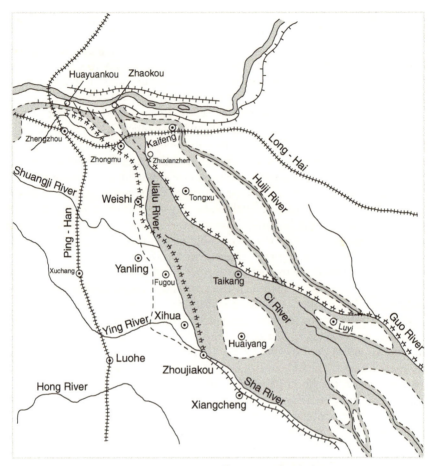

FIGURE 1.2 Henan's Yellow River flooded area

occupied and unoccupied territories, nor could they function in the vast flooded area created by the Yellow River.[19]

The damage caused by the strategic diversion was tremendous. The short-term benefits gained from the Nationalist gambit of turning the Yellow River into a weapon came at a staggering price. To halt the Japanese assault, floodwaters only needed to cut off transport along the Long-Hai railway, which ran just south of the river. But the Yellow River had its own momentum. Once unleashed, it flowed unimpeded across eastern Henan's landscape, which had a generally higher elevation in the north than in the south. This gradient gave the river the energy to leave the channel it had followed since 1855 and take a new course. No topographical divisions prevented the river

---

[19] Lary (2010): 78–79; Mitter (2013a): 171.

FIGURE 1.3 Chinese Nationalist soldiers walking barefoot through Yellow River floodwaters
Source: Guomin zhengfu zhongyang xuanchuanbu. Courtesy of Qinfeng lao zhaopian guan, *Kangzhan Zhongguo guoji tongxun zhaopian*. Guilin: Guangxi shifan daxue chubanshe, 2008.

from moving southeast to join the Huai River. Advancing at a steady rate of around 16 kilometers (10 miles) per day, floods spread into narrow, shallow beds of rivers and streams that flowed toward the Huai. Floodwaters filled these waterways and broke their embankments, causing them to overflow and inundate fields to the east and west.[20]

After its diversion, the Yellow River split into several channels. Its western branch – the largest – went from Huayuankou to Zhongmu and into the Jialu River, flowing south through Weishi, Fugou, Xihua, and Huaiyang counties before reaching Zhoujiakou, where it followed the Ci and Sha rivers into Anhui. These and other smaller rivers could not contain the Yellow River's waters, which overflowed and damaged cultivated lands nearby. An eastern branch formed when the Yellow River rose and burst through the initially unsuccessful Zhaokou breach. Floodwaters coming from Zhaokou split into two channels. One flowed southeast and merged with waters that poured out of the Huayuankou opening. The other passed north of Kaifeng

[20] Han and Nan (1948): 6.

FIGURE 1.4 Nationalist soldier directing laborers working on Yellow River dikes
Source: Guomin zhengfu zhongyang xuanchuanbu. Courtesy of Qinfeng lao zhaopian guan, *Kangzhan Zhongguo guoji tongxun zhaopian*. Guilin: Guangxi shifan daxue chubanshe, 2008.

and wound southeast into the Guo River and other waterways before entering Anhui. In early July 1938 the floodwaters entered the headwaters of the Huai River, turning northeast to cut across the Jin-Pu railway before pouring into Hongze Lake. The lake overflowed and waters burst into Jiangsu, flowing in three streams toward the Pacific Ocean. Nature's rhythms heightened the catastrophe, as summer precipitation increased the flooding's severity. Heavy rains fell throughout June and July. Waters surged as a result.[21]

As this point, the scale of destruction went uncalculated. Wartime instability made accurate quantification impossible.[22] Yet damage reports compiled after 1945 convey the magnitude of the catastrophe. Postwar investigations estimated that in the twenty counties of eastern Henan hit by the disaster, 32 percent of the cultivated land (7,338,000 *mu* = 489,200 hectares) was inundated.[23] The river also deposited approximately 100 million tons of silt, which spread

---

[21] Ibid: 1–2; Henan shuiliting shui han zaihai zhuanzhuo bianji weiyuanhui (1998): 95; Lary (2001): 199–201; Lary (2004): 149; Cheng et al. (2007): 284–285; MHS: 178–179.

[22] One investigation conducted in early July 1938 reported that floods affected 2,300 square kilometers of land, 2 million people, and 3,600 villages, destroying 50,000 homes. "Minguo ershiqi nian Huanghe juekou zaiqing diaocha biao" (1938): 144.

[23] Han and Nan (1948): 13–14, 18. See also Xu and Zhu (2005): 151, 154–155, 162. Note that 1 mu is equivalent to approximately 0.0666 hectares.

over vast areas of land.[24] Floods inundated 45 percent of the villages in the affected counties in eastern Henan. Over half the villages in eight of these counties were destroyed, with the total in Fugou County reaching over 91 percent.[25] Wartime flooding reportedly killed over 800,000 people in Henan, Anhui, and Jiangsu. In Henan alone, more than 325,000 people reportedly lost their lives. According to one postwar estimate, the civilian death toll in Henan's flooded areas amounted to 4.8 percent of the prewar population. This figure exceeded the numbers in the battle zones in China, where the civilian death rate was 0.6 percent. Death rates reached as high as 25.5 percent in Fugou and 26.8 percent in Weishi. Wartime floods also turned almost four million people – over 20 percent of the total population – in Henan, Anhui, and Jiangsu into refugees. In Henan the Yellow River floods displaced more than 1,172,000. Displaced people came to 67.7 percent of the total population in Xihua, 55.1 percent in Fugou, 52.2 percent in Weishi, 32.2 percent in Taikang, and more than 10 percent in Zhongmu.[26]

Like the numerous scorched-earth tactics that the Nationalists employed during the Sino-Japanese War, this "drowned earth" tactic, to borrow Diana Lary's term, was undertaken in an atmosphere of high-level desperation and panic.[27] Instances of self-inflicted destruction in China during World War II, as Keith Schoppa explains, "grew from the Japanese war of terror and were at the time deemed necessary, and even advantageous, by the Chinese victims."[28] On the other hand, the Nationalist regime's willingness to sacrifice people along with resources to keep them out of Japanese hands "showed a leadership callous to the needs of its people and all too ready to destroy its infrastructure, almost in automatic reflex in the name of stopping the Japanese."[29] Rana Mitter likewise identifies a "callous streak in the government's collective psyche, leading officials to regard the lives of individuals as expendable."[30] The breaking of the Yellow River dikes was the prime example of this tendency. In the eyes of Nationalist leaders, not unlike other high modernist regimes of the twentieth century, "saving the nation" could justify almost unlimited sacrifice on the part of the civilian population.

Throughout the war, the Nationalist government refused to take responsibility for the disasters caused by the Yellow River's diversion. Instead, the Nationalists claimed that Japanese bombing of the dikes had caused the floods, presenting the disaster as another example of Japanese atrocities against China's civilian population. Chinese newspaper reports published in summer of 1938 followed the official version of events. The Japanese denied

---

[24] Li et al. (1994): 255–256; Su (2004): 81; Xu and Zhu (2005): 153; Cheng et al. (2007): 287.
[25] Han and Nan (1948): 7.
[26] Ibid., 22–23; Xia Mingfang (2000b): 106; Xu and Zhu (2005): 159–160; MHS: 179–180.
[27] Lary (2010): 61.
[28] Schoppa (2011): 239.
[29] Ibid., 250.
[30] Mitter (2013a): 157.

these accusations, framing the flood as proof of China's disregard for human life. When the disaster's true causes eventually came to light after 1945, the Nationalist regime changed the narrative and presented the flood as evidence of sacrifices made by China's people to save the nation during the War of Resistance.[31]

DAMAGE CONTROL

After Nationalist military leaders destroyed the dike to halt their enemies in June 1938, communities in Henan and Nationalist hydraulic engineering personnel tried to build dikes to prevent catastrophe. As the 1938 summer rains caused the river to swell, local elites rushed to organize residents to construct new dikes to keep waters from spreading and doing greater damage. Centrally ordered destruction necessitated mobilizing labor and materials for local construction. As one contemporary recalled, "Residents along the new Yellow River's two banks, to prevent the disaster area from expanding, spontaneously organized in succession and invested large amounts of labor power and material power in building dikes along the banks to defend against floods and confine the waters so they would no longer overflow."[32]

In July and August 1938, initiatives were mounted in Fugou to contend with the Yellow River's waters. As floods moved southeast along the Jialu River, they flowed past Fugou's county seat. At its peak discharge in late July, the river surged to more than 4 meters in depth, threatening to break through the Fugou county seat's eastern and northern gates and inundate everything within. To prevent greater disaster, local authorities organized dike construction to protect the county seat. Qiao Guanghou, a representative from the Nationalist regime's Yellow River Conservancy Commission, went with the Fugou county magistrate to, as Qiao reported, "lead soldiers from each military unit in the county and several hundred able-bodied adult males, ordering them to transport bricks and dirt from faraway places and cut down trees for lumber, and devised a method of directing them in making emergency repairs." Repair efforts proved successful for a time. "By exhausting their power in this work, in several hours [the county seat] was out of danger and safety was temporarily secured." But victory could only be temporary in this struggle. With the onset of heavy summer rains, waters outside the county seat rose to a level about 2 meters higher than the ground inside. If waters continued to rise, the situation would turn dire.

At the same time, floods threatened several dozen villages on the Jialu River's eastern bank, more than 5 kilometers east of Fugou's county seat. As Qiao explained, defensive circular dikes that the villages had constructed

---

[31] Lary (2001): 199, 205; Qu (2003): 107–114; Lary (2004): 155; Mitter (2013a): 161; Edgerton-Tarpley (2014): 460–463.
[32] Xing (1986): 187. See also Xie (2002): 99.

reported emergencies and these localities requested assistance. Once again, Qiao and the county magistrate went by boat "to supervise the work of able-bodied adult males and pressured them to exert their utmost power to make emergency repairs." Fortunately, no danger emerged. But energy expended to make repairs in one locale made it unavailable elsewhere. The dike along the Shuangji River's southern bank also reported emergencies. Because attending to one crisis meant neglecting the other, the dikes burst. The torrents flowed southwest and devastated nearby villages. Many people and draft animals drowned. Residents clung to roofs and trees awaiting relief. Qiao instructed the magistrate to hire a boat and send police to rescue more than 300 flood victims. But a thousand or more people still needed assistance. And despite the severity of the flooding in Fugou, the central government's Yellow River Disaster Relief Commission (*Huang zai weihui*) had not sent emergency relief.[33]

When the high-water season ended in August 1938, residents who stayed in Fugou constructed civilian dikes to prevent additional floods. These projects were local initiatives. According to a report from Fugou, "To construct this dike the people along the dike collectively organized a commission and divided it into sections, directing nearby villages to take responsibility for closures and repairs." By late August, residents completed over 70 percent of the embankments.[34] Yet local measures had limited effectiveness, especially in autumn, when farming responsibilities drew labor power away from the work of dike maintenance. As a later report explained,

> For the civilian dike being constructed to the east of the county seat, in the recent busy agricultural season the number of workers has decreased and the rate of results on the dike has fallen. Also, many people who have no way of making a living have fled with their families, so recruiting laborers has been difficult. Together with the county magistrate, we are still exhausting our power in pressing them to complete the stipulated length [of dikes].[35]

Pressure on local labor supplies intensified as farm work and refugee flight rendered them scarce, hampering the effectiveness of emergency hydraulic maintenance. War-induced dislocations made it impossible to build dikes while sustaining agricultural production. By breaking the dike, the Nationalist regime used the river to avert military defeat, but ended up sacrificing sources of labor power, agricultural output, and building materials. At this stage in the war, immediate strategic victories, rather than long-term considerations, were the primary motivation.

---

[33] "Fugou xian zhu gong weiyuan Qiao Guanghou jing rong daidian" (July 25, 1938), in "Huangfanqu yan Huang kuishui ge xian beizai baogao" (August 1938): YRCC MG4.3.3–6.

[34] "[Fugou] nianyi zhi niansi ri diaocha ribao biao" (August 21–24, 1938), in "Huangfanqu yan Huang kuishui ge xian beizai baogao." See also Fugou xianzhi zong bianji shi (1986): 97.

[35] "[Fugou] ba yue nianwu ri zhi nianba ri diaocha ribao biao" (August 25–28, 1938), in "Huangfanqu yan Huang kuishui ge xian beizai baogao."

USING THE RIVER TO CONTROL THE ENEMY

The Nationalist regime did not, however, simply abandon the Yellow River after relocating to Chongqing. Alongside local initiatives, larger-scale struggles between human energies and nature's energies played out, with belligerents manipulating the river for strategic purposes. Hydraulic engineering became part of warfare; the river remained a tool for attaining military power.

Even before its armies broke the dike at Huayuankou, the Nationalists took the first step toward militarizing hydraulic management by granting military commanders control over water control agencies. Early in May 1938, as Japanese armies moved into eastern Henan and threatened Kaifeng, First War Zone commander Cheng Qian wired Chiang Kai-shek asking him to place Yellow River water conservancy under direct military direction. Cheng noted that river protection troops were stretched over a long distance, but work sites were sited all along the river and closely interconnected. As he explained:

> In previous ages, our nation's river control officials also commanded armies. The United States and Holland's water control organs and military organs are also combined for the same purpose. Normally it is done in this way. Now areas along the river have already become battle zones and the division of labor absolutely cannot handle this trend in the environment. In this war zone, a Provisional River Defense Commission should be established to directly oversee river defense organs to simultaneously attend to military affairs and river work. It will not be detrimental to [the Yellow River Conservancy Commission's] basic river defense work and convenience can be gained in military provisional river defenses.[36]

Cheng proposed that the Henan Repair and Defense Office's director serve on the First War Zone Provisional River Defense Commission, which would oversee river defense agencies. Chiang Kai-shek approved Cheng's plan and convened representatives from military and water control agencies to discuss its implementation. Opening the meeting on May 15, director of the Military Affairs Commission's administrative office, He Yaozu, reported that, "Yellow River defense is a great problem for our nation. Recently, since the War of Resistance has entered its second period, river defense and national defense have become intimately related. For this reason, when discussing river defense one must simultaneously pay attention to national defense."[37] All the meeting's participants supported Cheng's proposal. But given the urgent military situation it would take too long to organize a new river defense commission. Instead, they concluded that the Yellow River Conservancy Commission would remain responsible for river defense, with oversight from the First War Zone Command. That day, Chiang Kai-shek issued a

---

[36] Quoted in Bi (1995): 33. See also MHD: 130.
[37] Quoted in Bi (1995): 35.

directive ordering that the Yellow River Conservancy Commission accept direction and supervision from the First War Zone's military leadership "to closely cooperate with military affairs and adapt to the needs of the war."[38]

After June 1938, with Nationalist armies holding areas west of the river's new course and Japanese armies occupying territory to the east, Henan's flooded area turned into one of the war's most important frontlines. In this situation, the First War Zone Command and the Yellow River Conservancy Commission merged river defense and national defense by "using the Yellow River to control the enemy" (*yi Huang zhi di*). First, the Nationalists intended to keep the river's waters flowing through the Huayuankou breach, while preventing its multiple channels from combining into a single course. Second, the Nationalists would let waters southeast of Huayuankou disperse and form mudflats to impede the mobility of Japanese mechanized units. Third, the Nationalists would shore up the dike west of the Huayuankou breach to divert part of the river into its old bed and damage Japanese transport and communications links. To realize these goals, the Nationalist military built a new flood defense dike along the river's western bank, which shifted waters east to threaten Japanese positions on the other side. In addition to trying to take advantage of this new dike to restrain and redirect the river, Nationalist military and political leaders repaired and dredged other waterways to make the flooded area into as effective an obstacle as possible.

To prevent the flooded area from expanding west and to maintain it as an effective military impediment, in July 1938 the Yellow River Conservancy Commission and the Henan provincial government constructed 34 kilometers of dikes from Guangwu (west of Huayuankou) to the Long-Hai railway's roadbed in Zheng County. Construction was carried out as a "work relief" (*gongzhen*) project, mobilizing flood victims from Guangwu and Zheng County. Due to summer high waters and lack of funds, only a short dike section from Huayuankou into Zheng County was completed. Nevertheless, the new dike restricted the Yellow River's channel and caused its sediments to block the Long-Hai railway, making it impossible for the Japanese to move west.

In spring 1939, the Henan provincial government and the Yellow River Conservancy Commission organized laborers from disaster-stricken counties to construct a new dike from Zheng County to Henan's border with Anhui. The dike extended along the flooded area's western edge, passing through Zhongmu, Kaifeng, Weishi, Fugou, Xihua, Shangshui, Huaiyang, Xiangcheng, and Shenqiu counties. A former resident of Poxie village in Fugou recalled that civilian laborers from outlying areas came to build the dike, leaving no places in Poxie for people to live. Even villages two kilometers to the west were full of civilian laborers.[39] The dike had a total length

---

[38] Bi (1995): 35–36. See also MHD: 130; Cheng et al. (2007): 287–288.
[39] Xie (2002): 100.

of 316 kilometers and consumed some 3.4 million cubic meters of earth.[40] Yet wartime instability hampered its effectiveness. Work had to be done in a hasty fashion, so the dike was narrow and short. With labor power scarce, dirt was not thoroughly tamped down and construction quality was poor. The dike could only give limited protection to areas west of the river's new course.[41] As a later government investigation noted, "At that time, because of economic and time constraints, repairs to the new dike were insufficiently high and thick, and many were made of sand. When scoured by the 1940 high waters, many proved unusable."[42]

For the Nationalists, the confluence of warfare and water control militarized the river, making it the "line of national defense in the War of Resistance." As a former Yellow River Conservancy Commission hydraulic engineer named Xu Fuling put it, "The Nationalist government put forth the slogan 'river defense is national defense; controlling the river is protecting the nation' (*hefang ji guofang, zhihe ji weiguo*), making the western dike into a frontline position and demanding that they be tightly defended."[43] Achieving that task was a huge undertaking. After the dike was finished in July 1939, the Yellow River Conservancy Commission's Henan Repair and Defense Office (*Huanghe shuili weiyuanhui Henan xiufangchu*) oversaw maintenance, stationing personnel year round to oversee the repairs. At the same time, hydraulic engineering came under tighter military direction. The First War Zone Command Headquarters and the Lu-Su-Wan-Yu Border Area Headquarters stationed troops along the dike. The Fifteenth Group Army Commander, He Zhuguo, oversaw defenses. Because the western dike formed the "first line of national defense," the Nationalist military outfitted each section with a telegraph to report on local conditions and coordinate work.[44] Given this strategic importance, local administrations had to monitor hydraulic infrastructure and coordinate labor and materials to maintain it. The Yellow River Conservancy Commission enacted regulations in 1939 that called for the Henan Repair and Defense Office and administrative supervisors in areas along the new dike to press magistrates in counties under their jurisdiction to maintain defenses.[45]

---

[40] MHD: 132; MHS: 183–184. See also Fugou xianzhi zong bianji shi (1986): 97–98; Bi (1995): 58; Xu Fuling (1991): 24–25; Xihua xian shizhi bianzuan weiyuanhui (1992): 118; Li et al. (1994): 259; Qu (2003): 169–170; Cheng et al. (2007): 287.
[41] Fugou xianzhi zong bianji shi (1986): 97–98; Xu Fuling (1991): 24–25, Xihua xian shizhi bianzuan weiyuanhui (1992): 118; Li et al. (1994): 259; Bi (1995): 58; Xie (2002): 102; Qu (2003): 169–170; Cheng et al. (2007): 287; MHD: 132; MHS: 183–184.
[42] "Zhuan'an baogao: Huangfan digong qingxing," (July 27, 1941): HIA, KMT Project 003 Reel 212 File 1717.
[43] Xu Fuling (1991): 25.
[44] Ibid., Qu (2003): 171–172; Cheng et al. (2007): 287; MHS: 184–185.
[45] MHS: 185.

Hydraulic engineering and warfare were thoroughly intertwined. Following the 1938 Huayuankou breach, the northernmost portion of the Yellow River's main channel flowed toward Jingshui in Zheng County, making military installations there a main point of defense. As Nationalist reports described, "Zhengzhou is on the frontlines of national defense, bordering the Yellow River's Huayuankou breach in the north and the Yellow River floods to the east. We are separated from the enemy only by these waters. The town of Jingshui north of the city walls is scoured by the Yellow River's southern flood and an extremely important strategic position for our military."[46] To eliminate the threat posed to the dike and nearby military revetments, in spring and summer of 1939 the First War Zone Command and the Yellow River Conservancy Commission constructed six kilometers of military dikes, eight deflection dikes, and several dozen revetments between Huayuankou and Jingshui. To counter Japanese artillery across the river, thirty-two military blockhouses were built. Also for military purposes, deflection dikes were constructed to "deflect the river's stream and obstruct the enemy."[47]

JAPANESE COUNTERMEASURES

In Japanese-controlled territories, hydraulic engineering likewise intertwined with consolidation of military power and political authority. Between August and December 1938, the Japanese army mobilized Chinese workers to repair four kilometers of dikes near Kaifeng.[48] But Japanese-occupied areas in Taikang on the eastern bank of the river lacked dike defenses. If waters shifted east, the Japanese would have no way of securing their positions and protecting Taikang and other areas from flooding. Further inundations would disrupt social stability and jeopardize economic production. Local residents tried to shore up embankments. However, from summer 1938 to early 1939, breaches occurred at twelve places in Taikang. According to the Japanese report, "At the site of all these breaches villagers spontaneously made defensive closures." Where serious breaks took place, villagers closed them with earth and tree branches. But local labor and resources could not keep the river in check. Dikes were small and weak, so flooding was a constant threat.[49] Since its waters contained large amounts of silt, areas through which the river flowed grew higher due to sediment deposition and its levels

---

[46] "Huanghe shuili weiyuanhui Yu sheng hefang tegong linshi gongchengchu gongzuo baogao" (May 21, 1940): YRCC MG.1–134.
[47] Xu Fuling (1991): 27; Cheng et al. (2007): 291; MHD: 142; MHS: 185–186.
[48] Xing (1986): 187; Cheng et al. (2007): 288; MHD: 134; MHS: 190–191. See also "Shin Kōga karyū ibban kaikyo chōsa hōkokusho" (September 24, 1943): YRCC MG 10–140.
[49] "Taikō shin Kōga chihō chōsa hōkoku" (August 1939): YRCC MG10.29.

rose. The river either inundated or broke earthen dikes on its eastern bank during the 1939 high-water season, so floods spread and the disaster area expanded.[50]

For the Japanese, like the Nationalists, controlling the river had strategic importance. In territories under Japanese control, instead of governing directly the occupiers worked through collaborationist regimes manned by Chinese functionaries. For the Japanese and their collaborators, as Timothy Brook notes, the goals were to re-establish social order and stability to rebuild economies shattered by invasion, and to consolidate viable administration.[51] According to the reporter Xing Youjie, head of Henan's collaborationist propaganda office during the war, "to prevent the territories under their jurisdiction from shrinking and to keep disaster victims from causing disorder" (which would hamper implementation of local control), the Japanese deputed personnel to investigate dike construction and flood conditions. They also called on North China's collaborationist regime in Beijing to "quickly depute effective personnel, allocate special funds, relieve disaster victims, and construct new dikes" to consolidate their rule in Henan's occupied areas.[52]

Motivated by these imperatives, North China's Japanese power-holders prioritized dike construction. Japanese reports warned that Chinese guerillas in Taikang and the "false" (i.e. Nationalist) county magistrate intended to break dikes and divert waters to the east, which would inundate Japanese-held portions of the county. Once the rainy season arrived, waters would burst through embankments that the local populace had built, making it necessary to construct dikes at once to avert flooding.[53] In response to this threat, in spring 1939 the Japanese-controlled North China regime and Henan's collaborationist government oversaw construction and fortification of dikes on the eastern bank. Japanese water control specialists acted as consultants, the North China regime allocated funds, and Henan's collaborationist government was to "estimate its capabilities and supplement them."[54]

The Japanese intended to construct the dike through eastern Taikang, Tongxu, and Qi County – guerilla areas where Communist, Nationalist, and Japanese military forces jockeyed for influence. The Communist New Fourth Army's River East Independent Regiment (*Shuidong duli tuan*), based on the river's northeast bank in the Tongxu-Qi County-Taikang border

---

[50] Xing (1986): 187.
[51] Brook (2005).
[52] Xing (1986): 187.
[53] "Taikō shin Kōga chihō chōsa hōkoku."
[54] "Shin Kōga karyū ibban kaikyo chōsa hōkokusho"; Xing (1986): 187–188; Cheng et al. (2007): 288; MHD: 134; MHS: 190–191.

region, took cover and reorganized in villages that had not been inundated. These Communist forces harassed survey personnel, who requested that Japanese armies send military escort vehicles to protect them. All functionaries lived within the city walls at night. During the day, they took a roundtrip journey to survey the work site, returning home to eat and rest at noontime. Japanese troops also had to escort them back and forth.

For the first month, work proceeded slowly. Later, county headmen in occupied territories east of the river conferred and decided to divide the dike into sections (*fenduan baogan*). Each county conducted surveys and raised preliminary ideas, which were approved by the New Yellow River Dike Repair Commission before being implemented. Local leaders in Tongxu and Taikang eagerly anticipated the project's start because it was "intimately related to their vital personal interests" in fostering stability and some sense of wartime normalcy, as well as those of residents along the bank. After conferring with the area's populace, local Chinese Communist Party (CCP) military leaders agreed not to interfere with dike construction work.[55] With the Yellow River as part of the equation, opposing Japanese-led hydraulic management initiatives risked alienating the CCP from local society.

To keep floodwaters from moving farther east, the Japanese army and Chinese collaborators in Taikang made hydraulic engineering top priority. Japanese reports vividly illustrate how authorities in occupied territories secured and managed the limited local labor force. Labor conscription took the county as its primary unit, with each *bao* called on to send forty laborers between the ages of 15 and 40 to work on the dike. With all local organizations participating in recruitment, it was estimated that Taikang could provide 50,000 workers. In terms of the division of labor, workers from each *bao* would be organized into groups to construct dike sections about 66 meters in length. Group headmen directed work. In overseeing construction, troops from "friendly armies" (i.e. Japanese troops and their Chinese clients) handled defense and direction, while group headmen and commission members supervised work and pressed for its completion. To keep track of work, the headmen kept record books and investigated the efforts of each laborer twice daily, fining any workers who delayed.

Hydraulic management required huge investments. To pay expenses, areas in Taikang that were severely affected by flooding received 500,000 yuan; smaller amounts were allocated to lightly affected areas. Funds first went to the county magistrate, who distributed payments to headmen based on the number of workers in their group. Inspectors checked daily to make sure workers received wages and provisions, holding headmen responsible if they did not. Laborers who did not work diligently suffered

[55] Xing (1986): 188.

heavy fines. Each worker got 30 qian for provisions and headmen acquired the necessary supplies. The laborers resided in nearby villages or in tents along the dikes. Materials for cooking and heating were "borrowed" from the villages.[56]

The first stage of the project started in earnest in 1940 before winter ice floes arrived. Just as work got underway, the Yellow River rose suddenly, waters submerged a large portion of the newly constructed dike, and there was no way to move forward with the project. The only choice was to wait until autumn when waters had fallen and then continue work.[57] The 1940 floods inundated many villages near the riverbank and disaster victims fled.[58] After repair work resumed in autumn, civilian labor conscription became increasingly difficult. As Xing Youjie recalled, "Even if some civilian laborers could be found they were mostly sallow and emaciated. Moreover, their households lacked grain and they did not have enough to eat, so in doing heavy physical labor it was of course difficult for them to be highly effective." Since the main project sites were mostly located in guerilla areas, if overseers were too harsh young workers might join up with guerilla forces. Furthermore, waters submerged most of the previously selected dike routes, so others had to be found. Local residents strived to keep their villages "outside the dike," where levees would shield them from floodwaters and protect them from damage. Residents of villages that ended up "inside the dike" (between the levees and the river), because they were located in low-lying areas or had unsuitable locations, "all did everything they could to resist the project being carried out, so in winter 1940 the project could not make any progress."[59]

To prevent the river from returning to its original bed, thereby protecting the Japanese-held railway link from Xinxiang in northern Henan to Kaifeng, the Japanese army also set about enlarging the breach at Huayuankou. By widening the gap, Japanese forces could also threaten Nationalist military installations in Jingshui. The Japanese sealed off the Zhaokou breach, forcing all the river's waters to flow out through the Huayuankou opening. During a brief assault on Huayuankou in July 1939, the Japanese seized the opportunity to dig another opening east of the original one, which soon expanded to 100 meters across. In August 1941, high waters washed away the remaining dike segments and the two openings combined. Scoured by the main channel, the gap expanded farther east and by 1945 it was 1460 meters wide.[60]

---

[56] "Taikō shin Kōga chihō chōsa hōkoku."
[57] Xing (1986): 188.
[58] Ibid., 189.
[59] Ibid.
[60] "Shin Kōga karyū ibban kaikyo chōsa hōkokusho"; MHD: 139.

RIVER DEFENSE AS NATIONAL DEFENSE

In response to these Japanese actions, on January 1, 1940 the Nationalist government's Yellow River Conservancy Commission took to repairing militarily important river defense installations between Huayuankou and Jingshui. Despite constant shelling from Japanese artillery, eight willow and stone revetments were constructed, which shifted the river's channel toward the opposite bank and protected Nationalist-built dikes. Once completed, the defenses were taken over by the Third Group Army.[61]

However, heavy rains in late summer and fall of 1939 caused the river to burst through civilian dikes in Taikang and other nearby counties.[62] River defense units (*gongxundui*) in Nationalist-held territories enlisted civilian laborers to make repairs, but the Japanese re-occupation of parts of Taikang in late September disrupted work. Thereafter, Chinese troops opened civilian-built dikes at Wangpan and nearby areas in Taikang – which were on the frontlines closest to Japanese-held territories – unleashing floodwaters to secure their own safety. Water shifted east and the river's channel split into several streams. By decreasing the water volume in the main channel, as Nationalist investigators warned, this most recent breach jeopardized the river's ability to block Japanese incursions: "If in the future the river's position-power is decreased any more, there is concern that it will be possible for the enemy to wade across." To obstruct the Japanese, Nationalist investigators urged the Yellow River Conservancy Commission to send troops stationed in the area to enlist civilian laborers and close the Wangpan breach, "to decrease the flooded area and increase the main flood channel's flow, so as to protect the natural barrier of national defense (*guofang tianxian*)."[63]

When military hostilities along the river eased in February 1940, Chiang Kai-shek cabled the Yellow River Conservancy Commission with instructions on how to manage floodwaters to "use the Yellow River to control the enemy." First, his directive emphasized that the flood's purpose was to impede encroachments by the Japanese, and shield Nanyang and Luoyang in western Henan against attack. Logistical support for the several hundred thousand Nationalist troops on the Yellow River's banks and the safety of the outer perimeter of the Nationalist regime's "auxiliary capital" of Xi'an in Shaanxi Province also depended on the floods for protection. Given the primacy of attaining military victory, floodwaters could not, for the sake of the "people's livelihood," be dispersed by subdividing them into additional channels, which would decrease their power to impede the enemy. Since the

---

[61] "Huanghe shuili weiyuanhui Yu sheng hefang tegong linshi gongchengchu gongzuo baogao." See also Qu (2003): 175–176; Cheng et al. (2007): 291; MHD: 139, 145.
[62] Li et al. (1994): 251; MHD: 139.
[63] "Li Jingtang cheng" (December 17, 1939): YRCC MG.4.1–8.

river had been diverted for three years and most of the flooded area's residents had relocated or constructed dikes to protect their fields, at least as Chiang claimed, their hardships were not a great as in the past. If the river changed course again, people would suffer renewed hardships and have to flee once more. Based on these considerations, Chiang concluded, the Nationalists needed to uphold the current state of affairs.[64]

But the river had its own energies, which made it difficult for the Nationalist authorities to maintain this situation. Areas east of the Jialu River and north of the Sha River in Huaiyang County, for instance, were inundated in 1938 following the Huayuankou breach, leaving many fields under water. Because this portion of Huaiyang was not along the river's main channel, it flowed slowly and deposited its sediment load. Following two years of silt buildup, land in the area gradually grew higher. The change in the landscape caused the main channel to move east between Taikang and Huaiyang, almost cutting off its flow in territories west and south of Huaiyang.[65]

As a result, the flooded area shifted east and an earthen ridge formed between the Jialu River in the northwest and the Sha River to the southeast. In a triangular area west of this ridge, dry lands reemerged and people could turn swamps back into fields. In 1940, some displaced residents returned to farm. Flood refugees who got word that there was a chance to survive in their home villages returned. Some started to plant fields again and expected a good harvest. Unfortunately, the earthen ridge did not afford sufficient protection against summer floods. If waters inundated fields, disaster victims in Huaiyang would again be left in a hopeless situation. To avert this outcome, local residents held a meeting to discuss building a new dike along the earthen ridge. Impoverished disaster victims could not afford to undertake the project, however, so representatives from Huaiyang requested assistance from the Yellow River Conservancy Commission to construct the new dike.[66]

The Huaiyang residents' petition explained that the dike along the Jialu and Sha rivers had been built for the purposes of the War of Resistance to shield Zhoujiakou against Japanese attack. The dike was far away from the river's main channel, however, so it did not offer effective defense. Chinese troops had already moved away from the Jialu-Sha dike to defensive points along the earthen ridge in Huaiyang. Their positions lacked shelter and in the event of flood the armies would have no way to communicate, making it difficult to defend against Japanese incursions. Building a new dike along the earthen ridge would facilitate transport and form a "natural strategic barrier" against the Japanese. Alongside these strategic considerations, of course, the

---

[64] Cheng et al. (2007): 287; MHS: 186.
[65] "Yu Wan Huangfanqu chakantuan baogao."
[66] "Huaiyang xian zaimin daibiao ni qing bo kuan zhu di" (March 1940); "Chakan Huaiyang zaimin qingqiu xiuzhu xin di luxian baogao shu" (August 1940): YRCC MG4.1-51.

dike would also protect many fields in Huaiyang. Constructing it as a work relief project would assist the disaster victims.[67] This argument won over Nationalist authorities, who responded favorably to the request.[68] To prevent the Yellow River's connecting channels from entering the Sha River and to ensure the waters still impeded the Japanese, the Nationalist Military Affairs Commission and the Yellow River Conservancy Commission ordered the Henan Repair and Defense Office to seal channels and build a large dike north of the Sha. The project, which was completed in 1941, sealed nine channels and constructed a large dike of over 15 kilometers in length north of the Sha River from Zhoujiakou into Huaiyang County. In line with the original petition, the dike protected 300 villages and over 13,200 hectares of cultivated land.[69]

HYDRAULIC ENGINEERING AND LOCAL CONFLICT IN OCCUPIED AREAS

As Chinese soldiers and civilians built dikes along the river's new course, Japanese forces funded emergency dike construction and repair to consolidate their hold over occupied areas. The investment of labor and resources was huge. In July 1940, the river's main channel shifted east and broke through the Japanese-constructed dike at Jiangcun in Fugou, flooding nearly all of Taikang.[70] In December 1941, the water's "position-power" in Taikang decreased, and "in February 1941 the old Yellow River's northern bank dried up and the common people spontaneously constructed dikes along the bank." By June 15 they had completed over 35 kilometers of embankments.[71] When the civilian dikes broke on the eastern bank near Wangpan, waters surged southeast and overtook the Guo River. Dikes also breached at two other places between Zhuxianzhen near Kaifeng and Baitan in Fugou.[72]

After the levees broke, Japanese military authorities and Chinese collaborationist leaders in North China and Henan conducted research in early 1941 and concluded that dike construction in Taikang, Tongxu, and Qi County needed to resume. To recruit civilian laborers, they turned to work relief. Several hundred thousand kilograms of mixed grain were purchased in Xuzhou, shipped to Kaifeng, and transferred to work sites. Every five civilian laborers comprised a "big group" assigned to work on a specific dike section. Each worker received 1.5 kilograms of maize or sorghum per

---

[67] "Huaiyang xian zaimin daibiao ni qing bo kuan zhu di."
[68] "Chakan Huaiyang zaimin qingqiu xiuzhu xin di luxian baogao shu."
[69] "Zhuan'an baogao: Huangfan digong qingxing," Cheng et al. (2007): 291; MHD: 148–149.
[70] "Taikang xian xiu xin Huanghe di gailue shuoming," in Xie et al. (1942); Xu Fuling (1991): 27; MHD: 147–148; MHS: 186.
[71] "Taikang xian xiu xin Huanghe di gailue shuoming."
[72] Ibid. See also Xu Fuling (1991): 27; MHD: 147–148; MHS: 186.

day. For impoverished flood victims, working on the dike in exchange for relief grain must have been an attractive option. "When this new [work relief] method was first carried out civilian laborers grew more numerous by the day and their effectiveness also greatly increased," Xing Youjie recalled. In spring 1941, the dikes started to take shape. Personnel from the North China regime and Henan's collaborationist government oversaw difficult sections. Environmental conditions proved favorable, since in 1941 the river's water volume was relatively low.[73] In mid-March 1941, civilian laborers conscripted by the Japanese army and its Chinese clients in Kaifeng, Tongxu, Qi County, and eastern Fugou had constructed 200 kilometers of dikes and revetments.[74] Once completed, the dike effectively blocked the Yellow River's eastern floodwaters, confining them to the channel of the Ying River.[75] The new dike "showed its effectiveness" and 1941 was the only year since the Japanese occupation that flooded areas did not expand.[76]

Though this hydraulic engineering project achieved its goals, the resulting disruption of drainage systems ignited local conflict. In autumn 1941, the new dike obstructed the river's waters and prevented them from flowing out. Waters rose in areas located inside the new dike, causing buildings to collapse in many villages. As Xing Youjie described it:

The villagers – regardless of whether or not they had already moved away or stayed in the villages – saw that villagers outside the dike could still live peacefully as usual and felt that it was unfair. Residents of some villages inside the dike joined together and forcefully broke the new dike, villagers outside the dike organized and took up arms to protect the dike, and as the two sides fiercely struggled, it also endangered the new dike.

Xing Youjie was a native of a village in Taikang located inside the dike on the border with Qi County, and his cousin was among the leaders of the dike breakers. To protect the new dike, Xing decided to use position of influence to mediate the dispute.[77]

Xing Youjie got support from Henan's high-level Japanese leadership. Under the protection of several dozen Japanese soldiers, the Japanese military intelligence agency's vice-director, Kani Kenhei, went with Xing to the ward office in Gaoxian, 25 kilometers to the northwest of Taikang. The ward officials informed villages inside and outside the dike that they should select representatives to go to Gaoxian and discuss how to protect the embankments and relieve the disaster victims living within them. Among those representing each side in the dispute were Xing's former classmates and students, so he wielded a great deal of influence. Xing talked for close to

---

[73] Xing (1986): 189.
[74] MHD: 191.
[75] Han and Nan (1948): 1.
[76] Xing (1986): 189.
[77] Ibid., 189.

two hours, with Kani Kenhei standing at his side. Because of Xing's connections and the coercion implied by Kani's presence, the meeting came to three decisions. First, villages outside the dikes would provide residences for homeless people who fled from villages inside the dikes free of charge. Second, disaster victims from inside the dikes who had no way of maintaining a livelihood would be loaned relief grain. Each adult was to receive 375 grams per day and small children received 250 grams. When dike repairs began, disaster victims who borrowed grain would have to work on the project and part of their wages would be withheld as repayment. Third, all villagers had to make concerted efforts to protect the dike. If they were discovered, anyone who harbored intentions to break the dike would be severely punished along with everyone else in their village.

Representatives from villages inside the dikes thought these decisions would help them survive the period of dearth that came before the harvest every spring; villagers from outside the dike thought they would no longer have to worry about the dikes being broken, so all sides consented. When mediation concluded, Xing Youjie and Kani Kenhei told the Gaoxian ward headman and those responsible for work sections to resolutely enact the resolutions and protect the new dike. Both sides sent two representatives who traveled about 10 kilometers with the ward headman, work section heads, Xing, and Kani to inspect the dike, which was largely intact. Xing and Kani returned to Kaifeng the next day and reported the results to Chinese and Japanese leaders, who commended their efforts. All believed that the new dike would hold steady. But three months later several breaches occurred, including work sections in Gaoxian.[78]

When winter ice floes arrived in March 1941, the earthen dike did not have a sufficiently solid foundation or adequate shore protection structures, so it could not withstand the impact. Dike defense personnel were few, supplies were lacking, and surveillance was ineffective. Floodwaters spread to about 1 kilometer in narrower places and over 5 kilometers in wider ones. Taikang suffered most severely. Previously, about forty percent of the county was under water and sixty percent had not been flooded. After this breach, over half the county was submerged. Waters surrounded Taikang's county seat to the west, north, and south, so only the eastern gate was still passable. At the previously bustling western gate, half the buildings had collapsed and all merchants had fled. Taikang's collaborationist county magistrate, Guo Chengzhang, rushed to Kaifeng in early May to propose closures and relief methods to Henan's provincial governor. The provincial governor deemed relief an important matter and requested assistance from the collaborationist North China regime. Provincial authorities gave Guo 15,000 yuan, and ordered him to go back to Taikang and cope with the disaster. The 1.5 million

[78] Ibid., 190.

yuan in funds originally sent from Beijing for dike construction had been exhausted, so Henan also sent representatives to discuss dike repair methods with the North China regime. Following several negotiations, Henan received another 700,000 yuan in work funds and 100,000 yuan in relief funds, which the provincial government distributed to counties affected by the recent flooding. By that time, however, the spring flood season had already arrived and dike construction could not be carried out.[79]

MILITARIZED WATER CONTROL AND ITS LOCAL IMPACT

In Henan's Japanese- and Nationalist-held territories alike, the vast amounts of labor and resources mobilized for hydraulic management could not stand up to the Yellow River's energies. In early August 1940, the Nationalist-built flood defense dike broke in Weishi. Waters inundated Yanling and Weichuan counties, and the Yellow River overtook the lower Shuangji. The largest breaches, which occurred at Shilipu and other sites in Weishi, flooded over 1,400 square kilometers.[80]

A dike repair proposal brought before the Nationalist Party's Central Executive Committee in summer 1940 explained the implications of this rapid deterioration of hydraulic infrastructure: "Since the Yellow River changed course, we and the enemy have confronted each other across the river, making it the most important line of national defense." Flooding also influenced the people's livelihoods. From Huayuankou to the border with Anhui, new dike defenses had been built to check the water's flow. However, during the 1940 high-water season, frequent and heavy rains washed away the weak embankment at over fifty places, so areas to the west suffered flooding once again. Shore defenses and willow revetments constructed as emergency repairs were also washed away. These decayed defenses were insufficient to resist the river's surging waters. In the future, there would be many "hidden dangers" to worry about.

Japanese hydraulic engineering projects presented even greater threats. In the words of the Nationalist dike repair proposal, "In addition, the enemy used 500,000 yuan to coerce the people on the eastern bank to build and fortify dike defenses to check the water's position-power (*shuishi*) and disrupt our defensive lines. Although our army has devised methods to attack and block them, they have not been completed." With high-water season approaching, the situation was critical. Unless those responsible for the dike sections stepped up repairs, the river's traverse flow threatened to break through and cause emergencies. As the proposal concluded, "Not only will military affairs and national defense suffer great effects, but for several dozen kilometers the people's lives will defy contemplation. Therefore, to make

---

[79] Ibid., 191.
[80] Xu Fuling (1991): 27; MHD: 147–148; MHS: 186.

comprehensive preparations to simultaneously attend to national defense and flooding, shoring up the new and old Yellow River dikes is currently the most urgent work and cannot be further delayed." The proposal directed the Yellow River Conservancy Commission to make technical preparations for dike repairs, the Henan provincial government to take charge of labor conscription, and the central government to send funds for work relief.[81]

The Nationalist regime quickly moved to cope with this crisis. On August 10, 1940, the head of the Yellow River Conservancy Commission's River Defense Office Tao Lüdun, acting director of the Henan Repair and Defense Office Shi Andong, and the Zhengzhou Special Area Administrative Supervisor Yang Yifeng met with river defense personnel, military leaders, county government functionaries, and local elites at the Weishi county government offices to plan repairs. The meeting's minutes illustrate the demands for labor and materials that wartime hydraulic management placed on Henan's flooded area, as well as the avenues through which Nationalist authorities acquired these resources.

Securing adequate supplies of labor was a challenge. At the start of the meeting, Tao Lüdun, Shi Andong, and Yang Yifeng proposed methods for managing civilian workers conscripted to repair dikes in Weishi County. As they stated, "The river is torrential, the work situation is urgent, the peak flood season is long, and abnormal flooding is hard to predict. To protect the Weishi section dike defenses, [we] must close breaches and carry out emergency defenses, so that the flooded area will not expand and construction can be powerful (*shigong weili*)." To achieve this end, they proposed methods for organizing and managing civilian laborers "to avoid the malpractice of shifting responsibility and lax discipline." Each *bao* mutual-security unit in areas lucky enough to avoid flooding would provide one hundred able-bodied adult males; *bao* in flooded areas only had to provide fifty. The local *baojia* security unit headmen oversaw civilian work teams. Floods destroyed the homes and property of most civilian laborers, so the Yellow River Conservancy Commission had to give them food and shelter.

Given the project's scale, Administrative Supervisor Yang Yifeng raised the issue of how to "concentrate labor power" to complete it: "The Shilipu breach is a vast project and it should be closed at an early date to obstruct the water's flow. For the project to proceed smoothly we should concentrate labor power and the division of labor should be cooperative in order to achieve twice the work with half the effort." To this end, personnel from the Yellow River Conservancy Commission's River Defense Office and the Henan Repair and Defense Office would direct river defense troops and civilian laborers, while local organizations procured food. The county magistrate would press civilian labor conscription and collection of supplies.

[81] Wei Lihuang et al. "Beixiu Huang di zenggu guofang yi li kangzhan er wei minsheng an" (July 1940): HIA, KMT Project 003 Reel 64 File 658.

Obtaining resources for dike repairs was even more challenging. The amount of biomass required was tremendous, but wartime dislocations made it hard to obtain. The destructive power of the Yellow River eliminated the material resources needed to harness its waters. As Weishi county magistrate Lu Bingyin stressed, "Closing breaches and repairing dangerous sections requires large amounts of wooden stakes, willow branches, sorghum stalks, and ramie [plant fibers]. Currently, because the disaster in this county is severe, they cannot be supplied in large amounts." Responding to Weishi's call for neighboring counties to assist in obtaining materials, the meeting resolved that the government would procure ramie fiber elsewhere. The wooden stakes, willow branches, and sorghum stalks were to be requisitioned in Weishi to the extent that it was possible. If local supplies were inadequate, the Zhengzhou Special Area Administrative Supervisor would ask nearby counties to help take on the burden.

As temporary motions, the meeting's participants requested government subsidies to purchase and repair boats, which were scarce but essential for transporting labor and supplies. With commodity prices on the rise, the attendees also requested that the Yellow River Conservancy Commission provide rations for the military officers and mutual-security unit directors who oversaw dike repair work.[82] The closure ultimately took three months, consuming 170,000 cubic meters of earth, 50,000 kilograms of hemp, and 150,000 kilograms of willow branches.[83]

Hydraulic maintenance put pressure on local supplies of labor and resources, which the Japanese invasion and flooding had already rendered scarce. Archival documents show how localities tried to avoid these demands, as well as the Nationalist regime's rationale for making them. War did not eliminate contentious negotiations between different levels of government, but intensified them.

In September 1940, Yanling County's Financial Affairs Commission sent a petition to the Weishi Section Emergency Closure Provisional Project Commission, asking it to reduce levies of workers and materials for emergency dike repairs. Breaches in Weishi occurred during the wheat harvest, when Yanling's residents also had their hands full assisting with the construction and repair of other dikes along the Yellow River. For this reason, Yanling had difficulty supplying labor and materials for the Weishi repair project. They could attend to dike maintenance or farming, but not both at the same time. Though it sympathized with the plight of Yanling's residents, the Yellow River Conservancy Commission rebuffed their appeals. The Commission acknowledged that material costs might exceed the power (*liliang*) of a few mutual-security units. But the entire county shared the cost of materials and

---

[82] "Fangfan xindi Weishi duan qiangxian dukou huiyi jilu" (August 10, 1940): YRCC MG4.1-177.
[83] Xu Fuling (1991): 27; MHD: 148; MHS: 186.

the Yellow River Conservancy Commission gave compensation for them, so dike maintenance would not place an undue burden on the locality. The Yanling petition claimed that supplies of sorghum stalks had fallen to only one tenth of normal. The Commission asserted that, given the amount of land in Yanling planted with sorghum, it should have no difficulty coming up with the materials. The petition also claimed that Yanling could not meet the cost of providing wooden stakes. The Yellow River Conservancy Commission responded that if the task were shared by the entire county, each village would only have to provide ten stakes. The Yellow River Conservancy Commission stressed that its requisitions were completely different from "military river defense materials" (*junshi hegong cailiao*) in that payment was given for materials upon delivery, so the common people had no reason to fear. Because four-wheeled carts could be levied from each *lianbao* security unit to transport materials, there was also no need to hire handcarts.[84]

The crux of the debate was whether dike maintenance was a central or a local responsibility. The Yanling petition claimed that the closure was a "matter of the national treasury" to be funded by the central government, but the Yellow River Conservancy Commission maintained that it undertook the emergency closure to meet an urgent need. For this reason, the Commission made a few counties along the river responsible for repairs. For larger endeavors, the Nationalist central government would formulate a comprehensive plan to allocate materials and funds, but the present situation had to be handled differently. Waters from the Weishi breach inundated much of Yanling, and the Yellow River Conservancy Commission expressed compassion for the county's plight. Yet the Commission explained that it chose to requisition labor and materials in Yanling because the county was below Weishi at the endpoint of the floodwaters' drainage. As a result, Yanling had a closer connection with the project than other counties. To be self-reliant and avoid additional calamities, Yanling had to take advance precautions and assist with fortifications.

The fate of the nation called for selfless sacrifice in water control as well as warfare. Though Yanling residents built embankments to protect their own locales, according to the Yellow River Conservancy Commission, they showed little concern for larger-scale hydraulic management projects. As the directive admonished:

The common people are ignorant and do not know how to exhaust their power in comprehensive dike works and only construct dikes and make defensive closures. Likening this to resisting the enemy, exhausting ones power in comprehensive dike repairs is constructing national defense fortifications; constructing dikes and making defensive closures is heightening the walls around ones own home. What is advantageous and what is disadvantageous should be evident without explanation.[85]

---

[84] "Fangfan xindi Weishi duan qiangdu linshi gongcheng weiyuanhui zhiling" (September 21, 1940): YRCC MG4.2–71.
[85] Ibid.

According to the Yellow River Conservancy Commission, Yanling's residents had to look past narrow local concerns and devote their energies to the greater cause of national defense through water control.

The cruel irony, of course, was that the locality lacked this energy precisely because of Nationalist military actions. Conscription, the Yanling petition insisted, had taken more than half of the county's able-bodied adult males "to serve the nation." Working on military fortifications impeded farm work during the wheat harvest. Dike construction further disrupted planting, making it difficult for Yanling to take on additional responsibilities without harming agricultural production. From the local perspective, devoting energy to fighting a war and strengthening dike defenses left too little behind for farming. In response, the Yellow River Conservancy Commission stressed that the fate of the locality was bound to that of China's War of Resistance and larger-scale hydraulic management projects. As the Commission's directive warned, "once the county seat is occupied by the enemy, even if there is wheat it cannot be harvested. If a deluge of floodwaters arrives, how could grain be planted? In all matters one must distinguish relative importance and urgency."

To strengthen dike defenses during high-water season, the Yellow River Conservancy Commission urged Yanling to organize civilian laborer defense teams (*mingong fangxundui*) "to assist in making up for the inadequate power of flood defense troops."[86] The Commission maintained that river works did not require many materials and that trying to collect them over wide areas would lead to delays. To complete the closure in a timely fashion, it was necessary to gather materials in advance. Waiting until after the autumn harvest to start work would bring delays. The Commission repeated its sympathy for Yanling's hardships, but emphasized that higher levels of government had already approved levies of labor and supplies for the repairs. The exactions were "totally different from wantonly requisitioning labor power and material power." For this reason, the Yellow River Conservancy Commission refused to grant Yanling's plea to decrease material requisitions and waive its river defense responsibilities.[87]

Other counties endured similar demands. Wartime efforts to exploit the river's energies for military ends required extraction of labor and materials throughout the flooded area but due largely to the 1938 flood, resources were severely limited. As Nationalist hydraulic engineer Xu Fuling recalled, "During the War of Resistance the people faced hardship. Collecting and transporting materials was difficult and there was a shortage of stone. Flood defense projects mostly requisitioned supplies locally and were temporary undertakings that made do with whatever was available."[88] Wartime

---

[86] Ibid.
[87] Ibid.
[88] Xu Fuling (1991): 26.

conditions made it impossible to import materials from outside. As a result, counties near the dikes shouldered the burden.

In spring 1941, the collaborationist Henan provincial government conscripted laborers to repair the dike on the river's eastern bank and divert waters west to threaten Nationalist-constructed dikes. To figure out how to counter the Japanese initiatives, in April 1941 the Nationalist regime's Administrative Yuan convened a conference at which the First War Zone Command asked that branch channels above Jiangcun be blocked to augment the new dike's capacity to impede the Japanese. Following the conference, the Yellow River Conservancy Commission, the Military Affairs Commission's Xi'an office, and the First War Zone Command undertook dike repairs, with the Henan Repair and Defense Office responsible for construction work; the latter body started the project in April 1941 during the high-water season. Special offices were established to repair dangerous sections and to direct troops stationed in the area.[89]

In June 1941 the Yellow River again broke through its defenses at Xunmukou, causing eighty percent of its waters to flow into the Guo River. Its main channel passed through Weishi, Taikang, Huaiyang, and Luyi into the Huai. Because Huaiyang's county seat was located on high ground south of the Guo and north of the Sha, floodwaters never reached it. For this reason, Huaiyang was the only territory south of the flooded area that the Japanese had not occupied. If all the floodwaters entered the Guo, channels south of Huaiyang and north of the Sha would be cut off and Japanese armies in Huaiyang could move into Nationalist-held territory unimpeded. For defensive purposes, the Nationalists had to keep floodwaters south of Huaiyang in their present state and prevent the Yellow River from overtaking the Sha. Due to siltation, however, the Yellow River's main course shifted east between Taikang and Huaiyang in early 1940, causing its flow to dwindle southwest of Huaiyang. Without the barrier that floodwaters provided, Chinese armies in Huaiyang periodically came under attack by the Japanese. Under these circumstances, the Nationalists had to ensure that waters kept flowing to the south of Huaiyang in order to "simultaneously attend to national defense and the people's livelihood."[90]

In the spring and summer of 1941, the First War Zone Command and local governments closed two breaches near Wangpan, repaired six kilometers of dikes, and built ten willow revetments to decrease the river's flow as it entered the Guo and shift its main channel. Another project at Zhoujiakou blocked all but three of the eleven branch gullies through which the Yellow River entered the Sha and repaired 40 kilometers of dikes on the Sha's northern bank between Zhoujiakou and Huaiyang. These projects prevented floods from overtaking the Sha and kept waters south of Huaiyang from dissipating,

---

[89] Cheng et al. (2007): 292; MHS: 187.
[90] "Yu Wan Huangfanqu chakantuan baogao" (1941): YRCC MG4.1-124.

thereby obstructing Japanese troop movements.[91] At the same time, Fugou and other counties constructed thirty-seven military dikes (*jungongba*), along with revetments, bank defenses, and gullies to drain accumulated water. Local initiatives repaired almost 272 kilometers of dikes, using 800,000 kilograms of sorghum stalks and 8.3 million cubic meters of earth.[92]

A Nationalist investigation of counties in Henan's flooded area gives a vivid picture of how these projects were carried out. In 1941 the Yellow River Conservancy Commission requested funds to augment almost 300 kilometers of new flood defense dikes from Guangwu to Jieshou on the border with Anhui.[93] By June 1941, the Guangwu–Weishi section was completed and repairs were complete in Fugou. Other sections lagged behind. Xihua completed only 60 percent of its share and Huaiyang only 20 percent. Delays resulted in part from conflict between dike maintenance and agriculture: "The counties that undertook work early completed work before the wheat harvest. In counties that undertook work late, many delayed work during the time of the wheat harvest."[94]

Counties tried to ramp up the number of workers to complete repairs before high waters arrived. Central government funding was insufficient to purchase enough food for laborers, so localities incurred the cost of procuring it. "Flood defense dike works are undertaken by each county bordering the floods. For shoring up each cubic meter of earth the Yellow River Conservancy Commission pays four jiao as work relief. But this year grain prices have greatly increased and each worker needs two yuan per day (in Zhoukou [Zhoujiakou] hiring a worker requires four yuan) and each worker can only build one cubic meter each day. Therefore, each county's losses are extremely heavy."

At Hansiying in Fugou and other locations, workers rushed to complete military revetments and shore defenses. At Jiangcun, on the east bank opposite Hansiying, the Japanese had already constructed ten deflection dikes. "After these embankments were completed the main channel passed by Hansiying, which made breaches a great danger. Our side has also constructed sixteen deflection dikes near Hansiying to resist. Work is being carried out and is planned to be completed within one month." Along other dike sections, Nationalist hydraulic engineering agencies aimed to "Utilize existing civilian dikes, ordering the county governments to mobilize labor power to shore them up on their own and solidify them."[95]

---

[91] "Zhuan'an baogao: Huangfan digong qingxing"; "Chakan Taikang Huaiyang jingnei Huangfan qingxing baogaoshu" (December 31, 1941): YRCC MG 4.1-135; Xu Fuling (1991): 27; Li et al. (1994): 252.
[92] Cheng et al. (2007): 291; MHD: 156; MHS: 186–187.
[93] "Zhuan'an baogao: Huangfan digong qingxing."
[94] Ibid.
[95] Ibid. See also Xihua xian shizhi bianzuan weiyuanhui (1992): 117.

Efforts to close branch gullies between the Yellow River and the Sha did not always go smoothly. As a report on dike conditions in the flooded area related, "Sealing off Baimagou has failed twice, material losses have been great, and the local populace's complaints have been numerous." Nationalist inspections found that the river bottom at the work site was turbid and sandy. At the time of the closure, waters suddenly rose. Passing water destabilized the western embankment, causing it to collapse. Without adequate materials, there was no way to make emergency repairs. The project failed right when it was on the verge of success and material losses were heavy. The Yellow River Conservancy Commission selected another location about 1.5 kilometers upstream as the new closure site. On the northern bank, workers dug a diversion channel. On the opposite bank, they built a deflection dike to guide waters into the diversion channel "to divide the water's position-power (*fen shuishi*)." On nearby mudflats, small dikes were built to prevent water from flowing back into the gully. Investigators concluded that "If each county requisitions materials and sends them on time, within 20 days it can be closed. If materials are not acquired, the high waters will arrive, it will be difficult to complete, and the influence of national defense will be great." Inspectors met with the Seventh Special Area Administrative Supervisor and "instructed him to order each county to rapidly transport materials and send civilian laborers to complete work as soon as possible." As investigators emphasized, successfully completing the hydraulic engineering project would preserve floods as a defensive barrier against the Japanese. Since the main course of the Yellow River had shifted north of Huaiyang, its southern channel's volume had decreased, "so that if each branch channel is not sealed off all floodwaters' flow south of Huaiyang will enter the Sha River, and there will be no barrier to defend against the enemy in Huaiyang. Therefore, in terms of military affairs, sealing off each branch channel is extremely important."[96]

The Yellow River flooded area was never an impermeable barrier, however. In late August 1941, in tandem with a Japanese offensive against Changsha in central China, Japanese commanders in Henan increased troop strength and trained their engineering corps in ferrying operations and dike construction, preparing to move south across the river. Due to the difficulty of negotiating the river's summer high waters, military action did not happen until October, when the flood season had passed. Japanese armies built causeways and bridges to cross the Yellow River near Zhongmu and the Jing-Han railway bridge north of Zhengzhou that had been destroyed in 1938, easily breaking through Nationalist defensive positions. Japanese forces took the largely abandoned city of Zhengzhou on October 4 and built a bridgehead on the river's southern bank, deploying two infantry

[96] "Zhuan'an baogao: Huangfan digong qingxing."

regiments and one artillery regiment to defend it. Additional Japanese troops were stationed west of the river's main channel in Zhongmu's county seat. Following the Japanese action, on orders from the Military Affairs Commission, First War Zone Commander Wei Lihuang held a meeting with personnel from the Henan Repair and Defense Office to consider breaking dikes again to divert the river south and block Japanese westward encroachments. The Repair and Defense Office conducted surveys, but concluded that the site's terrain was unsuitable, water levels were too low, and the Japanese held nearby areas, so another strategic flood would be difficult to execute.[97]

At the end of October, the Japanese withdrew from Zhengzhou and Chinese armies moved back into the city. Japanese armies still controlled Zhongmu's county seat, which severely weakened Nationalist defenses. To eliminate this point of vulnerability, in November the commanders of the Third Group Army ordered the Henan Repair and Defense Office to send personnel to the front to conduct another survey and research the feasibility of diverting the Yellow River's waters southwest of the Zhongmu county seat. After conducting investigations, water control personnel dredged a branch gully west of Zhongmu to connect with the river's main channel. The project increased flow volume in the branch gully and make it harder for the Japanese to advance. The dredging required the movement of an estimated 428,300 cubic meters of earth. Nationalist river defense organs deemed the cost of paying workers too great, so local commanding officers ordered counties near the work site to conscript civilian laborers, giving them food subsidies as compensation. Starting in late November, more than 10,000 civilian laborers recruited for the project worked at night in freezing weather to avoid Japanese artillery fire. Dredging was completed at the end of the year.[98]

To prevent the Yellow River floods from overtaking the Guo, Nationalist military leaders recommended closing breaches in Taikang to make the waters return to their original position, but when work began in mid-December 1941, local sources of labor and materials had dwindled. An investigation conducted in late December found that "In the vicinity of [flood] gates in Taikang, all the willow branches were already completely cut last year when the breach at Wangpan was closed. Also, during this year's high-water season many willow trees were drowned and there are no materials. Moreover, most of this place's residents have already fled. Although there are still some residents, they are mostly women and children. Requisitioning labor and materials locally will be extremely difficult."[99] Labor and materials could be requisitioned 20 kilometers away from the work site but residents had little

[97] Chen (1986): 36–39; Bi (1995): 193–198; MHD: 157. See also Peck (1967): Chapter 13.
[98] Bi (1995): 198–202; MHD: 158.
[99] "Chakan Taikang Huaiyang jingnei Huangfan qingxing baogaoshu."

clothing, there were neither dwellings nor food for them, and winter was coming. Gathering large numbers of civilian laborers would be difficult. Even if materials could be procured from more distant areas, there were no navigable waterways in the area to transport them. The Japanese occupied positions near the site, which made work even harder to carry out.[100] By January 1941 the Nationalists somehow mustered enough energy to seal and stop the flow from ten dike breaches.[101] As a former resident of Fugou's Poxie village recalled, "The Nationalist government unceasingly sent civilian laborers from counties in western Henan to repair and reinforce dike defenses. Whenever they arrived, Poxie villagers' doors, wood, furniture, and trees were all taken without compensation."[102]

However, the weakly constructed new dikes did hardly anything to alleviate devastation caused by Yellow River floods.[103] As Xu Fuling recalled:

When repairing the new river defense dikes, work was carried out hastily, earth was sandy and loose, and it was not tamped down, so its ability to withstand water was poor. At the same time, the river's area was wide, the wind and waves were severe, there were many branch streams, and its flow's position-power often changed. Once [dikes were] scoured by the main channel or hit by strong winds and waves, if emergency defenses were not made in time there would be calamities due to breaches and for this reason breaches occurred year after year.[104]

The huge amount of sediment deposited by the river added to the instability. The width of the flooded area expanded from 1.5 kilometers between Jingshui and Zheng County to over 10 kilometers after it joined the Jialu River. By the time floodwaters entered Zhongmu their width had expanded to over 15 kilometers. In Weishi they were 50 kilometers wide. Flow velocity decreased as the river spread out across the flat plain, causing it to deposit its sediments. The threat of flooding grew as siltation caused the river's bed to rise. One year the terrain might be relatively low and full of accumulated water but as sediment accumulated, the terrain rose and floodwaters shifted to more low-lying areas.

Dikes constructed by Chinese and Japanese armies, along with the inability of hastily built structures to contain the Yellow River, influenced floodwaters' movements and distribution. Together, siltation and dike construction caused the river to meander and shift unpredictably, causing the total area impacted by floods to expand.[105] The river did not settle into a new course, but spread over the plain and continued to lay down its load of silt. With the deposition of this sediment every year, the area covered by floods shifted in an arc that

---

[100] Ibid.
[101] Cheng et al. (2007): 291; MHD: 156.
[102] Xie (2002): 100.
[103] Li et al. (1994): 260.
[104] Xu Fuling (1991): 28.
[105] Han and Nan (1948): 6–7. See also Xing (1986): 187; Li et al. (1994): 250.

swung to the south and west.[106] With the Yellow River's diversion, its sediments also damaged the hydrological system of the Huai River and its tributaries as well, clogging large sections of the Jialu, Sha, Ying, Guo, and Shuangji rivers. Siltation of the Huai's tributaries threw its drainage system into disarray. As drainage capacity drastically reduced, floods grew more severe and the potential for flooding in the Huai watershed grew.[107] Between 1938 and 1945, dikes along the Yellow River broke dozens of times at numerous spots in Henan.[108] The Yellow River, wrote the American reporter Jack Belden, "is out of control and cannot find a channel." Continually shifting its course, the river created disasters in Henan and nearby provinces. "In its unpredictable journeyings," according to Belden, "the new river has gone on a rampage" and caused untold damage.[109]

Initially, the river's unruly energies were precisely what the Nationalist regime wanted to rely upon to shore up its waning military power. Once they had been unleashed, these same energies caused enormous destruction regardless of how hard people tried to rein them in.

CONCLUSION

From the earliest stages of the Sino-Japanese War a web of sometimes cooperative and sometimes contentious interactions played out in Henan among armies, rivers, hydraulic engineering works, and local societies. Energy flowed through these webs in numerous forms. During the war's first year, the Japanese military depended on railway lines to move troops and supplies. Railroads, which facilitated energy flows across space and time, initially defined military strategy. The Nationalist army's diversion of the Yellow River in June 1938 temporarily repulsed the Japanese by transforming the river's energy into a weapon that disrupted North China's railway network, which converged in Henan. Flooding altered the environmental landscape and redefined military space. Unleashing the river's energy and altering its course safeguarded the Nationalist position until the Japanese army's 1944 Ichigō Offensive.

Following its 1938 diversion, pursuit of power continued to depend on channeling and exploiting the river's energy. All sides in the conflict struggled to control, redistribute, and drain the river's waters to gain advantage and advance their objectives. Ecologically, the Chinese Nationalists and the Japanese authorities acted on the river in essentially the same way. Militarily and politically, their hydraulic engineering initiatives were diametrically

---

[106] Barnett (1953): 11.
[107] Li et al. (1994): 256–257; Cheng et al. (2007): 286–287.
[108] SJZHFZ 63 (March 24, 1947): 4; Han and Nan (1948): 6; MHS: 181–182; Cheng et al. (2007): 287.
[109] Belden (1943): 180.

opposed, with each side trying to keep the river's waters out of the territories that they controlled and deflect them onto their adversaries.

Militarized hydraulic engineering demanded huge energy expenditures. To manipulate the river for strategic purposes, military actors and hydraulic management agencies that allied with them had to find ways to extract labor and resources from Henan's flooded area. The task of providing this energy placed a massive burden on localities that had already been devastated by war-induced disasters. Breaking the dikes and unleashing the river's waters against the Japanese benefited Nationalist armies in the short term, but floods led to energy losses of staggering magnitude. War-induced flooding destroyed agricultural landscapes, threw water control systems into disarray, and displaced vast populations. Neither Chinese nor Japanese armies had the power to command labor and materials in the quantities needed to counter the river's energies.

Effectively manipulating the Yellow River for military-strategic purposes proved futile. As it had for centuries, the river defied human efforts to control it. As in times past, "hydrological systems kept twisting free from the grip of human would-be mastery, drying out, silting up, flooding over, or changing their channels. By doing so they devoured the resources needed to keep them under control or serviceable."[110] In a time of war, when armies devoured or destroyed virtually all available resources, this cycle grew more vicious. Given the level of damage, Henan's flooded area had little energy to devote to hydraulic engineering, let alone for repairing ecological devastation. Energy is finite. If it is diverted for war, it is unavailable for the work of reconstruction. Military systems drained energy out of local society, making it virtually impossible to recover from war-induced disasters.

The state's agency in the intentional destruction of hydraulic infrastructure and extraction of finite energy sources for military purposes made these wartime disasters distinctive. When the Yellow River's southern dike broke about 16 kilometers east of Huayuankou in 1887–1888 and caused massive flooding, the Qing government for the first time consulted foreign engineers regarding "river training" techniques.[111] After merely two seasons, officially sponsored re-diversion projects sent the river back into its previous channel.[112] It is also worth noting that after disastrous floods struck the Yangzi River and Huai River basin in 1931, the Nationalist regime implemented relatively effective flood control measures. Extensive government relief also limited losses in 1935, when the next major floods arrived.[113] During the Sino-Japanese War, the state's altered priorities made a decisive difference.

---

[110] Elvin (2004): 164.
[111] Pomeranz (1993): 165, 167.
[112] Todd (1949): 40.
[113] Lillian M. Li (2007): 306–308.

In 1938, the Nationalist leadership created the Yellow River flood as a strategic calculation, trying to ensure their regime's survival by sacrificing the welfare of the rural populace. Thereafter, authorities deemed turning the river against their enemies a greater priority than relief measures. Chinese forces exploited huge amounts of energy waging hydraulic warfare. The Japanese and their Chinese collaborators, for their part, desperately tried to reimpose order and consolidate power. Neither side was successful. Despite the futility of the task, extracting labor and materials to wage war and manipulate waterways channeled scarce resources away from the work of repairing agro-ecological systems. Even as human populations migrated out of the flooded area, the destruction of North China's railway networks made it impossible to import materials from other regions. Ecological cataclysm was the result. Without energy devoted to relief and recovery, the Yellow River floods experienced during World War II lasted longer and had a greater impact than the disasters that had occurred in times of relative peace and stability.

This wartime distortion of energy flows to maintain militarized hydraulic systems had a catastrophic impact on local society. As China's military and political leaders trumpeted the absolute necessity of sacrifice to ensure national survival, the flooded area's residents had to find ways to cope with these war-induced environmental catastrophes.

2

Stories of Survival: Refugee Migration and Ecological Adaptation

Disruption of hydraulic infrastructure following the breaching of the Yellow River's dikes at Huayuankou by the Nationalist army in June 1938 displaced more than 1.17 million people in Henan. As Chinese and Japanese armies and their civilian allies battled to manipulate the river for military-strategic purposes, refugees struggled to secure the energy they needed to survive. This chapter examines how refugees from Henan's Yellow River flooded area confronted these war-induced disasters. Its focus is on the ecological strategies with which displaced people adapted to war-torn landscapes, as well as the environmental consequences of these activities.

By the early twentieth century, villagers in Henan and other parts of the North China Plain had plenty of experience with floods and other disasters. Life was always volatile. Rural residents viewed environmental unpredictability as the norm and developed ways of coping with it. After the 1938 flood, refugees from Henan's flooded area drew on a repertoire of survival strategies – some of which had existed for several centuries – that had often been employed in times past. This continuity blurs clear distinctions made between socio-ecological histories of wartime and peacetime. Nevertheless, war's environmental impact gave rise to disasters that were more acute, larger-scale, and of longer duration than those that occurred under "normal" circumstances. On top of flooding, people contended with the violence, danger, and instability derived from the military situation. Even after war had devastated agro-ecosystems, moreover, Henan's rural populace had to provide labor and materials to fuel warfare and to support militarized hydraulic engineering projects. In addition to making it harder for refugees to obtain the energy they needed to survive, the metabolic demands of military conflict siphoned off labor and resources needed to reconstruct Henan's war-damaged environmental infrastructure. In this manner, redirection of energy flows for military purposes compounded war-induced ecological catastrophes.

Multi-dimensional relationships existed between refugee survival strategies and wartime ecological change. The Yellow River's strategic diversion

59

and its place in the geography of the Sino-Japanese conflict created new ways of making a living for refugees in Henan who engaged in smuggling goods across the frontlines. Other ecological adaptations employed by refugees had a definite impact on the land. Many flood victims earned income collecting and selling energy stored in biomass as fuel for heating and cooking. Fuel gathering by refugees heightened demands on energy sources that human exploitation had already depleted, making them even scarcer.

Fallout from wartime displacement in Henan also triggered environmental changes in Shaanxi Province, where thousands of flood refugees fled. The most significant transformations occurred in the areas in Shaanxi where the Nationalist regime resettled refugees and mobilized their labor to reclaim land for agriculture. Land reclamation converted wooded landscapes to farms, simplifying ecosystems and damaging wildlife habitats. The impetus for these environmental changes was the wartime state's need to generate energy surpluses to fuel China's military resistance against Japan.

FLOOD REFUGEE DISPLACEMENT

Although few people received advanced warning, when Nationalist soldiers attempted to excavate the Yellow River dikes at Huayuankou in June 1938 local residents took notice. Feng Zhaoxue, who grew up near Huayuankou, recalled that,

> At the time when the Nationalists breached the Yellow River dikes, I was still small. Whenever I saw soldiers I got scared. Every day the soldiers guarding the Yellow River went to dig. Lots of soldiers passed through the village carrying guns and went to each household to take tools. Then they all went up onto the dike. That village of ours faced the dike. Right after the water came out it was not big. Some of the common people did not care, saying that after a while it would not come out any more. But afterward it got bigger and bigger, and the common people ran to high ground. As it turned out, the water even flooded high places, and then the common people finally knew the Yellow River's cruelty.[1]

> Once the torrent grew, houses collapsed and people were trapped on the high ground. Local residents, with encouragement from the local authorities, went to save disaster victims by boat, but as Feng put it "the area flooded was extremely large, the population affected by the disaster was extremely large, and there were few boats, so there was no way to attend to them all and some people drowned. There were also some people who could not part with their household things and were unwilling to leave, and as it turned out once the waters rose they also drowned."[2]

---

[1] Mei (2009): 207.
[2] Ibid.

When floodwaters first arrived in June 1938, local officials tried to organize dike repairs to contain damage and ordered people in disaster-stricken areas to evacuate. Many residents escaped by moving to high ground or to the tops of embankments. The river's surging waters left others stranded in trees or on the roofs of houses. As a report on flood conditions in Zhongmu and Zheng counties written in July 1938 described the catastrophe: "The people in the flooded region have mostly fled to villages and towns with higher terrain and are urgently awaiting relief. Their fields and houses have all been flooded and destroyed. If they were unable to flee in time, people and draft animals were carried away and it was utterly horrible."[3] Many disaster victims were trapped and had to wait for waters to subside before they could move to safety.[4]

The 1938 flood came during the peak agricultural season, on the eve of the summer harvest. At that time of year, farmers hesitated to leave their land and crops behind.[5] According to Jin Mancang, who also lived in a village near Huayuankou as a child, lots of residents escaped floods by moving to higher ground or to the tops of dikes. Once the deluge passed and things got back to normal, they expected to return home. But the flooding lasted much longer than anticipated. Since flood victims took only a limited amount of food and fuel with them, hunger set in quickly. "The people stuck in the high places did not have anything to eat, and after a while a lot of them starved. In the places where water was shallow the tops of the wheat showed through. The people who fled to the top of the dikes carried baskets and waded through the water to go pick the wheat sprouts." Once disaster victims ate everything they could salvage from fields and available fuel sources were exhausted, many of them had to flee and try to beg for food.[6]

With the disaster's severity not fully clear, many refugees assumed that – as had happened after previous floods – waters would soon subside and they could return home. In Weishi, as one flood victim recalled, "At first everyone still thought the waters would not flow for long and once the Yellow River breach was sealed they would have a way to stay alive. Practically no one in

---

[3] "Di yi zhanqu siling zhangguan Cheng daidian" (July 9, 1938), in "Huangfanqu yan Huang kuishui ge xian beizai baogao."

[4] "Luo zhuanyuan Zhen yang dian" (July 22, 1938); "Xihua xian zhugong weiyuan Wu Zhidao jing daidian" (July 24, 1938); "Fugou xian zhugong weiyuan Qiao Guanghou jing rong daidian" (July 25, 1938); "Zhongmu xian Huangzai fanlan quyu diaocha biao" (July 21, 1938); "Luo Zhen shi daidian" (July 31, 1938); "[Fugou xian] di shi hao diaocha biao" (August 5–6, 1938); "Fugou diaocha biao" (August 7–8, 1938) "[Fugou] ba yue nianwu ri zhi nianba ri diaocha ribao biao" (August 25–28, 1938), in "Huangfanqu yan Huang kuishui ge xian beizai baogao." See also Bo (1989): 119–120; Qu (2003): 256.

[5] Qu (2003): 254–255. See also Bo (1989): 119–120.

[6] Mei (1992): 259; Mei (2009): 205–206. Nationalist personnel who went to Henan's flooded area to administer relief in July 1938 commented disapprovingly on the initial reluctance of many local residents to leave. See report dated July 20, 1938 in "Henan sheng Zheng xian, Zhongmu, Weishi deng xian guanyu Huangzai jizheng gongzuo baogao" (1938): HPA M8-08-0194.

the village thought of fleeing." Their expectations did not prove realistic. "Then the floodwaters got bigger, and after two or three months people in the village had eaten what little grain they could, so there was nothing they could do but flee." Only the elderly stayed in the villages, left behind by family members who were able to move away more quickly.[7]

Most flood refugees traveled with family or neighbors to nearby villages and towns, or to other counties in Henan that the Yellow River had not inundated. Some found shelter in temples and begged, while the more fortunate lived with relatives and friends.[8] Fugou's county seat was located in a low-lying area and floodwaters ran along its northern and eastern edges. The local government organized construction of temporary dikes and earthworks to protect the county seat's walls, preventing waters from entering the town and inundating it. As a result, hundreds of refugees from Fugou, Luyi, and Taikang took refuge within the city walls, filling vacant buildings and roaming the streets.[9] Soon the number of refugees in the Fugou county seat increased to over a thousand, exhausting the limited grain stores. Without outside assistance, there was no way for the county magistrate to give relief to all the needy.[10] Dwindling food supplies could not support the expanding refugee population.

In the days following the June 1938 flood, the Nationalist regime deputed personnel to distribute relief in Henan's flooded area and try to evacuate victims.[11] Yet the exigencies of war and the sheer scale of disaster made adequate relief programs impossible. Tens of thousands of flood victims moved to the towns of Zhoujiakou, Xuchang, Luohe, and Zhengzhou. A mere fraction found shelter in refugee reception centers run by local governments, charitable associations, and foreign missionaries. By early August 1938, the Zhengzhou refugee reception center had taken in over 4,700

---

[7] Wang (1990): 67. For additional evidence on the situation in Weishi, see Lu (1990); "Luo Zhen gan daidian" (July 27, 1938), in "Huangfanqu yan Huang kuishui ge xian beizai baogao."
[8] Qu (2003):259.
[9] "Fugou xian zhugong weiyuan Qiao Guanghou jing rong daidian" (July 25, 1938); "Zhu Fugou diaocha weiyuan Qiao Guanghou" (August 13, 1938); "Zhu Fugou diaocha weiyuan Qiao Guanghou cheng song ba yue shisan ri zhi shiba ri diaocha ribao biao" (August 13–18, 1938), in "Huangfanqu yan Huang kuishui ge xian beizai baogao." See also "Shin Kōga karyū ibban kaiko chōsa hōkokusho."
[10] "Fugou diaocha biao" (August 7–8, 1938); "[Fugou] diaocha ribao biao" (August 17–20, 1938), "[Fugou] ba yue nianwu ri zhi nianba ri diaocha ribao biao" (August 25–28, 1938), in "Huangfanqu yan Huang kuishui ge xian beizai baogao." See also Wang (2003): 118.
[11] "Guomindang Henan sheng dangbu tepai Qu Yingguang deng banli fuji shiyi" (August 15, 1938): HPA M2-25-686; "Guomindang Henan sheng dangbu guanyu dangzheng jiguan qianyi, Huangzai jiuji gao minzhong shu, biaoyu" (July 1938): HPA M2-27-753; "Zhongguo guomindang wei juxing Huangzai jiuji juankuan yiri yundong gao dangyuan minzhong shu" (July 1938): HPA M2-25-690; "Henan sheng Zheng xian, Zhongmu, Weishi deng xian guanyu Huangzai jizheng gongzuo baogao" (June 29-August 8, 1938): HPA M8-08-0194. See also Qu (2003): 272–275, 291–298; Qu (2007): 57–63; MHS: 180–181.

people, but it had no way to accommodate all flood victims in the city.[12] Disaster victims heard rumors that assistance was being distributed in certain locales, only to find that relief programs had concluded by the time they arrived.[13] Henan's provincial government ordered counties that had not been hit by the disaster to take in flood refugees, distribute them among *baojia* mutual-security units, and to look after their welfare until they could support themselves. Though these arrangements gave some refugees a measure of assistance, most did not benefit from any relief and were left to their own devices.[14]

In places where flood refugees congregated, poor sanitation and overcrowding made infectious disease a constant threat. Cholera and other maladies spread rapidly.[15] Crowding of dense populations in confined areas exposed people to water that was contaminated by human waste and lice that spread typhus. As in past floods, pools of standing water made an ideal eco-niche for *Anopheles* mosquitoes that were vectors for malaria. Mosquitoes flourished in swamps of stagnant water that existed throughout eastern Henan's flooded area.[16] In July 1938, Nationalist representatives sent to distribute relief funds in Zhongmu found that, "In Zhongmu epidemic disease is rampant and it has recently spread to Zhongmu's county seat."[17] By August, the situation was worse. Epidemic disease spread everywhere, but no medicine was available to treat the ill.[18] In the Fugou county seat, unsanitary conditions in which refugees lived and their poor state of nutrition made typhoid, cholera, and dysentery pervasive.[19] In Xihua, "in villages that have not been flooded epidemic disease has appeared and people die every day."[20] A former flood victim from Zhongmu recalled that after the 1938 flood, "there was filth all over, lots of mosquitoes, lots of corpses, and disaster victims often had to live outdoors, so disease became widespread." For this reason, Zhongmu experienced particularly virulent cholera, typhoid, and dysentery epidemics. Cholera was especially harmful: "It caused vomiting

---

[12] "Qianwang Kong weiyuanzhang jiang daidian" (July 3, 1938); "Dong hai daidian" (August 2, 1938), in "Huangfanqu yan Huang kuishui ge xian beizai baogao."
[13] Mei (2009): 206–207.
[14] A.J. Parenti to Newton Bowles, "Part I, Survey of Flooded Area Refugees as basis for estimating post-UNRRA food requirements," September 7, 1947: UN S-0528-0543 A.R. 8B. See also Qu (2003): 299–304.
[15] Qu (2003): 256. See also Mei (2009): 214.
[16] Mosquitoes and infectious disease (most likely malaria) during the Song are referred to in Zhang (2011): 32–33.
[17] Report dated July 20, 1938 in "Henan sheng Zheng xian, Zhongmu, Weishi deng xian guanyu Huangzai jizheng gongzuo baogao."
[18] Proposal from Zhang Daqi dated August 1938 in "Henan sheng Zheng xian, Zhongmu, Weishi deng xian guanyu Huangzai jizheng gongzuo baogao."
[19] Wang (2003): 118.
[20] "Xihua Wu Zhidao hao daidian" (August 19, 1938), in "Huangfanqu yan Huang kuishui ge xian beizai baogao."

and diarrhea, and some died from it in half a day's time."[21] Some refugees who fled Fugou for Xuchang or elsewhere had to come back because they could not find shelter or contracted disease.[22]

By August 1938 waters had subsided in much of Yanling, but sand and silt deposits were "as deep as a person is tall." Houses collapsed and were hidden beneath the sediments. As a Henan newspaper reported, "The disaster victims make dried grasses they have gathered into shanties and live on top of dry mounds. The streets of the past have now turned into channels navigated by boat." On the road from Yanling to Xuchang, "Beside every village and in the shade of every big tree one sees the vagrant masses spreading out blankets that have been soaked by the Yellow River's waters. On one side are displayed small carts, poles for carrying baskets, bundles of firewood, and other broken down things."[23] When summer high-water season ended, floods receded in Weishi, Fugou, and other counties, freeing disaster victims who were trapped in high places and making it easier for people to move about. But floods washed away houses and sediment covered roads and fields, making it difficult for refugees to return to their villages and resume farming.[24]

Local governments tried to keep floodwaters in check. However, large-scale refugee migration rendered unavailable workers needed for effective hydraulic maintenance. Wartime conscription intensified these labor shortages, as many men were drafted or fled to evade military service. In August 1938, the Fugou County government tried to construct small dikes to protect villages and farmland against floods. But the precipitous decline in the county's population due to war and disaster hampered this undertaking. As a report on conditions in Fugou stated, "many residents cannot make a living and have fled with their families, so recruiting laborers is extremely difficult."[25] Labor shortages posed a problem for dike construction projects in Taikang as well. As investigation reports explained, "Although there are still some residents, they are mostly women and children. Requisitioning labor and materials locally will be extremely difficult."[26] As wartime dislocations made workers scarce, maintaining hydraulic infrastructure grew increasingly difficult.

---

[21] Xu Shouqian (1991): 25. More references are found in Fugou xianzhi zong bianji shi (1986): 92; Feng (1991): 36–37; Liu (1991): 6; Han and Han (1991): 59; Taikang xianzhi bianzuan weiyuanhui (1991): 94.
[22] "[Fugou] nianyi ri zhi niansi ri diaocha ribao biao"; "[Fugou] ba yue nianwu ri zhi nianba ri diaocha ribao biao," in "Huangfanqu yan Huang kuishui ge xian beizai baogao."
[23] Quoted in Li et al. (1994): 248.
[24] "Diaochayuan Wu Chaoliang ba yue si ri chengbao Weishi xian fanlan quyu diaocha biao" (August 4, 1938); "Fugou xian diaocha biao di jiu hao" (August 4, 1938), in "Huangfanqu yan Huang kuishui ge xian beizai baogao."
[25] "Ba yue nianwu ri zhi nianba ri diaocha ribao biao," in "Huangfanqu yan Huang kuishui ge xian beizai baogao."
[26] "Chakan Taikang Huaiyang jingnei Huangfan qingxing baogaoshu" (December 31, 1941): YRCC MG4.1-135.

Nevertheless, in 1939 the Nationalists gathered enough labor to construct a series of dikes along the western edge of the Yellow River's new course. By building the embankments, as detailed in the previous chapter, Nationalist leaders sought to utilize the floodwaters as a strategic barrier against westward Japanese encroachment, "using the Yellow River to control the enemy." Some residents of Henan's flooded area actually benefited from these militarized hydraulic engineering projects. Nationalist-constructed dikes shifted waters eastward, enabling flood victims from parts of Fugou to return and cultivate previously flooded land. Resettlement was difficult, however, since labor was scarce, returning refugees lacked tools and seed, draft animals perished, sediments covered fields, and flooding remained a perpetual threat.

Wartime instability threw water control systems into disarray. Without adequate defenses, the Yellow River underwent sudden shifts and its waters broke through temporarily repaired dikes, causing additional flooding that pushed the refugee population even higher.[27] In summer and early fall of 1939, torrential rainfall and flash floods made the Yellow River rise abruptly, causing the Jialu, Sha, Ying, Jingshui, and Shuangji rivers to overflow as well. Floods were most severe in Fugou, Xihua, Huaiyang, Shenqiu, Xiangcheng, and Taikang, which had a million or more disaster victims in need of relief. Each day tens of thousands of refugees congregated in Zhoujiakou, Xuchang, and Zhengzhou. Heavy rains fell again in the spring and summer of 1940, leading to equally serious dike breaks in Kaifeng, Zhengzhou, Zhongmu, Weishi, Yanling, Fugou, Xihua, Taikang, and Huaiyang.[28]

Because of this persistent flooding, some local residents had to flee multiple times. The family of one refugee left their home in Fugou after the 1938 flood had covered the 6.7 hectares of land that they owned. After living in a temple for a year, they returned to Fugou to plant their fields. In the autumn of 1939, dikes broke again and caused an even bigger flood. With their crops and homes washed away, four hundred villagers followed two local men who suggested they "might as well run far away from that damn place and never come back!"[29] Refugees who ventured back to Xiangcheng County met with similar misfortune. In October 1938, after the first floods passed, people who fled to nearby areas returned. Upon their arrival, they discovered that a thick layer of sediment covered the land and made it impossible for them to find their previous homes. The only alternative was to move to high ground, build grass shacks, and prepare for winter. When heavy rains caused the Yellow River to flood following the wheat harvest in 1939, they were forced to flee

---

[27] Fugou xianzhi zong bianji shi (1986): 97–99; "Henan sheng zhanshi sunshi diaocha baogao" (1990): 15; Xihua xian shizhi bianzuan weiyuanhui (1992): 118; Wang (2003): 119; Xu and Zhu (2005): 148–53; MHD: 136; MHS: 182–188.
[28] Li et al. (1993): 525–526, 532–533; Li et al. (1994): 251–252.
[29] Xing (1996): 216.

for a second time.[30] After the flood of 1938 and those that came in 1939, investigations found nearly 553,347 hectares of flooded land, more than 1,963,200 disaster victims (*zaimin*), and more than 1,285,500 people in need of relief (*daizhen renshu*) in Henan's flooded area.[31]

Other organisms benefited. As happened in times past, flooding that was utterly catastrophic from a human perspective came as a boon to certain wildlife species.[32] Without significant human populations, grasses and other vegetation overgrew lands that emerged when waters receded. Wild animals flourished in these habitats. Prior to 1938, birds such as crows and sparrows, which thrived in human-engineered agricultural settlements, were the dominant avian species. Before the flood, migrating wild geese spent the winter in Fugou, but not in large numbers. After 1938, the flooded area's water surfaces became a stopover on the flyways of migratory aquatic bird species. Every year over 10,000 wild geese wintered in Fugou. Egrets were also numerous. Fugou's Caoli township became known as "white egret village" (*bailu cun*) because so many egrets gathered there. Some mammals benefited too. Without humans around, rabbits thrived in the overgrowth that emerged in places where waters subsided.[33] War-induced flooding and population flight led to a contraction in cultivated land area, along with the resurgence of spontaneous vegetation and habitats that were home to wild animal species. Floodwaters and wastelands became a playground for geese, egrets, and rabbits.

Humans did not fare nearly so well. In addition to persistent flooding, the military situation in eastern Henan weighed heavily on the civilian populations that remained. Under unstable wartime conditions, much of the flooded area lacked effective civilian government. A motley assortment of armed contingents – Nationalist and Communist guerillas, regular forces, local militias, bandits, and secret societies – vied with one another for influence in the conflict against the Japanese, sometimes collaborating with the invaders as well.[34] From 1938 the Nationalist army stationed large numbers of troops in Zhongmu to defend against Japanese forces on the river's northern bank. A flood victim from Zhongmu's Zhanyang village later recalled that, "In Zhanyang village there were [Nationalist] soldiers everywhere. They seized males as soldiers and laborers, stole chickens and dogs, abducted women, held people up and robbed them, extorted the people's wealth, and forced men to

---

[30] Qu (2003): 260.
[31] "1939 nian Henan sheng ge xian shuizai sunshi diaocha tongji biao" (1940): HPA AB6-591.
[32] Zhang (2011): 32.
[33] After the Yellow River returned to its pre-1938 channel in 1947 the goose population gradually decreased. But even in the 1950s there were flocks of 3,000–4,000 geese that spent the night on the banks of the Jialu River. Many geese were caught and killed, so they eventually became scarce and no longer wintered in Fugou. After floodwaters subsided in the late 1940s, white egrets also left and did not return. Fugou xianzhi zong bianji shi (1986): 249–250.
[34] Lary (2004): 155–156.

FIGURE 2.1 Henan residents evacuating the Yellow River flooded area by boat
Source: Guomin zhengfu zhongyang xuanchuanbu. Courtesy of Qinfeng lao zhaopian guan, *Kangzhan Zhongguo guoji tongxun zhaopian*. Guilin: Guangxi shifan daxue chubanshe, 2008.

repair dikes and build roads, creating turmoil in the village."[35] These military demands made resumption of normal farming activities all but impossible.

As in other regions, Chinese troops tore down temples to obtain wood they needed to repair defensive fortifications. Shelling by Japanese artillery across the Yellow River reduced other buildings in the Zhongmu county seat to rubble.[36] Nearby Japanese installations bombarded Guangwu's county seat as well. The Japanese army occupied portions of Zhongmu and Guangwu when it advanced across the Yellow River in late 1941, leaving over 80,000 disaster refugees unwilling to return home. When the Japanese moved into Zhongmu, residents of the county seat and people in villages near the firing line fled to the south and southeast. The Japanese massacred villages in Guangwu, burning ninety percent of their buildings and killing 4,500 residents. Poorly disciplined Chinese troops placed additional burdens on the civilian populace by seizing their dwindling grain and fodder supplies.[37]

[35] Liu and Mao (1991): 49.
[36] Liu (1991): 7.
[37] Wang Bingjun, "Wei baogao shi ju bao Henan sheng Zheng xian, Zhongmu, Guangwu san xian zaiqing" (July 28, 1942): HIA, KMT Project TE 20, Reel 13 File 534. On seizure of wood for military construction projects in Zhejiang see Schoppa (2011): 253–254. On difficulties that arose in Shaanxi due to the presence of Japanese and Nationalist troops massed on opposite banks of the Yellow River see Hershatter (2011): 40.

FIGURE 2.2 Refugees in Henan's flooded area
Source: Guomin zhengfu zhongyang xuanchuanbu. Courtesy of Qinfeng lao zhaopian guan, *Kangzhan Zhongguo guoji tongxun zhaopian*. Guilin: Guangxi shifan daxue chubanshe, 2008.

REFUGEE LIVELIHOOD STRATEGIES

To cope with war-related catastrophes, refugees from Henan's flooded area drew on an existing repertoire of survival strategies. In Henan – as elsewhere on the North China Plain – migration was an established way to confront everyday hardship and periodic disaster.[38] Well before outbreak of the Sino-Japanese War, mobility characterized everyday life for many. Some of Henan's rural residents (most often young males) left to earn additional

---

[38] Migration due to flooding during the Song is referred to by Zhang (2011): 35. On other parts of North China during the Qing and Republican period see Huang (1985): 10–11, 30–32, 271–273.

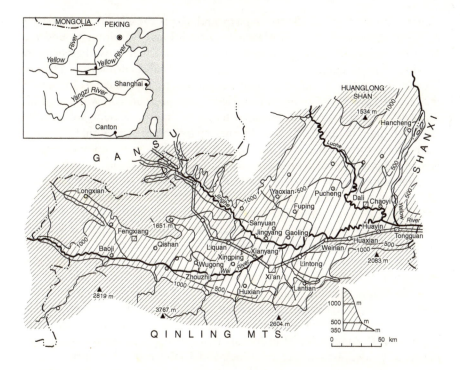

FIGURE 2.3 Map of central Shaanxi Province (Huanglongshan at upper right)

income by working in cities or other villages during the slack agricultural season, returning home to harvest and plant crops each spring. Some men went out to work as long-term hired laborers and remitted earnings to their families, leaving farming to women, children, and older men. When floods or famines struck, whole households took flight. Some disasters lasted longer than others, but these migrations were usually short-term. People left home for several weeks or months and came back to rebuild as soon as the disasters subsided.[39] Prolonged flooding that struck Henan after 1938, on the other hand, led to displacements of greater scale and duration, forcing hundreds of thousands of rural residents to leave their native places for months or years at a time. Environmental infrastructure collapsed and wartime demand for labor and resources rendered agro-ecological recovery impossible. Even without government assistance, however, displaced people found ways to adapt to these precarious circumstances.

A relief proposal brought before the Nationalist government in October 1939 enumerated the array of survival strategies employed by refugees from

---

[39] Zhu and Wang (2001): 134–142; Su (2004): 132–140; Hershatter (2011): 42–43.

Henan's flooded area.[40] Between 1937 and 1941, the Nationalist military conscripted more troops from Henan – a traditional recruiting ground for Chinese armies – than any province. Many adult males who lost their fields to flooding found employment by joining Nationalist armies in Henan. Wealthier families commonly hired substitutes to keep their sons out of military service. Flood refugees provided a vast pool of men who could fill this role.[41] Even in areas of Henan affected by floods, demand for recruits remained high. In late August 1938, a newspaper report stated that although many flood victims fled and populations dwindled, the Nationalist army demanded conscripts according to the original quotas set for each locality. If communities in the flooded area lacked able-bodied adult males, *lianbao* mutual-security units shared responsibility for hiring replacements, with each *bao* paying 100–200 yuan for them. Warfare compounded the effects of disaster for local residents. "In this way, the common people's land is flooded, their houses collapsed, their wheat is washed away, and every day they are busy making emergency repairs to the dikes to relieve disaster, but they still have to pay money to hire soldiers. There are really countless hardships."[42]

Wage labor, gleaning, and begging were other familiar survival strategies that assumed greater importance during the war years. When residents fled and males left to serve as military conscripts, flooded areas experienced acute population shortages. Relief proposals noted that people who remained in Henan's flooded area found work as menial laborers. When farmers harvested crops in summer and fall, many flood victims gleaned in fields. Relatively abundant grain supplies existed during that time of year, so refugees could also beg for food. But this strategy was only effective if food was readily available. Once winter arrived there was no way to glean and begging became difficult, so refugees went hungry.[43]

Flood refugees from Xihua, as a former refugee recalled, "depended upon working as long-term and short-term hired laborers, begging, street performing, pushing carts, carrying loads, and engaging in petty commerce to make a living." As during earlier disasters, some families had to sell children to stay alive. Desperation also compelled some women to turn to prostitution. In Xihua, "Some younger disaster victims were seized by the Nationalists as conscript laborers or soldiers, and tragic instances of local tyrants and bullies

---

[40] "Wei Huangzai canzhong jiuji wei zhou ni qing zhi bo ju kuan chedi jiuji an" (October 24, 1939): HIA, KMT Project 003, Reel 45 File 389.

[41] From 1937–1945, 1,898,000 people in Henan were recruited for the Nationalist standing army. See van de Ven (2003): 256. Military conscription and effects in Henan during the Sino-Japanese War of 1937–1945 are discussed in more detail in the following chapter. On military recruitment in Henan in earlier times, see Lary (1985): Chapter 1. Other examples can be found in Zhu and Wang (2001): 140. Conscription in Shaanxi during the 1930s and 1940s is taken up in Hershatter (2011): 51–54.

[42] Quoted in Li et al. (1994): 262.

[43] "Wei Huangzai canzhong jiuji wei zhou ni qing zhi bo ju kuan chedi jiuji an."

deceiving young women occurred frequently."[44] One foreign investigator writing in 1947 retrospectively listed "typical job descriptions" of Henan's displaced population during the war years as "coolies, hawkers, ricksha [sic] boys, migratory farm hands, water carriers, domestic servants, [and] the nightsoil brigade." For women and girls, "spinning, weaving, laundering, domestic service" were the most commonly cited occupations.[45]

Xu Guangdao and his extended family, flood victims from Zhongmu, broke apart after the 1938 flood with each member turning to different strategies to survive. Xu's paternal grandmother and grandfather went with his third uncle to stay with a friend in the southern part of the county, where the third uncle worked as a hired laborer. The eldest uncle and his family moved to another village, where they engaged in small-scale trade. Xu's younger brother went with his wife to live with her uncle and farmed land for a wealthy household. Xu Guangdao's younger sister was too young to flee and was given up to another family for adoption. Xu himself ended up joining the army.[46] Innumerable extended families disintegrated in similar ways during the war.

The change in the Yellow River's course and the deluges that followed dramatically transformed eastern Henan's landscape. Even when the floods receded, the river left behind sediment deposits that buried vast tracts of cultivatable land. Water accumulated in low-lying areas; grasses and vines grew on silt embankments.[47] Farm tools and draft animals were lost to floods, so reclaiming land for farming was difficult. In parts of Weishi, water filled the flooded area during the rainy season, but during dry months the sun parched the silt-covered earth. Unable to reclaim and cultivate land, most residents had to flee. When waters subsided, according to a former refugee from Weishi, "The ground turned as hard as brick, and there was no way to plant crops, which made it even harder for people to stay. It basically turned into an uninhabited area, and not even one out of ten people stayed."[48] Many Weishi residents migrated to Nationalist-held areas in southern and western Henan. Men worked as hired laborers or porters; women, elderly, and small children lived in temples at night and begged during the day. Wartime circumstances rendered some migration routes unavailable, as few refugees fled to Japanese-occupied territories. Fear of the enemy was too great.[49]

Other people found ways to keep living in the flooded area. Construction of dikes in Yanling, Fugou, and Xihua by the Nationalists in 1939 caused water levels in parts of Fugou and Xihua to fall. Some refugees returned. With

---

[44] Li (2003): 116.
[45] Parenti to Bowles, "Part I, Survey of Flooded Area Refugees." See also Wu (2004): 172–175.
[46] Ma et al. (1991): 45–46.
[47] Su (2004): 81; Xu and Zhu (2005): 151; MHS: 179–180.
[48] Xing (1996): 213.
[49] Jin (1990): 74–75.

disaster victims who had stayed in Xihua, they planted crops on this newly dried land in 1939 and 1940, bringing in fairly good harvests.[50] In Fugou, some refugees who had fled the 1938 flood came back to cultivate previously inundated lands that had dried up when new dikes were built along the river's western edge.[51] In parts of Fugou, as in other counties, waters receded during the winter and spring dry seasons, leaving silt embankments exposed. Local residents who had not fled planted crops on alluvial land, which they harvested in spring. When the summer rainy season arrived, however, their land flooded again. The single harvest was not much, but it gave some Fugou residents reason to stay.

In some locales, military and ecological conditions generated new economic opportunities, at least for a time. At the beginning of the 1900s, railroads had caused waterborne transport in eastern Henan to decline. The war against Japan led to its revival. As a Nationalist report on smuggling in the flooded area stated, "Since the fall of Xuzhou, Kaifeng, and Hankou in 1938, the Long-Hai and Ping-Han railroad transport lines have been cut off and the geographical environment has returned to its past condition. Transport between the Yangzi, Huai, and Sha rivers suddenly grew active and came to surpass that of former days."[52]

On a few "lonely islands" in Henan's flooded area people fished or engaged in small-scale commerce to pay for salt, oil, and other necessities. Residents traveled around in rafts and boats. Harbors formed at river crossings. Fugou's county seat turned into a particularly important harbor and one of wartime Henan's economic centers.[53] Lütan, a town east of the Fugou county seat, was on high ground and escaped flooding. Merchants and other residents from nearby towns and villages moved into Lütan, making it a bustling market.[54] Another harbor formed at the village of Poxie, also in Fugou, and it became the main transit point between the river's western and eastern banks. With Nationalist armies, guerilla units, and river defense personnel stationed in the village, amidst the desolation of the flooded area Poxie became "abnormally prosperous."[55]

This commercial prosperity derived mainly from a burgeoning smuggling trade with Japanese-controlled territories on the river's eastern bank. According to the Nationalist report on smuggling, "The Yellow River flooded area's waterways have no impediments, transport is convenient, and for this

---

[50] Li (2003): 114.
[51] Fugou xianzhi zong bianji shi (1986): 92, 98–99.
[52] Zhongyang diaocha tongjiju tezhong jingji diaochachu (1944). See also Chen (1986): 268–269.
[53] Han and Nan (1948): 42; Guan (1991): 111–112.
[54] Tian (2000): 84.
[55] Xie (2002): 100.

reason it is second to none as an important frontline smuggling area."⁵⁶ Trade restrictions, along with transport impediments created by the war, made goods extremely scarce and their prices soared. The lure of profit enticed some merchants to cross illegally into Japanese-occupied territory to engage in trade. Paying off Nationalist troops, guerilla units, and other personnel stationed in Poxie enabled traders to travel freely back and forth across the river.⁵⁷ Illicit trade facilitated the flow of goods between occupied and unoccupied areas. Nationalist troops in Fugou shipped restricted goods like pig bristles, raw lacquer, tong oil, and sesame oil to the occupied territories, bringing back opium, heroin, paper, and cloth to transport to Zhengzhou, Luoyang, Xi'an, and other cities.⁵⁸ Armies under Nationalist general Tang Enbo and Nationalist-affiliated guerilla units, which controlled the river passages in Taikang, likewise cooperated with collaborationist armies to smuggle goods from Japanese territories to sell in cities like Zhoujiakou, Xuchang, Zhengzhou, and Luoyang, or to export to other unoccupied provinces.⁵⁹

Smuggling that flourished along frontlines in eastern Henan gave some refugees opportunities for employment. Catastrophic floods made many local residents all too willing to risk defying the law to make a living. As the Nationalist report on smuggling put it, "In the early period of smuggling in the Yellow River flooded area, many disaster victims used 100–200 yuan to go back and forth to peddle goods."⁶⁰ Groups of refugees camped on the outer fringes of Zhengzhou, where smuggling Japanese goods was a big business, because they could make their living hauling smuggled goods into the interior.⁶¹

With the flooded area's proximity to Japanese-occupied Kaifeng, there was an abundance of imported goods. Towns in the flood zone became hubs for commercial exchanges across enemy lines. As another report on smuggling observed, "Things like salt from Haizhou [in coastal Jiangsu] as well as transport equipment, hardware, and cloth manufactured in Tianjin and

---

⁵⁶ Zhongyang diaocha tongjiju tezhong jingji diaochachu (1944). From 1939–1940, Zhengzhou and Zhongmu, were the major smuggling centers. When Nationalist defenses and the Japanese blockade tightened after 1941, smuggling around Zhengzhou declined and trade moved south to Jieshou, which became "the biggest smuggling center in the nation," rivaling even Jinhua in Zhejiang and Hong Kong. Zhoujiakou, once a major water transport hub at the convergence of the Jialu and Sha rivers, also gained commercial importance as a transshipment center. Ibid.
⁵⁷ Xie (2002): 100.
⁵⁸ Zhongyang diaocha tongjiju tezhong jingji diaochachu (1944); Fugou xianzhi zong bianji shi (1986): 94–95. The classic treatment of smuggling is Eastman (1980). See also Schoppa (2011): Chapter 11.
⁵⁹ Taikang xianzhi bianzuan weiyuanhui (1991): 93; Xihua xian shizhi bianzuan weiyuanhui (1992): 118.
⁶⁰ Zhongyang diaocha tongjiju tezhong jingji diaochachu (1944).
⁶¹ Peck (1967): 367.

Shanghai are imported in large amounts from here into the rear areas, which does quite a bit to balance the needs of the people's livelihood." In the town of Shuipoji in Weishi, daily commercial exchanges amounted to several tens of thousands of yuan. "However, on the negative side, the black market sale of white flour and opium, as well as tax evasion and smuggling rackets emerge in an endless stream." Shuipoji seemed "just like a big city, on the front side splendid and prosperous with many merchants, but on the back side full of dark trauma and groaning poverty. This is why many people who pass through call Shuipo[ji] the flooded area's 'Shanghai.'"[62]

Despite its profitability, military contingences could abruptly cut off this illicit trade. Floodwaters surrounded Jiangcun in northern Fugou, making the town a center for smuggling and drug running. With protection from more than one thousand guerilla troops and a Nationalist regular division, Jiangcun turned into one of the flooded area's most bustling markets. Yet Jiangcun's prosperity also attracted the attention of the Japanese army, which moved to occupy the town. The Japanese assault got underway in February 1941, but the floodwaters made Jiangcun difficult to attack. It took a day of fierce fighting, in which Japanese suffered high casualties, to drive out the Nationalist regulars and guerilla troops. Once they took Jiangcun, Japanese troops massacred over 200 civilians, burned more than 400 houses, and slaughtered over 800 chickens and 300 pigs and sheep.[63]

Environmental changes caused by flooding made more specific forms of smuggling possible as well. In certain parts of the flooded area, inundation by the Yellow River raised the water table and led to salinization of waterlogged lands.[64] As in parts of Henan affected by Yellow River floods in the past, salinization enabled flood victims to earn income by producing salt and selling it in areas where this necessity was in short supply.[65] Flood victims in parts of Zhongmu, for instance, hauled salt to Xinzheng and Mi counties for sale.[66] Refugees from Yanling and Fugou who migrated to Lushan County in western Henan regularly went back to their native places to obtain salt, which they then sold in Lushan.[67] Local women endured harassment by soldiers and smuggled salt across the floodwaters at Poxie in Fugou to earn

---

[62] Zhe (1942): 44. Schoppa finds that at least three villages in Zhejiang were nicknamed "Shanghai" after wartime conditions transformed them into bustling commercial towns. See Schoppa (2011): Chapter 11.

[63] Chen (1986): 100–102; Fugou xianzhi zong bianji shi (1986): 397–398.

[64] Su (2004): 81; UNRRA, "Survey Report on Yellow River Flooded Areas in Honan, Anhwei and Kiangsu" (July 14, 1947): 19, UN S-0528-0070.

[65] Sugimoto (1939): 458–459; Han and Han (1991); Liu and Mao (1991): 47–48; Li Yubao (1991): 71; Tian (1991): 73; Su (2004): 83. On salt production in flooded areas during the Song, see Zhang (2011): 35. On salt making in northern Henan villages affected by salinization in the early twentieth century see Thaxton (1997).

[66] Lei and Lou (1991): 57. On salinization in Zhongmu see Zhu and He (1947): 114.

[67] Zhang (1994): 134.

money for their families.[68] A flood refugee from a village near Huayuankou, named Shao Heniu, recalled that, "Our family at first lived in a temple in Ma village. Several dozen people lived in that temple. Some begged, some worked as laborers, and some who had money engaged in petty commerce. Our family at that time depended on making and selling salt to get by. During the day, I rowed a small boat to the eastern bank to scrape the saline soil to make salt, and in the evening I took the salt back and sold it."[69] Income from this illicit salt production was low, however, and refugees had to take care to avoid the salt police who enforced the government's monopoly regulations.[70]

Other refugee survival strategies put pressure on the flooded area's limited resource base. Many flood victims earned income by gathering and selling organic biomass energy as fuel for heating and cooking.[71] Displaced people gathered housing timbers, trees, grass, and "anything that can serve as fuel."[72] In Fugou, for instance, disaster victims who stayed in the flooded area lived in grass shanties built on dikes and ridges. When high waters arrived they fished. When the waters receded they farmed and cut grass, reeds, and other vegetation, pushing carts of dried kindling to the Fugou county seat and Yanling for sale, where they exchanged it for grain or sweet potatoes.[73] When flood victims migrated to Lushan, local governments took them in and gave them grain. But once refugees had settled down, they earned income by gathering fuel.[74] Many refugees scavenged for lumber and furniture from abandoned buildings to get wood.[75] In Huaiyang, disaster victims with no way to plant crops had to "sell beams and boards" to eke out a living.[76] After the war's end, flood refugees who lived in temples in Zhoujiakou were "living by selling brick and tiles from destroyed buildings and stealing trees which they sell for firewood."[77]

The few available trees in Henan's flooded area made prime targets. In December 1939, refugees near the Huayuankou breach felled more than two hundred willow trees planted to consolidate dike foundations, secure the soil, and supply materials needed for repairs. Wood poaching prompted the

---

[68] Xie (2002): 100.
[69] Mei (2009): 206.
[70] Lei and Lou (1991): 57–58; Liu and Mao (1991): 48.
[71] SJZHFZ 12 (April 1, 1946), 4; UNRRA, "Honan weekly report of Office of the Economic and Financial Advisor" 9 (May 28, 1946): 3–4.
[72] Robert Hart to Walter West, "Report on Field Trip to Flooded Area, 16 to 26 March, 1947" (March 28, 1947): UN S-0528-0543, A.R. 8. On fuel shortages see Mei (2009): 214–215.
[73] Han and Nan (1948): 42; Wu (2004): 173; Ren (1996): 149.
[74] Zhang (1994): 134.
[75] Reports quoted in "Nan yi duan zong duanzhang Yan Kai cheng" (n.d.); "Wang Qiuhang qiancheng" (January 15, 1940); "Quan Xianmiao cheng" (January 19, 1940); "Nan yi duan zong duanzhang Yan Kai cheng" (January 19, 1940): YRCC MG2.2-277.
[76] "Huaiyang xian zaimin daibiao ni qingqiu bokuan zhudi."
[77] "Notes on Information from Dick Hillis, H.I.R.C. Regarding Conditions in parts of the Flooded Area, Honan, March, '46" (March 1946): UN S-0528-0543, A.R. 8. Report reprinted in "Monthly Report, March 1946, Section 7 – Welfare Attachment (2)," UN S-0528-0540.

Zheng county government and dike section head to post a public notice in 1940 that forbid damaging these willow trees:

> Trees planted along the dikes are for consolidating river defense. The people's livelihoods and property depend upon them for protection. The masses should protect and must not wantonly destroy them. Cultivating [trees] is not easy and protection should be comprehensive. Yet lawbreakers cut firewood and graze their animals on the dikes. If it is not strictly prohibited it will impede the development of forestry policy. Each ward and *bao* are ordered to guard the trees and each dike section is directed to take strict precautions. Intentionally disobeying and damaging them will be punished according to relevant sections of the statutes.[78]

The prohibition could not have had much of an effect, since wartime instability in this contested frontline area would have made enforcing it difficult. Cutting down willow trees to get fuel added to the shortage of construction materials needed to repair and reinforce dikes, making floods even more of a threat.

But in a region of China that had been deforested for centuries, and where severe fuel shortages had existed since the nineteenth century, refugees took whatever biomass they could find.[79] Few refugees cut down trees, simply because there were so few to cut down. The fuel they gathered consisted of little more than brush, grass, chaff, and roots. Regardless of the type, refugees sold a good portion of what they gathered to the Chinese and Japanese armies in Henan, which had a voracious appetite for fuel.[80]

In Japanese-occupied territories along the Yellow River near Kaifeng, which had been subject to flooding for centuries, Henan's collaborationist provincial government tried to plant shelterbelts to prevent winds from blowing sands that had been deposited along the river's old bed and creating dust storms.[81] Dearth of biomass meant that neither the trees in the shelterbelts nor any other type of vegetation lasted long. According to a Japanese investigation report, "Because the farmers in this important protective forest did not have adequate fuel, they went around pulling up sand grass and left it on the sandy land to dry. In addition, they used axes to harm the sand-protection forests that were planted, let them dry, and used them as firewood."[82] Cooking food by stir-frying it at high temperatures in oil enabled rural residents to conserve fuel by using only small branches and dried grasses. But to remove the impediments that gathering wood and grass as fuel

---

[78] "Zheng xian zhengfu bugao" (1940): YRCC MG4.1-43.
[79] On deforestation in North China see Elvin (2004): Chapters 3–4. Fuel shortages during the nineteenth and early twentieth centuries are discussed by Pomeranz (1993: 122–127).
[80] "Nan yi duan zong duanzhang Yan Kai cheng"; "Wang Qiuhang qiancheng"; "Quan Xianmiao cheng"; "Nan yi duan zong duanzhang Yan Kai cheng." On military demand for fuel, see "Henan sheng zhengfu daidian" (November 1944): HPA M08-50-1469.
[81] Zhang (2009): 1–36; Marks (2012): 154–156, 233.
[82] Sugimoto (1939): 459.

presented to tree planting efforts, as the Japanese report concluded, Henan's rural populace had to be adequately supplied with other kinds of fuel.[83]

Acute fuel shortages had existed in North China for decades, as the region's dense population consumed more biomass than it could gather. Wartime refugee survival strategies made these fuel shortages even more severe. By the end of the conflict with Japan, the fuel situation in Henan's flooded area had become "critical." Displaced farmers struggled to make a living gathering grass and weeds, which they exchanged for sweet potatoes and other foodstuffs. But fuel had become "practically unobtainable in the area."[84] As foreign observers stated after the war's end, "There is no fuel in the area except grass which the people gather and sell in the nearby cities. There is little of this remaining."[85] Extraction of biomass deprived soils of organic material and subjected land that was jeopardized by erosion to even greater damage. The precariously fragile environmental conditions that existed in North China during the early twentieth century, perhaps as much as any other part of the world, made it vulnerable to the sudden, cataclysmic ecological shocks caused by warfare.

LOCAL VARIATIONS

As illustrated by an investigation of Henan's flooded area conducted in 1941 by the Nationalist government's Yellow River Conservancy Commission, the impact of wartime flooding and refugee survival strategies varied considerably according to geographical location. Between the Huayuankou breach and the Zhongmu county seat, the river carved out a new bed and for two years large floods had not occurred. In 1938 residents suffered considerably, but flood victims had moved to nearby villages or went to other places to find food. From the Zhongmu county seat to Weishi, the river split into several streams. This area had many hills and ridges, so each stream scoured out a definite channel and the flooding was not severe. Except for a minority of households whose fields were inundated, most found ways to eke out a living by cultivating high ridges and banks, or engaging in peddling. Below Weishi the landscape leveled out and the river's flow slowed, causing floodwaters to spread out. The amount of inundated land expanded and the number of flood victims increased accordingly. Although the Nationalist government administered some relief, "those who have benefited from it are only ten to twenty

---

[83] Ibid.
[84] John H. Shirkey to Walter West, "Recording Some Observations and Recommendations Made During a trip to Chengchow, Hsu-chang, Yen-ling, Fu-kou, Weishih, Hsi-hua, Chou-chia-k'ou, Lo-ho and Vicinities, 24 February to 3 March, 1947" (March 11, 1947): UN S-0528-0544 A.R. 17a.
[85] Walter West, "Report from Flooded Area Committee. Field Trip 16th March. Report No. 4" (March 19, 1947): UN S-0528-0544 A.R. 17a.

percent of those in need." Damage was especially severe from Weishi to Taikang, where waters covered almost all villages and fields.

In the wake of the repeated floods, young males left the area and females had to find ways to earn income. As the 1941 survey report on the flooded area put it:

> 80–90 percent of residents have fled; those left behind are either the old and weak or women and children, who all reside in the ruins of buildings, filling their stomachs with grasses and water plants. Although some fields have emerged due to sedimentation, because of lack of seeds and shortages of human and draft animal power, most of them are left to waste and there are reeds and wild willows all over.[86]

People who remained eked out an existence selling salt. "The women left behind sell salt in the occupied areas or dry saline soil in the marshes to make saltpeter for a living. Wading barefoot and half-naked through the floodwaters, their condition is as terrible as has ever been heard of." The ill received no medical treatment and were left to die. There was nowhere to bury the dead and they floated abandoned in the water. From Luyi County to Taikang, however, conditions improved slightly. During summer and fall, floodwaters covered a wide area, but in winter and spring they subsided. Farmers could plant a wheat crop on mud flats and bring in at least one good harvest a year.[87]

The Nationalist government issued orders to register disaster victims and escort them out of the flooded area, but river defense troops who were responsible for dike maintenance illicitly profited from their control of ferry passages. Unless disaster victims had money to pay they could not cross. River defense troops also confiscated boats that were supposed to take disaster victims to safety, using them to smuggle goods to and from Japanese-occupied territories on the river's eastern bank. Without boats to carry them across, many refugees had to trudge through the floodwaters to find safety. Some ended up stranded or died from disease along the way.[88]

The Nationalist central government allocated funds to maintain dikes on the river's western bank, but all labor and materials were provisional levies (*tanpai*) collected from local residents. Prices set by the Nationalist authorities fell far below market levels and those actually paid were even lower than those set by the government. Once official functionaries at each level took their cut, the amount of funds that made it to people who did the work and provided materials dwindled. For this reason, the total exacted from disaster area residents was several dozen times greater than what the government actually paid.[89] Even as many residents fled, inputs of labor and materials

---

[86] "Yu Wan Huangfanqu chakantuan baogao" (1941): YRCC MG4.1-124.
[87] Ibid.
[88] Ibid. See also Liu (1991): 7; Mao (1991): 74.
[89] "Yu Wan Huangfanqu chakantuan baogao." See also Xie (2002): 102.

needed to maintain Henan's hydraulic infrastructure grew. With much of the flooded area's population gone, the burden of hydraulic maintenance increased for residents who stayed and conscription of men for military purposes made it even more onerous.

REFUGEE RESETTLEMENT AND LAND RECLAMATION IN SHAANXI

Once the severity of the Yellow River floods became apparent and other survival strategies lost effectiveness, many flood refugees fled Henan for more distant places, especially Shaanxi Province to the west.[90] At least half of the approximately 1.2 million people originally displaced by wartime flooding moved beyond Henan's borders.[91] By the end of July 1938 over 900,000 refugees had moved west along the Long-Hai railroad to Shaanxi.[92] By the Sino-Japanese War's end, some reports claimed that perhaps as many as 1.7 million refugees from Henan and other provinces affected by Yellow River floods had migrated to Shaanxi.[93]

Nationalist armies had destroyed the stretch of the Long-Hai railroad from Zhengzhou to Luoyang to obstruct the Japanese invasion, so refugees walked this part of the journey. Upon arriving in Luoyang, some took a dangerous ride on trains bound for Shaanxi, which were frequently shelled by Japanese artillery installations north of the river. Others simply continued to Shaanxi on foot.[94] Displaced people settled in Xi'an, Xianyang, and Baoji, as well as smaller towns in Shaanxi along railroad lines and major roads.[95] Nationalist officials formed a relief committee and set up reception stations to assist the Henan refugees who had migrated to Shaanxi, but limited resources made it impossible to help more than a fraction of them.

After the 1938 flood, a Zhongmu resident named Mao Guangde moved with his mother, wife, son, and daughter to a village near Zhengzhou and found shelter with his maternal grandmother. After a few days, Mao pooled money with several men to buy a boat, enabling him to earn money operating a ferry across the floodwaters. Nationalist troops soon commandeered the boat, which cut off Mao's source of income. When an uncle who had gone to the town of Xianyang in Shaanxi to make a living by collecting junk came back, he advised Mao to move to Xianyang and find work. Mao's mother refused to flee, so he left his five-year-old son with her and took the rest of the

---

[90] Qu (2003): 259.
[91] Parenti to Bowles, "Part I, Survey of Flooded Area Refugees." See also Qu (2003): 299–304.
[92] Li and Wang (2006): 5.
[93] UNRRA, "Weekly Report for Economic Analysis Bureau, Honan Region" 6 (May 6, 1946): 2; Han and Nan (1948): 42.
[94] Tan (1991): 77–78.
[95] Li and Wang (2006): 5–6.

family to Shaanxi. Once they reached Xianyang, Mao failed to find work because many factories had closed due to Japanese bombing. At first he cut and sold reeds for a living, but the earnings could not support his family. Eventually, Mao was able to borrow money from another Henan native to buy a rickshaw. After pulling his rickshaw for several months, Mao and an acquaintance set up a stand selling fried buns (*shuijianbao*) at the Xianyang train station.[96]

Another flood victim named Shao Heniu related that after autumn 1938 the weather grew cold, so people had no way to beg and some starved. Government assistance was negligible: "When relief came from above, this department and that department plucked off a bit, so when it made it into the common people's hands there was nothing left. Once, we heard that relief was being distributed in Zhaolan village, so many disaster victims rowed boats over to get relief. But once everyone made it to Zhaolan village not even a trace of people distributing relief could be seen." As circumstances got harder, many people fled. Shao Heniu's family had a total of eighteen people, sixteen of whom eventually starved to death. As she remembered, "My oldest brother and his wife took their two children and walked from Zhengzhou to Luoyang. As they walked they begged. Halfway, one of the children died. Then, in Luoyang they got on a train and fled to Xi'an, and relied on grinding bean curd and doing casual labor to make a living."[97] Thousands of other Henan residents who migrated west to Shaanxi found similar ways to stay alive.

As the refugee population in Shaanxi swelled, China's Nationalist regime turned to resettlement and land reclamation as favored relief methods. Immediately following the breaking of the dikes in 1938, land reclamation was put forth as an optimal way of providing relief to flood refugees. On June 28, 1938, the newspaper *Dagongbao* declared, "In addition to emergency relief, work relief and land reclamation should be carried out in the future to give refugees a lasting way of making a living."[98] The Nationalist military leader Zhang Fang, himself a native of Henan, was adamant about the importance of relocating refugees to reclaim land. If the Chinese government failed to assist flood victims, Zhang warned, they might ally with the Japanese. "The enemy will use this opportunity to carry out small acts of kindness to drug our people, which will have a great influence on social order in rear areas of the War of Resistance." Resettling farmers displaced by the Yellow River flood was the only way to avert this possibility. Flood victims, as Zhang asserted, differed from other refugees:

Regular refugees from war zones only flee temporarily, and every one of them intends to return to their native place after the national emergency has been resolved.

---

[96] Mao (1991): 74–75.
[97] Mei (2009): 206.
[98] "Dagongbao de baodao" (June 28, 1938): 28–29.

Furthermore, their backgrounds are mostly in the fields of academics or business and they come from families with a little bit of property, who have never personally engaged in farming. Yellow River flood refugees, by contrast, have no way to make a living aside from plowing fields.

The nation, Zhang Fang maintained, had a responsibility to help restore the livelihoods of the victims of this "extraordinary disaster." Handing out relief funds was a temporary solution. Relocating refugees to open uncultivated land for farming promised to make them self-sufficient and give them a more permanent livelihood.[99]

To the Chinese state, land reclamation was more than just a way of assisting displaced people. Expanding cultivated acreage through land reclamation played a critical role in China's wartime economy by capturing energy through agriculture. Especially with the Japanese occupying China's main grain-producing regions, food supplies were critical for waging war.[100] To meet these demands, the Nationalist regime resettled refugees to reclaim land and increase agricultural production in unoccupied territories. Seen in ecological terms, state-directed land reclamation mobilized the dispersed labor power of refugees to convert landscapes to agriculture and generate energy surpluses needed to wage war.

As tens of thousands of flood victims migrated west from Henan, Shaanxi's Huanglongshan region became the prime destination for resettlement and reclamation. Huanglongshan is a rugged upland area that makes up part of the string of mountain ranges that separate northern Shaanxi's loess plateau from the Wei River Valley to the south. Huanglongshan covers an area of approximately 3,000 square kilometers, with a topography made up of deep valleys with steep slopes and narrow ridges. Above 1,400 meters, the landscape consists of steep, rocky hillsides. Below 1,300 meters, loess soils spread out on the valleys, gentler slopes, and ridge tops. Huanglongshan also has relatively abundant forest cover, which sets it apart from the severely deforested northern Shaanxi plateau and Wei River Valley.[101]

For much of the Qing dynasty (1644–1911), Huanglongshan supported a sizable farming population. During that period, fields covered Huanglongshan's hillsides. By the 1800s, farming activities had reduced the area's vegetation cover. Clearing trees and other vegetation to cultivate hillsides accelerated soil erosion. After several years, soil fertility and productivity decreased and residents

---

[99] "Zhang Fang guanyu Huanghe juekou beizai nanmin ying guangchou yiken ti'an" (1940): 43.
[100] Farm Credit Division of the Farmers Bank of China, "Land Reclamation in War-time China: A Memorandum for the U.S. Technical Experts to China" (October 1942): HIA, Walter C. Lowdermilk Papers, Box 9.
[101] Lowdermilk (1944): 205–206; Shaanxi shifan daxue dili xi Yan'an diqu dili zhi bianxie zu (1983): 37. For a more detailed history of this reclamation project see Muscolino (2010).

moved on to farm other areas.[102] By the early nineteenth century, Huanglongshan's landscape displayed the legacy of this exploitation pattern. Erosion corrugated upper slopes and cut deep gullies into lower slopes. Topsoil on hillsides washed away, exposing sandstone and shale underneath.[103]

Internal warfare that racked China during the late nineteenth century gave Huanglongshan's environment a chance to recover. The Muslim Rebellion (1864–1877) devastated the region, causing virtually all of Huanglongshan's residents to flee and abandon their land. Others fled when drought and disease outbreaks struck, leaving Huanglongshan virtually depopulated. Villages established in valleys and along mountain ridges in the eighteenth and nineteenth century lay in ruins. Farmers feared they might fall prey to bandits who roamed Huanglongshan's hills and forests, so the area remained practically devoid of settlement in the early twentieth century. To most Chinese observers, Huanglongshan reverted to desolate, uncultivated "wasteland."[104]

From a nonhuman perspective, depopulation was an opportunity for trees and other wild vegetation to thrive and for eroded landscapes to recover. Abandonment may have initially increased soil loss, but after several decades the return of vegetation cover eliminated the problem. By the twentieth century, grasses spread over corrugated upper slopes, while shrubs and trees grew in gullies. Dense stands of birch, aspen, maple, and oak returned to Huanglongshan's hillsides. By the 1920s and 1930s, this secondary growth gave Huanglongshan more extensive forest cover than any other part of Shaanxi. After several decades without intensive agricultural cultivation, soil erosion no longer took place under Huanglongshan's regenerated vegetation cover.[105] Decomposed grasses, leaves, and other organic matter accumulated as green fertilizer that enriched soil nutrients. During the 1930s, the content of nitrogen and other nutrients in Huanglongshan's soil was several times higher than soils in other parts of Shaanxi.[106]

The Muslim Rebellion had given the environment a respite by depopulating Huanglongshan. The Sino-Japanese War of 1937–1945 had the opposite effect. During the war years, the Chinese Nationalist regime encouraged renewed human exploitation of Huanglongshan's landscape by resettled refugees to reclaim uncultivated lands. In early 1938 the Shaanxi provincial government founded the Huanglongshan reclamation office, sending the first group of 300 refugees to reclaim wasteland in the region. The refugee settlers were to receive about 0.66 hectares of land per person, along with monthly food rations and loans to purchase draft animals, seed, and other farming

---

[102] Wang (2005): 285; Yang and Hou (2005): 127–129.
[103] Lowdermilk (1944): 204; Yang and Hou (2005): 130.
[104] Lowdermilk (1944): 203; Wang (2005): 286.
[105] Lowdermilk (1944): 204–205; Shaanxi sheng difangzhi bianzuan weiyuanhui (1994): 24.
[106] Zhou Changyun, "Huanglongshan zhi turang" (1938): SPA 9-5-285.

supplies. Refugees were exempted from taxes and conscription for five years.[107] Following the breaching of the dikes in June 1938, land reclamation took on even greater importance as a relief method. Starting in October 1938, the Nationalist regime relocated refugees from the flooded area to Huanglongshan to reclaim land. By the year's end 12,130 refugees from the flooded area had settled in the reclamation area, along with 13,000 other war refugees.[108]

During the Huanglongshan reclamation area's first year of existence, resettled refugees lacked adequate food and clothing. To remedy the situation, the Nationalist central government took over Huanglongshan from Shaanxi Province, making it a "nationalized" reclamation area.[109] Subsidies from the central government were essential. In January 1940 the National Relief Commission and the Ministry of Economics loaned grain, clothing, draft animals, and farm equipment to refugees to enable them to make it through the severe Shaanxi winter. In spring 1941, some refugee settlers left the reclamation area because they felt the material support was insufficient. Others refused to take the long journey to Huanglongshan, since they could earn more money as wage laborers hauling coal along the Long-Hai railroad in Shaanxi. The Huanglongshan reclamation area depended on government support until 1941, but a good harvest that year and income from hemp production and other side employments ended refugees' dependence on relief funds.[110]

For the Nationalist regime, the purpose of land reclamation was more than relieving China's displaced population. Maintaining food supplies in Nationalist-controlled areas was a serious concern, which made expanding cultivated acreage by opening up wasteland a critical part of wartime economic mobilization. According to a Nationalist memorandum,

> To meet the urgent and wide-spread demand for staple food supplies for both the civilian population and the armed forces, crop production in all the interior provinces had to be stepped up. It was to achieve the latter aim that nation-wide land reclamation has been deemed of utmost importance. It was also thought that the best way to carry out the construction program was to finance it with government loans.[111]

Between 1937 and 1940, the Ministry of Economics loaned 8.7 million yuan to Shaanxi and other unoccupied provinces to fund reclamation projects.[112] Land reclamation, as a Nationalist military leader later recalled, utilized refugees to promote economic mobilization in unoccupied territories and

---

[107] Shaanxi sheng difangzhi bianzuan weiyuanhui (1994): 420.
[108] Ibid., 661–662, 665.
[109] He (1940): 16; Shaanxi sheng difangzhi bianzuan weiyuanhui (1994): 420.
[110] "Nonglinbu Huanglongshan kenqu gaikuangshu" (December 31, 1941): SPA 9-2-823.
[111] Farm Credit Division of the Farmers Bank of China, "Land Reclamation in War-Time China," 2.
[112] Ibid., 3. See also Guo (1940): 6.

"arouse the people's vital energies (*minqi*) to increase grain production."[113] Huanglongshan was not wartime China's only land reclamation initiative, but it was easily the most successful. From spring 1938 to summer 1944, settlers in Huanglongshan reportedly reclaimed over 22,060 hectares of land for agricultural production.[114]

Along with the economic importance of expanding cultivated acreage, the Nationalist military also had strategic reasons for garrisoning Huanglongshan. Holding the location made it possible to flank a possible Japanese thrust westward along the Wei River to Xi'an and beyond.[115] From 1939 onwards the Nationalist army also maintained a military blockade around the Chinese Communist Party (CCP)'s Shaan-Gan-Ning Border Region in northern Shaanxi. Because Huanglongshan was to the immediate south of the Communist base area, developing the "mountain stronghold" tightened the Nationalist grip on the CCP's power center in Yan'an.[116]

Much of Huanglongshan's uncultivated land consisted of fields abandoned in the nineteenth century, which made it relatively easy to reclaim. Many refugees took residence in villages deserted during the late Qing, inhabiting hillside cave dwellings and using grinders, millstones, and other tools left behind decades before.[117] To be sure, the life of refugees in Huanglongshan was far from idyllic. Wildlife such as leopards, jackals, wild boar, and Mongolian gazelles (*Procapra gutturosa*; Ch: *huangyuang*) had taken possession of Huanglongshan's forests. Leopards sometimes attacked settlers. Other animals trampled and ate crops. In 1940, wild boar reportedly damaged about 466 hectares of maize, sorghum, and wheat fields. When the reclamation area's leadership organized 3,000 refugees into crop protection and hunting regiments, the area damaged by wild animals decreased to a mere 46.6 hectares. Along with boar hunting, conversion of "wastelands" that were once wildlife habitats into farmland likely accounted for much of the decrease.[118]

In addition to its animal inhabitants, resettled refugees also had to contend with Huanglongshan's tattered social fabric. For decades, Huanglongshan had been a haven for bandits who colluded with "local bullies" from nearby counties, calling themselves "lords of the mountain" (*shanzhu*). Local strongmen had grown accustomed to exploiting Huanglongshan's resources for

---

[113] Ma (1989): 15.
[114] Sun (1993): 172; Lu (2005): 89. Another reclamation area in western Henan's Deng County took in about 5,000 flood refugees, who reclaimed 22,000 *mu* of land. Unlike Huanglongshan, documentation on the Deng County reclamation area is rather limited. See Henan sheng zhengfu (1938); Su (2004): 164–165.
[115] Lowdermilk (1944): 203.
[116] Vermeer (1988): 75, 86.
[117] "Shaanxi sheng Huanglongshan kenqu banshichu gongzuo baogaoshu" (September 30, 1939): SPA 7-1-2.
[118] "Nonglinbu Huanglongshan kenqu gaikuangshu" (December 31, 1941): SPA 9-2-823; Zhu (1986): 224.

their own gain. They profited from tree cutting, occupying publicly owned wastelands, burning charcoal, and gathering plants for medicinal ingredients. To stop these activities, the Huanglongshan reclamation office persuaded neighboring counties to prohibit illegal woodcutting. Poor people could burn charcoal to sell as fuel in neighboring counties only if they applied to county officials for permits, which were checked by local *baojia* headmen.[119] After prohibitions were put in place, refugees were still permitted to gather firewood and medicinal ingredients to supplement their incomes. These regulations were a point of tension with neighboring counties, which did not have forests of their own and depended upon Huanglongshan for their fuel supplies. Once the reclamation office restricted woodcutting, nearby counties had difficulty meeting their fuel demands.[120] Huanglongshan was, in effect, an island of forest, of biofuel, in a sea of energy-starved populations. As later chapters make clear, land clearance and fuel gathering had a tremendous impact on this area's landscape.

CONCLUSION

The 1938 strategic diversion of the Yellow River forced hundreds of thousands of people in Henan to seek livelihoods far away from their native places for extended periods of time. In areas of Henan that flood refugees abandoned, population decline contributed to war-induced disruption of hydraulic and agro-ecological systems. Refugee flight cut off the labor and investment needed for intensive maintenance of anthropogenic landscapes, leading to rapid and prolonged deterioration. Managing complex hydraulic and agro-ecological systems required dense flows of energy, much of which came in the form of human muscle power. Without those energy inputs, fragile human-constructed landscapes spiraled into chaos and disorder. Some other organisms benefited, as wartime flooding and displacement of human population created new eco-niches in which wildlife and disease microbes thrived. For humans, however, World War II triggered what they perceived as massive ecological decline. More unexpectedly, war-induced transformation of eastern Henan's environment generated new economic opportunities for some – albeit precarious ones – in the form of smuggling.

Warfare generated environmental effects that reached far beyond sites of actual military engagements. Many of the survival strategies that refugees employed to adapt to wartime conditions had an environmental impact. But understanding the baseline for those changes is essential for grasping their significance. War's ecological consequences are neither straightforward nor

---

[119] "Shaanxi sheng Huanglongshan kenqu banshichu di yi nian gongzuo baogaoshu" (January 1938): SPA 7-1-2; Huanglong xian difangzhi bianzuan weiyuanhui (1995): 660–661.
[120] "Nonglinbu Huanglongshan kenqu gaikuangshu" (December 31, 1941): SPA 62-2-50; Wu (1944): 32.

unambiguous. Environmental degradation on the North China Plain did not start with World War II, which by the late-1930s had been mired in a century or more of ecological crisis. Yet the Sino-Japanese War's impact on this fragile, intensively exploited landscape was especially catastrophic, as military conflict and displacement intensified pre-existing environmental problems. With biomass extremely scarce, eastern Henan's displaced population exploited any and all organic material they could sell as fuel, aggravating shortages that had plagued Henan and other parts of northern China for decades.

Other environmental changes associated with refugee migration resulted directly from the reception and relief programs undertaken by China's wartime state. The Nationalist regime's resettlement efforts sought to mobilize displaced people's labor power to attain its economic and military objectives. With funding and assistance from the Nationalist regime, flood refugees from Henan resettled in Shaanxi's Huanglongshan region, where they cleared land for agricultural production. In addition to making refugees self-sufficient, this state-directed drive to open up "wasteland" and boost grain output aimed to generate energy surpluses to fuel warfare. Farmlands extended at the expense of trees and other spontaneous vegetation, encroaching on wildlife habitats. Meanwhile, back in Henan, the military's voracious appetite for energy caused even greater devastation.

3

Military Metabolism and the Henan Famine of 1942–1943

From 1942 to 1943, in the midst of China's war against Japan, Henan suffered a famine that killed between 1.5 and 2 million out of Henan's population of approximately 30 million and forced another 2–3 million residents to flee.[1] Famines are frequently associated with war and other military activities. Like numerous other famines that have occurred during times of military conflict, the Henan famine of 1942–1943 highlights connections between war, environmental change, and shifting patterns of food production and distribution. From antiquity to the present, military conflict and famine have occurred together. No formulaic connection exists between war and famine. But the threat or reality of war can precipitate famine even without a poor harvest and increase damage inflicted by harvest shortfalls. In many instances, belligerents have deliberately induced famine to weaken or kill their enemies.[2]

After 1900, as economic historian Cormac Ó Gráda argues, the connection between warfare and famine grew even stronger. Many of the twentieth century's largest famines, he asserts, would have caused less damage or would not have taken place in times of peace and stability. Previously, he contends, famines were mainly linked to harvest shortfalls. What distinguished the twentieth century was that famines were more often linked to war or political upheaval than poor harvests. Given the ties between military conflict and the twentieth century's most terrible famines, he concludes, "Human action had a greater impact than, or greatly exacerbated, acts of nature."[3]

---

[1] The low-end estimate comes from an official investigation conducted in 1943, which reported 1,484,983 famine deaths in Nationalist-controlled counties in Henan. "Ge xian zaiqu siwang shumu zhi diaocha tongji," attached to "Zhang Guangsi guanyu Henan hanzai qingkuang ji jiuzai qingxing de diaocha baogao" (September 27, 1943) in Zhongguo dier lishi dang'anguan (1991): 565–566.
[2] Ó Gráda (2009): 12, 230. See also Sen (2000): 10–26.
[3] Ó Gráda (2009): 11.

From an environmental historian's perspective, an interpretation of war's role in the causation of famine premised on an artificial distinction between human actions (war) and acts of nature (poor harvests) affords little insight into these relationships. Edmund Russell and Richard Tucker criticize the tendency to see "war and control of nature (exemplified by agriculture) as belonging to separate categories."[4] Ecologically informed interpretations of wartime famines must view military conflict and nature as continually interacting in a co-evolutionary relationship. Human actions reshape the physical environment. Nonhuman elements also shape social processes, sometimes in line with human intentions, but usually in unexpected and unpredictable ways. In light of these inextricable connections between the human and nonhuman, social processes can never be divided from natural ones.[5]

By focusing on this combination of diverse forces, my analysis of the Henan famine draws its inspiration from Brett Walker's notion of "hybrid causation," premised on a recognition that "Everything on Earth, living or otherwise, is integrated into one interconnected, bufferless web that is neither artifice nor nature."[6] War-induced famines, though certainly not the same as famines that result entirely from harvest failures, have environmental dimensions. Famine results from complex interactions between anthropogenic and non-anthropogenic elements. Rather than upholding artificial dichotomies, this chapter analyzes dynamic linkages between environmental systems and human societies – including military establishments that they support. All these linkages were permeated by energy flows.

Previous writings on the Henan famine of 1942–1943 have explained it primarily in terms of human agency. American journalist Theodore White's influential coverage of the famine attributed it to callous indifference and administrative incompetence on the part of the Nationalist regime, which failed to ameliorate disaster. Despite drought and poor harvests in 1942, the Nationalist regime taxed Henan's farmers and robbed them of their grain reserves. Shaanxi and Hubei provinces possessed ample grain supplies, White suggested, but the government did not deploy relief grain.[7] Other historians put less emphasis on Nationalist administrative failings, instead stressing the war's role in precipitating the famine. Lloyd Eastman observed that the nearly one million troops in Henan had to be fed. Since war had devastated transport facilities, armies had to find food locally. The government's choice was to

---

[4] Tucker and Russell (2004): 1.
[5] Mitchell (2002): 27–30; Latour (2005).
[6] Walker (2010): 16.
[7] White and Jacoby (1980): 172–177; White (1978): 150, 152, 155–156. Though the Henan famine of 1942–1943 is not her primary concern, Lillian M. Li (2007: 307) directly follows White by noting that it "was unambiguously caused by human factors" and points to the Nationalist regime's suppression of reports about the famine as evidence of "the government's certain complicity in this tragedy." Bose (1990) likewise characterizes it as a "man-made famine."

"either starve the troops or starve the peasants."[8] Odoric Wou, for his part, emphasizes the forcible expropriation of grain by Japanese armies.[9] While also noting that military demand took primacy over civilian needs, Diana Lary stresses that warfare ruled out effective state interventions to relieve famine.[10] Despite their merits, all these interpretations overlook the complex ways in which human and nonhuman elements combined to precipitate famine. The environment, if it appears at all, remains external to the analyses, functioning as a static backdrop with little independent force. To comprehend the ecology of war and famine, one must focus on the interactions between human actors and a dynamic environment that changes in unpredictable ways even as anthropogenic forces act upon it.

Few have considered war's ecological dynamics – the changes that military conflict brings for human relations with a changing environment – as a variable in the occurrence of famines that occur during wartime. The social metabolism approach, with its focus on the interplay between human and nonhuman elements, provides a useful framework for examining these relationships.

Warfare carries at least three sets of metabolic consequences with implications for the environmental history of famine. First, damage caused by military conflict, whether intentional or unintentional, can reduce food production through agriculture or severely disrupt its circulation. Population losses due to wartime conscription, displacement, and death further cut into agricultural output by critically reducing supplies of human labor power. And with people weakened by hunger, output per unit of labor declines even more. Second, the military's voracious appetite for energy intensifies pressure on food supplies, often diverting calories away from civilian populations. War at once radically simplifies ecosystems and demands extraordinarily large concentrations of energy. The strain of providing food for militaries from war-devastated agricultural landscapes can easily give rise to famine. Third, warfare increases wastage of food energy in various ways. Ships, trains, trucks, and carts carrying food get destroyed. Food spoils during long periods of transport and storage. And in wars of movement, armies deliberately destroy food stocks to deny them to enemies.

The Henan famine of 1942–1943 illustrates these ecological dynamics. The Nationalist army's strategic breaching of the Yellow River's dikes in 1938 threw intricate, human-engineered environmental infrastructure into disarray. Wartime ecological damage significantly reduced food production, while also impeding its circulation via transport networks. Short-term

---

[8] Eastman (1984): 78. While stating that Chiang's regime "must be held responsible for the famine in Henan," Mitter (2013a: 273–274) gives equal weight to fiscal strain caused by the "unraveling of the Nationalist state after 1941 following China's entry in the global war."
[9] Wou (2007).
[10] Lary (2004): 160–162; Lary (2010): 124–126.

climatic changes added another shock, when in 1941–1942 North China experienced unpredictable weather and low levels of rainfall linked to a global El Niño Southern Oscillation event, which caused agricultural output to decline even more precipitously. Locust infestations took an additional toll. But as a strategically vital frontline region, Henan had to supply vast amounts of energy and resources for military consumption. Satisfying the metabolism of the military required extracting energy from agro-ecological systems in Henan that were already in a highly degraded condition due to war's devastating impact. Military grain consumption increased demand for food at a time when agricultural production had markedly declined.

Under these circumstances, all combatants had to violently compete for food supplies, which took on the utmost military-strategic importance. In Hans van de Ven's words, "Battles for the harvest followed between the Nationalist state, its armies, local militaries, and the population, which the Japanese also joined."[11] The Chinese Communist Party's military forces actively participated in these food struggles as well. As military and state actors tried to capture more and more energy to fight a war, energy available for other life forms dwindled. Channeling energy to the military distorted food entitlement relations in Henan and made grain scarce or unavailable for vulnerable segments of society. The result was an "energy crisis" in which millions of people could not obtain the caloric intake needed for their minimal subsistence. Famine resulted from a web of interconnections among war, water, climate, agriculture, and insects. What tied these elements together was energy.

Famine also had military and political implications. With the Nationalist regime unable to create structures to channel and coordinate large energy flows, its military forces crumbled. The Chinese Communist Party's (CCP's) military units in Henan, on the other hand, responded to the famine of 1942–1943 by improvising more stable and effective ways of extracting energy from the environment, which benefited the CCP and civilian populations alike. As famine paved the way for the eventual collapse of the Nationalist armies in North China, a more symbiotic relationship between the military and its host society undergirded expansion of Communist influence in Henan's flooded area during the last two years of the Sino-Japanese War.

THE YELLOW RIVER FLOOD'S IMPACT ON AGRICULTURE

The persistent flooding that followed the 1938 diversion of the Yellow River disrupted hydraulic infrastructure and led to transformations in Henan's landscape that dealt a blow to agriculture. Floodwaters inundated fields; sediment covered previously cultivated land.[12] Refugee displacement caused

---

[11] van de Ven (2010): 458.
[12] Xu and Zhu (2005): 151; Zhang (2005): 146.

by floods led to outflows of labor power that was badly needed on farms, which further decreased harvests. As the river branched into numerous shallow channels that were more susceptible to evaporation, floods also ended up depriving much of eastern Henan of its drought resistance capacity.[13] Given the area of farmland in Henan that was abandoned, one postwar survey estimated that flooding in Henan from 1938 to 1945 led to average annual decreases of 17,463,000 *shidan*[14] in grain output (more than 20 percent of the normal annual production).[15]

Populations displaced by Yellow River floods put an added strain on food supplies in areas where they sought refuge. As a former Henan official recalled, "People whose houses and land had been flooded were left homeless, and those who did not want to stay in the flooded area to suffer the depredations of the enemy fled to the west of the floods, relying on friends and neighbors or roaming around begging for a living, which also increased Henan's food burden."[16] By summer 1942, counties behind the front lines that had taken in several thousand flood refugees began to experience acute grain shortages. As chairman of the Henan provincial government, Li Peiji

---

[13] "Yu Wan Huangfanqu chakantuan baogao."

[14] Chinese grain measures are notoriously confusing. The Nationalist government employed a "market system" (*shizhi*) of measurement. The units of measure were the *shidan* 市石, *shidou* 市斗, and *shisheng* 市升.

   1 *shidan* = 10 *shidou* = 100 *shisheng*
   1 *shidan* = 1 hectoliter = 2.84 U.S. bushels
   1 *shidou* = 1 dekaliter = 1.14 U.S. pecks
   1 *shisheng* = 1 liter = 1.8 U.S. pints

Usually, the character *dan* 石, a unit of volume, is pronounced *shi*. By the twentieth century, this word had become thoroughly confused with the character *dan* 擔, a unit of weight. Both the unit of volume and weight were often pronounced *dan* and although they were not interchangeable they were sometimes written with the same character. Eventually, in 1929 the Nationalist government officially designated *dan* 石 as a unit of volume, while *dan* 擔 was defined as a unit of weight equal to 100 *shijin* (50 kilograms). In this text, I use *shidan* to refer to the former measure and simply *dan* for the latter. In practice, moreover, units of volume were still often assigned fixed weights. For example, one *dan* (unit of volume) of unhulled rice weighed around 60 kilograms (about 132 pounds), while a *dan* (unit of weight) equaled 50 kilograms (110 pounds). For useful explanations see Eastman (1984): 51–52; Rawski and Li (1992): xiii; Wilkinson (2012): 559–561.

[15] The survey that arrived at this figure assumed that floods destroyed 8,731,500 *mu* of farmland and that each *mu* could produce two *shidan* of grain each year. "Henan sheng zhanshi sunshi diaocha baogao" (1990): 15. According to one estimate, from 1938–1946 crop production in Henan's flooded area fell by a total of 103,447,078 *dan*, or over 90 percent of normal production. Han and Nan (1948): 30, 32. Based on figures for total production of all grains compiled by Wou (2007: 177) output fell from 211,045,000 *dan* in 1936, to 147,363,000 *dan* in 1937, to 105,880,000 *dan* in 1938, to 101,205,000 *dan* in 1939. Garnaut (2013: 21) finds that sown area in Henan was relatively stable at 9.4 million hectares before the war, but from 1938 to 1945 it fell to 4.2–4.4 million hectares, a decrease of 55 percent compared with prewar levels.

[16] Zhang (2005): 146.

stated, "Recently, because of the severity of the famine, [the counties] do not have the power to take on this burden and their livelihood has turned into a problem, so many people from these counties have fled to neighboring provinces to find food."[17]

The burgeoning illicit trade across enemy lines in Henan also had a deleterious effect on food supplies. A 1944 report on smuggling in the flooded area related that "Along the Ping-Han railway many fields are planted with cotton and tobacco, so there are shortages of grain. But what the smuggling merchants export to the enemy is grain, cotton, and tobacco, and what they import are daily items needed in the rear areas and cosmetics. Most of it does not go to Henan's people. Therefore, in the 1941 drought disaster the Yellow River flooded area suffered the greatest calamity."[18]

CLIMATIC SHOCKS

Naturally occurring climate fluctuations further contributed to declining agricultural output. In 1942 precipitation levels in Henan and other parts of North China sharply declined. Drought was linked to a climatic anomaly that coincided with the strong El Niño event that occurred around the world between 1939 and 1942. El Niño is characterized by unusually warm ocean temperatures in the eastern Equatorial Pacific, which influence how solar energy drives global climate via winds and ocean currents. The El Niño started in 1939, reached full strength in January 1940, and lasted with varying intensity until spring 1942. Influenced by this El Niño phenomenon, the period 1940–1942 witnessed an extreme climatic anomaly of hemispheric to global extent.[19] The Henan famine partly resulted from this global shift in weather patterns. For areas along the middle reaches of the Yellow River, such as Henan, years when these El Niño events occur typically experience lower than normal precipitation due to disruption of the Asian summer monsoon system.[20]

El Niño events occurred with a fair degree of regularity during the late nineteenth and early twentieth century, typically leading to droughts in North China.[21] The El Niño of the late 1930s and early 1940s led to similar outcomes, as 1941–1944 saw successive years of low precipitation or drought in much of Henan. Available data indicate that rainfall in Henan for 1942

---

[17] Petition from Li Peiji to Chiang Kai-shek (September 7, 1942): AH 00100004790A.
[18] Zhongyang diaocha tongjiju tezhong jingji diaochachu (1944).
[19] Brönnimann et al. (2004): 971–974.
[20] In the lower and middle reaches of the Yellow River, the 1940 precipitation anomaly was −4.74 percent. In 1941 it was −22.29 percent. Hao et al. (2008): 17–25.
[21] According to Marks (2012: 255), the most serious El Niño droughts came in 1876–78, 1891, 1899–1900, 1920–21, and 1928–30. On El Niño and its global effects see Davis (2001): 341–376.

amounted to only forty to sixty percent of average.²² In historian Anthony Garnaut's estimation, when summer rains failed in 1941 and 1942 Henan experienced the worst drought seen since the Great North China Famine of 1876–1879.²³ As in earlier times, the harsh drought that hit Henan in 1942 undoubtedly resulted from the climatic anomaly that was related to global El Niño effects. It comes as no surprise that drought seriously damaged agricultural output. Winds and unexpected hailstorms came at harvest time in 1942, slicing wheat production deeply.²⁴ In counties that remained under Nationalist control, which accounted for about half of Henan's arable land, the 1942 wheat harvest reportedly totaled around 17,996,530 *shidan*, only 28 percent of normal output. Henan provincial government surveys estimated that the meager wheat harvest could support the population of its unoccupied regions for only three months and nine days.²⁵

Henan cultivated two crops per year: wheat, which farmers sowed in late autumn and harvested in mid-May, along with millet and corn, which they sowed in late May and harvested in the fall. Rural households normally sold wheat on the market or handed it over to the state as tax payments, consuming primarily the summer crops. After the poor 1942 wheat harvest, Henan's populace could still count on the fall millet and corn crops to supplement their diets and get them through the year. But nature dashed these hopes. No rain fell during summer, and the millet and corn withered.²⁶ Fall harvests of sorghum, millet, and barley were only about 20 percent of normal. Sweet potatoes and peanut harvests were around 50 percent. Failure of the 1942 summer crops especially damaged the welfare of Henan's rural populace, since it was their main food source. With this shortfall, in October 1942 it was estimated that food stocks would only last until the end of the year – more than four months before the 1943 wheat harvest.²⁷ Garnaut estimates that in

---

²² Henan sheng shuiliting shui han zaihai zhuanzhuo bianji weiyuanhui (1998): 182, 188–189; Garnaut (2013): 6–14.
²³ Garnaut (2013): 11.
²⁴ "Henan sheng zhengfu jiuzai zong baogao" (December 1943), 1: HPA AB6-588, "Henan sheng zhenwu baogao," 1944: IMH 20-00-03 9–1. See also Garnaut (2013): 15–16.
²⁵ The report assumed every individual consumed three *dou* of grain per month, arriving at a total of 5,527,390 *shidan* per month. "Henan sheng sanshiyi nian mai shou ji xiaofei shuliang tongji biao," HIA, KMT Project, TE 29 6.2. See also *Henan nongqing* 1:4/5 (1942): 1, 7. Service (1974: 11) estimated that the 1942 wheat crop was about 20 percent of normal. Wampler (1945: 288–229), a missionary active in famine relief, stated that Henan had "about a fifty-per-cent wheat crop all over the territory, and in some very small areas only a thirty-per-cent crop." According to Wou (2007: 177), total grain output for Henan in 1942 was 46,856,000 *dan*, only 22 percent of prewar output. Wheat harvests totaled 24,708,000 *dan* (23.4 percent of prewar output).
²⁶ "Henan sheng zhengfu jiuzai zong baogao," 1; White and Jacoby (1980): 172; Zhang (2005): 144; Yang (2005b): 56. See also Yang (2005a); Yang (2005c): 52–62. Garnaut (2013: 16) finds that 1942 yields for summer crops were one-third of the prewar average.
²⁷ *Henan nongqing* 1:4/5 (1942): 1, 7; Service (1974): 11; Garnaut (2013): 5, 16–17, 37.

1942 average crop yields per unit of sown area in Henan fell 40 percent below the prewar average – "an extreme case of crop failure."²⁸ Wartime circumstances magnified the effects of climatic fluctuations, as war-related disruption of hydraulic infrastructure made poor weather all the more damaging.

Along with drought, locust swarms did additional damage to crops. In 1941 locusts appeared in Fugou, Huaiyang, Yanling, and Weishi counties in Henan's flooded area.²⁹ A larger swarm of locusts emerged from the eastern edge of the flooded area in summer 1942 and spread west to nearby counties. Infestation grew even more severe the following year.³⁰ Migratory locust outbreaks typically strike areas on the North China Plain when wetlands in river basins dry up due to prolonged drought. Locust plagues frequently follow flood and drought, when waters fall and create habitats where locusts can lay their eggs. In these periods, locust breeding conditions improve and absence of rainfall increases the survival rate of the eggs they lay in the soil. The large inundated areas created by the breaking of the Yellow River dikes, when dried by drought conditions, produced landscapes that were ideal habitats for locust breeding. Given the strong connection between El Niño and droughts in North China, locust outbreaks usually occur one or two years after an El Niño event.³¹ The early 1940s were no exception. Locusts from overgrown, abandoned land in the flooded area spread throughout Henan in 1942 and 1943, meeting their own energy needs by consuming the crops in their path. Locust disasters took place almost every year throughout the rest of the war.³²

Locust infestations were nothing new in China. To cope with them, local populations and government officials had over the centuries developed an array of locust-abatement strategies.³³ But implementing anti-locust measures required considerable labor and material resources. Depopulation and labor shortages caused by war and floods in Henan allowed locusts to run rampant. As a postwar investigation observed, "The areas where locusts breed are mostly in abandoned and peripheral areas. The Yellow River flooded area is where the locusts reproduce most."³⁴ With too few people

---

²⁸ Garnaut (2013): 16.
²⁹ Li et al. (1993): 545–546; Li et al.(1994): 257–258; Li Yanhong (2007): 25–28; Zhang (2008): 46.
³⁰ Locusts first appeared in June 1942, and by August they had affected Xihua, Fugou, and 67 other counties in Henan. The insects consumed sorghum, corn, soy, and black bean crops. Only mung beans and sesame were spared. "Henan sheng zhengfu jiuzai zong baogao," 80. See also Li et al. (1994): 258; Su (2004): 172–174; Zhang (2008): 46–47.
³¹ Locust outbreaks also appear one or two years after floods, when water dries in inundated areas, creating wet habitats in which locusts can lay eggs. Zhang and Li (1999); Zhang (2008): Chapter 4.
³² Yang (2005b): 156; Zhang (2005): 144; Li et al. (1993): 573–574; Zhang (2008): 46–47, 412–415.
³³ Marks (2012): 233–235; Zhang (2008): Chapter 7, 9.
³⁴ SJZHFZ 13 (April 8, 1946): 5.

to eradicate them, the locusts that flourished in the flooded area devoured standing crops to feed their own metabolisms. Locust swarms resembled passing armies, siphoning up all the food energy they could get.

Henan provincial government reports described damage caused by locusts in 1942: "During the summer locusts sped across the river from east of the flooded area and expanded to the west. Although each county has already mobilized the army and the common people to work together to catch and kill them, there are too many and it is difficult to eradicate them completely."[35] Similarly, a Nationalist government investigator noted that in 1943: "Just when the autumn grain was growing, large amounts of locusts emerged in each county, blocking out the sun in an area over five kilometers wide. In every place they passed through the autumn grain was eaten up.... After grain was eaten, people replanted it and waited for it to sprout, but it was once again eaten. Now grain has been planted for the third time and it is being eaten by the newborn locust nymphs." Locusts reportedly destroyed over half the fall crops. Lightly affected areas lost over 50 percent; severely affected areas lost over 90 percent.[36]

ENERGY FOR THE ARMY

Nature was not kind to Henan in 1942, as drought and locusts reduced the amount of food energy produced through agriculture. According to provincial investigations, the 1942 wheat harvest and fall crops for the 68 unoccupied counties in Henan came to about 26 percent of normal (an estimated 23,019,609 *shidan*), more than 68,491,151 *shidan* below the amount necessary to feed the area's population.[37] But as a contested region, Henan had to feed armies stationed in the province. On the frontlines between the Nationalists and the Japanese, the burden was especially great. To secure energy for the military in the form of food grains, China's Nationalist regime enacted a series of grain taxes, compulsory purchases, and miscellaneous levies. Grain procurement systems prioritized the military, seeking to ensure that soldiers had sufficient rations.

When it assumed power in 1928, the relatively weak Chinese Nationalist regime had to leave land tax revenues in the hands of the provinces. After the war against Japan broke out in 1937, this fiscal arrangement left China's central government without adequate sources of funds. The Japanese occupied China's major revenue-producing regions in 1940–1941 and reduced government revenues at a time when expenditures were growing tremendously. The

---

[35] "Henan sheng zhengfu jiuzai zong baogao," 80.
[36] "Zhang Guangsi guanyu Henan hanzai qingkuang ji jiuzai qingxing de diaocha baogao," 565.
[37] "Henan sheng sanshiyi nian ge xian hanzai diaocha biao," in "Henan sheng zhengfu jiuzai gongzuo zongbaogao."

Nationalist regime paid for the war against Japan by printing money. The volume of currency vastly expanded, leading to one of the most serious hyperinflations in history. Terrible inflation continued after 1945, truly spiraling out of control during the Civil War period.[38]

China's wartime inflation crisis had at least one environmental consequence, in that it fundamentally altered how the Nationalist regime procured food grain for the army. In July 1941 the central government nationalized the land tax and began to demand payment in grain rather than cash. Prior to that time, the government bought food for its troops on the open market, which contributed to China's spiraling inflation. By collecting land taxes in kind (*zhengshi*), the Nationalist regime limited inflationary pressure to an extent, while gaining the ability to secure grain for the military with less difficulty. But the most important consequence of taxation in kind was to shift financial responsibility for the war onto the rural population, whose direct access to food was reduced. The burden of feeding the troops now fell on the farmers.[39]

Since land taxes did not meet the army's food demands, moreover, the Nationalist regime made compulsory purchases of grain (*zhenggou*) in areas under its control to meet local needs. Prices paid for compulsory grain purchases were usually far below market value. Theoretically, the government paid for 30 percent in cash and the rest in grain bonds or other promissory notes. In reality, few if any notes were honored. In effect, compulsory purchases added an additional grain levy to the land tax.[40] In 1941, the Nationalist government set Henan's land tax quota at 1.3 million *shidan* of wheat, but the province needed to supply 3.5 million *shidan* to the military. As a result, an extra 2.2 million *shidan* had to be purchased. In 1942, Henan's land taxes and compulsory purchases together totaled 5 million *shidan* of wheat.[41] In normal years, according to one estimate, official levies amounted to 15–20 percent of the crop.[42] As war-induced devastation and climatic anomalies reduced harvests, these levies grew all the more burdensome.

Farmers expended additional energy transporting tax grain to collection stations. The two main railroads in Henan that might have been shipped grain – the Ping-Han and the Long-Hai – were torn up by the Nationalists earlier in the war to impede the Japanese. Armies seized the few automobiles in the province. They also commandeered most large carts for military use, so grain transport depended on small ox-carts. Taxpayers hauled tax grain over great distances to fulfill their quotas, and transport costs were high. Most

---

[38] Young (1965); Eastman (1984): Chapter 2; Eastman (1986): 584.
[39] Meng (1941): 11–15; Peng (1942): 384–390; Eastman (1984): 49–54; Eastman (1986): 587–588; Xu (1997): 672–673; Jin (2001): 162–164; van de Ven (2003): 276–278; van de Ven (2010): 458; Mitter (2013a): 267–268.
[40] Lu (1942): 33; Xu (1997): 673–675; Jin (2001): 166.
[41] Lu (1942): 37–38.
[42] Garnaut (2013): 19.

Nationalist armies were stationed in western and northern Henan along the Yellow River, but Henan's main grain production centers were in the southeast and southwest corners of the province. Thus, the amount of grain produced where armies were garrisoned did not meet demand and most grain had to be transported from the southeast and southwest. The amount of military grain shipped across Henan each year came to over 1.2 million bags. The routes taken to transport this grain covered 300–600 kilometers. A two-yoked ox-cart could carry five bags of grain and travel 20 kilometers per day, so some 240,000 carts – as well as almost 500,000 men and 500,000 oxen – also had to be conscripted. Tax grain shipments took around a month, or even longer in poor weather. Along with delaying acquisition of military grain, this inefficient transport system diverted carts and labor power away from agriculture.[43]

Logistical problems hampered flows of energy to the army and put greater burdens on the rural populace. Transport costs frequently exceeded the value of grain delivered. At the same time, local functionaries embezzled funds that were supposed to be paid to farmers for transport services.[44] Japanese bombing raids frequently targeted grain transport caravans, leading to the death of people and draft animals, as well as loss of precious grain. According to officials in charge of grain tax collection, "Because of the people's patriotic eagerness they never complain, but if this waste of labor power (*xiaohao minli*) persists it will be especially detrimental to the War of Resistance."[45] Tax grain shipments employed "oxcarts requisitioned from the people, and oxen are farmers' primary draft animals, so requisitioning them to transport military grain greatly influences agricultural harvests."[46] This wartime grain procurement system shouldered the civilian population with the energy costs of transporting military food supplies. Provincial government functionaries advocated reforming transport arrangements, but there is no evidence that the ideas were ever adopted or that they did anything to decrease the burden on Henan's rural residents.[47]

Along with land taxes and compulsory purchases, Henan's populace also had to pay a wide assortment of provisional levies (*tanpai*). After the central government nationalized the land tax in 1941, local administrations grew more dependent on these informal exactions for revenue. Armies instituted their own provisional levies as well. These exactions drained additional energy sources. In addition to grain, military garrisons demanded pigs, chickens, and other livestock as food for soldiers, wood for fuel and construction, as well as grass for fodder. Armies obtained all these resources through

---

[43] Lu (1942): 35–36.
[44] Ibid., 33, 34; Eastman (1984): 54, 58; Zhang (2005): 146.
[45] Lu (1942): 36.
[46] Ibid., 37.
[47] Ibid., 36–37.

provisional levies. Whenever tax grain was inadequate or transport problems impeded grain deliveries, moreover, army commanders made up for shortages by obtaining grain locally via compulsory purchases. Local government functionaries assigned quotas to residents, supervised collection, and conscripted labor to transport grain to military garrisons. In the rare event they actually paid for it, armies purchased grain below market prices. More often, soldiers seized crops for themselves and their animals without payment. Large amounts of energy were expended to transport these impromptu grain exactions as well. Military grain levies differed from regular grain taxes only insofar as the former might come at any time and in any amount depending on military exigencies.[48]

Provinces with especially large troop concentrations during the Sino-Japanese War, such as Henan, paid a disproportionate share of military grain levies compared with other parts of China. According to John S. Service, who visited Henan in October 1942, "Due to the difficulty in free China of transporting grain (the Japanese hold nearly all important transport lines), it is the practice to require each area to feed the troops stationed in it. Thus the closer to the front, generally speaking, the larger number of troops and the greater impositions on the farmer."[49] In 1942 and 1943, the approximately 500,000 Nationalist soldiers stationed in Henan outnumbered any other province. To sustain this presence, military grain levies took precedence over civilian food entitlements. As a former provincial official described, the army "ate Henan out of house and home," leaving civilians with limited grain reserves.[50] In summer 1941, before the situation in Henan became truly desperate and grain was still on the market, "some farmers who had eaten all their wheat were actually buying it for the tax collectors, pawning their winter clothes or cutting down and selling their farmyard trees to raise the money."[51]

From 1941 to 1944, land taxes and compulsory purchases in the seventy unoccupied counties of Henan reportedly totaled around 11,927,200 *shidan*.[52] This figure did not include miscellaneous levies or military grain exactions. Data on precisely how much grain these levies amounted to are not available. But a petition presented by Henan's representatives to the People's Political Council in 1942 suggests that the amount was staggering. According to petition, military grain and other levies for 1941 came to 11,000,000 *shidan*. The central government's land taxes and compulsory purchases totaled 5,683,000 *shidan*. After deducting transport costs, these

---

[48] Eastman (1984): 55–57; Taikang xianzhi bianzuan weiyuanhui (1991): 93; Xu (1997): 675–676; van de Ven (2003): 278–279.
[49] Service (1974): 12. See also Peck (1967): 313.
[50] Zhang (2005): 146. See also Garnaut (2013): 20.
[51] Peck (1967): 311.
[52] Zhao (1985): 304–305.

exactions left precious little to feed the people.⁵³ When harvests decreased even more due to inclement weather in 1942 and the army's demand for food resources only grew, it was a recipe for disaster.

Along with the food energy exacted by Chinese forces, Henan's countryside also bore the brunt of grain raids that the Japanese army launched to obtain food. These raids grew in intensity from 1941 to 1943, as Wou notes, when poor harvests led to grain shortages in Japanese occupied regions as well. Food shortage influenced military strategy, as grain raids became a key part of the mopping-up campaigns the Japanese launched in Henan and other parts of North China to wipe out guerilla resistance.⁵⁴ The Japanese raided and looted Zhengzhou and surrounding counties in fall 1941, making it into a "skeleton city" and devastating nearby villages. Seizure of food and destruction of infrastructure by the Japanese put additional pressures on energy stores that war-induced disasters and climatic fluctuations rendered extremely scarce.⁵⁵ When the Japanese army withdrew, Nationalist tax collectors announced that since the Japanese had stolen all the grain collected that summer as taxes, an emergency autumn tax would be collected from farmers around Zhengzhou to feed government officials and the army. "Shortly afterwards, the first of the caravans of wheat-loaded wheelbarrows – pushed by peasants from many of whom this levy took the last of their own grain reserves – began arriving in the city under armed guard."⁵⁶

Henan's rural populace provided additional energy for the military by working as soldiers and laborers. From 1937 to 1941, Nationalist armies recruited more troops from Henan than any other province. Henan was a key recruitment area until 1943, when famine made recruiting in Henan difficult and it was overtaken by Sichuan Province as a source of conscription. From 1937 to 1945, some 1,898,000 men from Henan entered the Nationalist standing army.⁵⁷ A vicious cycle was at work: poor and hungry young men

---

⁵³ The petition stated that in 1941 the central government's Ministry of Grain set Henan's military grain quota at 3,733,000 *shidan*. The Fifth War Zone made its own compulsory purchases of 1,027,000 *shidan*, the Thirty-First Group Army made compulsory purchases of 280,000 *shidan*, and guerilla forces in the First War Zone made compulsory purchases of 650,000 *shidan*. Military grain exactions for 1941 totaled some 7,200,000 *shidan*. In addition, local requisitions by the army and reduced-price grain purchases for police and other government functionaries came to 3,400,000 *shidan*. "Guomin canzhenghui erliuer ci dahui canzhengyuan Guo Zhongkui deng ershier ren ti: Henan junliang ji zhengshi fudan guo zhong minli bu dai qing zhengfu su yu jianqing yi wei difang er li kangzhan an" (November 1941), in Zhu et al. (1990): 246–248. Service (1974: 13) stated that normally taxes and various other levies, including military grain, totaled 30–50 percent of the crop.
⁵⁴ Wou (2007): 192–194. See also Lu (1942): 37; Wang (1943): 70; Chen (1986): 210–228.
⁵⁵ Peng (1942): 385, 386–387; Wampler (1945): 230; Peck (1967): 336–340.
⁵⁶ Peck (1967): 344.
⁵⁷ van de Ven (2003): 256.

joined the army, which meant less labor on farms, which meant less food and more hunger.

Besides taxation and military conscription, rural households also feared and suffered from compulsory labor service obligations.[58] In frontline areas of eastern Henan near the Yellow River's new course, "Garrisons were set up along the river and armies gathered. Defensive fortifications were repaired every year. Civilian laborers and materials were conscripted in large amounts. The heaviness of the burden on the common people is hard to describe."[59] Conscription of able-bodied males, whether as soldiers or workers, kept their labor out of the agricultural sector. Diversion of energy to the military meant it could not be used to maintain agro-ecosystems, and this had deleterious effects on harvests.

For mutual-security unit headmen (*baozhang*) responsible for collecting grain levies and requisitioning materials for the military, the task could prove unbearable.[60] In fall 1942, for example, the headman of Pingxin township in Shangcai County (southeast of the flooded area in Henan) informed the provincial government that,

The headman of this township's thirteenth bao, Di Fengzhu, and the headman of the sixteenth bao, Li Xiangtang, have had their financial power completely exhausted because the wheat and barley harvest was poor, drought has been extraordinarily heavy, the autumn crops were hopeless, and the people were left miserable and destitute [literally: "nine out of ten houses stand empty and forsaken" *shishi jiukong*]. At this time, the War of Resistance is serious and official affairs are as numerous as the spines of a hedgehog (like conscription of porters, carts, workers, materials, and collection of various types of military grain, etc.). In addition, every day locally garrisoned armies send squads of three to five people to sit at the bao headman's home to demand fodder, utensils, and other goods that they need. Also, at the present time military grain exactions are an urgently important military matter. [Di] Fengzhu and [Li] Xiangtang thought carrying out compulsory purchases in a limited time was difficult. On September 20, Fengzhu secretly fled, and Xiangtang sealed up his door with bricks and his entire family went into hiding. Fengzhu and Xiangtang did not

---

[58] Pei (1942): 45; Eastman (1984): 58; Zhang (2005):148.
[59] "Henan sheng di yi qu xingzheng ducha zhuanyuan jian baoan siling gongshu wu nian lai gongzuo jiyao," 1 (July 1, 1947): ZMA 6-1-37. See also Wang (1943): 70.
[60] In addition to grain levies, the Henan provincial government found that in 1940 the military requisitioned 453,174 large carts, 35,666 livestock, 6,306,306 civilian laborers, 57,894 rickshaws, 130,345 wooden planks, 14,424 burlap sacks, 245,593 kilograms of wood, 23,814 kilograms of hemp, 25,574 civilian porters, 465,688 bricks, 307,417 meters (or 587 kilograms) of iron wire, 381 boats, 145,132 dowels, 53,027 meters of rope, 2,263 handcarts, 776 carrying poles, 22 pouches, 258 kilograms of dynamite, 119 pieces of steel, 39 steel hammers, 3,300 meters of hemp cord, 30,500 sorghum stalks, 1,518 wheelbarrows, 203,493 steel nails, 571,283 kilograms of willow branches, 693 kilograms of dried grass, 1,332 kilograms of wheat straw, 822 reed mats, and 22,382 beasts of burden. These figures only account for items reported to the government, so actual amounts must have been even higher. Henan sheng zhengfu (1941): 59–61.

purposely abandon their posts. It was actually because handling official business was difficult.⁶¹

But mutual-security unit leaders were hardly mere victims, as other headmen increased burdens on the local populace. Oftentimes, *baojia* personnel resorted to extortionate measures to meet quotas of grain, fuel, draft animals, and human labor. Many local functionaries gained a notorious reputation for making false returns and embezzling funds and supplies.⁶²

China, an overwhelmingly agrarian country with a fledgling industrial sector trying to wage a modern war, depended on massive concentrations of grain, animals, and people in battle zones. Extracting those energy sources from a war-devastated environment influenced by climatic anomalies threw ecological balances into disarray and yielded catastrophic results.

FAMINE'S HYBRID CAUSES

A Nationalist government investigator who visited Henan in fall 1943 identified climatic shocks and warfare as the dual causes of the famine. In his evaluation, "If Henan Province only had drought and no war, the famine would not have been as severe as it was this spring." Hundreds of thousands of troops were garrisoned in Henan and they needed food. Since the start of the war against Japan, common people had given up "labor power, financial power, and material power" to the nation in large amounts for the war effort. For this reason, the report stated, "nine out of ten houses are stripped bare and households have little grain stored, so once the drought occurred the rich had no way to live, and the poor had even more difficulty supporting themselves."⁶³

In a time of drought, taxes and levies drained what little food was left. Henan's wheat crop was poor and much of the harvest was taken out of the province for the military.⁶⁴ As a former Henan official recalled, "Whether great or small households, they had no grain stored. Once the famine arrived, it was panic and there was nothing they could do."⁶⁵ Mobilization for war extracted available food resources, leaving Henan's civilian population a precariously thin buffer against environmental downturns. When drought struck in 1942, civilian food reserves could not suffice to prevent famine. After several years of military devastation, floods, and the heavy taxes and levies demanded for the War of Resistance, "The localities' vital energies have

---

⁶¹ "Henan sheng Shangcai xian Pingxin xiang xiang gongsuo cheng" (October 1942): HPA M02-25-692.
⁶² Van de Ven (2003): 278.
⁶³ "Zhang Guangsi guanyu Henan sheng hanzai qingkuang ji jiuzai qingxing de diaocha baogao," 560.
⁶⁴ Christensen (2005): 95.
⁶⁵ Zhang (2005): 146.

been completely exhausted and the hardship of the people's livelihood has reached its utmost." When harvests failed and food supplies dwindled, residents had no way to make a living.[66] Military grain exactions had "drained the pond to get the fish and households among the populace who have grain are only one or two percent."[67]

Armies had an insatiable appetite. As central government investigators put it, "Henan Province is an area near the front lines. All military food supplies and fodder are supplied locally. For this reason, even though the common people do not light their kitchen fires for a day, they still pay grain taxes, in addition to all the firewood, grass, and fodder to supply the army."[68] Henan's limited energy surplus went to the war effort, leaving little behind for civilian consumption. Troops were stationed in largest numbers in the western section of the province, which was now famine-stricken. Henan "already suffered in various ways as a result of the war," devastated by military hostilities and the floods that followed the breaking of the Yellow River dikes.[69] With agricultural production declining, grain exactions taken to feed the hundreds of thousands of troops in Henan threatened the civilian populace. After the spring wheat and autumn harvest failed in 1942, with output below 20 percent of normal, people in Henan still had to pay grain taxes and make compulsory sales. Taxes and military food procurements exhausted the 1942 wheat harvest, leaving only the autumn crops. When these failed, the situation grew desperate.[70] Rough estimates indicate that in 1942 per capita grain availability for Henan's farmers fell to one-third of the prewar average of 250 kilograms per capita. With little household surplus to begin with, this diminished level of grain availability left most rural residents on a "starvation diet."[71]

Grain prices skyrocketed. Rampant inflation that plagued virtually all parts of China after 1941 makes it difficult to analyze available price data. Wartime inflation had primarily monetary causes, but factors such as resource scarcity and disruption of transport networks contributed as well.[72] In Henan during 1942–1943, inflation merged with wartime devastation, poor harvests spawned by an El Niño drought, and state intervention in food markets in order to supply the military to create catastrophe. Rates of inflation seen in Henan were among the highest in all the country. Due to a

---

[66] "Henan sheng di yi qu xingzheng ducha zhuanyuan jian baoan siling gongshu wu nian lai gongzuo jiyao."
[67] Wang (1943): 70.
[68] "Zhang Guangsi guanyu Henan sheng hanzai qingkuang jiuzai qingxing de diaocha baogao," 560.
[69] Service (1974): 12.
[70] Wampler (1945): 229.
[71] Garnaut (2013): 23–24.
[72] Eastman (1986): 584–587; Lary (2010): 121–124; van de Ven (2010): 458. Classic works on the inflation are Chang (1958) and Young (1965).

TABLE 3.1 *Price indices for wholesale goods in Henan's main counties and towns (1942 average) January 1941 = 100*

County/town	Total index	Foodstuffs	Clothing and textiles	Fuel	Hardware/ construction materials	Willow branches
Nanyang	521.71	591.69	407.16	561.21	464.99	506.68
Luohe	545.29	682.19	332.39	634.02	378.83	560.90
Huangchuan	553.01	639.35	421.36	575.09	377.02	731.19
Xuchang	523.39	631.48	363.70	461.62	535.05	496.03
Zhoujiakou	594.49	733.37	424.78	661.52	405.05	625.07

"Henan ge zhuyao xian zhen pifa wujia fenlei zhishu biao (1942)," *Henan ge zhuyao xian zhen wujia zhishu niankan* (Henan nonggong yinhang jingji diaocha shi, 1942–1943), 1, 3.

combination of factors, from 1941 to 1942 increases in the price of food in Henan outstripped all other commodity categories (See Table 3.1). This inflation can be thought of as a distortion in chains of energy conversion that made it impossible for people to exchange their labor or commodities that they produced for food grain.

In spring 1943, a Nationalist investigator reported skyrocketing grain prices in Henan: "In each county, all civilian households have run out of grain. Their food supply is mostly dependent upon imports. Because of the difficulty of transport, prices have increased by the day." Before the war, 10 liters of wheat cost about six yuan. Prior to the 1942 wheat harvest, this amount cost approximately twenty yuan. On the eve of the 1943 wheat harvest, the going price for 10 liters had increased to 300 yuan.[73] Grain price indices for all urban centers in Henan showed similar increases (See Table 3.2).[74] As of 1943, grain prices in Zhengzhou and Luoyang were 150 percent greater than the average in other cities in Nationalist China.[75]

Large-scale speculation and hoarding do not seem to have played a major role in the Henan famine because, as a foreign observer later explained, "Most of the grain that goes into public distribution is handled by small merchants who have neither the capital nor the storage capacity to accumulate large quantities. In a sense, however, every farmer and land owner is a hoarder: because of the present uncertainty of currency he will not release his surplus until he has to purchase something, and naturally he will hold out for the most favorable prices." Normally, farmers unloaded stocks right before the spring harvest when grain was most scarce, which caused prices to fall.[76]

---

[73] "Zhang Guangsi guanyu Henan sheng hanzai qingkuang jiuzai qingxing de diaocha baogao," 560. For additional price information see Su (2004): 48–51.
[74] See also Chen (1986): 236–237.
[75] Garnaut (2013): 26.
[76] George Dickey to Will B. Rose (May 16, 1946): UN S-0528-0091.

TABLE 3.2 *Grain prices in Henan cities, November 1941–September 1942 Units:* Guobi yuan *per* shidan

1941–1942	Nov.	Dec.	Jan.	Feb.	Mar.	Apr.	May	Jun.	Jul.	Aug.	Sep.	Oct.
Luoyang	149.30	148.33	150.33	164.00	221.67	235.25	248.78	264.64	383.37	515.20	570.00	722.33
Zhengzhou	133.00	140.00	135.67	141.67	201.00	222.12	253.47	311.54	426.50	511.50	590.00	963.35
Hengchuan	48.00	53.00	75.00	112.50	115.00	117.50	120.00	148.08	176.06	204.25	210.00	264.37

"1941–1942 nian quanguo ge zhongyao shi xian liangshi jiage biao" (November 12, 1942), Zhang Bofeng and Zhuang Jianping, eds. *Kang Ri zhanzheng, vol. 5: Guomin zhengfu yu da houfang jingji,* 760.

That no such drop occurred in 1942–1943 indicates genuine dearth. People did not have money to purchase the little grain on the market, and transport difficulties ruled out importing sufficient quantities of food from other areas.

Even as people starved, army officers in Henan pressed civil officials to fulfill tax quotas. White surmised that the "army's tax ... was usually equivalent to the full crop, but in some cases it was higher – and where the grain tax was higher than the yield, peasants were sometimes forced to sell animals, tools, furniture for cash to make up the difference."[77] A missionary who observed conditions in famine-stricken areas wrote that, "In many homes we came across people already unconscious and whose lives were ebbing out, due to starvation. Going past the front doors of these homes were carts loaded with grain for military use."[78] If taxpayers delayed, local authorities placed them under arrest. Farmers sold once-valuable farmland at cut-rate prices to obtain wheat for tax payments. Speculators – merchants, officials, army officers, or landlords – gladly bought up this land.[79] Most farmers had no seed grain, having handed it over as taxes or eaten it all. Those who did have seed loaned it out at exorbitant interest rates.[80] According to Nationalist investigators, "common people in each county tearfully reported that some people had sold their wives and daughters but it was still not enough for the land tax and compulsory purchases. Some had no way to pay the land tax and compulsory purchases and were compelled to hang themselves and commit suicide."[81]

OBSTACLES TO RELIEF

To ensure access to grain taxes, the Nationalist regime punished officials suspected of falsely reporting famine conditions to evade payment and commended those who successfully met their quotas. Faced with these bureaucratic pressures, many local officials in Henan reported only a modest harvest shortfall to superiors or informed them that the famine was light. Even after crops failed, Henan's provincial leaders initially believed counties that reported famine were making exaggerated claims to avoid taxes. When famine conditions grew undeniable in the summer of 1942 and Henan had

---

[77] White (1978): 151.
[78] Quoted in Christensen (2005): 112.
[79] White claimed that land that yielded 20–30 pounds of wheat per *mu* was being bought for the equivalent of a mere 16–18 pounds of wheat. White (1978): 152. See also White and Jacoby (1980): 174.
[80] Wampler (1945): 241.
[81] "Zhang Guangsi guanyu Henan sheng hanzai qingkuang ji jiuzai qingxing de diaocha baogao," 562. On sale of wives and children, see Su (2004): 63–66.

to ask for tax reductions and disaster relief, the initial misinformation delayed the central government response.[82]

Once informed of the famine in fall 1942, the Nationalist regime remitted a portion of Henan's land taxes and compulsory purchases. But the army's demand for energy never waned and grain levies had to be collected. In late September 1942, Chiang Kai-shek decided to reduce Henan's land tax and compulsory purchase obligations from 5 million to 2.8 million *shidan* of wheat. But this waiver did not apply to back taxes, which farmers still needed to pay.[83]

Nationalist military leaders Zhang Zhizhong and Zhang Dingfan immediately voiced concern that provinces in battle zones north of the Yangzi River had not paid military grain quotas called for by the central government on time. Inability to fulfill military grain obligations, they warned, "directly influences war-making discipline and actual power (*shili*)." To assure adequate provisions for the army, provincial governments had to meet military grain obligations in full by the appointed time.[84] The Nationalist regime had reduced Henan's grain obligation, but military grain was essential for the war effort. Military leaders asked that Henan promptly make compulsory purchases and provide the reduced grain quota by year's end.[85] Nationalist leaders ordered Henan's provincial authorities and local elites to make announcements to the common people, "explaining the importance of military grain and urging them to diligently send it forward." The Nationalist government allocated famine relief funds to "placate the people's hearts," but hastening payment of military grain levies in kind remained top priority.[86]

---

[82] "Zhang Guangsi guanyu Henan sheng hanzai qingkuang ji jiuzai qingxing de diaocha baogao," 561–562; Yang (2005b) 157; Yang (2005a): 165–170. See also Li et al. (1993): 553; Li et al.(1994): 270. White (1978: 153–154) claimed that even in early 1943, "In Chungking [Chongqing], literally no one had any sense of dimension about what was happening in Honan [Henan]. By the time layer upon layer of officials in Honan had covered their tracks and layer upon layer of reports had been softened on their way up to Chungking, not even Chiang K'ai-shek knew there was anything more than a food shortage for which he had appropriated two hundred million dollars in paper money."

[83] "Henan sheng zhengfu jiuzai zong baogao," 7; Chen Bulei, "Guanyu Henan junliang wenti zhi jingguo qingxing yu chuli banfa" (October 26, 1942); "Xingzhengyuan daidian" (October 5, 1942): AH 001000004790A. See also White (1978): 152; White and Jacoby (1980): 173. The central government sent 200 million yuan in paper currency for famine relief, but by March 1943 only 80 million made it to the famine area. Funds came in the form of 100 yuan bills, which bank branches discounted by up to twenty percent to change into notes of smaller denomination needed to purchase grain. See Wampler (1945): 259–260; Christensen (2005): 112.

[84] Petition from Zhang Zhizhong and Zhang Dingfan (September 9, 1942): AH 001000004790A.

[85] "Junliang gaishan yijian" (September 1942): AH 001000004790A.

[86] Chen, "Guanyu Henan junliang wenti zhi jingguo qingxing yu chuli banfa." See also Zhang (2005): 149.

In the following weeks, two inspectors sent by the central government visited Henan.[87] Though the inspectors acknowledged the famine's severity, they stressed the absolute importance of military grain. At a meeting with Henan's civil and military leaders, the inspectors gave assurances that the central government would mobilize relief. But as the inspectors made clear, "Henan is a vital military area and military grain supply cannot be lacking for even a day." For this reason, Henan needed to collect its reduced obligation of 2.8 million *shidan* of wheat in full. The conclusion was straightforward: "First look after military grain then attend to civilian food supplies. This is a principle that definitely cannot be changed."[88] The tax and compulsory purchase reduction did not apply to back taxes from previous seasons, which farmers still had to pay.[89] Even in times of famine, military grain collection had to go forward.

Nationalist leaders had legitimate reason for concern about military food supplies. The Chinese army could not meet its own energy needs. After 1941, most Nationalist armies lived off the land.[90] During the latter stages of the war with Japan, food shortages decreased the fighting capabilities of Chinese troops, who frequently suffered malnourishment. During the famine, soldiers fared only slightly better than farmers. Armies were poorly motivated and hungry. British consular reports describing famine conditions in Henan during fall 1942 observed that "Maintenance of Chinese troops in forward zones became a problem in this connexion, and many were found by foreign observers to be suffering from disease and wastage caused by malnutrition."[91] In this situation, the Nationalists were less than willing to release grain from military storehouses. The guiding principle for relief, as Henan provincial government directives stated, was to "Do the utmost to decrease the burden on the people and localities, but do not influence the War of Resistance's progress and implementation of the province's administrative measures."[92]

The energy demanded was not for humans alone. When the famine was at its worst, Henan's farmers also had to supply fodder and straw for the over 50,000 army horses in the province. This fodder contained more nutrition than the famine foods (peanut shells, tree bark, dirt, etc.) that many common people had taken to consuming.[93] Petitioners asked that fodder levies be

---

[87] "Henan sheng zhengfu jiuzai zong baogao," 2; Chen, "Guanyu Henan junliang wenti zhi jingguo qingxing yu chuli banfa."
[88] "Zhang Ji and Zhang Lisheng dian" (October 21, 1942): AH 001000004790A. See also Zhang (2005): 152.
[89] Service (1974): 15.
[90] Wang (2010): 416–417.
[91] "Sir H Seymour, Chungking to Mr Eden, Foreign Office, June 22, 1943, Political Review for China for the year 1942 (prepared by Mr GV Kitson, Chinese Secretary to HM's Embassy), [FO371/35831]," in Jarman (2001): 157.
[92] "Henan sheng zhengfu jiuzai zong baogao," 3.
[93] White (1978): 151; White and Jacoby (1980): 174; Eastman (1984): 76; Su (2004): 55–59.

waived because localities in Henan did not have the ability to supply horse feed. The government decided that, although the famine in Henan was severe, "fodder is the main food for horses and mules, and has to do with military requirements. Waiving local compulsory purchases and changing to supplying [fodder] through compulsory purchases from other provinces in which production is abundant will not only waste financial power, but will also be impossible at present in terms of transport." The government forbade armies from seizing grass and fodder directly from the common people, but localities had to "do their best" to supply these resources through approved channels.[94]

Famine conditions presented the dilemma of whether people or horses would obtain the energy needed to stay alive. As the Nationalist military commander Jiang Dingwen explained in early 1943, "Henan Province had a severe famine last year and straw is scarce." The government increased funds for purchasing fodder to 100 yuan per horse, but the amount was far below the market price. Jiang Dingwen came to the grim conclusion that humans and horses alike might not survive. "The people's burden is so heavy that it is unbearable. In the future, it is feared that there will not be actual goods to purchase, and horses and mules will starve to death, decreasing transport abilities and influencing war-making capacity."[95]

The Nationalist government tried to ship grain into Henan from surplus areas like Shaanxi. Initially, however, Shaanxi and other neighboring provinces would not allow grain to leave their borders to ensure availability of food supplies for armies that they too had to feed.[96] Henan's provincial government eventually succeeded in making grain purchases in Shaanxi and other provinces to sell in famine areas at reduced prices. But transport bottlenecks slowed the arrival of this relief grain.[97]

War had severely disrupted North China's transport system. Cutting railroad links paralyzed the government's capacity to import grain and relieve famine. Another buffer against environmental shocks was lost. The Japanese held the Long-Hai railroad's eastern branch, as well as the northern and southern branches of the Ping-Han railroad. Part of the Long-Hai railroad's western branch was within range of Japanese artillery and regular shelling limited the ability to import grain. By itself, the normal volume of freight required for military needs overtaxed railroad capacity.[98]

Roadways were broken and the Japanese presence on the Yellow River's eastern and northern banks ruled out riverine shipments. Lack of transport

[94] "Junzheng buzhang He Yingqin qiancheng" (February 11, 1943): AH 001000004791A. See also "Henan sheng zhengfu jiuzai zong baogao," 85.
[95] "Jiang Dingwen dian" (February 22, 1943): AH 001000004791A.
[96] White and Jacoby (1980): 173; Zhang (2005): 144; Mitter (2013a): 269.
[97] Some 3,160,935 *jin* of grain borrowed from Shaanxi for famine relief never reached Henan due to "transport matters" (*jiaotong guanxi*). "Henan sheng zhengfu jiuzai zong baogao," 27.
[98] "Xingzhengyuan daidian" (December 25, 1942): AH 001000004791A; Li (1942): 35; Wampler (1945): 242–243, 255–256; Service (1974): 15; Zhang (2005): 146.

facilities hampered ability to import grain from Shaanxi or Gansu Province, which had good harvests.[99] As an American missionary active in famine relief in Henan recalled, "Train service was cut north, south, and east, which made it difficult for food to come from other areas. Some grain came in by wheelbarrow, but it was very expensive."[100] Securing muscle power to do the work of moving grain was not any easier. When local grain supplies ran low, relief agencies had to get animals and men to transport grain purchased in other areas. But as another American missionary recalled, "So many of the draft animals had died or been killed that officials often could not get enough to haul supplies for the army. This resulted in drafting men. When we went on the market to hire carts or men to transport grain, prices began to climb."[101]

When Henan had met with poor harvests in the past, grain stores from previous years and grain imports from other regions made up for losses. When harvests failed in 1942, wartime conditions ruled out this option. "In the [first] five years of the War of Resistance, middle- and lower-level households' grain, aside from what was eaten, was mostly contributed to the nation. Wealthy households that stored grain in the past, because of local conditions, were not calm and almost all of them sold their grain stores." After two seasons of dearth, people had no way to live. "Moreover, because of the needs of the War of Resistance, railroads have already been torn up and transport implements are extremely scarce. Grain prices are more than a hundred times higher than normal. Even if some grain funds are acquired, it is still difficult to obtain the necessary grain. Under these conditions, speaking of disaster relief is extremely difficult."[102]

As reports from Henan's provincial government noted, "For this province to purchase and ship grain from Shaanxi to distribute to various counties is not only circuitous and time consuming, but also wastes the people's power."[103] As the report explained,

Disaster relief and transport are intimately connected. Using this place's surplus to relieve that place's shortfall is no less effective than living things naturally coming to fruition (*shengwu chengwu*), but it depends on good transport and shipping to be beneficial. In this province, since the start of the War of Resistance, many railroads have been damaged and road vehicles are also scarce. Relief grain previously purchased in Shaanxi, Hubei, and Anhui, because of these transport limitations, met with shipping difficulties and the influence on disaster relief effectiveness was considerable.

---

[99] "Henan sheng zhengfu jiuzai zong baogao," 90; Pei (1942): 49; Wampler (1945): 247–248. Transport disruption is also stressed by Garnaut (2013): 37–39.
[100] Katie Murray, "God Working in Chengchow, Honan: Interior China Baptist Mission, 1936–1950" (August 14, 1970): Wake Forest University Archives, Katie M. Murray Papers, Box 2, Folder 161.
[101] Wampler (1945): 260. On "slow inefficient methods" of transport, see Christensen (2005): 104.
[102] Li (1942): 35.
[103] "Henan sheng zhengfu jiuzai zong baogao," 35.

To maintain control of scarce food sources, some counties in Henan restricted trade as well, refusing to ship grain to areas where it was more badly needed. For this reason, the provincial government's report concluded, "From now on there should be close contact between provinces and between counties to facilitate transport, so that grain can circulate freely and goods can be used exhaustively."[104]

As Service explained after visiting Henan, "The problem therefore becomes one of an insufficiency of grain – with no means of shipping in large enough quantities to effectively relieve the situation."[105] Famine-stricken regions, British consular reports found, "are in close proximity to the enemy, who occupy a considerable portion of Honan [Henan] province, and that the problems of relief must be immeasurably complicated by the necessities of the military situation." Further distress resulted from Japanese military operations, which "have for the past year or two consisted mainly of raids for supplies." These factors made famine nearly impossible for the central authorities to ameliorate: "When, as in the case of Honan, the incidence of drought is added to the depredations of the enemy and the burdens of intermittent warfare and the exactions of the Chinese armies, a situation of terrible suffering results which it is quite beyond the resources of the Chinese Government to control."[106] As an area that passed back and forth between Chinese and Japanese control, relief programs in Henan "lacked substance."[107]

Missionary Ernest Wampler listed the array of factors that in 1942 "brought on one of the worst famines China ever experienced: an autumn failure of all crops; the closeness of the territory to the battle line; the Japanese raid into part of that territory the year before, in which all surplus grain was destroyed and many villages burned; the breaking of the Yellow River dikes, flooding great portions of the rich valleys of Honan, driving out thousands of farmers who had settled just back of the battle line, the great number of Chinese soldiers stationed around the rim of this partial-failure area." Famine came suddenly "and was really a famine blitz."[108] The Nationalist government "heavily burdened by the war effort," was slower than the few remaining foreign missionaries and local Buddhist relief agencies "in getting relief machinery going, but by late winter and spring of 1942–1943 it helped more than any other agency did."[109] Relief committees in Henan made some seed loans without interest, but many farmers still did not have the grain they needed for planting.[110]

---

[104] Ibid., 90. See also Christensen (2005): 138.
[105] Service (1974): 15.
[106] "Sir H Seymour, Chungking, to Mr Eden, Monthly Summary for 1943, dated May 7, 1943," in Jarman (2001): 191.
[107] Mitter (2013a): 273.
[108] Wampler (1945): 229.
[109] Ibid. See also Su (2004): 156–158, 167–168.
[110] Wampler (1945): 229.

TABLE 3.3 *Military grain loans from armies in Henan and grain obtained by abstaining from food to assist famine relief (1 jin = 500 grams)*

Army commander	Military grain loaned for famine relief		Abstaining from food to assist relief	
	Type	Amount (*jin*)	Type	Amount
Jiang Dingwen	Wheat	9,400,000	Wheat	3,000,000 *jin*
Hu Zongnan	Wheat	4,000,000	Flour	5,166 bags
Tang Enbo	Wheat	2,900,000	Wheat	1,950,515 *jin*
Total	Wheat	16,300,000	Wheat	4,950,515 *jin*
			Flour	5,166 bags

"Yu jing ge jun bojie junliang jiu zai ji jieshi zhu zhen shuliang," July 9, 1943: AH 001000004791A.

In spring 1943, with conditions in Henan at their worst, relief grain from neighboring provinces had not yet arrived. What is more, Theodore White's gripping coverage of the famine in the international press embarrassed the Nationalist regime and necessitated more decisive official action. Nationalist leaders took the drastic step of ordering armies in Henan to loan part of their stored grain for famine relief until the time of the wheat harvest. Commanders ordered troops to eat even less than usual so military food supplies could be used to feed hungry civilians (See Table 3.3).[111]

However, army supply organs cautioned that because military grain had not arrived on time or in the proper amounts, provisioning the army presented difficulties. Given the amount loaned for famine relief in Henan, "military grain can only barely be maintained until the new wheat is harvested."[112] As soon as the harvest arrived in spring 1943, the Nationalist government insisted on repayment of all military grain that was loaned for famine relief to avoid shortfalls in the army's food supplies.[113]

A BITTER HARVEST

Even after the spring 1943 wheat ripened, Henan's agro-ecological system had not recovered. Crops initially looked promising, but erratic rains, ongoing flooding, locust swarms, and loss of work animals caused new problems, as did shortages of human labor. In some places crops were growing well. But as missionaries observed, "The sad thing is though, that many

---

[111] "Henan sheng zhengfu jiuzai zong baogao," 21–24, 35; "Junzhengbu daidian" (June 14, 1943); "Henan sheng zhengfu kuaiyou daidian" (July 1943): AH 001000004791A; Yang (2005a): 169. See also Wampler (1945): 243; White (1978): 148, 152, 155; Christensen (2005): 120.
[112] "Junzhengbu daidian."
[113] Ibid.

who planted will not be here to reap. Thousands have died and none of those who fled last autumn when they realized what lay ahead have as yet returned and most of them will never return."[114] Labor power was necessary to harvest grain, but it was not available. Villages were devoid of people, as populations dwindled to from one half to one fourth of what they had been a year before. Some disaster victims who had fled gradually returned home to farm. But military demand for energy and resources hampered recovery.

Henan's provincial government telegraphed Nationalist military leaders in summer 1943, asking that "armies stationed in counties within Henan Province temporarily stop requisitioning labor and supplies, unnecessary fortifications, and compulsory purchases of mules, horses, military shoes, military socks, and miscellaneous goods during the time of the wheat harvest and the planting of the autumn crops." The provincial government also requested an increase in the "standard of payment for hiring [labor] power" (*zuli jiyu biaozhun*) to maintain the livelihoods of people and draft animals. Nationalist leaders granted these requests, stopping collection of shoes and socks for the soldiers, temporarily waiving compulsory purchases of mules, horses, and other supplies, and agreeing to consider increased payments.[115] Henan provincial government relief plans ordered that "Grain transport and compulsory purchases of flour and grass, as well as human and draft animal power, should be verified and paid for."[116] Death and displacement during famine also led to a dearth of able-bodied adult males, which had a negative effect on military conscription. To maintain an adequate supply of farm labor, Henan negotiated to forgo its military conscription obligations during the harvest period.[117]

Famine-related dislocations reduced the human and nonhuman muscle power needed for agricultural recovery. Missionaries wrote that, "Cattle and donkeys they say perhaps 8/10ths have starved or been slaughtered in desperation."[118] Unable to afford feed for their livestock, many households sold them; desperate for food, famine victims killed untold numbers of draft animals. County governments in Henan prohibited slaughtering oxen, but their orders were often ignored.[119] This prompted an official directive to warn, "It must be known that oxen are not only the primary motive power (*yuandongli*) for agricultural production, but are also important as transport

---

[114] Quoted in Christensen (2005): 128. See also Pei (1942): 52. On persistent disaster conditions in Yanling during summer 1943, see "Yan min kunku xianzhuang zhong zhong" (1943): 2.
[115] "Zhongguo guomindang Henan sheng shixing weiyuanhui xunling xingzutuan zi 68 hao" (August 9, 1943): HPA M2-25-690. See also "Henan sheng zhengfu jiuzai zong baogao," 83, 85. See also Pei (1942): 45, 48.
[116] "Henan sheng zhengfu bennian jiuzai jihua" (1943): 70.
[117] "Henan sheng zhengfu jiuzai zong baogao," 85.
[118] Quoted in Christensen (2005): 128.
[119] "Henan sheng zhengfu jiuzai zong baogao," 6–7. See also Pei (1942): 52–53; Wang (1943): 75; "Yan min kunku xianzhuang zhong zhong," 2.

power for transportation. If they are slaughtered in excessive numbers the influence on cultivation and transport will be hard to imagine."[120] Another provincial relief plan urged residents to: "Conscientiously protect oxen, mules, and horses, and strictly prohibit people from slaughtering them. If disaster victims do not have the power to care for them themselves, they should be publicly raised by the *baojia*."[121] A contradiction existed between short- and long-term survival strategies. Killing draft animals to obtain food calories eliminated the energy stores required to fuel agriculture and commerce.

NATIONALIST MILITARY COLLAPSE

The ecological catastrophes that accompanied the Henan famine of 1942–1943 had military and political implications. Energy burdens that Nationalist wartime mobilization placed on local populations in Henan did much to damage the regime's legitimacy. It did not take long for popular resentments to come to a head. In mid-April 1944, the Japanese launched the Ichigō Offensive to drive Chinese armies out of Henan and clear transport links along the Ping-Han railroad as part of its effort to open up transport links between northern and southern China. The Ichigō campaign was the largest operation undertaken by the Japanese army during the war. Nationalist defenses under the command of Jiang Dingwen and Tang Enbo collapsed in the face of the assault. The Japanese occupied Zhengzhou on April 23, and Xinzheng and Mi counties fell the next day. Over the next month, Japanese forces advanced west along the Long-Hai railroad toward Luoyang and on May 25 they captured the city.

Two years of famine severely weakened Nationalist military forces and made Henan's starving populace hostile toward them. Heads of villages and mutual-security units ran away, taking grain supplies with them and leaving Chinese armies without food.[122] Because Tang Enbo and Jiang Dingwen's soldiers lacked supplies, they had to "borrow" grain from farmers. Even after the troops found a way to mill the grain, its poor quality left them undernourished and their will to fight was exhausted. The relationship between the civilian population and the military "was now utterly hollow." When the Japanese captured previously unoccupied areas in Henan, they seized grain that had been left in Nationalist government granaries. According to Rana Mitter, "the million bags of flour captured could have nourished 200,000 soldiers for five months."[123] As Nationalist armies fled the Japanese onslaught, Henan's

---

[120] "Henan sheng di er qu xingzheng ducha zhuanyuan jian baoan siling gongshu daidian Zheng Erjian zi di 1769 hao" (December 1945): ZMA 6-1-13 18.
[121] "Henan sheng zhengfu bennian jiuzai jihua," 59.
[122] Mitter (2013a): 323.
[123] Ibid., 325.

farmers turned on retreating Chinese troops and disarmed entire companies.[124] Upon hearing this news, a dismayed Chiang Kai-shek lamented, "The local population attacked our own forces and seized their arms, just as happened with the czar's army in imperial Russia during World War I. Such an army cannot win! Our military trucks and horses carry smuggled goods, not ammunition... During the retreat, some lost discipline, looting and raping women."[125] As the Japanese advanced, social disintegration gave way to "open anarchy." Evacuees robbed and murdered one another as they struggled to escape. Bandits, deserters, and hungry farmers "roamed in hordes, pouncing on the road whenever they saw groups of evacuees weak enough to attack."[126]

As the Henan famine made evident, inability to secure the energy flows needed to wage war eroded the Nationalist military structure, as well as the Nationalist regime's political legitimacy. The Communists did not hesitate to capitalize on this popular disaffection. The Nationalist regime's authority in Henan had all but fallen apart, paving the way for its demise in North China.

FROM PREDATION TO PROTECTION IN COMMUNIST TERRITORIES

Up to this point, our narrative has focused on Henan's Nationalist-controlled territories. But gaining access to food energy posed the same challenges for troops in the province's Communist base areas. By the time of the famine, the Communist movement in eastern Henan was in dire straits. Confined to a narrow strip of land west of the Guo River between the Japanese army and the hostile Nationalist forces, Communist mobility was extremely limited. Worse yet, the small area of land under Communist control – only 25 by 100 kilometers – could not provide enough food for a large armed force. The Nationalists maintained an army in Henan ten times larger than that of the CCP. A series of defeats by larger Nationalist armies and Japanese "three all" (burn all, loot all, kill all) eradication campaigns in 1941 and 1942 virtually destroyed the Communist military presence in eastern Henan, making it necessary for CCP forces to withdraw. The flooded area was taken over by the Nationalists, the Japanese, and their collaborators.[127]

The arrival of famine in 1942–1943 did additional damage to the Communist powerbase. The small Communist force that stayed in the flooded area found it nearly impossible to procure food supplies. Reports

---

[124] On the offensive see Chen (1986): 42–59; Hara (2010); Wang (2010); Mitter (2013a): 322–326. Popular hostility is described in White (1978): 153; White and Jacoby (1980): 178; Eastman (1984): 69; 141–142; Eastman (1986): 606; Wang (2010): 417.
[125] Quoted in Wang (2010): 417.
[126] Peck (1967): 259.
[127] Taikang xianzhi bianzuan weiyuanhui (1991): 117; Wou (1994): 224–226.

from cadres in the CCP's River East Independent Regiment (*Shuidong duli tuan*), based in northwest Taikang, stated that the 1942 drought and locust disasters caused grain harvests to fall to less than thirty percent of normal. At the same time, "unlimited plunder" by Nationalist and collaborationist troops increased the severity of the famine.[128] Supplying food for the Independent Regiment's 1,936 soldiers grew incredibly difficult. All expenditures stopped, including payments for food. It was considered "special treatment" for soldiers to get rations of 125 grams of grain every two days. In early 1943, CCP troops in River East devoted all their energies to finding food, usually through raids on Nationalist-held and Japanese-occupied areas. But with food resources unavailable, even these raids grew difficult. As local cadres reported,

In the army's movements, the enemy's situation was secondary and whether one could eat at a certain village was primary. Under these circumstances, once a call was given to levy grain (*zhengliang*) from enemy-occupied areas all other work suddenly stopped. At all levels, a levy grain movement began. Initially, one platoon could levy what was needed for one company. Later, the enemy intercepted small armies and the masses sealed their stockade gates and made things difficult by hiding, so close to 1,000 men had to be gathered to force collection.[129]

The Communists engaged in fierce competition with Nationalist and Japanese adversaries for food. Like their opponents, Communist armies lived off the local populace. Villagers' reaction indicates that they feared rapacious CCP armies just as much as they did the Nationalists. Farmers did not simply hand over grain to the Communists. It required coercion. During the famine, CCP forces gave up coordinated food allotment and adopted a laissez faire system of raising provisions. Commanders were responsible for feeding subordinates. Troops requisitioned any food they could get from the civilian populace. In the parlance of local cadres, ordinary people functioned as the army's "natural supply office." A CCP report from River East summed up the procedure: "One true man with a gun; where you went was where you ate."[130]

When food grew more abundant after the 1943 wheat harvest, however, the CCP was gradually able to put its supply system in order. Initially, Communist military units adhered to a "chaotic preparation and unified distribution system," trying to exert at least some centralized control over food distribution.[131] According to this principle, it did not matter how army commanders obtained food for the troops as long as it was allocated and reported in a unified fashion. In reality, "chaotic preparation and independent consumption" were the norm.

---

[128] "Yijiusisan nian Shuidong dulituan yijiusisan nian gongzuo baogao" (1985): 203–204. Wou (1994: 240–245) refers to this document, but translations and interpretations here are my own. See also Taikang xianzhi bianzuan weiyuanhui (1991): 117.
[129] "Yijiusisan nian Shuidong dulituan yijiusisan nian gongzuo baogao," 204.
[130] Ibid., 216–217.
[131] Ibid., 217.

Armies levied grain for their own consumption and superior officers had no way of knowing about it. Local cadres in eastern Henan had to accept this practice out of necessity, "Those who were a little bit better; a little bit more honest, reported what they had demanded, but if it was a little bit short then it didn't matter."[132]

Only after the harvest was reaped did the CCP reform its provisioning system and impose centralized control over food supplies. As a CCP report stated, "we proceeded from all sides, strengthening each company's supply personnel and placing emphasis upon the preliminary calculation system (*yu juesuan zhidu*), as well as convening a battalion-wide work conference and opening a work personnel training class. Now there is a model and the recognition of supply organs has changed."[133] Communist military units also defended the harvest against raids by the Nationalists, Japanese, and Chinese collaborators. Thanks to these measures, the party managed to bring the food supply problem under control.[134]

Although the metabolism of CCP and Nationalist troops put similar demands on Henan's strained agro-ecosystems and the region's human inhabitants, military contingencies worked in favor of the Communists. In spring 1944, the Japanese advance during the Ichigō Offensive and the subsequent Nationalist retreat lifted military pressure on eastern Henan's Communist forces. Taking full advantage of this opportunity, CCP cadres perfected a strategy of securing food supplies through their leadership of local collective defense against grain raids launched by pro-Japanese and pro-Nationalist guerillas. As Odoric Wou has pointed out, "It was in common defense against enemy grain raids (*qiangliang*) that the Communists built the long-lasting relationship between the party and the peasants that eventually formed a solid base for the Communist triumph in this area." CCP military work teams penetrated enemy-occupied areas, vigorously denouncing grain seizures by the Nationalists, the Japanese, and their collaborators to arouse popular sentiment against them.[135]

Communist mobilization in Henan utilized pre-existing local organizations, such as clan bands, village pacts, and neighborhood pacts. What the CCP gave them was effective leadership and coordination.[136] Carefully organized defensive efforts offered local residents protection against hostile elements, safeguarding the Communist military's access to food supplies and

---

[132] Ibid.
[133] Ibid.
[134] Ibid., 204. When the CCP-liberated area government carried out its first grain levy in Taikang after the grain harvest in 1943, it collected 150,000 kg of grain. That summer Communist authorities also issued a land redemption order that allowed farmers to buy back land sold during the famine for the original selling price. By 1945 this policy resulted in the redemption of over 50,000 *mu* of land. See Taikang xianzhi bianzuan weiyuanhui (1991): 117.
[135] "Yijiusisan nian Shuidong dulituan yijiusisan nian gongzuo baogao," 208, Wou (1994): 246.
[136] Wou (1994): 252.

depriving its enemies of these resources. Largely due to their collective defense initiatives, after 1944 the Communists began to expand their influence in Henan's flooded area.[137] The CCP integrated local defense with agricultural production, mobilizing soldiers and local residents to "form mutual aid teams to increase production and to fight."[138]

In several instances, Nationalist military forces opened dikes in an attempt to contract Communist-held territories and take advantage of the floods to seize grain. CCP armies built embankments to block assaults and defend their positions.[139] Ultimately, the flooded area's topography worked to the advantage of CCP forces. Overgrown with vegetation and covered with sediments, this landscape obviously favored guerilla warfare tactics. The flat floodplain, dissected by small streams, gave Communist troops plenty of places to hide. Inundated and swampy land, which posed obstacles for conventional mechanized warfare tactics, likewise hampered Japanese and Nationalist attacks.[140]

The Communists' ability to devise new ways of harnessing energy and resources had significant implications. Defensive activities gave the CCP a presence in Henan local society that the Nationalists never established. Taking over pre-existing community organizations, the Communists took hold of scarce food resources in Henan's flooded area and kept them out of the hands of its enemies. The CCP, in short, had started to forge effective systems for seizing power in local society. The precondition for this achievement was the ability to effectively extract energy from the population and the environment. Ultimately, this power proved impossible for the Nationalists to dislodge.

CONCLUSION

The Henan famine of 1942–1943 grew out of a complex interplay between non-anthropogenic changes in North China's fragile, unpredictable environment and the impact of human actions on that landscape. War severely distorted energy flows, aggravating the effects of climate fluctuations. Efforts to mobilize the environment as an instrument of warfare and keep vital resources out of the hands of enemies – exemplified by the breaking of the Yellow River dikes in 1938 – dealt a severe blow to production of food energy through agriculture, while war-related devastation impeded its circulation. Short-term climatic changes added another shock in 1941–1942,

---

[137] Ibid., 248–249.
[138] Ibid., 249. See also Taikang xianzhi bianzuan weiyuanhui. (1991): 117.
[139] "Yijiusisan nian Shuidong dulituan yijiusisan nian gongzuo baogao," 205.
[140] Wou (1994): 235–236; "Yijiusisan nian Shuidong dulituan yijiusisan nian gongzuo baogao," 208. For an earlier example of CCP forces in Xihua exploiting floods to counter Nationalist mechanized cavalry, see Zhonggong Henan shengwei dangshi yanjiushi (2001): 77.

when North China experienced unpredictable weather and low precipitation levels connected to a strong El Niño event. These naturally occurring environmental changes caused even greater declines in agricultural output.

As Peter Perdue observes with reference to the Great North China Famine of 1876–1879, which took the lives of 9–13 million people in Henan and several other provinces, "Whether or not famine happens depends on the effect of climate conditions on interactions between officials, peasants, relief agencies, and markets for labor and grain." People's ability to sell labor and resources on markets, not simply the aggregate availability of food, determines life or death. In late imperial times, Chinese officials effectively mobilized relief programs to deliver food, cash, and work opportunities to starving communities. But in the 1870s, as Perdue argues, state security interests linked to suppressing a rebellion in Xinjiang overrode the need to rescue millions of starving peasants.[141] During the early 1940s, the direct impact of warfare once again combined with the state's military imperatives to rule out effective interventions to assist Henan's rural population and avert famine.

Five years of war and dislocation left Henan with little buffer against the drought and locust infestations that came in 1942. Nevertheless, food energy remained vital for waging war. For this reason, Nationalist forces – like those of the Japanese and Chinese Communist Party – had to channel and control supplies of food grains and other forms of energy for military purposes. Ecological collapse and grain seizure by military and political actors emptied grain stores, translating into scarcity, hunger, and starvation for millions of Henan's civilians.

William McNeill once conceptualized consumption of food energy by armed forces as the "macroparasitism of military operations." To sustain themselves, militaries must rob agriculturalists of part of their harvests. Seizing harvests for the military, "if it led to the speedy death of the agricultural work force from starvation, was an unstable form of macroparasitism."[142] No parasite will last long if it kills its hosts. Just as some disease-causing viruses evolve less virulent strains that exploit hosts without killing them, armies have usually learned to protect the agriculturalists they exploit. Shared interests soften exploitation and restrain predation. In some situations, primary producers become as dependent on militaries as the militaries are on primary producers.[143] But this symbiotic ecological balance has certainly not always existed. Oftentimes, extraction of crops for the military has not left enough energy behind for cultivators to survive. In times of acute crisis, as David Christian observes, "even the most able rulers become brutal and destructive predators. Rulers who were less able,

---

[141] Perdue (2010): 114. The authoritative study of the famine of 1876–1879 is Edgerton-Tarpley (2008).
[142] McNeill (1977): 72.
[143] Ibid. See also Christian (2005): 250–251.

or more desperate, used destructive fiscal methods as a matter of course, even when they or their own advisors knew that they were undermining the basis of their own power."[144] For the Chinese Nationalist regime, the Henan famine of 1942–1943 was an instance of "military macroparasitism" that fatally disrupted the host society.

Unlike the Nationalist military, Communist armies in Henan's flooded area made a successful transition from predatory to protective strategies, to borrow Elizabeth Perry's terminology, as the famine subsided. CCP local defense forces evolved a more stable form of macroparasitism, lending protection to the farmers they exploited and thereby consolidating the CCP's local powerbase.[145] In part, the Communist forces benefited from military contingencies that gave them room to maneuver after the Ichigō Offensive. Of necessity, CCP cadres in Henan's villages had to be flexible, adjusting organizational strategies to the givens of the new environmental conditions that the war created. At the same time, Communist local defense forces were of much smaller size than the complex, bureaucratic, and unwieldy Nationalist military structure, making it easier for them to adapt new ways of harnessing energy flows needed to wage warfare. To a large extent, this capacity to innovate and extract more energy from the environment explains the CCP's success in eastern Henan during the latter stages of the war against Japan.

But energy was not simply needed to feed armies; wartime hydraulic management initiatives still demanded it as well. The following chapter returns to the ongoing efforts to harness the Yellow River's power for military purposes, as well as the strains and disruptions that the energy expenditures needed to carry out this work caused for the shattered remnants of local societies.

---

[144] Christian (2005): 322.
[145] Perry (1983).

4

Against the Flow: Hydraulic Instability and Ecological Exhaustion

At a moment when millions of Henan's residents could not meet their own basic metabolic needs, they had to keep supplying massive quantities of energy for wartime hydraulic engineering projects. When the famine was at its most horrific in 1942–1943, the Nationalist and Japanese militaries still extracted energy stores from local societies as they tried to channel and manipulate the Yellow River for strategic purposes. What little labor power and material resources that localities in Henan had left were appropriated by combatants for their ongoing struggle to harness the Yellow River. Nationalist and Japanese hydraulic engineering initiatives continued to work with, on, and against the river to harness its energy and deploy it against their enemies. Competitive dike building went on unabated, with Chinese and Japanese forces trying to divert floods into the territories held by their adversaries.

For the Nationalist government, river defense and national defense remained inextricably linked. The Japanese likewise perceived the river as militarily vital. For this reason, water control remained a foremost priority for Chinese as well as Japanese wartime leaders. The technological imperatives of hydraulic maintenance were the same for both sides, though neither could by any means conquer or tame the river. Nature's energies thwarted their undertakings. As in peacetime, sediments deposited by the river unceasingly elevated its new bed. The Yellow River's restlessness threatened Nationalist-constructed dikes on its western bank as well as the Japanese-built dikes to the east, leading to more flooding that damaged agricultural settlements and at the same time jeopardized military positions.

Harnessing the river for military purposes demanded power – the ability to gain advantage by commanding energy and benefiting from the work of others. Energy sources extracted to feed armies and for militarized hydraulic engineering were a net withdrawal from the energy at the disposal of the rural populace. With the military's hunger for resources and the sheer devastation caused by war-induced floods and famine, localities in Henan's flooded area lacked energy surpluses needed to effectively carry out river defense. At this stage in the war, militarized hydraulic engineering assumed an even more coercive character. Even as army commanders took over dike maintenance responsibilities and organized civilian labor conscripts along militarized lines, however, extracting adequate quantities of labor and resources from flood- and famine-stricken localities in Henan grew more and more difficult. War-induced breakdown of hydraulic infrastructure added to the effects of famine, further devastating agro-ecosystems and subjecting the rural residents who had not fled to even greater dislocations.

DIKE CONSTRUCTION AND MAINTENANCE IN NATIONALIST AREAS

By 1942, the new bed that the Yellow River overtook after its strategic diversion had risen considerably due to sediment accumulation and recently built dikes were no longer high enough to contain it. Floods broke through embankments every year as siltation caused the river to gradually shift west and impinge upon Nationalist-held territories. In order to cope with this situation, in late 1942 Nationalist general Tang Enbo gathered representatives from the Fifteenth Group Army Command, the Yellow River Conservancy Commission, the Huai River Conservancy Commission, and Henan, Anhui, Jiangsu, and Shandong's provincial governments to discuss river defense. The meeting's attendees formed a team to inspect river conditions and dikes in the flooded areas from Weishi southeast into Anhui. The investigators' report stressed that the new dike on the Yellow River's western bank needed to be strengthened. Unless the dike was reinforced, the river would change course and threaten military installations along with the people's livelihood. To keep the floods in their current position, the Nationalist government launched work relief projects to repair over six million cubic meters of embankments.[1] But calamity struck before any repairs were completed. After the Yellow River froze in January 1943, ice floes assailed a 10-kilometer dike section near Rongcun in Weishi, threatening to break through it. Labor and materials were scarce, so emergency repairs were not made sufficiently quickly to keep the embankments from breaking. Along the dike section between Fugou and Daolinggang in Xihua more breaches occurred.

This crisis prompted immediate official action. Again under general Tang Enbo's direction, the Su-Lu-Yu-Wan (Jiangsu-Shandong-Henan-Anhui) Border Area General Command and the Fifteenth Group Army Command met in Luohe with the Yellow River Conservancy Commission's director Zhang Hanying, representatives from the Henan provincial government, and magistrates from counties along the river. Heads of Henan's dike defense

---

[1] Xu Fuling (1991): 29; MHD: 166; MHS: 189; Cheng et al. (2007): 292.

sections also attended. This conference allocated five million yuan in military work funds to strengthen the flood defense dike. Work was to be completed using military labor prior to the spring 1943 wheat harvest. To oversee this project, the conference established the Yellow River flood repair engineering office, with military commander He Zhuguo as director. By mid-May, after several months of work, most repairs spelled out at the conference had been finished.[2]

In that same month, however, sudden winds and heavy rains collapsed embankment works along the river's western bank at Daolinggang in Xihua, causing the dike openings to expand. Surging waters also burst through poorly constructed dike sections at Rongcun in Weishi. Dikes broke in Fugou and Yanling as well, flooding low-lying areas and destroying crops. By the end of May 1943, dikes had broken at seventeen places in Weishi, Yanling, Fugou, and Xihua counties, flooding nearly 86,670 hectares of cultivated land, destroying over 59,700 houses, and turning more than 186,100 more people into disaster victims. Floods wiped out the spring wheat harvest and prevented farmers from planting fall crops. Xihua and Fugou were most severely affected, followed by Yanling and Weishi, but floodwaters threatened parts of Xuchang and Luohe as well.[3]

Together with inclement weather conditions, the susceptibility of Henan's hydraulic infrastructure to war-related disruption brought on this series of disasters. According to a Henan provincial government report, the Rongcun breach in Weishi had "remote causes" and "immediate causes":

The remote causes were that from 1940 to 1941 the Yellow River flood's main channel originally flowed east through Huaiyang and Taikang, and then, for military reasons, at Wangpan to the northwest of Taikang a gully was dug to divert the river to the west, flowing closer to the flood defense dike. On the opposite bank, the enemy constructed dike defenses, making the riverbed silt up, and the main channel shifted completely to the west. The dike that our side initially built was not sturdy, and wherever and whenever the Yellow River scoured it dangerous sections could appear. The immediate causes were that dike defenses were not solid. In the spring the water's position-power increased, but labor and materials for defending dangerous sections were not adequate. In addition, there was a strong northeast wind, waves pounded against the dike, and there was no way it could be saved. The dike first breached at Daolinggang in Xihua County. But because the water's position-power was small, only part of that area was flooded and there was no great obstruction to the water

---

[2] Xu Fuling (1991): 28–29; Xihua xian shizhi bianzuan weiyuanhui (1992): 117, 118; MHD: 168; MHS: 189.
[3] "Henan sheng zhengfu jiuzai zong baogao," 78–79; "Zhang Guangsi guanyu Henan sheng hanzai qingkuang ji jiuzai qingxing de diaocha baogao," 564–565; "Long-Hai tielu tebie dangbu nanmin fuwudui canjia sanmin zhuyi qingniantuan Shaanxi zhibu Yu zai fangwen gongzuo baogao" (June 1943): SPA 9-2-823; Xu Fuling (1991): 28; MHD: 168; MHS: 182, 189–190.

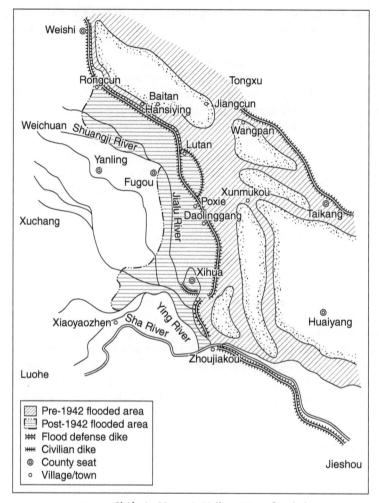

FIGURE 4.1 Shifts in Henan's Yellow River flooded area

flowing back into the old flooded area. Because of the terrain at the Rongcun breach, however, the waters overflowed southward, leading to a great disaster.[4]

Nationalist and Japanese attempts to consolidate their military positions and destabilize those of their enemies increased the river's usual tendency to wander. Wartime dislocations made labor and resources scarce, so there was no way to prevent the river from breaking dikes and flooding even more farmland. Despite this persistent drive to manipulate the river, military conflict caused a shortfall in the energy needed to keep it in check.

[4] "Henan sheng zhengfu jiuzai zong baogao," 78.

The Rongcun breach took place in Weishi, east of the Jialu River. With this area's low-lying terrain, waters spread southeast and southwest along the Jialu, inundating parts of Yanling, Fugou, and Xihua. The floods were tens of kilometers across at their widest point and a kilometer or so across at their narrowest, branching off from the Jialu River near the city of Zhoujiakou, where the deluge entered the Sha River. Waters surrounded Xihua on three sides. Only the southwestern part of Xihua, where terrain was relatively high, escaped flooding. In Fugou, floods flowed to the north and northeast of the county seat. Gates were sealed shut to keep waters from inundating the town.[5] But protection was insufficient. Seepage through dikes and earthworks erected to protect the walls left at least 15 percent of the county seat under water. As foreign investigators later described, "The south-eastern quarter of the city looks not unlike pictures we have seen of Venice .... Fishing is carried out within the city walls." People lived in houses that had not collapsed, but brackish water covered streets and yards to a depth of up to a meter. During the high-water season people moved to higher ground, but returned whenever waters receded.[6]

This most recent flood further disrupted hydraulic systems. Unless the breach at Rongcun was closed and dike structures repaired, the Jialu River would end up flowing entirely into the Sha River. If sediments carried by the floodwaters silted up the Sha's bed, its downstream tributaries would be blocked. The Shuangji, Hong, and Ying rivers would then overflow as well, inundating the autumn crops. For this reason, it was imperative for the Nationalists to close the Rongcun breach and strengthen dikes on the eastern edge of the Jialu River to make the Yellow River's floodwaters return to their previous path, which would prevent the Sha River and the Yellow River from rising together during high water season. These repairs would stop the Sha from overflowing and spare counties to the south of it from experiencing additional floods.[7]

Contending with the Yellow River and making repairs demanded huge energy surpluses in the form of human muscle power. Responsibility for providing that labor fell on counties already stricken by flood and famine. Henan's provincial government planned to "Order the flooded area and neighboring counties to mobilize civilian laborers and requisition materials to make a common effort (*heli*) and carry out emergency repairs to dangerous sections and reinforce the dike to prevent the disaster area from expanding."[8] At first, dike repairs were to enlist over 400,000 civilian laborers from areas

---

[5] "Henan sheng zhengfu jiuzai zong baogao," 78–79. See also "Shin Kōga karyū ibban kaikyo chōsa hōkokusho"; Cheng et al. (2007): 291–292.

[6] Harold Johnson to Lucile Chamberlin, "Survey and Report on Administrative District 9, South Honan" (June 1946): UN S1021 Box 58 File 7.

[7] "Henan sheng zhengfu jiuzai zong baogao," 78–79.

[8] "Henan sheng zhengfu bennian jiuzai jihua," 55.

up to 100 kilometers away from the dike. But since the more distant counties had difficulty sending laborers, Yanling and Weishi alone ended up having to bear most of the burden of making repairs.

Refugee flight made workers scarce, so mobilizing labor power demanded strict discipline. Dike repair work assumed a highly militarized character. Henan's provincial government chairman, Li Peiji, noted this trend when he observed that: "Each county's civilian laborers are all led by the assistant regimental commander of the county's citizen militia corps (*guomin bingtuan*) using militarized management (*junshi guanli*). Each small group is based on a military company and platoon structure. Organization is extremely tight and order is excellent. Based on what managerial personnel say, this is truly the first time it has ever been seen." Militarized interactions with the environment facilitated militarization of civilian populations. Yet Li was not entirely optimistic. Summer was fast approaching and, "with many civilian laborers gathered in severe heat there is deep concern that epidemics will occur."[9] Labor conscription started during the busiest agricultural season, before the wheat harvest finished and when autumn grain had to be planted. But farmers who delayed going to work on the dike repairs were forcibly detained. Work continued through the autumn harvest, diverting labor needed to bring in grain to feed famine victims.[10] "What is more," stated Li Peiji, "the cost of mobilizing civilian laborers from over twenty counties has been huge. At this time, disaster conditions are severe and the common people's power will truly have difficulty bearing the burden."[11] Most of the populace had migrated to other areas, so labor power was limited. Energy burdens increased for those who remained.

DIKE MAINTENANCE IN JAPANESE OCCUPIED AREAS

Authorities in Japanese-held areas to the east found it no easier to master the river and make it yield to their will. In late 1941, the recently appointed head of the collaborationist Henan provincial government's Reconstruction Department, Qu Chuanhe, set his sights on repairing the dikes on the river's eastern bank. Qu's friend Xing Youjie, the reporter and propaganda office head who mediated feuds caused by the Japanese-built dike's disruption of drainage systems in the previous year (see Chapter 1), assured him that Chinese Communist Party (CCP) guerilla forces would not interfere with repairs and personnel would be safe at the work site, which strengthened

---

[9] "Henan sheng zhengfu jiuzai zong baogao," 79.
[10] "Zhang Guangsi guanyu Henan sheng hanzai qingkuang ji jiuzai qingxing de diaocha baogao," 564–565.
[11] "Henan sheng zhengfu jiuzai zong baogao," 79. See also "Long-Hai tielu tebie dangbu nanmin fuwudui canjia sanmin zhuyi qingniantuan Shaanxi zhibu Yu zai fangwen gongzuo baogao."

Qu's confidence. The Reconstruction Department had sent 700,000 yuan in work funds and many construction materials were left over from earlier projects. Qu also orchestrated the transfer of Ji Luhuan, a Japanese-trained hydraulic engineer, from Manchukuo to Henan to oversee repairs and deputed Yu Benyi, a graduate of the Henan Water Control Technical School who had worked for nearly ten years in the Nationalist regime's Reconstruction Department, as Ji's assistant.[12]

In January 1942, the collaborationist provincial government sent technical personnel to survey dike defenses.[13] A February directive spelled out the project's rationale in terms of national prosperity and social welfare: "Constructing new Yellow River dike defenses is connected to the nation's veins and arteries (*guomai*), and linked to the people's livelihood. If there is not thorough defense, it will end up being a sorrow for the country (*bangjia zhi you*)." For these reasons, the provincial government started dike construction the previous year. However, the river's bed was rising and repairs had to go forward. Henan's collaborationist authorities deputed the necessary technical personnel, and they were rushing to the scene. Taikang was ordered to "conscientiously follow the technical personnel's leadership and rapidly depute civilian laborers to go to the work area and diligently work without delay."[14]

Technical personnel formed teams and surveyed dike sections to select appropriate paths for dike construction based on terrain and water flow conditions to, as Xing Youjie put it "confine the waters and prevent them from overflowing, utilizing old dikes that had not collapsed, and straightening meanders (*jiewan quzhi*)." Plans were made in winter and work got started in the spring, so that repairs could be made before the high waters came. With guidance and encouragement from the project's leaders, functionaries that county governments in Henan's occupied areas sent to assist "all exhausted their power." Plans for conducting surveys and selecting dike routes were completed on time, materials arrived, and grain for workers was transported to the site. By 1942 repairs were underway along the whole eastern dike.[15]

The work site spanned over 50 kilometers from Tongxu to southeast of Taikang. Tens of thousands of civilian laborers worked every day under the direction of technical personnel and overseers. Each worker received 1.5 kilograms of coarse grain per day as wages. The person in charge of each section gave this grain to large-group headmen, who oversaw fifty workers, and they passed it on to small-group headmen to distribute to civilian laborers. For the first few weeks, this arrangement functioned well and the project progressed quickly.[16]

---

[12] Xing (1986): 191.
[13] "Taikang xian xiuzhu xin Huanghe di gailue shuoming."
[14] Ibid.
[15] Xing (1986): 192.
[16] Ibid., 194.

After a month, however, problems and disputes arose. Some headmen used the pretext of needing funds to "entertain" project personnel as an excuse to decrease laborers' wages; others engaged in malfeasance by withholding grain whenever workers did not complete tasks on time. Some headmen claimed to have made payments to fictitious small-group headmen, which they pocketed. Others said they needed funds "to get in touch" with local guerilla forces and, with overseers' agreement, withheld wages for their personnel engrossment. Workers' daily grain allotment of 1.5 kilograms fell to 1.25 kilograms and some did not even receive 1 kilogram. Food energy did not reach those who needed it to do heavy labor. As a result, "Civilian laborers were hungry and of course did not do good work." Once the project's directors found out, they investigated and discovered that their subordinates were implicated in these schemes. After they punished a few of the headmen whose offenses were particularly serious and dismissed two other personnel, malpractices decreased.[17]

On the surface at least, dike repairs seemed to be going well. Henan's recently appointed collaborationist provincial governor organized an investigation commission to keep tabs on the quality of the dike and ensure its sturdiness.[18] Xing Youjie recalled that, "By expending the power of nine oxen and two tigers [i.e. working incredibly hard] the dike construction project was hurriedly completed half a month later than originally planned."[19] Taikang's county gazetteer, published under the Japanese occupation, boasted that, "After only five months' time a gigantic dike spanned majestically (*weiran henggen*), protecting the people." Taikang "shouldered most of the labor power," with the rest provided by Zhecheng and Luyi counties. With the new dike, people were able to "settle down a bit." The gazetteer's editors concluded by confidently asserting that, "'Human power excels heaven (*renli sheng tian*)' is indeed not an empty phrase."[20] They were mistaken.

As the collaborationist Henan provincial government was preparing a ceremony to commemorate the dike's completion, heavy rains fell, winds and waves came, and dikes in Taikang broke. Eastern Henan's circuit attendant (*daoyin*), Zhao Xiuchun, rushed to Kaifeng to ask for emergency relief. When he met with the collaborationist provincial governor, Zhao urged him to take money earmarked for the ceremony to Taikang and use it to relieve disaster victims. Zhao asked Qu Chuanhe what he intended to do about the situation, but Qu was at a loss. The project ended in failure.

By the end of 1942, Japan's fortunes in World War II had taken a turn for the worse, "and North China's Japanese leaders were unwilling to invest large amounts of labor power and material power in maintaining the new Yellow

---

[17] Ibid.
[18] Ibid., 193.
[19] Ibid.
[20] "Taikang xian xiuzhu xin Huanghe di gailue shuoming."

River dike." In 1943, the collaborationist Henan government's Hydraulic Engineering Office sent the water control specialist Yu Benyi to oversee dike construction matters and directed counties along the river to "do everything in their power (*jin li zhi suoneng*) to close breaches and prevent the disaster area from further expanding." But Yu cleverly used this reassignment to slip into Henan's unoccupied territories. After Yu absconded, except for occasionally ordering counties along the river to report on dike repairs and river defense, the collaborationist provincial government's Reconstruction Department devoted hardly any attention to dike maintenance.

As Xing recalled, "Officials in counties along the river that suffered disasters did not have the power to relieve disasters (*jiuzai wuli*), let alone repair the dike. Some villages simply built a few earthen embankments to prevent the Yellow River waters from entering their villages." At this time, the flooded area's widest place was 35–40 kilometers across and at its narrowest it was 20–25 kilometers. Villages on higher ground had dried up and disaster victims who were fortunate enough to survive returned and reclaimed abandoned land. The Yellow River's waters no longer overflowed, so defense work in Japanese-held territories came to a close. Despite all the money and resources initially invested, hydraulic engineering yielded meager results. Everyone familiar with the project saw it as having nothing more than "a tiger's head and a snake's tail" – it had started out strong but in the end it amounted to nothing.[21]

MILITARIZED RIVER DEFENSE AND ITS ECOLOGICAL COSTS

In late May 1943, the Nationalist Yellow River Conservancy Commission's director, Zhang Hanying, visited Xihua to inspect the county's dike defenses.[22] During his visit, Zhang held a meeting with Yellow River Conservancy Commission personnel, Xihua's Nationalist Party members, local government officials, and a group of local elites. The meeting's transcript vividly illustrates the level of war-induced ecological damage in the county. At the same time, the meeting's records capture the tensions that emerged between the Nationalist government and its local subordinates as they engaged in competition for increasingly scarce energy sources.[23]

In his opening statement, Zhang Hanying related that wind, waves, and siltation caused dikes to deteriorate, making their "defensive power weak." In light of the recent dike breaches, Zhang had invited local notables from Xihua to voice their ideas about flood control. The meeting also gave Zhang a chance to express his concerns about the difficulties that Xihua had experienced over

[21] Xing (1986): 193–194.
[22] MHD: 168; 170; MHS: 189–190.
[23] "Huanghe shuili weiyuanhui ji Xihua xian dang zheng jiguan shishen zuotanhui" (May 25, 1943): YRCC MG4.1-218.

the previous year. As he remarked, "This year counties along the river have contributed a great deal to repairs and defenses, especially in Xihua. As for requisitions of labor and materials, this Commission has made great efforts to make them fair and equitable, but it has unfortunately not been able to make gains." For this reason, Zhang invited everyone in attendance to discuss ways to eliminate malfeasance and ensure that funds actually benefited the people. During the preceding year, the price of goods had inflated tremendously. The amount paid by the government for labor and materials increased somewhat, but had not kept pace with soaring prices. The meeting, as Zhang stated, needed to come up with better payment methods.[24]

Xihua's representatives openly voiced their dissatisfaction about the demands imposed by Nationalist hydraulic management initiatives. Local authorities pointed to the strains river defense placed on the county's limited finances and dwindling resources. As the Xihua Nationalist Party branch secretary explained, "Xihua has suffered most deeply from the disaster and has also put forth the most labor power and financial power... Moreover, we have not complained at all because we know that river defense is national defense, so expending power for river defense is also being diligent in the War of Resistance. But over the past several years, power has been exhausted."[25]

Despite its military-strategic importance, the burden of river defense had grown too heavy. As explained by Nationalist People's Political Council member (*canyiyuan*), Gao Zhaolin, military considerations had fundamentally altered Xihua's drainage system. The wartime situation necessitated hydraulic maintenance that Xihua could not carry out alone. The Yellow River's western dike had become "the frontline of national defense." Nationalist-constructed dikes shifted the river's flow to the east. Mud and waters in between prevented the enemy from sneaking across. The Japanese augmented dikes on the eastern bank in opposition to those that the Nationalists constructed. Farmers who had not abandoned their land built civilian dikes as well, which impeded drainage and caused dangerously weak dike sections to appear. To strengthen river defenses, Gao proposed planting willow trees along the dikes to block the wind and waves. Because the circuitous layout of the western dike created many dangerous sections, it was necessary to import stone from Mi County (southwest of Zhengzhou) and construct additional embankments as reinforcement. And since counties along the river like Xihua shouldered the heaviest river defense responsibilities, Gao Zhaolin hoped that other areas would help make the situation more equitable.[26]

---

[24] Ibid. See also "Zhi Huanghe shuili weiyuanhui xiudu hefang zai shi yuangong ci" (November 1943): YRCC MG4.1-298.
[25] "Huanghe shuili weiyuanhui ji Xihua xian dang zheng jiguan shishen zuotanhui."
[26] Ibid.

Appeals from Xihua's representatives tried to turn the language of patriotic sacrifice during China's War of Resistance on its head. If local hydraulic maintenance carried national significance, then it was only right that the nation and other administrative jurisdictions should pay for it. External support was essential. Hu Minying, chairman of the Xihua county government's Financial Commission, reported that over the past several years Xihua had "expended especially large amounts of power and money" for river defense, but the county had not yet fulfilled its responsibilities to the nation. In his view, river defense problems consisted of those of a "national defense character" and those of a "local character." As Hu explained, "Those of a local character are discussed from the perspective of the people's livelihood. Those of a national defense character are truly of the first importance. Yet local power (*difang liliang*) is inadequate, so defense techniques cannot display their accomplishments. This aspect needs to be clearly understood by the common people and government alike."[27]

Xihua County could not accomplish the task of river defense alone, so Hu urged the central government and neighboring counties to help fund it. With no way of knowing when flood disasters would end, "Military and political power (*junzheng liliang*) should be concentrated so they can be utilized flexibly. Currently, Xihua already has this kind of organization. If Xihua can conserve part of its power to prepare for Yellow River floods, whenever there is an emergency there can be surplus power for emergency repairs." Flooding and famine combined to make river defense an increasingly heavy burden. Only outside assistance would give Xihua the capacity to make adequate preparations for unexpected disasters.[28] As things stood, scarcity of labor and resources hampered Xihua's ability to fulfill its hydraulic maintenance responsibilities. Shortages caused delays. As the Xihua county magistrate Zhang Weiya reported, "This year the project to fortify the dike at Daolinggang experienced delays because obtaining dirt was difficult and civilian laborers were scarce." High winds had caused emergencies. But military commanders still made Xihua and other counties in the flooded area conduct dike repairs and carry out river defense on their own.[29]

As explained by Zhu Guoheng, Henan's Seventh Special Area Administrative Supervisor, "Counties along the river have suffered too great a disaster. After the drought, labor was once again requisitioned for river works and the common people's power has been worn out." Problems occurred along the dike because it was too low and thin. Only by making the dike higher and thicker could they rectify these shortcomings. Xihua and other counties in the area did not want to shirk their responsibilities, said

---

[27] Ibid.
[28] Ibid.
[29] Ibid.

Zhu, "yet the projects are so enormous that they do not have power to undertake them."[30]

In light of this situation, Zhu Guoheng requested assistance from the Yellow River Conservancy Commission and Henan Province. Zhu maintained that Henan should send high-level personnel to direct dike repairs. The Seventh Area had "already exhausted its power bearing [the burden]," so Henan's provincial leadership needed to order other areas to assist. The Yellow River Conservancy Commission had to attend to technical matters. Only by doing their utmost to acquire central government funds and exploit local labor could the undertakings prove effective. Yet the center did not have much to give. Zhu recognized that the Nationalist government's economic difficulties meant it could not provide funds in large amounts. Half the laborers would have to be conscripted and the other half could receive wages.[31]

Despite these appeals, the Nationalist regime's water control agencies refused to yield to local concerns. Wang Heting, a technician from the Administrative Yuan's Water Conservancy Commission, acknowledged the losses that had been suffered during the five years since the Yellow River's diversion. New dikes constructed using central government funds had achieved the military goal of impeding the enemy, but he admitted that they had not done enough to protect local lives and property. Xihua endured the greatest disaster, "but had also put forth the most power."[32] In 1943 flood conditions had gotten even worse. Military personnel and civilians took positive steps and did their utmost, but failure came when they were on the verge of success. On May 18, heavy winds broke the dike at more than ten places within two hours. Damage was "unprecedented." Floods moved closer to the dikes along Jialu River. If the Jialu dike was not defended, floodwaters would enter the Sha River. According to Wang Heting, "The flooded area will then certainly shift and the influence on military affairs will be great." Upholding dike defenses had strategic importance, necessitating additional expenditures for their maintenance. River defense personnel, local military and political leaders, and the common people made great efforts to avert accidents.[33]

But, as Wang noted, they had not been able to prevent recent breaches, which resulted from a combination of factors. The new dike that had been constructed was low and thin, because "at the time, it was thought that it would be a temporary project and it was not expected that the mission would be this great." In the past, said Wang, the Yellow River's sediment was carried to the sea, but now all of it was deposited in the flooded area. Every year the river silted up by about half a meter, causing water levels to rise. And the river

[30] Ibid.
[31] Ibid.
[32] Ibid.
[33] Ibid.

did not have a set path. In 1940 the main channel shifted east. Then silt accumulated on the river's eastern side, and during the previous year it again shifted west. The new dikes faced directly northeast, so whenever a northeasterly wind blew, waves reached a height of more than one meter and the scouring action was severe. Famine had struck the locale, so "labor and materials are both scarce." Following the breaches that took place, there had not been the opportunity to put dike works in order. Wang explained that "in terms of military affairs" he hoped to stabilize the flooded area, "while at the same time attending to the people's livelihood to better protect agricultural land."[34] Before deciding on a plan to improve river defenses, however, several matters had to be considered.

First, Wang noted that at the present time "the common people's power is extremely limited." In the short run, they could only complete the most important river defenses. With the high-water season coming, the future held greater dangers. Essential dike defenses had to be completed in time to keep disaster from spreading. Moreover, realistic estimates of the "power (*liliang*) and time" required to close each of the openings between Lütan and Daolinggang had to be made. After repairing the dike, river defense needed to receive adequate attention to avert additional floods.[35]

Second, Wang Heting reminded everyone in attendance that the flooded area was continuously silting up. The crises of the coming year could surpass the present emergencies. Fundamental river control and defensive methods were the only solution. Reinforcements to the Jialu River dike for 1943 had been made provisionally to meet an urgent need and could not be used as a second line of defense. All other breaches had to be closed in the shortest time possible. The dike also had to be strengthened by making it higher and thicker. Wang recommended that areas along the dike should "plant willow trees all over, construct shore defenses, and drain water in each area to form alluvial land to resist the danger from wind and waves."[36]

Third, civilian dikes that harmed the government's new flood defense dike had to be removed. Civilian dikes that were beneficial for the larger dike needed to be restored as shelter and reinforcement. At suitable points upriver, embankments were to be constructed to divert waters east and reduce pressure on the new flood defense dike.

Fourth, Weishi still confronted the greatest flood crisis. That county's terrain consisted of "high areas facing low areas," so if an accident took place the losses would be unimaginable. For this reason, Weishi merited special attention. As Wang emphasized, they needed to "formulate a comprehensive plan and cannot simply pay attention to defense at single points. It

---

[34] Ibid.
[35] Ibid.
[36] Ibid.

is necessary to pay attention to comprehensive arrangements and strictly allocate time and power to achieve the goal of defense."[37]

Wang Heting noted that the Yellow River Conservancy Commission already increased prices paid for materials, but it was imperative to ensure people actually received the funds. To this end, localities had to find better ways of distributing them. On behalf of the Water Conservancy Commission, Wang explained that, "In the future, there must be a self-sufficient plan (*zili gengsheng zhi jihua*) for river-works materials and only then will they be prepared to avert peril. Willows are to be planted in places along the dike to prepare for urgent needs. As for work funds, the central government should exhaust its power in raising and distributing funds to decrease the burden on the localities." The localities had to understand the central government's difficulties and "make a concerted effort to cooperate in order to make it through the present difficulty."[38] Given the Nationalist regime's fiscal predicaments, of course, counties in the flooded area would assume most of the burden.

The widening disparity between central expectations and diminished local capacities gave rise to disagreement and tension. Though Xihua's county magistrate Zhang Weiya agreed with the ideas Wang Heting put forward, he stated that in Xihua and nearby counties material resources had already been completely exhausted. In the future, materials would have to come from areas at least 50 kilometers north of the Sha River. Huang Yanli, head of Xihua's Reconstruction Department, likewise stressed the difficulty of filling in and transporting earth, observing that "requisitioned civilian laborers are tired out," and recommended that in the future they should receive payment for their work. Perhaps trying to soften his critique, Huang conceded that Yellow River water control was "part of the great enterprise of reconstruction during the War of Resistance." The common people had to come to understand this fact "in order to pursue psychological reconstruction."[39]

In his concluding remarks, Zhang Hanying explained that in 1943 the central government sent ten million yuan for Yellow River water control, with five million yuan going to Tang Enbo's army and five million yuan going to the Yellow River Conservancy Commission's Henan Repair and Defense Office. In the future, it would still be necessary to "exhaust their power" by requesting funds from the central government and preventing malfeasance. It was also important to promptly plant willow trees and re-divert the river's channel.[40]

At the end of the meeting, Chen Ruzhen, head of the Yellow River Conservancy Commission's River Defense Office and director of the Henan Repair and Defense Office, tried to spell out ways to maintain vital environmental infrastructure, which had fallen into disarray, with dwindling local

[37] Ibid.
[38] Ibid.
[39] Ibid.
[40] Ibid.

resources. His comments point to the futility of the undertaking. Chen's inspections revealed that the dike section south of Lütan was in extreme danger. Prior to the war, materials for river defense works were prepared in advance. "This year, although there was such a plan, due to last year's floods emergency repairs had to be made as needed and could not wait. The reason for the floods was that sediment accumulation was too great and the main channel moved west." In the old flood area, which was now dry land, many common people had already returned and started planting crops. But the new dike was not solidly constructed and once it broke it could not be repaired. "Also, last year there was famine and the common people fled, so there is little labor power." The winds that struck earlier in the month moved 160,000 cubic meters of soil in a mere two hours, "How could human labor power have resisted it?" In Weishi as well, dike repair projects had not been completed because "labor power and financial power are limited." To make hydraulic management effective, local personages had to assist without regard for territorial divisions and "exhaust their power in defenses."[41]

All the statements made at this meeting pointed to one conclusion. Warfare made the labor and resources – the energy – needed to maintain the human-engineered landscape that was Henan's hydraulic infrastructure grossly inadequate. Combined with environmental factors like inclement weather and the river's tendency to silt up, floods were all but unavoidable. Newspaper reports claimed that hydraulic maintenance costs in Henan outweighed all other wartime taxes and levies, which were of course considerable. For dike repairs in counties along the Yellow River, "The workers employed every year, compared to military conscripts, are at least more than ten times greater. The food and fuel that the common people provide, when compared to the taxes and levies they pay, is several times greater."[42] One Fugou resident stated that even in flooded areas the common people had to perform miscellaneous labor duties. In 1942, when he was fourteen years old (fifteen *sui* by Chinese reckoning), he was sent to assist with dike construction. Under famine conditions, he recalled, the workers "did not have the power to carry soil, and the overseers even used willow switches to beat us."[43]

War-related dislocations rendered the energy inputs needed to maintain environmental infrastructure impossible, leading to severe ecological damage. Efforts to channel and redirect the Yellow River grew less effective and production of food energy through agriculture declined. Refugees fled war, famine, and flood, leaving localities in Henan with little labor power. As a result of these transformations, local societies lacked energy to devote to hydraulic maintenance. But the persistent energy demands for wartime hydraulic engineering would not wane.

[41] Ibid.
[42] Cited in Li et al. (1994): 262.
[43] Wu (2004): 173.

The Nationalist government had no way to subsidize the costs of river defense and wartime conditions made it too difficult to import materials, so demands on counties nearest to the river grew. It comes as no surprise that one of the main reasons people took flight was to escape hydraulic maintenance duties. Xihua and other counties in Henan's flooded area could not acquire labor and resources needed to repair damage and sustain the hydraulic system. There was simply insufficient energy available. Yet, no matter how onerous the task, these localities were still expected to carry out intensive ecological maintenance.

THE LOCAL COSTS OF RIVER DEFENSE

In early June 1943, Tang Enbo convened another meeting on hydraulic repairs in Zhoujiakou. The attendees resolved to allocate another 4.5 million yuan in military work funds to seal breaches in dike sections that had not been closed, repair the Jialu and Shuangji river dikes, and reinforce the Sha River's northern dike from Zhoujiakou west to Xiaoyaozhen. The most important task was to fortify the dike along the southern bank of the Sha River to the east of Zhoujiakou and prevent the Yellow River from flowing into the Sha. In July, with the second round of work mostly done, Tang held yet another conference, at which Henan's provincial government, the Yellow River Conservancy Commission, and armies stationed in the Henan–Anhui border region formed a Yellow River flood repair commission, electing Henan provincial government chairman, Li Peiji, as director. In a joint report to the Nationalist government's Military Affairs Commission and Administrative Yuan, army commanders Tang Enbo and He Zhuguo and hydraulic engineer Zhang Hanying requested an additional 30 million yuan to use to close breaches, repair dikes, and fortify defenses against high waters.

Large-scale dike repairs began in February 1943 and finished that October. In eight months, the project consumed 9.5 million yuan in military work funds and spent 30 million yuan to mobilize civilian laborers from 28 counties in Henan, along with 400,000 troops from the Nationalist army's 193rd Command and local military units. The project employed hundreds of thousands of workers, who completed over 9 million cubic meters of earthworks. They reinforced the Yellow River's flood defense dike, repaired dikes on the Sha, Ying, and Jialu rivers, and finally closed the Rongcun breach. Several military diversion dikes, earthen embankments, and shore defenses were also constructed. These structures eliminated the threat of the Yellow River's main channel shifting south and moving west, thereby altering the Nationalist lines of defense in Henan and Anhui.[44]

---

[44] Xu Fuling (1991): 29–30; MHD: 168–171; MHS: 190; Cheng et al. (2007): 291–292.

As before, the cost of hydraulic maintenance fell primarily upon counties in Henan's flooded area. In November 1943, representatives from Weishi, Yanling, Fugou, and Xihua petitioned the central government asking that funds for Yellow River dike repair come from the national treasury instead of from localities, so as to relieve disaster victims and to strengthen national defense. The petition vividly describes the deepening wartime ecological crisis in these counties. At the same time, the document offers information about the sheer quantity of materials extracted in the name of hydraulic maintenance. The petition's language cast this burden in terms of the strain placed upon the various forms of "power" available in local society. As its authors explained,

Last year and this year drought, heavy rain, Yellow River floods, and locust disasters have come in succession. Labor power, material power, financial power, and livestock power have all been exhausted in river affairs. Families have broken apart, people have perished, and the number of households has markedly decreased. For several years there has been famine. Villages are abandoned and fields lay waste. There are hardships upon hardships. Weishi, Yanling, Fugou, and Xihua counties have suffered directly from these disasters.[45]

With the autumn low-water season at hand, "everyone in the nation" viewed repairing dike breaches as a matter of great importance. However, Weishi, Yanling, Fugou, and Xihua all experienced catastrophes that made it hard for them to repair river works.[46]

Weishi had endured disasters for several years and 1943 was especially severe. Before the spring harvest nearly 10,700 famine victims in the county ate peanut shells, wheat chaff, wood, and picked through goose droppings to find undigested grain and seeds. The Rongcun breach flooded 5,760 hectares of land, destroyed 14,960 houses, and displaced over 7,600 people in the county. Breach closures enlisted 200,000 civilian laborers and requisitioned 2.75 million kilograms of willow branches, 6,000 wooden posts, and 160,000 bricks. Transporting materials occupied all carts and draft animals, and left people with no time to attend to agriculture. In Weishi's Dazhu township alone, more than 730 hectares of land lay waste. Embankment construction initiated in May requisitioned another 250,000 bricks and 2,000 wooden posts. In addition, 1.5 million kilograms of willow branches that were supposed to be collected from Zheng County, Xinzheng, and Mi County had to be purchased in Weishi, "so the willow branches originally needed for firewood have all been exhausted." In August, dikes on the north bank of the Shuangji River broke in Weichuan County and inundated 50 villages in Weishi's Shuitai and Dazhu townships, flooding 4,000 hectares of land and destroying over half the autumn crops. Standing water

---

[45] "Henan sheng Xihua xian zhengfu cheng" (November 11, 1943): YRCC MG4.1–340.
[46] Ibid.

rendered 200 hectares in Shuitai township uncultivable and displaced 10,000 more disaster victims. In June and August, locusts plagued the county, decreasing autumn harvests to less than 5 percent of normal. The common people had no way to pay grain taxes or make compulsory sales, so many families fled.[47]

Yanling experienced a poor wheat harvest in 1941 and the following year's crops failed. After the county's residents had paid grain levies, their storehouses were empty. First people sold their goods, then they abandoned their property. Men sold wives and children. People abandoned the elderly, left children orphaned, and drifted from place to place. After several days without anything to eat, people turned to ingesting tree bark, wheat sprouts, grass, and seeds picked out of goose droppings to satiate their hunger. After several months without grain to eat, the wealthy turned poor and the poor died; then the wealthy died as well. Following the 1943 wheat harvest, Yanling's population fell from over 287,350 to only about 113,030. During the famine, residents ate or sold 34,860 draft animals and tore down over 59,930 wooden houses to obtain fuel. Famine-related deaths caused 38 villages and 2,363 households to disappear completely.[48]

Famine was followed by floods. As the 1943 wheat harvest ripened, the breach at Rongcun inundated 56 *bao* in Yanling. Floodwaters drowned more than 2,900 people and nearly 140 draft animals, and destroyed nearly 15,290 houses. Repairing the breach following the wheat harvest cost the county 103,542,500 yuan. Repair work enlisted 1,400 civilian laborers, each of whom received 20 yuan per day, for a total of 84,000 yuan. Feeding the workers required 4.5 million kilograms of wheat, costing 90 million yuan. The closure used 4,250 wooden posts costing 212,500 yuan, 2.9 million kilograms of willow branches costing 580,000 yuan, 150,000 kilograms of sorghum stalks costing 210,000 yuan, and 10,300 carts costing 4,120,000 yuan. Management expenses came to 100,000 yuan. As if that were not enough, locusts soon descended and ate the autumn crops. The situation in Yanling showed little sign of improving:

> The people were busy with river works and in autumn many fields were left to waste. Although abundant rains have fallen, since labor power, material power, and financial power are all inadequate, the wheat crop could not be planted in its entirety. The Yellow River floodwaters are also in the county and soldiers advancing east of the flooded area come and go. When they pass through the county, the army recruiting offices require fuel and fodder worth at least 20,000 to 30,000 yuan per month.[49]

---

[47] Ibid.
[48] According to the petition, out of Yanling's original population of 287,357 people, 100,277 reportedly died and 68,849 fled. Only 802 returned, leaving a population of 113,033. Ibid.
[49] Ibid.

Warfare and hydraulic maintenance devoured energy desperately needed for agricultural recovery and the disaster grew more severe. All in all, Yanling experienced less severe flooding than Weishi, Fugou, and Xihua. But the 1942 famine was worse in Yanling than the other counties.[50]

The 1938 flood inundated practically all of Fugou. With the closing of the Hansiying breach and the construction of the new dike, waters subsided and two-thirds of the fields emerged. However, the receding of floodwaters did not bring agricultural recovery. "If there are not mudflats there are mounds [of sediment], and everything is buried under a sheet of sand. If there is not flooding there is drought and disasters are common. At the same time, since [Fugou] is on the frontline of river defense and national defense, annual repairs are a huge undertaking." Annual exactions of labor and materials amounted to 50,000,000 yuan, while supplying river defense troops cost 70,000,000 yuan. "The exhaustion of labor power, material power, financial power, and draft animal power has already led to extreme impoverishment."[51]

Due to severe drought in autumn 1942 and spring 1943, the able-bodied fled and the old and weak wallowed in gullies, subsisting on famine foods. Residents counted on the wheat crop to survive. But on May 18, 1943 heavy winds and rains came and the Yellow River rose violently, causing dikes to break at Poxie and Rongcun. The river's main course flowed from Yanling into Fugou, flooding over 90 percent of the latter county. The entire wheat crop was washed away and houses were left in ruins. Disaster victims lived outdoors on dikes or ridges with no clothing and nothing to eat. Higher lands escaped floods, but experienced drought followed by locust infestation.[52]

On August 2, heavy winds and rain caused the river to rise even more dramatically. Water from the Poxie and Rongcun breaches converged in Baitan and several other townships in Fugou. Civilian dikes built along levees and ridges broke, flooding over 10,000 hectares. On September 24, waters rose again and the river's position-power was even greater than before. Ridges south of the county seat broke and higher land to the southwest was flooded as well. Of Fugou's population of 100,000, over 80,000 were affected by the disaster. More than 30,000 residents fled, while over 50,000 old, weak, disabled, and sick disaster victims flocked to towns seeking relief.[53]

In Xihua the 1938 flood inundated about half the farmland and 180,000 residents fled. When the new dike was completed, the flooded area contracted. Yet whenever the level of the Yellow River rose, as it frequently did, the new dike broke and the flooded area expanded. The amount of labor and materials needed to shore up embankments increased until the costs were incalculable. Worse yet, drought struck Xihua in fall 1942 and

[50] Ibid.
[51] Ibid.
[52] Ibid.
[53] Ibid.

spring 1943, leading to famine. Violent wind and rain came in April when the wheat was nearly ready to harvest, causing the river to rise. Dikes broke at Poxie and Rongcun. Floods passed from Yanling through Fugou and converged in Xihua, washing away the wheat crop. Locusts struck in August, followed by severe winds and rain. The Yellow River's floodwaters caused the Sha, Ying, and Jialu rivers to overflow at several dozen points along their western banks. Flooding inundated all of Xihua and the water's position-power was several times higher than in the past. An area of 58,660 hectares was affected, almost 39,400 buildings were destroyed, and the financial losses amounted to 535,879,600 yuan. More than 137,890 people in Xihua were victims of the disasters and nearly 68,720 were in need of relief.[54]

As the petitioners reminded the central government, the Yellow River had caused catastrophes for China and proven difficult to control throughout history. In the past, they claimed, China's rulers went to great lengths to generate funds to meet the cost of hydraulic engineering projects. But this time labor and materials needed to close the Rongcun breach were requisitioned from counties along the river. The demands were not only too much for disaster-stricken localities to bear, but were even more than Henan as a whole could bear. "The Yellow River is currently extremely important to national defense. In Weishi, Yanling, Fugou, and Xihua counties labor power, material power, financial power, and draft animal power have already been contributed in the past. Now the disaster is severe, people are scarce, and there is no chance to rest." To equalize the burden and make it easier to complete this project, petitioners asked that labor and materials for closing the breach be taken from nearby counties where the disaster was lighter and requested that the central government pay the costs.[55]

Once river defense work started that summer, requisitions were made one after another. The common people spent all their time working on the dike and gave up their occupations, suffering exhaustion and incurring incalculable losses. Although the central government intended to pay for requisitions of labor and materials, a tiny fraction of the funds it distributed actually benefited the common people. The petitioners asked that the central government prepare special funds and depute honest, capable officials to the worksite to make payments. They also called for inspections to root out malfeasance by unscrupulous personnel. Since the expenditures were necessary for national defense, they could be combined with grain taxes and compulsory purchases, and collected together with them rather than as provisional levies. Petitioners concluded by recommending that, "This matter relates to the entire nation. Use the entire nation's power to respond to it so that it will be easy to undertake."[56]

[54] Ibid.
[55] Ibid.
[56] Ibid.

Before any of the requests were acted upon, however, the Japanese army's Ichigō Offensive of spring 1944 routed Nationalist forces and cleared them out of counties in the flooded area, as well as other parts of Henan, bringing river defense to a sudden halt. The Nationalist regime's hydraulic engineers could not resume work along the Yellow River until after World War II's end. As with the extraction of grain to feed the army, channeling energy into futile efforts to harness the river for military ends destabilized the Nationalist position and added to popular disaffection. For counties in the flooded area like Weishi, Yanling, Fugou, and Xihua, these massive energy demands intensified the state of ecological crisis. Given river defense's militarized character, wartime hydraulic engineering represented another form of "military macroparasitism" that undermined Nationalist power and legitimacy by damaging the society it depended on to survive.

By the end of World War II, Henan's hydraulic infrastructure was badly in need of comprehensive repair. In its eight years of meandering through the countryside, the Yellow River flooded the channels of dozens of smaller rivers and broke levees that, under normal conditions of stress, might have proven fairly adequate.[57] Hydraulic infrastructure needed to be rebuilt and strengthened. Dikes along the Jialu, Shuangji, Ying, and the Sha rivers between Zhongmu and Zhoujiakou deteriorated across the Yellow River's flood plain. From the western edge of the flooded area to their mouths, the rivers needed reinforced dikes to confine them until they could develop new channels. The Jialu had no outlet because of the Yellow River dike and flooded a large area to its west, leaving much of the land between Zhongmu and Fugou under water. The Shuangji River wandered north of Yanling into Fugou, where it obliterated all dikes and channels. South of Fugou, the Yellow River's floodwaters followed the old channel of the Shuangji River. The Ying River wandered over a large area northwest of Zhoujiakou and required dike work to prevent it from continuing to flood. Dikes had managed to control the Sha River, on the other hand, which no longer flooded above Zhoujiakou. Because dikes had recently been built below Zhoujiakou, the Sha did not flood in that area either. But streams that originated east of the Yellow River's new course did not have outlets and wandered over the area.[58] The work of humans, even on a large scale, had not overcome the Yellow River. Human-constructed hydraulic systems – even highly militarized ones – proved no match for nature's energy.

---

[57] Burlin B. Hamer, "A Study of the Yellow River Flooded Area in Honan Province by Regional Office C.N.R.R.A. and Regional Office, U.N.R.R.A." (December 1946): UN S-1021 Box 58 File 6.

[58] "Recording Some Observations and Recommendations Made During a Trip to Chengchow, Hsu-chang, Yen-ling, Fu-kou, Weishih, Hsi-hua, Chou-chia-k'ou, Lo-ho and Vicinities, 24 February to 3 March" (March 11, 1947): 3, UN S-0528–0544 A.R.-17a.

CONCLUSION

During the Sino-Japanese War of 1937–1945, the Yellow River possessed a distinctive agency, acting unpredictably even as it was being acted upon. Humans constantly intervened to shape and reshape the river with their labor, but they never bent the river to their will. Despite Nationalist hydraulic engineering projects aimed at manipulating the river's energy in defense of the nation, and the Japanese and their collaborators' construction of dikes in pursuit of their own strategic goals, the river surged and shifted without regard for human intentions. Controlling the Yellow River's waters was impossible without capacity to command the energy of people and nature. Nationalist military leaders and hydraulic engineers, like the Japanese and collaborationist authorities, devoted constant attention to extracting and coordinating labor and materials needed to harness the river for strategic purposes.

Militarized water control had to mobilize and consume huge quantities of energy, but in the end it proved unsuccessful and even politically counter-productive due to popular resentment of corvée labor and resource extraction. Labor scarcity, financial shortages, and resource exhaustion, as well as sedimentation and the river's proclivity to wander, translated into ecological instability. For the Nationalists, the war against Japan dragged on; the war with the river was clearly being lost. When they created the Yellow River flood in 1938 and constructed hydraulic works to impede the Japanese, Nationalist military leaders tried to enlist the river as a natural ally. Ironically, their actions also unleashed a natural enemy. As they fought the Japanese in the early 1940s, the Nationalists engaged in an extremely costly struggle against the river.

This conflict impacted all levels of society. For disaster-ravaged localities in Henan that were charged with providing the energy to fuel this conflict, the demands of wartime hydraulic maintenance led to deepening ecological disruption and ruled out the possibility of agricultural recovery. The power of local societies – their capacity to do work – was exhausted.

5

The Ecology of Displacement: Social and Environmental Effects of Refugee Migration

As the previous two chapters have shown, China's military resistance against Japan had by 1942–1943 pushed much of Henan to the brink of ecological collapse. When combined with climatic fluctuations linked to an El Niño event, battle destruction and the military's insatiable appetite for energy led to famine. The Chinese Nationalist regime's efforts to mobilize human labor to manipulate the Yellow River for military purposes required extracting even more energy from Henan's war-ravaged environment. But wartime depletion of resources and population loss that resulted from refugee flight made effective hydraulic maintenance impossible. This chapter returns to the question of how human residents of Henan's flooded area coped with war-induced environmental destruction and obtained the energy to sustain their own metabolisms.

The array of survival strategies that refugees relied on to endure wartime catastrophes altered the social and environmental landscape. Displacement caused by war-induced disasters destabilized and often destroyed kinship units, as family members perished or were forced to move to different places. Henan's rural populace endured loss, separation, and death or disappearance of kin. In response to these traumas, women as well as men were in constant motion. Wartime dislocations resulted in conspicuous absence of able-bodied males, large numbers of whom joined the army or sought work away from their home villages. Many other men disappeared or died. In areas of Henan struck by wartime catastrophes, in a departure from gender ratios typical of twentieth-century rural China, women came to outnumber men.

This instability changed what was expected of female household members. With male family members gone, many women and girls became sole supporters of households. Females relied on their own labor to survive, while also caring for children and elderly family members. As a result, woman took on a greater role in agricultural work or ventured out to find other ways of making a living. In China – as elsewhere – fuel gathering was typically the work of women and children. In comparison with other parts of the world, extreme shortage of wood and other types of fuel in North China made the refugee experience especially arduous. Far from providing opportunities for liberation, war-induced social dislocations shouldered rural women with greater burdens. The evidence from Henan confirms Gail Hershatter's assertion that "women often were not confined to domestic space during the 1930s and 1940s. They were out and about in a chaotic landscape in which physical mobility signified not emancipation but rather, hardship, danger, exposure, and shame."[1]

There were ecological consequences as well. When the Henan famine of 1942–1943 sent another wave of refugees into Shaanxi province, in-migration coincided with deforestation and intensified soil erosion. Rather than spontaneous migration, however, the most far-reaching environmental changes occurred in areas of Shaanxi where China's wartime state resettled refugees to reclaim "wasteland" and support wartime economic mobilization. Because wartime land clearance targeted marginal and highly erodible lands, this drive to harness the environment to wage warfare led to significant loss of vegetation cover and land degradation. In addition to altering landscapes, cultivation of marginal land jeopardized the health of the most vulnerable refugee groups, especially women and young children of low socio-economic status. These outcomes shed light on the complex relationships between refugee migration and environmental change.

THE SECOND WAVE: FAMINE REFUGEES

As armies extracted ever greater amounts of resources from the flooded area's devastated environment, these became scarce or unavailable for civilians who still resided there. Local governments in Nationalist-held territories in Fugou sent personnel to the flooded area in boats to collect grain and money from inhabited villages. Nationalist guerilla units in Fugou, which enlisted a motley array of bandits in their ranks, lived off the land and acquired food, fodder, and supplies from local villages. After taking what they wanted from a particular locale, guerilla forces moved on to some other area. Once the mutual-security unit headman and local gentry saw them off, other guerillas arrived soon thereafter. For obvious reasons, the local populace referred to these guerillas as "locust armies" (*mazha dui*) that swarmed through villages and ate up all they could. To rural residents, soldiers – like flood and drought – represented yet another type of disaster.

With food supplies scarce, many more local residents migrated to find ways to stay alive. The drought and locust swarms that struck in 1941–1942, together with grain taxes and other levies, pushed the people who had

---

[1] Accounts of these traumas also appear with great frequency in the oral history interviews that Hershatter (2011) conducted with rural women who lived in Shaanxi province during the 1930s and 1940s, many of whom had migrated from Henan.

previously been unwilling to flee to abandon their homes. Fugou's county seat, in particular, became a gathering point for famine refugees. At first, the refugees crowded into temples. As more displaced people poured into the county seat, they had to reside in caves dug around the city wall as shelters against Japanese bombing or on the streets. As the county seat's population expanded, grain grew scarce and prices soared. Some families migrated west in search of food, but the poorest could not afford to make the journey. Refugees lined up at soup kitchens set up by the local government. But with the sheer number of people who needed relief, these initiatives could not forestall famine.[2] Disaster victims sold off their property. Other households sold wives and daughters, many of whom ended up having to become prostitutes in Luohe, Luoyang, or Xi'an.[3]

The famine of 1942–1943 added to the devastation caused by wartime disruption of Henan's hydraulic infrastructure. Famine took an especially heavy toll in the counties affected by Yellow River floods. Yanling, according to a Nationalist investigation, originally had a population of 260,000. During the famine, about 56,580 people died and 65,850 fled. Fugou had a population of 340,000 prior to the war. After the 1938 Yellow River flood, which inundated over 90 percent of the county, 170,000 residents remained. During the famine of 1942–1943, Fugou's population fell to only 120,000.[4] By 1945, the number of people in Fugou dwindled even further. Residents who stayed behind made their living scavenging for organic material to sell as fuel. Others worked as porters; some wandered the street aimlessly.[5] Some 250,000 people from Xihua migrated elsewhere due to flood and famine, finding work as hired laborers, porters, and peddlers.[6]

As many localities experienced a dearth of food, supporting refugees became more burdensome than usual. During 1942 and 1943, flood victims exacerbated food shortages in the areas of Henan where they had taken refuge by placing added strain on dwindling grain supplies. After 1938, large numbers of flood refugees moved to Lushan, where they lived in temples, schools, and other public buildings. In keeping with higher-level directives, local government functionaries in Lushan requisitioned grain and clothing to distribute to refugees. After the crops failed, however, Lushan and other counties had difficulty feeding the recently settled refugee population.[7]

---

[2] Fugou xianzhi zong bianji shi (1986): 91–95, 99; Guan (1991): 112–114. See also Bo (1989): 120.
[3] "Long-Hai tielu tebie dangbu nanmin fuwudui canjia sanmin zhuyi qingniantuan Shaanxi zhibu Yu zai fangwen gongzuo baogao."
[4] Ibid. Famine deaths may have been even higher. Another Nationalist investigation from September 1943 reported 108,498 deaths in Yanling and 44,210 in Fugou. "Ge xian zaiqu siwang shumu zhi diaocha tongji," 565–566.
[5] SJZHFZ 12 (April 1, 1946): 4.
[6] Xihua xian shizhi bianzuan weiyuanhui (1992): 118.
[7] Ma (1993): 100; Zhang (1994): 133–134.

Disease is likely to have claimed as many lives as starvation. Nationalist investigators found that by spring 1943 epidemic disease was widespread in Henan's famine-stricken regions. As an investigation conducted by the Long-Hai railroad's Nationalist party branch observed, "The number of dead [due to disease] is equivalent to those who starved to death before the wheat harvest. In Xuchang, Yanling, and Fugou infectious diseases like 'relapsing fever' (*huiguire*) and 'cholera' (*huoluan*) have been discovered. The sick can die after only a few hours." Henan lacked disease prevention and medical care facilities, so people had few ways to cope with such maladies.[8] A local newspaper reported that in Yanling, "because of the disaster the masses' nutrition is inadequate and large numbers have died of starvation and disease. There are many corpses left unburied or buried in shallow graves, so diseases like typhoid, relapsing fever, and other illnesses are common in cities and villages. The speed of infection and severity of harm are truly unbelievable. It is hoped that personages of all sorts will come together to wipe out pestilence and ensure the masses' health and happiness."[9] Contrary to what this report implied, dead bodies most likely had little to do with the spread of epidemics, but the famine certainly did.[10] Malnourishment lowered resistance to diseases of all kinds. The gathering of dense populations in places with poor sanitation eased transmission. Weakened by months of hunger, people in Henan's famine area succumbed to epidemics of cholera and dysentery.[11]

The experience of a woman from Weishi County, née Wang (*Wang shi*), exemplifies the tribulations that forced famine refugees to take flight. Prior to 1938, she lived with her husband Li Hezhi, his mother, and their three daughters in Weishi's Zhangtie village. The Yellow River's floodwaters had washed away their grass house and inundated their land. They sought refuge with her husband's family in nearby Guacun, but after living there for a few days her mother-in-law passed away. The arrival of displaced family members strained their relatives' limited food reserves. As the woman explained, "Our relatives had all of a sudden added several people to their household and the little grain that they had stored was not enough for everyone to eat, so life got harder and harder." Things got even more difficult when members of her natal family came to seek refuge in Guacun as well. The woman's father urged her husband to flee to Shaanxi, where grain was cheaper and it would be easier for them to make a living. But her husband Hezhi hesitated. It would be hard to live without relatives, they might encounter bandits, and returning home would be difficult if they went so far away. His wife reminded him that "The grain in our relatives' household will soon be eaten up, and I can't be a burden

---

[8] "Long-Hai tielu tebie dangbu nanmin fuwudui canjia sanmin zhuyi qingniantuan Shaanxi zhibu Yu zai fangwen gongzuo baogao."
[9] "Jiuzai yu fangyi" (1943): 2.
[10] Watson et al. (2007).
[11] *The Times* (April 1, 1943): 4.

on them. Living here is not a long-term plan." Hezhi thought it over and realized they had no way to survive, so he got a cart and set out with the family and its few possessions to Shaanxi.[12] His wife's bound feet did not stop her from making the trek: "I had bound feet, and normally at home it was fine, but when going far away it was trouble. I swayed back and forth behind the cart and after a day my ankles were swollen and the soles of my feet were rubbed raw. But I gritted my teeth and moved forward step by step." Their relatives gave the family a little grain when they departed, but they had consumed it all by the time they got past Zhengzhou. She and Hezhi begged for food, but it was not easy. Many people in the area they traveled through did not have grain either. "Some people took small persimmons that fell on the ground, mixed them with tree bark, and ground them into flour to eat. Some people started eating white soil. Being able to beg for a chaff cake (*kangpi bingzi*) was like eating a rare delicacy. They did not have enough food for themselves. Who could pay attention to beggars?!"[13]

One day their eldest daughter Xiulan, age nine, dug up some carrots from a field. The field's owner caught the girl and insisted that her father, Hezhi, go to the *lianbao* office, where he was beaten so severely that he could not walk.[14] Following this incident, the family went to live in a dilapidated Earth God Temple (*tudi miao*). Due to Hezhi's injuries, they could no longer walk or beg. After much deliberation, the woman and her husband decided they had no alternative but to give Xiulan to another family as a child daughter-in-law to obtain food. The girl did not want to leave her family, but her parents reassured her that if she joined the other household she would no longer go hungry. Once they got to Shaanxi and had a better life, the parents promised, they would come back for her.[15] Leaning on his cane, Hezhi went with his wife and Xiulan to find out whether anyone wanted a child bride. A wealthy household agreed to take the girl in exchange for two bags of grain chaff and a bit of cash. A few days later, Hezhi's injuries got a little better and they took to the road. He could walk only with great difficulty, so his wife – with her bound feet – pushed their cart. They walked for a while and rested for a while, covering only about 10–15 kilometers per day.

Disasters, displacement, and the hard work she had to undertake due to her husband's injury did not leave this woman with adequate energy for childrearing. "At that time, my third girl was nursing. I ate chaff and swallowed vegetables, having one meal and skipping one meal, and during the day I also pushed the cart. After a few days, I was dizzy all the time and looked thin." Fearing that in his wife's physical condition she would not make it to Shaanxi, Hezhi decided to abandon their infant daughter to protect her

---

[12] Mei (1992): 330; Mei (2009): 260.
[13] Mei (1992): 331; Mei (2009): 260–261.
[14] Mei (1992): 332; Mei (2009): 261.
[15] Mei (1992): 332–333; Mei (2009): 261–262.

mother. The couple left the infant at a crossroads in a market town, and soon they saw a woman in her forties come and take her away.[16]

Later, Hezhi and his wife heard people saying that even after refugees went to Shaanxi their lives were still hard and many starved to death, so they gave up the idea of going there. With their remaining daughter, the couple did menial labor and begged for half a year. Before the wheat ripened the following year, the family decided to go back to Weishi. But the wife's health deteriorated. As she recalled, "my head ached, I had a fever, my stomach was swollen, and I did not even have the power (*liqi*) to walk." Hezhi borrowed a donkey, letting his wife and daughter ride ahead. Hezhi stayed behind and pushed the cart. In a rainstorm, the woman and her daughter rode to Weishi's county seat, where they found shelter with one of her relatives.[17]

That night her illness got worse and she was delirious with fever. Other members of her relative's family feared she would die in their home and wanted to send her to the City God Temple. The relative would not consent, however, and he hired a doctor to stay overnight and care for her. The woman later learned that she had typhoid fever. In a few days, her illness subsided and she was able to walk. But when she went back and looked for her husband, he was nowhere to be found. Several years passed and she did not know whether he was dead or alive, so she finally remarried.[18] As the rest of the chapter makes evident, this story was not at all atypical.

FAMINE, FLORA, AND FAUNA

After grain supplies dwindled, starving people scavenged for weeds, roots, immature wheat sprouts, and "anything green to be found to cook."[19] By stripping leaves and bark to try to satiate their hunger, famine victims damaged the few trees that were still standing in Henan. Theodore White recalled that during his trip to famine-afflicted areas, "One saw, as one traveled, people chipping bark from trees, with knives, scythes and meat cleavers." They stripped bark from the elms that had previously been planted by the provincial government. As White speculated, "The trees would then die and be chopped down for firewood; perhaps all China had been deforested that way."[20]

Along the road north of Xuchang, wrote a foreign missionary, "the elm trees were peeled of all bark as high up as the people could reach; also the leaves and the small branches had been cut off and used as food." In this way, famine led to destruction of thousands of trees. Hungry people attacked a tree

---

[16] Mei (1992): 333; Mei (2009): 262.
[17] Mei (1992): 334; Mei (2009): 263.
[18] Mei (1992): 335; Mei (2009): 264.
[19] Wampler (1945): 257.
[20] White (1978): 148.

by peeling off bark, "thereby stopping its circulation," and stripping leaves, "destroying its lungs." The "pulmonary disease" attacked "more than ninety percent of all the trees in that section, and a great number of them have their circulation cut also. They will soon be dead." People and trees suffered the same fate. A few of the trees' "pulmonary" ailments had started to heal: "if they are not attacked again by this disease, and if they are able to eat plenty of wholesome food they may still become mature trees .... In the case of some baby trees, having had their respiratory systems injured, having had a hard time getting started in life, and their resistance being low, the severity of the injury will practically destroy them .... They are caught between the millstones of war and famine and no one has time to protect them against exposure to these threats."[21] Warfare and famine were obviously not the original causes of deforestation in Henan, but they aggravated the problem as starving people collected leaves and bark to eat.

Famine took a toll on Henan's livestock population as well, as hungry humans sacrificed animal power necessary for agricultural production to secure essential foodstuffs in the short term. "Donkeys, mules and oxen, after practically starving, were killed and the bones with the little flesh were cooked, making broth to eat with other food."[22] In spring 1943 a Nationalist investigator explained that, "Last winter and this spring, because the famine was severe, many people slaughtered and sold oxen and other livestock. According to investigation statistics, about seventy percent of livestock have been slaughtered." Once the famine ended, livestock shortages were pervasive.[23] According to newspaper reports published at the time, "This year in Henan's agricultural villages, one no longer hears dogs barking or chickens clucking. Even oxen and mules have been killed by their hungry owners out of desperation. So pushing millstones and plowing fields must depend entirely upon human labor power."[24]

Consequences for canines were more ambiguous. During the famine years many villagers killed and ate their dogs.[25] At the same time, however, stray dogs fed on the bodies of the human victims of starvation and disease. White recalled that: "The dogs were also there along the road, slipping back to their wolf kinship, and they were sleek, well fed. We stopped to take a picture of dogs digging bodies from sand piles; some were half-eaten, but the dogs had already picked clean one visible skull."[26] During her time on the road with her husband Hezhi, the woman from Weishi remembered seeing large

---

[21] Wampler (1945): 257–258.
[22] Ibid., 257.
[23] "Zhang Guangsi guanyu Henan sheng hanzai qingkuang ji jiuzai qingxing de diaocha baogao," 564.
[24] Cited in Zhang and Zhuang (1997): 803.
[25] Wampler (1945): 257.
[26] White (1978): 147.

numbers of dead bodies. "Once I saw three corpses in a wheat field beside the road. One was a grey-haired old person lying face down in the wheat field. The cotton jacket on his body had been taken by someone. One was a woman, lying with her face to the sky. Beside her there was a cane for hitting dogs and a bamboo basket. There was also a teenage child. Perhaps they were a family. A black dog was chewing on that child's leg." Her husband chased away the dog with a rock, but as they walked away the animal returned to feed on the corpses.[27]

DISASTER AND GENDER

For many Henan refugees, the 1942–1943 famine was the most recent in a series of war-induced displacements. The plight of another unnamed woman from Fugou illustrates the combination of factors that made it necessary for Henan residents to flee multiple times. Prior to the 1938 flood, she lived in a family of seven with her husband, a daughter, two sons, a daughter-in-law, and a granddaughter. The household owned about 0.33 hectares of hilly land and a small orange grove. They also rented an even smaller area of inclined fields. Her husband wove reed mats, which he sold during the slack agricultural season for additional income. When floods inundated their hilly land in 1938, her eldest son fled with his wife and daughter to Hankou. When the Japanese occupied the city they seized her son as a forced laborer. He soon died and the daughter-in-law remarried. The rest of the family stayed in Fugou. Even though their land had been flooded, yams grew in the fields they rented, plenty of fruit grew in their orchard, and their house was intact.

The family's situation deteriorated when the local mutual-security unit headman selected them to provide an adult male for military enlistment. Since their first son was gone and the second son was still too young to fulfill the task, they had to sell part of their flooded land to pay the headman and settle the matter. Soon thereafter, swarms of locusts that spread from the flooded area ate the sorghum the family had planted on its rented land. The landlord still wanted his rent, so they had to give him the harvest from their orchard as compensation. With the household unable to get by financially, the woman took her daughter and younger son to Luohe and lived at a Red Cross refugee reception center for almost three years. Her husband stayed behind and made a living by selling firewood or whatever other fuel he could gather.

When the Yellow River's dikes broke again in 1942, floodwaters inundated the family's orchard and house. At that point, her husband also went to Luohe to live at the Red Cross reception center. After staying for eight or nine months, the husband went back to Fugou to make reed mats for a living.

---

[27] Mei (1992): 333; Mei (2009): 262.

He died of disease soon after his return. With her husband gone, the woman tried to flee to Shaanxi with her son and daughter, but when they reached Xuchang all their money was spent and they had to beg. Unable to feed her children, the woman had to sell them. She made it to Luoyang and took a train to Xi'an, but when she reached the city she too fell ill. She lived in a cave next to Xi'an's train station. One of her neighbors took pity on her and brought her tea and leftover food. After a month she recovered and moved to a village southwest of Xi'an, where she lived in a temple for four years before going back to Henan.[28]

Another woman named Wang Ruiying had entered a household in Weishi at age thirteen as a child bride. She lived in a three-room grass house with her husband Liu Huan, his two younger brothers, and their mother. When the Yellow River dikes broke in 1938, their village was flooded.

> When the water had just arrived, people in the village fled to a big temple in Beigang. Those who owned fields waited for water to go down, so they could plant their fields and rebuild their houses. I was poor and did not have any belongings, so when the water subsided for the first time I left home and fled the disaster. When I left there were seven people in total: my mother in law, Liu Huan and I, his second brother Liu Huo and his wife, as well as my daughter Xiaoen and my son Dean.

The family crossed the Jialu River and headed southeast, begging for food as they walked to Xihua, where they settled in a temple. Liu Huan and his brother did menial labor to earn money, while Wang Ruiying and her sister-in-law took the children to beg for food. The elderly mother-in-law stayed in the temple and looked after their things. "Life was such that if you earned something or begged for something then you ate; if you couldn't earn anything or beg for anything you went hungry. When the weather was cloudy and rainy [so they could not go out to beg], the whole family faced hunger."[29]

At that time, Wang Ruiying had another daughter, but she could not even eat dried bread or rice during the lying-in period after giving birth. Their situation only grew more difficult. Local residents in Xihua did not have any grain, which made begging impossible. Liu Huan and his brothers could not find work, so the family often went without food for days at a time. As Wang Ruiying recalled, "I did not have anything to eat, so I could not produce breast milk. The baby girl was so hungry that she constantly cried. She could not suck out a mouthful of milk, so she fiercely chewed my nipple. I saw how poor the child was and could not pay attention to the soreness, so I let her hold it in her mouth. The child endured for only a few days before starving to death. When she was on death's door, she still held my nipple in her mouth."[30] The rest of the family made it past the lunar New Year, but they

---

[28] Liu (1947): 7–8. Similar tribulations are described in Wu (2004): 173–174.
[29] Mei (1992): 336; Mei (2009): 265.
[30] Mei (1992): 336; Mei (2009): 265.

had dug up all the wild plants and stripped the tree bark available for food. Risking punishment, Wang Ruiying took her son and snuck into fields to pick wheat sprouts to eat. Her mother-in-law was so hungry she could not move and no longer had the power to groan. With no other options, Wang Ruiying and her husband decided to give their daughter Xiaoen to another family as a child daughter-in-law. Only a few days after her daughter was given away, Wang's mother-in-law died.[31]

Even though Wang Ruiying's household lacked the food necessary to sustain life, they had to contribute labor power to hydraulic maintenance projects. As she remembered,

Four or five days after my mother-in-law died, the local *bao* headman came around saying that he had to send Liu Huan as a worker to build the Yellow River dike (the new river course after the Yellow River flood). I said, "He has already been tortured almost to death by illness and hunger, how could he have the strength to go to work building dikes?" The *bao* headman said: "Eight out of ten families in our village are all in this condition. If you don't go, what am I supposed to tell the higher-ups? Go. This time the higher-ups are deputing workers to build dikes as work relief. Every day you can earn a few *jiao* and you will also be given grain."

Once Liu Huan heard that he could get money as well as grain he insisted on accepting the task, "I'm going. If the bones in my body can hold out for a day, I'll work for a day. Being able to earn 500 grams of grain to give to you and Dean [our son] to eat two meals of flour will be good. If we go on eating this bark and grass roots our family will starve." With that, Liu Huan dragged his body out the door and left to work on the dikes.[32]

Wang Ruiying worried that her husband, who had endured illness and hunger for several months, would not be able to carry earth for dike construction. If anything happened to him, she would have no one to rely on. The following day, someone delivered a letter stating that after Liu Huan had walked 15 kilometers to the work site at Daolinggang he collapsed on the ground and could not get up. Upon receiving the news, Wang Ruiying rushed to see him. When she arrived her husband had already been dead for several hours. "Once Liu Huan died I became a widow with an orphaned child. When fleeing disaster, there was no one to carry the baggage. When begging, there was no one to beat away the dogs." She felt there was no way to live and she wanted to commit suicide. In her words, "When the goodhearted people beside me saw that I was crying so pitifully and also wanted to kill myself, they said, 'You absolutely cannot take the short-sighted view. If you die, what will become of the child?'" Two women looked after Wang while the others wrapped her husband's body in a bundle of sorghum stalks and buried it. Both her husband and mother-in-law thus "became ghosts in strange place

---

[31] Mei (1992): 337; Mei (2009): 265–266.
[32] Mei (1992): 337–338; Mei (2009): 266.

(*yixiang gui*)." Not long after Liu Huan died, his younger brother, Liu Huo, also starved to death. As Wang Ruiying recalled, "To stay alive, his wife had to remarry. My sister-in-law and I wept bitterly when we parted. Once younger brother's wife left, when I begged I did not even have a partner."[33] The household that Wang's daughter Xiuen married into was also poor. After returning to Xihua to see her mother one last time, the girl died of starvation. Left on her own, Wang Ruiying took her son and moved to Suiping County. One day while they were out begging, her son found some beans. A rich man insisted that the boy had stolen them from his land and whipped him with a sorghum stalk. Only when Wang knelt on the ground and pleaded for mercy did the man let her son go. Wang could not go on living in Suiping, so she returned to Xihua. But after a while she could not stay in Xihua any longer and so she went to live with her younger sister, whose family also lived by begging for food. Wang and her sister begged together until 1947 (when the Yellow River breach was repaired) and she took her son back to their home in Weishi.[34]

The plight of a male flood refugee from Fugou named Liu Dongmin further illustrates the destructive effect that wartime migration patterns could have on families. In fall 1938 Liu and his wife, Jiang Xiuying, came to a small village in Lushan with their two young sons. The local mutual-security unit (*jia*) headman arranged for them to stay in an abandoned building. The family's livelihood depended upon charity from the headman's provisional levies. During Liu Dongmin's first few months in the village, getting grain was not much of a problem. But after a while locals came up with excuses to avoid contributing. Liu had to go from household to household with the mutual-security unit functionaries and try to convince locals to give him a little grain. Eventually, Liu Dongmin had no other way to make a living, so he left his family to sell his services as a substitute military conscript.

By the time of the 1942 famine, Liu's wife Jiang Xiuying had spent the money Liu received when he enlisted in the army, so she had to beg for food. With Liu Dongmin away, a man named Cao Wenzhang often accompanied Jiang Xiuying when she went to look for food, carrying grain for her and sometimes even buying her rice or bread. The two soon grew inseparable and wanted to get married. But supporting three people would be hard for Cao Wenzhang, especially since Jiang Xiuying's younger son suffered from favus (a chronic inflammatory dermatophytic infection) all over his scalp. Wanting to marry Cao and join his household, Jiang Xiuying took the most extreme steps imaginable. In October 1942, Jiang took her children to the county seat to beg for food. On the way back she pushed her younger son off a bridge. The nine-year-old boy survived and climbed out of the river, so Jiang went down to the riverbank and beat him to death with a rock. After killing her

---

[33] Mei (1992): 338; Mei (2009): 266.
[34] Mei (1992): 340; Mei (2009): 267.

second son, Jiang sent her elder son to the county seat to find food. He never returned. Only a few days later, Jiang Xiuying went to live with Cao Wenzhang. In the fall of 1943, Liu Dongmin deserted the army and came back to Lushan. Liu was enraged when he heard what happened. But because he was a deserter he dared not complain to local officials. Cao Wenzhang arranged for several villagers to give Liu Dongmin a sum of money so he could remarry. Liu had no choice but to take the money and agree to dissolve his marriage with Jiang Xiuying.[35]

This level of human suffering is hard to fathom, but evidence indicates that it was widespread. A survey of 94 families from Fugou and Xihua counties conducted in 1946 offers quantitative information regarding the effects that wartime flooding, famine, and the social dislocation that they generated had at the village and household levels. The sample size is small, but the information is rich. The 94 households had a total of 404 people, for an average family size of 4.3 per household. Households with four members accounted for 20.2 percent of the sample, and families of three made up 18.08 percent. Families of two and six people each made up 17.02 percent.[36] Since the start of the Sino-Japanese War in 1937, 358 of the individuals surveyed (88.56 percent) had fled at some point.[37] In most of the families (64.93 percent), everyone had managed to flee and return without incident. However, 26 households (27.6 percent) had experienced the death of a family member, and in five households as many as four family members had died.[38] The vast majority experienced displacement and almost one-third of all families experienced the death of one of their closest kin.

In terms of age, 25.7 percent were in the 0–14-year-old cohort, the 14–44-year-old cohort accounted for 40.85 percent, and those over the age of 44 made up 33.45 percent. Children and the elderly predominated, combining for 59.2 percent of the total population. Young adults, on the other hand, made up the clear minority.[39] In all likelihood, the low percentage of young adults in Henan's flooded area resulted primarily from their migration to other areas. People with the ability to move during times of flood and famine fled and left children and the elderly behind, resulting in a skewed age distribution.

Females accounted for 52 percent of the sample population and males only 48 percent.[40] The mostly female population of Henan's flooded area was anomalous in early twentieth-century rural China, where female infanticide and neglect of daughters typically biased sex ratios toward males.[41] The

---

[35] Lin (1996): 143–144.
[36] Wang Kejian (1947a): 3.
[37] Ibid., 4.
[38] Ibid., 6.
[39] Ibid., 4.
[40] Ibid.
[41] Lee and Wang (1999): 57–59.

predominance of females in the flooded area resulted in part from wartime demands, which drew males into military service as soldiers or conscripted laborers. Men also found it easier to leave their families and take flight. Compared with women, young males had a better chance of finding work and faced less risk of becoming victims of violence during their travels. Gender norms dictated that women look after dependent children, which also limited their mobility. As a result, men had an easier time migrating to find employment in other places than did women.[42] Following the 1938 flood, to cite one example, many able-bodied males from Fugou migrated to find jobs as farmhands and laborers or went to the army, leaving their children, wives, and elders behind in their native-place as beggars.[43]

As they destabilized family units, wartime migration patterns and demographic trends in Henan's flooded area had a great effect on the gender division of labor in rural society. As able-bodied young men abandoned the region or joined the army, women assumed a greater role in agricultural labor. Despite gender norms that discouraged it, women in North China routinely engaged in various kinds of farm labor during the early twentieth century, especially if they came from poor households. Yet female farm work was equated with poverty, shame, sexual vulnerability, abuse, and violation of norms dictating that women stay out of public sight. At a time when soldiers and bandits roamed the countryside, going out to work in the fields exposed women to immediate danger.[44] As war-induced catastrophes led to impoverishment, however, it became necessary for greater numbers of women to engage in farm work. The result was an increasingly feminized agricultural sector. The wartime trend in Henan coincides with what Hershatter finds in Shaanxi, where "in the 1930s and 1940s, the presence of women and girls in the fields was not just a supplement to male labor at harvest time. Given the general absence men, farming was becoming women's work."[45] With this feminization of agriculture, China followed a pattern frequently seen during periods of military conflict.

A 1941 report on agriculture in Henan as a whole stated that since the war began approximately 1.5 million able-bodied men from the province's villages had entered military service. Hence, "productive labor power" had greatly decreased, with negative consequences for agricultural production.[46] A later report noted that Henan had a pervasive shortage of labor power, which made intensive farming impossible. In addition to able-bodied males who were conscripted into the army, many other men fled to avoid military or

---

[42] Ó Gráda (2009): 83–84.
[43] Wou (1994): 220.
[44] Hershatter (2007); Hershatter (2011): 42–45.
[45] Hershatter (2011): 43.
[46] Yao (1941): 6. See also Henan sheng minzhengting (1941): 23.

labor service obligations. Able-bodied male farmers in the prime of their lives grew extremely scarce. With no one to cultivate it, large amounts of land were left to waste. As the survey concluded, "Now those who are left in the villages are either the old and the weak or women and children."[47] As many as three-quarters of the able-bodied males in some villages were taken as conscripts, as Graham Peck observed, so "most families could get along only if the old people, children, and pregnant women worked in the fields."[48] This pattern reflected a general trend in wartime China, as the departure of males pushed women to support themselves and their families.[49]

Refugee migration during the 1942–1943 famine further encouraged this shift in the gender division of labor. Zhang Guangsi, sent to investigate the famine conditions in Henan on behalf of Nationalist China's central government, found that: "Too many people have died or fled because of the famine, so henceforth the farmers needed to cultivate the fields are going to be in short supply. This kind of problem is growing more and more severe." Among the people cultivating fields in the famine-stricken areas of Henan that Zhang surveyed, "one already finds many women, while young adult men are already extremely few."[50] At the famine's height in 1943, a foreign missionary likewise noted that: "The men are either in the army, or they build roads and they build dikes, and only the women are left to take care of the farm and fight the locusts, and most of them don't have the strength for it."[51]

Warfare and the environmental disasters that it generated significantly reduced the number of able-bodied adult males in Henan's flooded area. The proportion of females, as well as the young and the elderly, increased accordingly. Due to this demographic shift, families came to depend increasingly on the labor power of their female members and women had to shoulder a greater share of agricultural work.

HENAN FAMINE REFUGEES IN SHAANXI

Like the Yellow River floods, the 1942–1943 famine stimulated a wave of mass migration out of Henan. With the famine taking its toll, word circulated that Shaanxi and other provinces in the northwest had good harvests. Thousands of famine victims began to trek west in search of food. In Yanling, residents who recognized the famine's severity early on sold their household possessions after planting the 1941 wheat crop and fled with their families to

---

[47] Yao (1942): 2. See also Xihua xian shizhi bianzuan weiyuanhui (1992): 118.
[48] Peck (1967): 348.
[49] Lary (2010): 97.
[50] "Zhang Guangsi guanyu Henan sheng hanzai qingkuang ji jiuzai qingxing de diaocha baogao," 563–564.
[51] Quoted in Christensen (2005): 133.

Shaanxi. Many, especially the elderly, were too attached to their homes to leave. Other farmers assumed that they had enough grain, sweet potatoes, and dried vegetables to hold out until the next harvest. When famine conditions were at their worst in 1942, many people who hesitated to leave faced starvation.[52]

In August 1942, about 500 refugees passed through Luoyang every day en route to Shaanxi. Numbers grew larger in the fall and winter months. By 1943, according to one estimate, more than three million people fled Henan to find relief in other provinces, with most ending up in Shaanxi.[53] Many of the famine refugees had only a few years earlier left their homes because of the breaking of the Yellow River dikes. Some worked in villages as farm laborers, but when crops failed they had no work and no food. Hearing news of good crops in Shaanxi, Henan refugees decided to migrate west.[54]

In the winter of 1942, Theodore White described huddled masses of refugees gathered at train stations waiting to go west to Xi'an. Most did not make it onto trains and traveled by cart, wheelbarrow, or on foot.[55] Villages in Henan's famine areas were left empty and deserted. White stated that Zhengzhou had a prewar population of 120,000, but after the famine it dwindled to only 40,000.[56] Journalist Harrison Forman, who traveled alongside White to the famine region, reported seeing, "roads and trains packed with haggard, half-starved refugees in a mass exodus already numbering more than 3,000,000. The highways are strewn with unburied corpses. Villages are deserted, and for miles trees have been stripped of their bark, which has been eaten by those too weak to join in the trek westward and southward for food." Henan's "blighted area," Forman wrote, covered approximately 20,000 square miles. The worst-afflicted districts bordered the Yellow River or were near Zhengzhou, only twelve miles from the Japanese lines.[57] Forman described "train after train encrusted with humanity, which was huddled on the slippery roofs of the cars: men, women, and children, boxes, bundles, pots and pans, ploughs [sic], and wheel-barrows were all jumbled together. They overflowed on to the sides, where they hung on precipitously. They were jammed between the cars sitting on the couplings or underneath the riding-rods, or they lined the catwalk of the engine, hugging the steam boiler as near as they dared for warmth." Many famine refugees fell to their deaths from the speeding trains.[58]

---

[52] Cui (1992): 63.
[53] Wojniak (1957): 162–163. Examples of women who fled Henan and married into families in Shaanxi during the famine can be found in Hershatter (2011): 49–50.
[54] Wampler (1945): 233; Mao (1991): 76.
[55] White and Jacoby (1980): 167–168.
[56] Ibid., 169–70.
[57] *The Times* (March 29, 1943): 4.
[58] *The Times* (April 1, 1943): 4.

TABLE 5.1 *Refugees from Henan transported on the Long-Hai railroad, August 1942–June 1943*

Month	To the west	To the east	Total
1942			
August	84,950	–	84,950
September	171,708	–	171,708
October	164,798	–	164,798
November	192,862	11,530	204,392
December	166,170	36,440	202,610
Total	780,488	47,970	828,458
1943			
January	157,606	77,980	235,586
February	170,016	113,420	283,436
March	155,390	148,950	304,430
April	58,000	216,650	274,650
May	4,500	197,110	201,610
June	220	53,560	53,780
Total	545,732	807,670	1,353,402
Grand total	1,326,220	855,640	2,181,860

From August 1942 to June 1943, the Long-Hai Railway Special Nationalist Party Branch (*Long-Hai tielu tebie dangbu*) tabulated the refugees moving between Henan and Shaanxi on the railroad. Out-migration peaked in November 1942, when 192,862 refugees took the train west. The flow reversed prior to the spring harvest in 1943, when refugees started to return to Henan in large numbers. Beginning in April 1943, the population going east exceeded the number going west. In June 1943, however, the population that had gone west was still greater than the population that returned east by 470,580. These people either stayed in Shaanxi or proceeded to migrate to other parts of northwest China (Table 5.1).[59] Even larger numbers of famine refugees made the journey on foot. Roads in Henan "were jammed with blue-clad humanity pushing wheel-barrows which were piled high with the most precious belongings: bundles and babies in baskets were slung from the ends of bamboo shoulder-poles, while women with bound feet and staves in their hands trudged painfully along ankle-deep in the yellow dust. In the heart of the famine area the villages were deserted and starving people were dropping like flies in the streets of the bigger cities."[60]

[59] "Long-Hai tielu yunshu Yu sheng nanmin renshu zongbiao, sanshiyi nian ba yue -sanshier nian liu yue" (July 1943): SPA 9-2-823.
[60] *The Times* (April 1, 1943): 4.

Looking at wartime China as a whole, the refugee relief situation was regionally determined. In areas of southwest China that were firmly under Nationalist control, government institutions and other relief organizations made "significant efforts in the field of social rehabilitation and welfare," though tangible successes resulting from the efforts proved far from adequate.[61] In eastern China's Zhejiang Province, one of the war's fiercest battlefields, the meager refugee relief initiatives did not offer much in the way of actual relief.[62] In Henan, "where control passed back and forth between the Nationalists and the Japanese, with the Communists always waiting in the rear," as Rana Mitter points out, the relief programs "lacked substance."[63] Once refugees from Henan reached Shaanxi, the limited resources at the disposal of relief agencies simply could not meet their needs.

When they visited Shaanxi in 1943, relief investigators reported 150,000–200,000 famine refugees along the section of the Long-Hai rairoad from Huayin to Baoji, as well as 12,000 inside the town of Baoji itself. Most refugees "would surely die during these winter months unless something was done at once to provide them with food, proper housing and medical help."[64] Most Henan refugees had neither relatives nor friends in Shaanxi, and no place to stay. Missionaries and Chinese relief agencies distributed grain to Henan refugees and the Shaanxi poor, some of whom lost their jobs to migrants from Henan. Large numbers of refugees congregated in western Henan when authorities in Shaanxi tried to slow the flow across the border.[65]

The Nationalist general Zhang Fang, who hailed from Henan, and other notables from the province founded the Henan Disaster Relief Committee (*Yu zai jiuji weiyuanhui*) in Xi'an, setting up two reception centers for his refugee compatriots. Foreign observers claimed that all Henan natives had heard of Zhang Fang, "and know him to be a successful and powerful figure who has devoted the recent years to his provincial fellows, giving liberally of his own funds, soliciting contributions, negotiating with governmental and railroad authorities, planning reclamation schemes and projects which could employ the refugees and campaigning for their rights."[66] However, material shortages in wartime Shaanxi impeded this relief work.

On the morning of November 13, 1942 the Henan Disaster Relief Committee had an emergency meeting at Xi'an's Nationalist Party Branch to discuss establishing a reception center for famine refugees in the city.

---

[61] Mitter and Schneider (2012): 179.
[62] Schoppa (2011): Chapter 2.
[63] Mitter (2013a): 273.
[64] Ling and Xu (1943): 4.
[65] Wampler (1945): 256.
[66] A.J. Parenti to Newton Bowles, "Honan Flooded Area Survey, Part II: Shensi and Northwest" (October 1947): UN S-1021 Box 55 File 4.

Buildings for the center were hard to find. The Relief Committee decided to utilize empty land outside Xi'an's city walls and collected reed matting and hemp rope that factory owners and shopkeepers used for wrapping goods to put up temporary grass shacks to shelter refugees from the elements. As the Henan Disaster Relief Committee explained in a petition to Shaanxi's provincial government, they needed bamboo poles to prop up the grass shacks and support their roofs. Since the price of materials had grown exceedingly high, the Relief Committee did not have funds to buy bamboo poles. The Relief Committee noted that it was currently winter time, when local villagers around Xi'an cut branches from trees. To give refugees shelter, the Relief Committee asked the Shaanxi provincial government to order Chang'an County (outside Xi'an) to direct each township and village (*xiangbao*) to persuade local villagers to take thin branches that they had cut and "make contributions according to their capability."[67] But the villages around Xi'an needed this biomass for other purposes. Villages in the area had hardly any public or private woodland. With firewood extremely expensive, villagers used all the small branches and twigs that were available as fuel. For this reason, as Shaanxi's Department of Civil Affairs explained, asking them to contribute branches would pose serious difficulties. Because it was a charitable undertaking, however, the provincial government grudgingly agreed to make Chang'an do its utmost to encourage donations.[68] Scarcity of biomass made twigs precious.

Henan refugees who settled around Xi'an ended up living in makeshift shelters of various sizes and types of construction. Some lived in caves dug into hillsides and the embankments of the moat around Xi'an's city wall. Shaanxi's loess soil proved easy to excavate, but capillary action kept cave floors damp and they had little ventilation.[69] Shaanxi's provincial government periodically tried to fill in caves and ordered refugees to move, leaving many homeless. Other refugees lived in shelters made of mud, straw, and sorghum stalks.[70] Wood shortages "necessitated economy in construction." Their dwellings used saplings as braces to support roofs, which were arched to transfer stress to the mud walls. Because even the straw needed for thatching had become "scarce or prohibitively priced," refugees had to patch mud lost from underlying sorghum matting after each rain. Most shelters had excavated floors to economize on construction material for walls, so many of the dwellings were really "nothing more than protected pits." Families of seven commonly lived in these tiny, cramped spaces.[71] Refugee dwellings

---

[67] "Yu zai jiujihui Xi'an shi fenhui han" (November 14, 1942): SPA 9-2-805.
[68] "Shaanxi sheng minzhenting daidian/qianhan" (November 24, 1942): SPA 9-2-805.
[69] Parenti to Bowles, "Honan Flooded Area Survey, Part II."
[70] SJZHFZ 15 (April 22, 1946): 6; SJZHFZ 18–19 (May 20, 1946): 10; UNRRA, "Honan weekly report of Office of the Economic and Financial Advisor" 5 (April 29, 1946): 2.
[71] Parenti to Bowles, "Honan Flooded Area Survey, Part II."

stretched around Xi'an on all four sides, with the oldest near the city walls and the newer ones on the city's periphery.

Rather than a haphazard collection of shelters, the settlements formed an aggregation of displaced rural communities. Unsurprisingly, refugees congregated together based on native-place ties. As a foreign observer explained immediately following the war's end,

> At the south of the city is what might be called "Little Fukou" [Fugou]; in the section the refugees from [F]ukou hsien [xian] have camped together; incoming refugees from that hsien have gravitated toward the original nucleus of Fukou people and found a measure of security in the company of others with their own background. So it is with the displaced from other hsien; as one proceeds around the city one finds little Weishih [Weishi], Little Sihwa [Xihua], Little Yenling [Yanling] .... side by side, each with its recognized leaders, its own dialect, and its special character.

This settlement pattern facilitated mutual-assistance "even if the security it affords were only mental, but it appears that the misery common to all has produced a community spirit which has mitigated the indignity and hardships of refugee status and has motivated the people to share what little they have with their more needy brethren." Native-place organizations, together with each group's compatriot associations (*tongxianghui*), gave refugees a basis for negotiating legal and other difficulties. Even with the assistance from the Henan native-place associations, "babies still starve, children display the symptoms of malnutrition, the able-bodied are rarely robust. Typhus, typhoid, cholera take their toll with ease in the humid, closely grouped huts along the moat filled with green flecked-sewage."[72]

Local authorities in Shaanxi, for their part, did little to accommodate the displaced population from Henan. Xi'an's municipal authorities forbade refugees from entering the city without passes, granting this documentation only when native-place associations interceded to register refugees based on their professions and capabilities. Some refugees found employment as rickshaw pullers and others worked sporadically at temporary jobs. "The refugee population provides an inexpensive, always eager pool of workers, and city people, including the army, never lack labor when they want it."[73]

The Henan Disaster Relief Committee's reception centers registered many of the refugees who came to Xi'an, organizing them into "teams" and "small groups." Refugees either lived at the centers or in other temporary residences that the Relief Committee arranged for them. A school for refugee children was opened near Xi'an's famous Drum Tower. Every five days, refugees above twelve years of age received rations of 500 grams of maize, while those under twelve received 187.5 grams. The reception center helped find work for refugees who were in good health and provided medical care for

[72] Ibid.
[73] Ibid.

the ill. The Relief Committee also resettled some refugees to more distant parts of northwest China or sent them back to their original homes. All in all, the reception center took in about 2,000 refugees and resettled about 400 to participate in land reclamation in Gansu Province. Refugees from Yanling and Fugou, whose homes were flooded, mostly moved to Gansu. Refugees from other parts of Henan went home after the 1943 wheat harvest.[74]

A mere fraction of the refugee population in the vicinity of Xi'an benefited from these relief measures. In March 1943, Chinese investigators estimated that over 300,000 famine refugees had migrated from Henan to areas in Shaanxi around Xi'an. Relief projects assisted at most 20,000. Monthly subsidies of 26 yuan distributed by the reception centers only bought enough grain for six meals. Most refugees did not have access to any form of relief and were left to their own devices: "The vast majority of refugees have scattered in various counties in Guanzhong [central Shaanxi's Wei River Valley], and either find their own occupations or beg." Officials in Xi'an, Baoji, and other urban areas were mainly concerned with maintaining order within their jurisdictions and neglected relief work. Shaanxi's provincial government secretly instructed military and police to prohibit refugees from entering cities. But more than 40,000 refugees from Henan somehow found a way to sneak into Xi'an.[75] By 1945, over 100,000 refugees from Henan were living in Xi'an, where they begged or did menial labor.[76] About half were under 15 years old.[77]

Not only did refugees rarely get handouts, they frequently incurred the animosity of Xi'an's local residents. As investigators stated, "Worst of all, there are some ignorant residents who despise refugees and even beat them up. At the Number One Henan Disaster Reception Center (*Yu zai di yi shourongsuo*) there were two or three girls who were beaten and injured. They say it was so terrible that from now on they would rather starve to death than beg." During the daytime refugees begged; when night fell they slept on the street. Passersby rarely paid them any mind. If refugees died no one buried them. Some refugees went out to beg in villages as far as 10 kilometers away from Xi'an. But refugees who tried their luck in the countryside did no better than those who stayed in the cities, "When there are a few of them they are cursed or beaten. When there are many of them the stockade gates are closed to turn them away."[78]

---

[74] Zhang Jinxing (1987): 173–174. See also Parenti to Bowles, "Honan Flooded Area Survey, Part II."
[75] "Ju zhanqu jun fengji di wu xunchatuan jianyi gaishan jiuji lai Shaan nanmin banfa dengqing dianyang zunzhao" (April 2, 1943): SPA 64-1-280.
[76] SJZHFZ 18–19 (May 20, 1946): 4.
[77] UNRRA, "Weekly Report for Economic Analysis Bureau, Honan Area" 5 (April 29, 1946): 2. Others estimated as many as 160,000 refugees in Xi'an and 2–3 million in Shaanxi as a whole. UNRRA, "Honan weekly report of Office of the Economic and Financial Advisor" 6 (May 6, 1946): 2–3.
[78] "Ju zhanqu jun fengji di wu xunchatuan jianyi gaishan jiuji lai Shaan nanmin banfa dengqing dianyang zunzhao."

Relief agencies tried to prevent tensions between Henan refugees and Shaanxi locals from breaking out into conflict. Every few days, workers from the Henan Disaster Relief Committee's reception center visited the refugees it had taken in and made it absolutely clear that: "When we come to Shaanxi, it's not like our hometowns in Henan. You have to follow the rules and dare not misbehave; otherwise you'll have a hard time." Because Henan refugees lived dispersed throughout Xi'an, reception center workers counseled them on how best to avoid "unfortunate incidents."[79]

Of particular importance to Nationalist leaders was keeping Henan refugees from migrating to northern Shaanxi and joining the Communist forces in the Shaan-Gan-Ning Border Area. Making sure that Nationalist-controlled counties took in refugees would keep them from "going astray" and slipping into Shaan-Gan-Ning.[80] To counter refugee relief measures already enacted in the Chinese Communist Party (CCP) base area, the Nationalist leadership ordered counties in north-central Shaanxi to instruct locals to share housing with refugees, loan them grain, give them land to cultivate, and refrain from conscripting refugees as soldiers. Mutual-security unit personnel were to take strict precautions to stop refugees from entering the Communist-held territory.[81] Despite Nationalist efforts to keep them out, however, by 1944 nearly 11,900 Henan refugees had ventured north into Shaan-Gan-Ning, where local CCP authorities accommodated and resettled them.[82]

Shaanxi's Provincial Relief Commission (*Shaanxi sheng zhenhui*) ordered counties and local mutual-security units (*bao*) in the province to take in 21,000 refugees and give them shelter. Shaanxi residents, who tended to see Henan refugees as competitors for limited food supplies and other resources, were less than welcoming. Local governments in Shaanxi complained about the burden of supporting this displaced population, but Nationalist authorities feared that refugees would harm law and order – or worse yet strengthen the CCP – if they were denied relief.[83]

---

[79] Zhang Jinxing (1987): 174.
[80] "Shaanxi sheng di san qu xingzheng ducha zhuanyuan jian baoan siling gong daidian" (November 30, 1942): SPA 9-2-800; "Junshi weiyuanhui Xi'an banshiting kuaiyou daidian" (February 26, 1943): SPA 9-2-800; "Di san qu xingzheng ducha zhuanyuan gongshu bugao" (June 15, 1943): SPA 9-2-815; "Xingzhengyuanzhang Jiang Zhongzheng xunling gao" (June 28, 1943): AH 062 673.
[81] "Wei jiuji Henan nanmin bao quan qu bao jiao renyuan ji quanti minzhong shu" (December 21, 1942): SPA 9-2-800; "Li Shanji cheng" (December 28, 1942): SPA 9-2-800; "Shaanxi sheng di san qu xingzheng ducha zhuanyuan jian baoan siling gongshu daidian" (March 22, 1943): SPA 9-2-808; "Shaanxi sheng zhengfu kuaiyou daidian" (July 1943): AH 062 673. On local implementation, see "Shaanxi sheng di san qu xingzheng ducha zhuanyuan jian baoan siling gongshu daidian" (February 3, 1943): SPA 9-2-722.
[82] Shaan-Gan-Ning bianqu caizheng jingji shi bianxiezu (1981): 646.
[83] "Jiuji ru Shaan Yu ji nanmin shenchahui zhaiyao" (December 17, 1943); "Xingzhengyuan mishuchu gonghan" (December 25, 1943): AH 271 2984.

The Ecology of Displacement

Slogans printed by Shaanxi's Third Special Area Administrative Supervisor and distributed to county governments to encourage them to provide relief for Henan refugees – and admonish locals against mistreating them – captured the frictions that existed between outsiders from Henan and Shaanxi locals:

1. We must do our best to vacate houses (or caves) for refugees to live in!
2. Do not bully refugees!
3. Relieving refugees is a benevolent act!
4. Do not wantonly impress refugees for military service!

Nationalist authorities tried to employ patriotic language to overcome tensions and push locals to give up a share of their limited resources to refugees. As another set of slogans proclaimed:

1. Relieving refugees is strengthening the power of the War of Resistance!
2. Welcoming refugees to reclaim land can increase grain supplies and lighten the locality's burden![84]

It is unlikely that these exhortative slogans and admonitions proved convincing. The wartime experience did not do much to energize a social consciousness "reaching beyond family and local ties toward a redefinition of community."[85] Instead of pulling people together in new ways, war heightened tensions between locals and outsiders. Nevertheless, it is clear that during the Henan famine, as in the aftermath of the 1938 Yellow River flood, refugee relief overlapped with discourses of national resistance and wartime mobilization. In particular, land reclamation in Shaanxi would make it possible to "exhaust the people's power and exhaust the earth's benefits."[86]

THE ENVIRONMENTAL IMPACT OF FAMINE REFUGEE RESETTLEMENT

As famine caused the number of Henan refugees in Shaanxi to swell, the Chinese state yet again turned to resettlement and land reclamation to assist them. Starting in 1938, as discussed in Chapter 2, the Nationalists relocated refugees from the Yellow River flooded area and other war-torn regions to reclaim uncultivated land in Shaanxi's Huanglongshan region.[87]

Land reclamation dramatically altered Huanglongshan's environment. Refugee settlers cleared highland areas covered in brush, grass, and trees.

---

[84] "Shaanxi sheng di san qu xingzheng zhuanyuan jian baoan siling gongshu dai dian" (February 10, 1943): SPA 9-2-800.
[85] MacKinnon (2008): 54. A similar argument is advanced by Lary (2010). For a contrasting perspective, see Schoppa (2011).
[86] "Yichuan xian jiuji nanmin huiyi jilu" (January 28, 1943): SPA 9-2-722.
[87] Lu (2005): 89. See also Zhang (2006): 199.

FIGURE 5.1 Refugee settlers and draft animals at Huanglongshan
Source: Walter C. Lowdermilk. Courtesy of *The National Geographic Magazine*, Vol. LXXXVII, No. 6 (June 1945), page 670 [plate XIV].

Without sufficient level land suited for farming, refugees pushed the cultivation line up slopes, clearing valley floors and "the loessial cappings of border ridges," as well as steep slopes. On this hilly land, refugees cultivated corn, potatoes, hemp, and buckwheat.[88] Land clearance destroyed vegetation that had flourished in Huanglongshan since it was abandoned following the rebellions of the late nineteenth century, leading to accelerated soil erosion. Early summer rains washed crops off inclined fields and sent gravel and boulders tumbling onto farmland below.[89]

In addition to land reclamation, other economic activities favored by refugees also had an impact on the land. In February 1943 the administrative supervisor of Shaanxi's Third Special Area, encompassing Huanglongshan and surrounding counties, published a pamphlet titled "The Refugee Livelihood Guide" (*Nanmin mousheng zhidao*). This text, which was distributed in localities throughout the Special Area, instructed Henan famine refugees on how best to earn a living. The pamphlet listed a number of side-employments with which "refugees should, based on their own labor power (*laoli*), find their own subsistence." All the subsistence strategies listed put pressure on the area's forests and other vegetation. Among these occupations

---

[88] Lowdermilk (1944): 205, 207; Walter C. Lowdermilk, "Preliminary Report to the Executive Yuan, Government of China on Findings of a Survey of a Portion of the Northwest for a Program of Soil Water and Forest Conservation" (November 26, 1943), 9: HIA, Walter C. Lowdermilk Papers, Box 4.
[89] Lowdermilk (1944): 206.

were cutting wood and grass to sell as fuel, burning charcoal (though the guide urged refugees not to burn "good materials"), collecting branches and vines to weave baskets, and gathering medicinal plants and dyestuffs in the mountains. The guide also recommended firing pottery, which demanded organic material for fuel. "Straightening up the forests" (*zhengli senlin*) in Huanglongshan's wooded lands held particular importance:

> No one straightens up [the forests], so their sparseness and density is uneven, and the branches are overgrown, which impedes their proper development so they cannot grow into good materials. Branches and waste wood are abandoned on the ground, which is also a pity. Refugees can consult with the local lords of the mountain (*shanzhu*) or the people in charge to let them straighten up [the forest]. The materials that you straighten up are yours to sell. Moreover, they can be made into handles for ploughs, mattocks, and hoes, which can also be sold for a good price.

On the other hand, the guide forbade what it termed "bad roads for refugees to make a livelihood" like begging, secretly gathering weapons, dealing opium or other drugs, and selling children or wives.[90] Yet all the good ways of making a living took an environmental toll. The prevalence of timber cutting and charcoal burning among refugees who resettled in Huanglongshan indicates that these livelihood strategies were commonly practiced.

Huanglongshan had abundant forests prior to the war, but after the land reclamation project's inception the actions of refugee settlers made a huge dent in them.[91] Forests along transport routes and near inhabited villages suffered extensive damage. All trees on reclaimable lands had been felled, as well as some trees on land that was not suitable for reclamation. Fires started by refugees, whether to clear land or out of mere carelessness, led to huge conflagrations that did additional damage. Settlers in the reclamation area and residents of neighboring counties burned charcoal for heating, which destroyed many trees. After arriving in the mountains, settlers also cut down trees to get materials for building houses, barns, irrigation works, and other structures.[92] The reclamation project had regulations that prohibited setting fires on mountainsides and unrestrained woodcutting, but forest fires and over-cutting still occurred. Due to loss of vegetation cover, soil erosion and accumulation of silt in waterways grew more serious. "When the mountains erode and the rivers [fill up with silt and] grow murky, the harvests from agricultural production are not abundant and erosion problems occur."[93]

---

[90] The guide advised refugees to haul coal or work as mine laborers, open food stands, carry water, plant vegetables, dig caves, work as farm laborers, make rope, peddle goods, make shoes, spin and weave, raise chickens, and work as female domestic servants. It also cautioned refugees against trying to save money by avoiding medical treatment when ill. "Nanmin mousheng zhidao" (February 1942): SPA 9-2-819.
[91] "Huanglongshan kenqu guanliju shicha baogao" (June 1943): IMH 20-26 60-12.
[92] "Shaanxi sheng Huanglongshan kenqu senlin shicha baogao" (1943): IMH 20-26 60-12.
[93] "Huanglongshan kenqu guanliju shicha baogao."

At the current rate of exploitation, as official reports warned in 1943, in about ten years Huanglongshan would not have any forests left.[94]

Loss of forest cover in Huanglongshan was not exceptional. Similar environmental changes occurred throughout Shaanxi, as China's wartime state struggled to boost agricultural output by reclaiming land. In Nationalist-controlled regions of Shaanxi, by 1943 reclamation projects opened up well over 100,000 hectares of land. Resettled refugees accounted for much of this total.[95] Between 1937 and 1943, Communist-initiated reclamation efforts in northern Shaanxi brought an alleged 160,000 hectares under cultivation. Refugees and other migrants reportedly reclaimed over 133,330 hectares, or over 83 percent of the total.[96] Although the figures are likely inflated, the ecological effects were clear. One foreign observer reported that areas reclaimed in Communist-held regions of northern Shaanxi were "all marginal land, bound to become useless from erosion in the course of years."[97] Whether in Nationalist- or Communist-controlled parts of China, land reclamation initiatives depleted woodlands and other vegetation cover in favor of grain-yielding plants. In Shaanxi as a whole from 1937 to 1945, forests reportedly decreased from 25 to 16 percent of land area and as a result soil erosion accelerated on many marginal lands.[98]

How does one explain this ecological damage? The American soil conservationist Walter C. Lowdermilk, who visited the reclamation area, stressed displaced people's unfamiliarity with their host environment, arguing that refugees employed cultivation techniques poorly suited to Huanglongshan's hilly landscape. Since their native regions were practically level, refugees from Henan's flat plains were unaccustomed to farming steeply inclined land. Settlers farmed in straight rows and "took no account of topography or of contour farming."[99] To a certain extent, the explanation is convincing. Yet most refugees did not have any way to make the costly investments of labor and resources required to implement soil conservation measures. Before they could reclaim and harvest their land, refugees depended on government assistance for their food and clothing. For this reason, it is hard to imagine that refugees could have afforded to put soil conservation techniques (such as terracing) into effect.

According to other government reports, land degradation in Huanglongshan resulted from rising population pressure. In this view, the area had simply taken in more refugees than the limited amount of land suitable for reclamation could

---

[94] "Shaanxi sheng Huanglongshan kenqu senlin shicha baogao."
[95] Vermeer (1988): 138; 480; Lu (2005).
[96] Huang (2005): 325–333; Zhang (2006): 200.
[97] Stein (1945): 166.
[98] Wen (2006): 82–83. See also Chen and Chen (2009). For discussions of deforestation in Shaan-Gan-Ning and its ecological consequences, see Huang (2005): 358–359; Huang (2006): 186–197.
[99] Lowdermilk (1944): 206.

support. As of July 1942, the reclamation area had resettled 29,500 refugees, who reclaimed 11,925 hectares (178,886 *mu*) of land (an average of 6.06 *mu* per person).[100] Refugee flight due to the Henan famine of 1942–1943 led to a jump in Huanglongshan's population. Surveys taken during the Henan famine in early 1943 stated that 52,377 refugees had settled in Huanglongshan and reclaimed around 16,766 hectares (251,496 *mu*, or 4.8 *mu* per person).[101] Having taken in 20,000 famine refugees, the reclamation area's population reached "saturation levels."[102]

By filling up the reclaimable land in Huanglongshan, refugee resettlement threatened to cause land degradation. As government investigators warned, "If too many refugees are taken in, then the land will certainly be used inappropriately. In addition to forests being destroyed, water and soil conservation will not be possible, and people's livelihoods will also grow more impoverished."[103] Another report held that settlers had exhausted the limited amount of land suitable for reclamation. "Land reclamation has been carried out in this area for over five years. There is a lot of hilly land, and many forests on the hills have been chopped down. In the future, soil erosion will increase and it will be difficult to conserve rainwater."[104]

However, this purely demographic explanation fails to capture the socio-economic forces that drove these environmental changes. Refugee populations were dynamic and complex rather than homogenous. Among the Henan refugees who settled in Huanglongshan, living standards tended to vary depending on how early they arrived. Refugees who came to Huanglongshan immediately after the 1938 Yellow River diversion benefited more from state-sponsored resettlement programs and appear to have done more to transform the area's natural landscape. Those who came following the 1942–1943 Henan famine lived under more desperate circumstances, but had less impact on the environment. It was these more impoverished groups who suffered disproportionately from the effects of environmental damage.

Villages founded by refugees who arrived earlier in the war produced large amounts of grain and enjoyed relatively good living conditions and nutrition. Villages inhabited by famine refugees who came to Huanglongshan after fall 1942 experienced greater deprivation and residents were frequently malnourished.[105] By all accounts, settlers who arrived prior to 1942 reclaimed

---

[100] "Qin Liufang guanyu kangzhan zhong de houfang kenzhi shiye de diaocha baogao" (November 30, 1942), in Zhongguo dier lishi dang'anguan (1991): 220.
[101] "Huanglongshan kenqu guanliju shicha baogao."
[102] "Nonglinbu Shaanxi Huanglongshan kenqu guanliju daidian" (February 15, 1942): IMH 20-26 31-8; "Nonglinbu Shaanxi Huanglongshan kenqu guanliju saner niandu gongzuo jihuashu caoan" (1943): IMH 20-26 60-12.
[103] "Huanglongshan kenqu guanliju shicha baogao."
[104] "Nonglinbu Shaanxi Huanglongshan kenqu guanliju saner niandu gongzuo jihuashu caoan."
[105] "Huanglongshan kenqu guanliju shicha baogao," Liu and Qi (1988): 180. New arrivals often had friends or relatives among old settlers, so they relied on assistance from earlier

more land and accounted for a disproportionate share of the damage to Huanglongshan's forests. According to an official report, "The old settlers have made a large amount of progress in land reclamation, but Huanglongshan does not have a lot of reclaimable land. The new settlers lack farm tools, and to open up land they can only rely on human labor power and progress is slow. The old settlers have more capital and can utilize their savings, so reclamation is more rapid."[106] With neither grain to eat nor tools to reclaim land, many new settlers gave up their fields and worked for older settlers as wage laborers. Land tenure grew uneven, as some refugees became tenants for the earlier arrivals: "The old settlers are well established, and use money to hire the new settlers to reclaim land (here they are called 'land companies' (*dibanzi*)). Under these conditions, the rich get richer and the poor get poorer. Before long, this creates big landlords."[107]

Even though the established, better-off settlers benefited more from land reclamation, the new refugees suffered more from its negative ecological consequences. Low living standards increased vulnerability to disease. In the early 1940s, the northern reaches of Huanglongshan experienced deadly outbreaks of Keshan disease – a poorly understood type of cardiomyopathy associated with selenium deficiency, which appears to increase the virulence of certain virus strains.[108] Keshan disease's most serious symptoms include cardiac arrhythmia, heart palpitations, and congestive heart failure.[109] Because of one of Keshan disease's most noticeable symptoms, in Shaanxi it was referred to as "vomiting yellow water disease."

Incidence of Keshan disease is highest in regions of China where soils have low selenium levels. Large-scale displacement due to war-induced disasters threatened human health by pushing people to cultivate marginal lands, like Huanglongshan's hillsides, with low selenium content. The earliest evidence of Keshan disease in China comes from stele inscriptions from Huanglongshan that date back to the seventeenth and eighteenth centuries, and the presence of this disease was likely one of the reasons why people had not inhabited the area since the late Qing.[110] Henan refugees who settled in Huanglongshan during the war did not possess this local knowledge, and Keshan disease took a heavy toll on the most vulnerable.

Official reports connected the prevalence of Keshan disease in Huanglongshan to human nutrition: "The staple food of people in the reclamation area is maize, with few vegetables and little salt. Drinking water is

---

arrivals to avoid starvation. "Huanglongshan kenqu nanmin shourong jiuji qingxing ji muqian kenmin gaikuang shicha baogao" (1943): IMH 20-26 60-12.
[106] "Huanglongshan kenqu nanmin shourong jiuji qingxing ji muqian kenmin gaikuang shicha baogao."
[107] "Huanglongshan kenqu guanliju shicha baogao."
[108] Beck and Levander (2000); Xia Yiming (2000).
[109] World Health Organization (2004): 197–198.
[110] Huanglong xian difangzhi bianzuan weiyuanhui (1995): 581.

high in minerals, but low in iodine and calcium, which has a great influence on health. Women and children frequently suffer from goiters, rickets, and vomiting yellow water disease."[111] During a Keshan disease outbreak that struck Huanglongshan in 1944, deaths only occurred in villages inhabited by recent refugees, who suffered from poor nutrition and farmed marginal land with less fertile soils. In older villages, which had higher living standards and better land to farm, no one died.[112] Keshan disease was endemic to Huanglongshan during the mid-1940s, with outbreaks occurring each winter and spring. The disease took a particularly heavy toll among women and children. The threat of Keshan disease led to a steady outflow of settlers from Huanglongshan before the reclamation project dissolved in late 1946.[113] On the other hand, the dwindling of the region's human population in the late 1940s and 1950s gave secondary growth forests a chance to recover.[114]

CONCLUSION

War-induced ecological catastrophes were clearly among the most important catalysts for refugee migration from Henan. In places refugees left behind, rural infrastructure collapsed, crop cultivation came to a near standstill, and previously settled areas turned into desolate wastelands. Farmers fled, land was abandoned, homes crumbled, farm tools were lost, and draft animals were killed. Attaining and maintaining order and structure in agro-ecological and hydraulic systems – as with all complex structures – takes energy. Protracted military conflict between China and Japan ruled out investments of labor and resources needed to maintain and reconstruct environmental infrastructure. Warfare left a devastated landscape in Henan's flooded area that was sparsely inhabited by people and badly in need of rehabilitation.

The trauma of war frequently displaces populations, curtails economic productivity, and damages the health and nutrition of society's most vulnerable members.[115] In social terms, the migrations sparked by military conflict and ecological upheaval during World War II drastically altered the fabric of local communities. Life stories of rural men and women were punctuated by forced separation, hunger, illness, and death. Warfare, flood, and famine tore

---

[111] Ibid.
[112] Tan (1996): 64. Scientific investigations have revealed a belt of low-selenium areas extending from northeast to southwest China consistent with the geographical distribution of Keshan disease. Xia Yiming (2000): 943.
[113] Liu and Qi (1988): 180.
[114] In the 1960s and 1970s afforestation and conservation measures restored Huanglongshan's forest cover. Liu and Dang (2001): 32–34. Forests in Huanglongshan reportedly increased from 47 percent in 1965 to 65 percent in 1977. In other parts of Shaanxi, however, a much larger area of original forest cover was lost to reclamation over this period. Vermeer (1988): 138–140, 480.
[115] Wadley (2007).

asunder household units and led to lasting changes in gender roles. Young men joined armies stationed in Henan, were conscripted to work on hydraulic engineering projects, or left to find employment elsewhere. The number of able-bodied males decreased relative to females, children, and the elderly. Some girls were sent away as child daughters-in-law or sold into prostitution, which may have kept them alive at a time when other family members perished. Many women had to support households with fathers and husbands absent or deceased. The gender division of labor shifted and agriculture grew more feminized, as women from rural households took on the burdens, humiliation, and danger of working in the fields.

On the ecological level, the impact of war-induced flood and famine generated cascade effects that reached far beyond the sites of military engagements. Wartime Henan resembled other situations in which military conflict deprives people of access to resources near their homes and forces them to rely on resources in accessible areas.[116] As refugees from Henan moved to nearby villages and towns in search of food and shelter, they put additional pressures on food and fuel supplies that warfare had already subjected to tremendous strain. Refugees did not cause deforestation in Henan, simply because human activities had destroyed North China's forests centuries before the war with Japan broke out.[117] Such problems did emerge in parts of Shaanxi like Huanglongshan, where land clearance by refugees led to deforestation and intensified soil erosion. Relatively well-off refugees did most of the damage to the environment and reaped the most benefits from its transformation, while cultivation of selenium-deficient land threatened the health of the most vulnerable, especially impoverished women and children.

Discussions of refugees and the environment tend to fall into two approaches informed by either Thomas Malthus or Ester Boserup. In the Malthusian view, heightened population density in areas that take in displaced populations strains available resources. Refugees rely on their host environments for food, fuel, and other essentials, so population pressure results in ecological degradation due to deforestation and cultivation of marginal lands. In the Boserupian view, ecological stability derives from active maintenance and management, which tend to be labor intensive and thus more easily undertaken in thickly populated lands.[118] The Malthusian and Boserupian positions are often seen as diametrically opposed. But in certain ways the consequences of refugee flight from Henan's flooded area fits with both perspectives. The appropriate analytical perspective depends on the environment under consideration. War-induced disasters left the

---

[116] Jacobsen (1997); Kibreab (1997); Kreike (2004a); Kreike (2004b).
[117] Elvin (2004): chapters 3–4.
[118] The Malthusian view is exemplified by Myers (2002) and Myers (1997); the Boserupian view by Black (1998). The notion of Malthusian and Boserupian perspectives comes from McNeill and Winiwarter (2006).

landscape of Henan largely depopulated, eliminating labor power needed to maintain human-constructed agricultural landscapes and causing acute ecological degradation. At the same time, these upheavals heightened pressures on environments – like the upland areas of Shaanxi – that took in refugee populations, leading to deforestation and accelerated erosion.

Yet population was not the only variable. Political power mattered as well. Without taking account of the state's role in reception and relief, the ecological effects of refugee flight in wartime China are incomprehensible. Typically, the state power does not figure prominently in analyses of interactions between refugees and the environment. Historians have detailed struggles by displaced people to recreate war-torn environments in the absence of external assistance.[119] But in the lands where refugees from Henan resettled, the most severe environmental impacts resulted directly from efforts by China's wartime state – in its Nationalist as well as its Communist guises – to mobilize refugees in order to realize economic and military objectives. Refugee migration cannot be isolated from the many other military, political, and economic factors that lead to ecological damage in wartime, which complicates the notion that displaced people have an unmediated impact on the environment. Given the character of the drive to reclaim "wasteland" and boost grain production in China, the environmental changes connected with refugee migration, as well as their indirect effects on human health, must be seen as another ecological casualty of mobilization for war.

---

[119] Kreike (2004a); Kreike (2004b).

6

The Land Needs the People; the People Need the Land

The Beginnings of Post-Conflict Recovery

Warfare degrades environments in countless ways. World War II's impact on North China's vulnerable, human-constructed environments was especially great. This chapter and the one that follows examine the extent of this war-induced destruction, as well as the process of postwar agro-ecological recovery. Nearly eight years of war, flood, and famine devastated the elaborate system for capturing and using energy that was Henan's human-engineered agricultural landscape. The Yellow River's floodwaters destroyed environmental infrastructure such as farms, fields, and waterworks. Concentrated, usable energy changed into forms less easily captured and exploited by humans. Militaries devoured what little usable energy remained, leaving scarcely any behind for the civilian populace. In response to war-induced disasters, hundreds of thousands of refugees flowed out of Henan. Labor supplies dwindled, rendering intensive maintenance of agro-ecological and hydraulic systems impossible. Wartime loss of draft animals further eliminated sources of energy and productive power. By the time the Sino-Japanese War ended in 1945, warfare had depleted the food, labor, and other resources needed for post-conflict reconstruction. Huge energy subsidies drawn from outside Henan's flooded area were necessary to give the rural populace the capacity to restore agro-ecosystems to productivity.

A significant portion of those inputs were of transnational origin. After Japan's withdrawal from China in 1945, the reconstruction of the Henan's flooded area garnered large-scale assistance from the United Nations Relief and Rehabilitation Administration (UNRRA). This international organization administered assistance to countries beset by socio-economic dislocations after World War II, providing food, fuel, clothing, shelter, and medical assistance. UNRRA also sought to lay the groundwork for postwar economic recovery and growth by providing materials and expertise to rebuild communications, agriculture, and industry. Redeveloping war-damaged areas in China became the largest single-country component of UNRRA's global project. In 1946 and 1947, UNRRA sent some two thousand foreign experts to China, along with $17 million worth of supplies. To administer relief, UNRRA worked through a partner agency formed by the Nationalist regime, the Chinese National Relief and Rehabilitation Administration (CNRRA). The most visible endeavor undertaken by UNRRA-CNRRA was reconstructing the Yellow River flooded area.[1]

From May 1946 to March 1947, tens of thousands of laborers supervised by UNRRA, CNRRA, and the Nationalist government's Yellow River Conservancy Commission worked to close the Huayuankou breach and return the river to its pre-1938 course. To oversee the closure, UNRRA appointed O. J. Todd, an American engineer who had previously worked in China for twenty years on other water control projects, as chief adviser to the Yellow River Conservancy Commission. In addition, UNRRA and CNRRA offered material assistance to refugees who returned to the flooded area and assisted them in bringing land back under cultivation.[2] Todd cast this endeavor as "an opportunity to increase the world's food supply by an estimated two million tons annually through the rehabilitation of nearly two million acres of good farmland that had been partly or entirely taken out of dependable production." UNRRA-CNRRA would also relieve Shaanxi and western Henan of the burden of feeding refugees by returning them to their old lands. First the Yellow River had to be "thrown back into its old course, the flooded area drained, and the tributaries of the Huai River cleaned of the new mud and sand deposits carried into them from the Yellow River basin during the years that 'China's Sorrow' had been trespassing over another river's territory."[3] Closing the breach, re-diverting the river, and rehabilitating the flooded area's farmland fit perfectly with UNRRA's larger goal of making China self-sufficient in agricultural production. Through these initiatives, the international relief agency contributed vast energy subsidies to Henan. Even though the energy inputs provided by UNRRA-CNRRA were a necessary precondition for agro-ecological recovery, they were not sufficient. It was the labor of Henan's rural populace that accomplished the task of repairing Henan's war-ravaged environmental infrastructure.

DEFERRED HOMECOMING

Even after 1945, eastern Henan's flooded area remained mostly depopulated. Statistics compiled by UNRRA in 1946 indicated that the population of the

---

[1] Todd (1949): 38. On the UNRRA in China, see Mitter (2013b): 51–69.
[2] Formulation of plans to return the river to its pre-1938 course is covered in MHS: 216–222. For their execution, see Barnett (1953): 15; Bao (2011); MHD: 196. Todd's earlier career is discussed by Lillian M. Li (2007): 303.
[3] Todd (1949): 40.

twenty counties of Henan affected by Yellow River floods had fallen by over 22 percent compared with prewar levels.[4] In addition to refugees scattered throughout Henan, as many as two million refugees from various parts of Henan were living in Shaanxi and more distant parts of northwest China.[5] With fields, houses, farm tools, and draft animals obliterated, most refugees opted to stay away. Late in 1945, immediately after Japan's surrender, refugees were traveling eastward from Shaanxi to their homes in Henan at a rate of 4,000–5,000 per day. However, a mere 20 percent of Henan refugees in Shaanxi left the province and 80 percent stayed.[6] Of the 400,000 flood refugees gathered in Xi'an, only 90,000 returned home. Some went back to Xi'an after realizing they had no way to make a living in their native place.[7] In May 1946, one UNRRA investigator found that, "Most refugees are not too anxious to leave [Xi'an] at the present time. A few who have visited their former homes in the flooded area have returned to await better conditions." Better housing facilities and food supplies existed in Shaanxi than anywhere between Kaifeng and Xi'an, and charitable organizations in Shaanxi were better equipped to render assistance.[8] For displaced people who did go back to the flooded area, CNRRA's Henan branch office set up six reception stations to offer food and shelter along the way.[9] But without fields and houses in Henan, it made better sense to stay put in Shaanxi. Returning to an energy-starved landscape was not an attractive option. Refugees hesitated to go back until floodwaters fell, stability was assured, and the land could support them.

In Henan's flooded area, farmland required reclamation "from scratch." As UNRRA relief personnel noted, "if the land is to be restored it will require years of patient toil; the land needs the people. But on the other hand, the people depend upon the land; and they will not return until there is promise that the land can support them." Refugees knew that as they worked to reconstruct the agricultural landscape they would have to live under harsh conditions. But, "if living is too precarious, if it is not certain that they can survive the initial period, they are unwilling to take the risk, for the consequences can be starvation or another forced retreat; and retreat would

---

[4] Han and Nan (1948): 22–23.
[5] Chinese relief organizations in Xi'an claimed that three million former residents of Henan were living in Shaanxi. UNRRA estimated two million. UNRRA, "Honan weekly report of Office of the Economic and Financial Advisor," 6 (May 6, 1946): 2–3; China Office, UNRRA, Office of the Economic and Financial Advisor, "Honan CNRRA – UNRRA Food Report" (1946): 3.
[6] "Survey Through Honan Province – Mildred Bonnell, 12 Dec. 1945," attached to "UNRRA History – Honan Region," UN S1021 Box 58 File 7.
[7] Tian (1946): 10.
[8] UNRRA, "Honan weekly report of Office of the Economic and Financial Advisor" 6 (May 6, 1946): 2. See also Parenti to Bowles, "Honan Flooded Area Refugee Survey, Part II," Tian (1946): 10; Wang Kejian (1947a): 5.
[9] Xiong Benwen (1947a): 16; Han and Nan (1948): 81; MHD: 195–197.

entail expense and great hardships. Until conditions improve, the interdependent factors of land and population will persist in a deadlock, with the land requiring population for its restoration, and the population hovering in the distance, where they find a measure of security." Breaking this deadlock called for "an unhampered program of supply and distribution in the Flooded Area and an organization equipped to transfer and provide for the population, a coordination of the needs of the land and its inhabitants – prospective as well as actual."[10] Wartime population loss led to collapse of human-constructed environmental infrastructure, and repairing it required labor power. Yet most displaced people had no desire to return if the flooded area's environment lacked sufficient energy to support their own metabolisms. For this reason, reconstructing agro-ecosystems required flows of energy that could not be acquired or produced locally.

THE POSTWAR LANDSCAPE

When refugees ventured back to Henan's flooded area after 1945, they confronted an environment transformed beyond recognition. An estimated 615,510 hectares of land in eastern Henan had been flooded at some point during the war. By 1946, however, inundated areas had contracted significantly. Areas that were once flooded but were now dry because waters had shifted course and no longer reached them, or because silt deposition made land rise above flood level, covered about 326,050 hectares. During peak flood season in 1946, floods reportedly covered 228,120 hectares. When waters receded during the dry season, inundated areas contracted to a mere fraction of this total, only to flood again when the Yellow River's waters rose. CNRRA and Nationalist river defense agencies undertook projects to strengthen dikes and to prevent floods from expanding. Waters had shifted progressively westward, so areas that had flooded in 1938 or soon thereafter had mostly dried up. Farmers began to resettle and reclaim some of the lands. But with few refugees willing to come back, the area remained largely uninhabited.[11]

The ecological impact of reckless human violence necessitated the evacuation of nearly all human beings, and as Julia Adeney Thomas writes of Korea's demilitarized zone, the unintended result was "a zone left free for other species." The consequences for humans were tragic, but other creatures

---

[10] Parenti to Bowles, "Honan Flooded Area Refugee Survey, Part II." For similar observations, see Liangshibu canshiting, "Jiuji jianyi" (May 1947): AH 212 1368.

[11] The largest flooded areas were in Xihua (649,000 *mu*), Huaiyang (1,028,000 *mu*), Fugou (550,500 *mu*), and Weishi (54,100 *mu*). Burlin B. Hamer, "A Study of the Yellow River Flooded Area," 4. See also W. S. Chepil, "Report of Survey of the Yellow River Flooded Area of Honan" (November 11, 1946), 3: UN S-528-0357 AR17a; Barnett (1953): 11; Shi (1947): 22. The same categorization of land types appears in Ma (1947): 1-2. On dike repairs, see MHD: 195, 196, 197, 214.

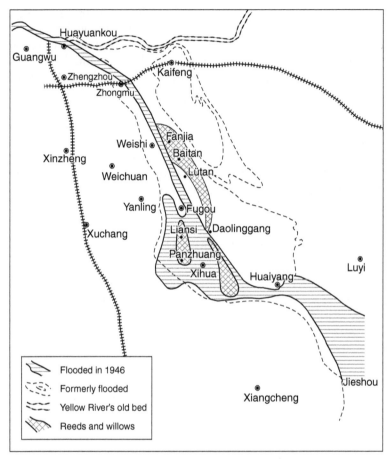

FIGURE 6.1 Land types in Henan's Yellow River flooded area, 1946

flourished because of the relative absence of people.[12] Disturbance of the flooded area's landscape due to warfare altered pre-existing ecological communities and led to secondary succession, as opportunist, fast-growing plant species colonized the habitat.

Willows and reeds overgrew a narrow strip of about 64,000 hectares east of the Yellow River in Weishi, Fugou, Xihua, and Taikang, where waters receded between 1939 and 1942.[13] This land was covered by "a thick jungle of willow seeding up to 8 feet tall and 1 to 2 inches in diameter, with swamp

---

[12] Thomas (2009).
[13] Chepil, "Report of Survey of the Yellow River Flooded Area"; Hamer, "Study of the Yellow River Flooded Area," 3. See also Han and Nan (1948): 6; Barnett (1953): 11; Ma (1947): 1–2; SJZHFZ 71 (May 19, 1947): 3; Wang Kejian (1947b): 2.

reed interspersed in the wetter places."[14] Dense expanses of willows and reeds appeared endless. In parts of Fugou, as one flood refugee recalled, "People went through the willow forests and could not walk out of them for a day and a half. The reed and club grass areas were also considerable, appearing in plots. Small ones were as large as a field, while big ones were several *mu*, ten or so *mu*, or several tens of *mu*. Of the 1,000 square kilometers of land in the entire county, aside from a few places that had not been flooded, most areas were in this condition. At that time, wild rabbits were especially numerous, looking for food or running away, rushing and jumping about freely."[15] For humans, these changes in the land posed an obstacle to socio-economic recovery. UNRRA surveys estimated that a farmer with twenty *mu* (1.3 hectares) would need to spend one hundred man days clearing overgrown land and preparing it for cultivation. Since most local residents were gone, human labor did not exist in sufficient quantities to reclaim the overgrown areas for agriculture.[16]

Lighter grasses grew on land that had been inundated until 1942–1945, but which was now dry, extending a fair distance east and west of the Yellow River's course. This grassy area comprised the largest percentage of land awaiting reclamation. Many people returned to these grass-covered lands immediately after the war against Japan ended. In other areas, which were still flooded, groups of several hundred refugees from the same native place camped on dikes for the winter. In a few places, people resettled small villages. Returned refugees lived in temporary huts made of sorghum stalks, which they plastered with mud. Most found work repairing dikes and pushing wheelbarrows, or made a living as petty merchants in towns and villages.[17]

Soon after Japan's military defeat, in March 1946 China once again plunged into the Civil War between the Nationalist regime and Chinese Communist Party (CCP). As noted in Chapter 3, the CCP's influence in eastern Henan expanded from 1944 onward. By the end of the Sino-Japanese War in 1945, the CCP controlled significant parts of Taikang, Huaiyang, Xihua, Fugou, and Weishi counties. Nationalist armies typically controlled towns and cities, while Communist forces held the surrounding countryside.[18] As of 1946, UNRRA sources indicated that the CCP claimed an area covering about 576,000 acres (233,099 hectares) – or about one-third of Henan's flooded area – inhabited by a population of 750,000–1,000,000. This section made up a block of about 30 square miles (over 77.6 square

---

[14] UNRRA, "Survey Report on Yellow River Flooded Area in Honan, Anhwei and Kiangsu" (July 4, 1947), 19: UN S-0528-0070.
[15] Song (1996): 153. See also Bo (1989): 127–128.
[16] Hamer, "Study of the Yellow River Flooded Area," 5; Ma (1947): 2; Xihua xian shizhi bianzuan weiyuanhui (1992): 118.
[17] Chepil, "Report of Survey of the Yellow River Flooded Area," 3–4; Chen (1947): 4–5; Shi (1947): 23. In early 1947 most of Xihua and Fugou counties were still flooded. Ma (1947): 2.
[18] Han and Nan (1948): 36.

kilometers), covering most of the willow and reed area, along with much of the land that was recently flooded but now cultivable.[19] At this point, the Communists did not exert particularly tight control over areas they claimed. CCP territory was "controlled by a government with no fixed headquarters, which moved frequently from one village to another and included one city of any size." Only limited radio and messenger communication existed with other Communist-held regions.[20] Most of Henan's flooded area had not undergone redevelopment. Depopulated territories, controlled by neither the Communists nor the Nationalists, fell between the lines and were accessible to both.[21] With much of the landscape depopulated and uncultivated, militaries had no incentive to control the territory directly.

For the few refugees who went back to the flooded area in 1945 and 1946, years of neglect generated what they perceived as tremendous ecological decline. Fugou experienced the heaviest damage, followed by Xihua and Taikang.[22] An eyewitness described former settlements in Fugou, where: "Some of the trees in the villages had been cut down, and some had their bark scraped off [for consumption during the 1942–43 famine] and died. As far as the eye could see, all that appeared before people's faces was a bleak, dreary, and ruined scene. The only clearly living things were the flocks of crows and magpies that flew up and down in the sky crowing wildly. At night foxes, badgers, grass foxes (*caohu*), and other wild animals appeared." Without humans and livestock, wild animal species flourished. For these creatures, war and its initial aftermath brought opportunity rather than destruction.[23]

Wherever the river's main channel passed – as in Weishi, Fugou, Xihua, and Taikang – huge amounts of silt had been deposited. Even after floods receded, sediments buried people's houses, buildings, possessions, and land. In Weishi the ground had risen four meters higher than before the flood.[24] Fields were buried beneath. Sediment deposits were especially thick in low-lying areas and places where the Yellow River had entered other waterways, obstructing the water's flow and causing suspended particles to settle. Such was the case in Fugou and Xihua, for instance, where the Jialu River entered the Ying River.[25]

Xihua lacked villages, trees, or any trace of people. As one former resident recalled, "Disaster victims who returned had no wells for drinking water, no homes to rest in, no draft animals for cultivating land, and no markets for

[19] "Outline of Plan for Rehabilitation of Yellow River Flooded Area," (1946), 5: UN S-1021 Box 55 File 4; Barnett (1953): 11.
[20] Barnett (1953): 9
[21] Ibid., 11.
[22] MHD: 196.
[23] Song (1996): 153.
[24] Liu (1990): 66.
[25] Xiong Benwen (1947b): 17; Han and Nan (1948): 20.

commerce, so their livelihoods were extremely difficult. Streams flowed all over, there were sandy lands everywhere, the wind blew up sandstorms, and travelling was difficult."[26] UNRRA observers marveled that Xihua had "nothing but farms buried '2 men deep' in silt, and scattered villages, some buried to their roofs." During the rainy season, waters covered the landscape. The ground stayed swampy for the rest of the year, but was dry enough to walk across.[27] Elderly people and others who had been unable to flee – numbering about 6,000 – gathered in Xihua's county seat. Together with returned refugees, the county's population amounted to around 15,000 people.[28] The few residents took "cart load after cart load of furniture and farm implements" to Zhoujiakou, where they sold these possessions to get enough money to feed their families. Others sold their landholdings and opted to work as menial laborers.[29] Swamps of stagnant water and carelessly deposited human waste littered Xihua's county seat. When hot weather arrived in the summer, malaria, typhoid, and cholera prevailed.[30] People lived in rooms with six inches of "slimy green water on the floor. Their beds are built up on bricks, their spinning wheels are also set up on piles of dirt and bricks."[31] Standing water covered much of Fugou's county seat as well.[32] During the flood season, people moved to higher ground and returned to houses that were left standing once the water receded.[33] Merchants in the Fugou county seat's previously bustling commercial district had closed up shop, leaving nothing more than a few peddlers along the streets.[34]

Throughout the flooded area, whole villages had moved onto dikes, living in acute congestion. "Houses have been constructed of straw and mud – floors are always wet. There is not even ground to bury the dead. There are no sanitary conditions whatsoever – the edge of the dike is a cesspool. It is bitter cold. People are without adequate clothing. One whole

---

[26] Li (2003): 116.
[27] "Memorandum from Mildred Bonnell to R. Van Hyning dated 3 April, 1946, Hsi Hua," attached to "UNRRA History – Honan Region," UN S1021 Box 58 File 7. Also quoted in UNRRA, "Honan weekly report of Office of the Economic and Financial Advisor" 3 (April 15, 1946): 1.
[28] Xiong Xiangyao (1947): 2–3.
[29] "Memorandum from Mildred Bonnell to R. Van Hyning." See also UNRRA, "Honan weekly report of Office of the Economic and Financial Advisor" 3 (April 15, 1946): 2.
[30] "Memorandum from Mildred Bonnell to R. Van Hyning"; UNRRA, "Honan weekly report of Office of the Economic and Financial Advisor" 4 (April 22, 1946): 2–3; "Preliminary Report on Flooded Area – Oct. 17–26" (November 11, 1946): UN S-0528-0541 A.R. 8.
[31] Robert Hart to Walter West, "Report for Flooded Area Committee, Field Trip. 16/3/47 – Report No. 3" (March 18, 1947): UN S-0528-0544 AR-17a.
[32] Fugou xian zhengxie wenshi ziliao weiyuanhui (2004): 121. See also Yang (1991).
[33] Harold T. Johnson to Lucile Chamberlin, "Survey and Report on Administrative District 9, South Honan" (June 1946), attached to "UNRRA History – Honan Region": UN S1021 Box 58 File 7.
[34] Fugou xian zhengxie wenshi ziliao weiyuanhui (2004): 121.

village is living packed on a bridge."³⁵ Dikes east of Zhoujiakou had "hundreds of mud and straw (or just straw) shelters grouped in small thin villages." The shanties formed inadequate barriers against winter weather, especially in their exposed position atop dikes. People living in the shelters found work constructing dikes, pushing wheelbarrows, or working as petty merchants in Zhoujiakou and villages south of the dike. On higher ground, people lived in houses with small areas of dry land adjacent to them, but had no means of support.³⁶ At least for some residents, food and other assistance provided by UNRRA-CNRRA partly alleviated this dire need.³⁷

ENERGY BALANCE AND THE DISEASE ENVIRONMENT

With resettlement slowly beginning in Henan, the return of refugees made it necessary to attend to their health and prevent disease outbreaks. As war transformed relationships between people and environment, disease-producing parasites took advantage of new opportunities to occupy ecological niches opened up by violent human action and the upheavals that it caused. Diseases drew additional energy away from the bodies of their human hosts. People's lives, to borrow William McNeill's phrase, were "caught in a precarious balance between the microparasitism of disease organisms and the macroparasitism of large-bodied predators," specifically human military systems.³⁸ Energy extracted by armies, like energy consumed by microparasites within human bodies, drew it away from the rural populace. That energy drain further decreased the surplus available for agricultural reconstruction.

More than eight years of warfare, a lack of food, and adverse living conditions seriously undermined human health and weakened immune systems. Population movements connected to the Civil War between the Nationalists and the Communists created additional difficulties. As an internal history of UNRRA put it, "With the return of large groups of war refugees to the crowded living conditions in the Flooded Area, and the mass movements of troops connected with the Civil War, the control and eradication of epidemic diseases was a very serious problem facing all health organization[s]."³⁹ UNRRA-CNRRA and Henan's health administration had to control the spread of disease, provide adequate medical care along repatriation routes, and re-establish health facilities.⁴⁰

---

[35] "Notes on Information from Dick Hillis, H.I.R.C. Regarding Conditions in parts of the Flooded Area, Honan, March, '46": UN S-0528-0543 A.R. 8. Report also reprinted in "Monthly Report, March 1946, Section 7 – Welfare Attachment (2)": UN S-0528-0540.
[36] "Preliminary Report on Flooded Area Survey – Oct. 17–26." See also Shi (1947): 23.
[37] Chen (1947): 5, 7; Fugou xian zhengxie wenshi ziliao weiyuanhui (2004): 131; MHD: 195–196.
[38] McNeill (1977): 24.
[39] "UNRRA History – Honan Region. Health Section," 17: UN S1021 Box 58 File 7.
[40] Ibid., 2–3. See also Zhang (1947): 19. By July 1947 "hygiene work teams" run by CNRRA's Henan branch office in Fugou and Zhoujiakou reportedly treated 340,000 people. Shi (1947): 23.

As refugees migrated in pursuit of the energy they needed to stay alive, human mobility facilitated spread of infection. Dissemination of diseases, as an October 1946 report observed, resulted from "a steady influx of displaced persons and political refugees" into Henan. Large bodies of Nationalist troops had been transferred into the province in connection with the military situation. The armies played a role in spreading disease microbes as well. Poor sanitary and living conditions existed in the flooded area, "and as a result a large proportion of the people are suffering from various forms of illnesses. With the arrival of cold weather and with the unavailability of food to the people for various reasons, economically and otherwise, malnutrition in serious proportions is expected."[41] Threat of epidemics was especially severe in Henan's main transport hubs. As a CNRRA report noted, "Zhengzhou is the crossing point of the Ping-Han and Long-Hai railways. After victory [in the war against Japan] demobilized personnel passed through in droves, so the population rapidly increased and epidemics could easily break out."[42]

Along with epidemics that spread among returning refugees, disease outbreaks frequently occurred among populations that remained in the flooded area. Though most residents boiled drinking water, people in some areas consumed it directly (most likely because they lacked fuel). As a result, cholera, dysentery, and typhoid spread due to water contamination. Poor housing and sanitary conditions were the norm. Wherever flooding and warfare made it impossible to cultivate land, poor nutrition existed. According to UNRRA reports, in some areas ongoing military operations linked to the Civil War "hindered peace-time cultivation of land, thus causing poor nutrition and in many instances contributing to the spread of illnesses."[43] Eye ailments affected 30–40 percent of the population and lung ailments another 10–20 percent.[44]

Typhus and relapsing fever posed the greatest threats. But the diseases "were controlled very effectively by the delousing of refugees entering the province at refugee stations, especially along the routes of repatriation. In 1946 only a small number of typhus and relapsing fever cases were reported."[45] Diphtheria, meningitis, and relapsing fever broke out sporadically. Inflammatory eye infections and skin conditions were common.

---

[41] "Health. Honan Regional Office Month of October, 1946": UN S-0528-0540. See also Tian (1946): 10.
[42] SJZHFZ 66 (April 14, 1947): 4.
[43] "Health. Honan Regional Office Month of October, 1946." See also SJZHFZ 18/19 (May 20, 1946): 11; Xiong Benwen (1947b):17.
[44] Shi (1947): 23.
[45] "UNRRA History – Honan Region. Health Section," 18. See also SJZHFZ 18/19 (May 20, 1946): 11; "Report and Recommendations on Joint Flooded Area Survey of Fukow Hsien by Representatives of CNRRA, Provincial Government, Hsien Governments & UNRRA 10 August to 10 September 1946": UN S-0528-324; Tian (1946):10.

Kala-azar (leishmaniasis), which even before the Sino-Japanese War had been a serious problem in Henan, was aggravated due to lack of medical facilities and drugs. Spread by the bite of a female sandfly, different forms of kala-azar lead to sores on the skin and mucous membranes, as well as potentially fatal damage to the immune system. Surveys carried out by UNRRA-CNRRA medical personnel estimated that half a million people in Henan were infected by kala-azar, but admitted that even larger unreported numbers suffered from the disease.[46] Wartime dislocation and mobility augmented the problem. Before the Japanese invasion, kala-azar infection was limited primarily to the easternmost section of Henan, adjacent to northern Jiangsu. As a CNRRA publication put it, "Since the War of Resistance, population movement, natural disasters, and human calamities have caused this disease to spread west, reaching the entire province."[47] In Henan's flooded area, kala-azar afflicted more than 30 percent of the population.[48]

Based on nutritional surveys that UNRRA-CNRRA conducted during spring 1946 in Fugou, "Over 60% of the people examined, which comprised largely children but also considerable numbers of adults, were found to be badly nourished. An additional 20–25% were in a very bad state of nourishment. Evidence of such malnutrition was shown by poor growth in the children, and by vitamin deficiency in general. The infants suffered particularly from inadequate nutrition."[49] Other reports claimed that just 2.6 percent of the flooded area's population had adequate nutrition, while 97.4 percent were malnourished. The young, elderly, and weak went hungry. Only men and women in the prime of life (*zhuangnian nan nü*) who took part in work relief had enough to eat.[50]

In March 1946, a smallpox outbreak occurred in Xinyang. A few weeks later the disease spread along Henan's transport routes and hit Zhengzhou. Local authorities took steps to contain the epidemic. UNRRA-CNRRA likewise dispatched supplies of smallpox vaccine and basic medical supplies to afflicted areas. During the outbreak in Zhengzhou, according to UNRRA's internal history, the city's refugee camp "was the focus of the infection. Quarantine was essential to avert the spread. Satisfactory control was accomplished and the incidence of the disease diminished rapidly." In June 1946, cholera outbreaks took place in Zhengzhou and Kaifeng as well, gradually spreading to five other cities. UNRRA took the lead implementing "stringent public health measures to cope with the rapid dissemination of the

---

[46] "UNRRA History – Honan Region. Health Section," 2–3. See also SJZFHZ 18/19 (May 20, 1946): 11; Xiong Benwen (1947b): 18; Shi (1947): 23. Kala-azar infection was particularly widespread in Xihua. SJZHFZ 66 (April 14, 1947): 2.
[47] Wang Boou (1947): 27.
[48] Tian (1946): 10.
[49] "Report and Recommendations on Joint Flooded Area Survey of Fukow Hsien."
[50] Tian (1946): 10.

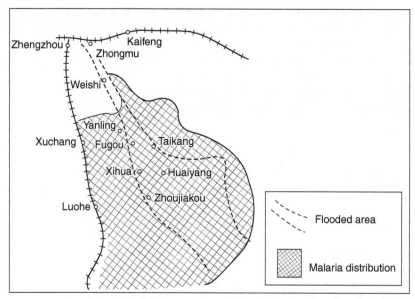

FIGURE 6.2 Malaria distribution in Henan Province, 1946–1947

disease" and "solicited the co-operation of local and military authorities in establishing public health measures to combat further spread of the disease."[51]

In late summer 1946, malaria reached epidemic proportions in the flooded area and contiguous parts of Henan, with over 10,000 people afflicted.[52] Incidence of malaria in Fugou reached fifty percent among the county seat's population and even higher in the villages.[53] Collapse of environmental infrastructure and flooding that resulted made people more susceptible to infection. As UNRRA reports noted, "In the Flooded Areas, swamps exist throughout the region, making breeding places for mosquitoes which has been one of the main causes of malaria in the area." With such extensive mosquito breeding grounds, effective anti-malarial control was beyond the means of authorities. Along with refugee movements, deployment of Nationalist troops to Henan to fight in the Civil War against the Communists helped spread the

---

[51] "UNRRA History – Honan Region. Health Section," 17–18; "Henan sheng di yi qu xing zheng ducha zhuanyuan jian baoan siling gongshu wu nian lai gongzuo jiyao." On smallpox, see SJZHFZ 18/19 (May 20, 1946): 11. On cholera, see SJZHFZ 32 (August 19, 1946): 2; SJFHFZ (September 16, 1946): 5; SJZHFZ 66 (April 14, 1947): 3; "Henan sheng sanshiqi nian bian xiaji fangyi jihua" (1948): ZMA 6-1-7 10.
[52] "Health. Honan Regional Office Month of October, 1946," "UNRRA History – Honan Region. Health Section," 18; SJZHFZ 18/19 (May 20, 1946): 11; SJFHFZ 48 (December 9, 1946): 2.
[53] "Report and Recommendations on Joint Flooded Area Survey of Fukow Hsien." See also "UNRRA History – Honan Region. Health Section," 2–3.

disease. Prevalence of the "malignant tertian form of malaria" was attributed to "the influx of large groups of refugees, as well as large bodies of troops from Yun-nan [Yunnan] Province, where this form of malaria commonly exists."[54] UNRRA- CNRRA personnel and other medical units investigated epidemic conditions and distributed anti-malarial drugs to institutions in the area.[55] Yet despite efforts to contain them, malaria and other infectious diseases continued to pose a grave threat to human health.

SOIL CONDITIONS IN THE FLOODED AREA

Since its diversion in 1938, the Yellow River deposited enormous amounts of sediment in eastern Henan, thoroughly altering the contours of the landscape. Water erosion turned places that were once high ground into lowlands; silt accumulation turned previously low-lying areas into high ground. At the same time, the Yellow River's sediments filled waterways like the Jialu and the Sha rivers. Due to the area's uneven topography and because silt clogged drainage systems, floods occurred whenever heavy rains fell.[56] Sediments raised land by one to five meters in some places, so territory impacted by flooding expanded as waters shifted from higher to lower terrain. Over an area 96.5 kilometers long and 16–40 kilometers wide in Weishi and Xihua, sediment deposits reached their greatest depth, averaging about three meters.[57]

Soil structures that existed in the flooded area after 1945 were an artifact created in large part by war-induced floods and sedimentation patterns. Postwar investigators explained that composition of sediment deposits was "extremely complicated." Some types of sediment were detrimental to agriculture and others beneficial, depending on specific conditions in a given locality and its distance from the river's main channel. For example, sediments consisted of gravel near the breach at Huayuankou; farther away they consisted of finer sands. Thickness of sediment deposits also varied, with Henan's flooded area tending to have thicker deposits than flooded areas in Anhui and Jiangsu. As soon as the flow of water from the Huayuankou breach slowed, the coarsest materials such as sand and gravel were deposited. As noted in a 1947 report on conditions in the flooded area,

---

[54] "Health. Honan Regional Office Month of October, 1946." See also "UNRRA History – Honan Region. Health Section," 18. On malaria in Yunnan, see Marks (2012): 245–246.
[55] "UNRRA History – Honan Region. Health Section," 18. With thousands of workers gathered at Huayuankou, additional health problems emerged. UNRRA advisors pointed out that sanitation, epidemic control, and adequate medical care were necessary among laborers compelled to live in close quarters while carrying out the project. "UNRRA History – Honan Region. Health Section," 2–3.
[56] Shi (1947): 22.
[57] UNRRA, "Survey Report on Yellow River Flooded Areas," 19. See also Chen (1947): 4; Wang (2003): 120.

coarse and poor-quality sediments sometimes made it impossible to return previously fertile land to agricultural production. But areas in which sedimentation made soil quality deteriorate were in the minority.

In most places, since this sediment was deposited the soil's productive power has not decreased. In some places, because loamy sands (*fenshatu*) and clay soil have accumulated to form layers, in the future after it is plowed the soil's physical properties will definitely be especially suited for crop production. At the same time, in some areas, because of the accumulation of this new mud and sand (*nisha*) brought from the upper reaches of the Yellow River, the villagers say that even if crops are planted and fertilizer is not used it will not lead to decreased crop production. Therefore, most sediment conditions, except for a very small part, are not as bad as most imagine.

Years of sediment accumulation made the surface soil hard and firm, so it needed to be plowed and loosened "to take advantage of the land's fertility and make crops produce the highest yields." Due to the scarcity of draft animals, however, plowing had "become a big problem."[58]

Some commentators worried that sediments deposited by the Yellow River consisted entirely of sands, and once they were eroded by winds during the winter and early-spring dry season deserts would form. But Chinese soil specialists cautioned against this view: "Sediments in the flooded area are of different types and are not only sandy soils. Moreover, wind erosion of sandy soil is not as serious as imagined, and the area of sandy soil distribution in the flooded area is not extremely large either."[59] The threat of "sandization" (*shahua*) – deposition of sandy soils susceptible to wind erosion, which tend to blow and form dunes – was real in parts of Henan's flooded area, but not new. In the words of one UNRRA agricultural rehabilitation officer, "The land that appeared after the flood waters receded is exactly the same as all of the Honan [Henan] plain. It had the same origin and was deposited in the same way. It was not 'a new and different land raw and dangerous, a potential dust bowl and desert' as they say."[60] Sedimentation did not harm soil quality everywhere. Much of the landscape was well suited for cultivation. In some locales, new sediment deposits actually alleviated problems that had previously existed, "such as poor drainage, excess salt and heavy clay areas" by covering land with several feet of good soil.[61] UNRRA reports claimed that much of the area between Weishi and Xihua was "probably more potentially

---

[58] Quotations are from Chen (1947): 4. See also Han and Nan (1948): 45; Xiong Benwen (1947b): 17.
[59] Xi et al. (1947): 33. See also Zhu and He (1947): 110; Han and Nan (1948): 18; Wang Kejian (1947c): 2.
[60] John H. Shirkey to William J. Green, "Evaluation of the Report prepared by Professor A.A. Stone and Professor H.F. McCaulley" (June 2, 1946): UN S-528-0356.
[61] UNRRA, "Survey Report on Yellow River Flooded Areas," 19; Shirkey to Greene, "Evaluation of the Report." New sediments of about two meters in depth covered many areas in Zhongmu that were previously sand dunes, eliminating the threats that sand storms posed to nearby fields. Zhu and He (1947): 107.

productive than before the Yellow River floods." Sediments deposited north of the Sha River near Zhoujiakou would also be beneficial for wheat production.[62]

On the whole, the Henan flooded area's soils experienced major changes, but new sediments were of various types. According to postwar investigations, "One type is alluvial land (*yuni zhi di*). It is the richest and most fertile, most suitable for cultivation, and its area is also the widest. This situation is just like Africa's Nile River. This is the floodwaters' only gift. One kind is sandy land. All of it is mostly in places where riverbeds have dried up or in areas near them. This kind of sandy land is not suitable for planting and it has created a serious problem in the flooded area. Because this sandy land will gradually expand, forests should be planted to prevent its area from spreading and expanding ... Another type is saline soil, and saline soil is also unsuitable for planting." Local residents explained that in places where water flowed rapidly, sediments had turned into sandy land and where water flowed slowly they did not. In limited areas that water had flowed through and then flowed back into, soil was mostly alkaline.[63]

The texture of sediments varied considerably depending on the depth of the Yellow River's waters and their flow velocity, the physical terrain, and proximity to the riverbed. In general, sandy soils were deposited near the river's main channel, where its rapid flow removed fine material and left sands behind. Some coarse sand was stratified in the deep sub-soils. But most soils in Henan's flooded area tended to have a fairly uniform texture ranging from fine to very fine sandy loam and did not form dunes. Sands tended to be coarser upstream, where rapidly moving waters deposited larger suspended particles. Sands became finer downstream, where slower-moving waters deposited smaller particles. Stretches of coarse sands were found in upper reaches of the flooded area adjoining the channels of large watercourses, such as the Jialu River. Areas farther away from main channels tended to have clay soils. Coarse sands that would drift with the wind and create sandstorms existed mainly near the flood's source at Huayuankou or at bends in the river's meandering channel. The largest stretch of sandy land covered a relatively narrow area between Huayuankou and Zhongmu.[64] In those territories, "The land is poor indeed,

---

[62] Chepil, "Report of Survey of the Yellow River Flooded Area," 7. See also Todd (1949): 54; Huang and Wang (1954): 316.

[63] Shi (1947): 22–23.

[64] Chepil, "Report of Survey of the Yellow River Flooded Area," 8; John H. Shirkey to Walter West, "Recording Some Observations and Recommendations Made During a Trip to Chengchow, Hsu-chang, Yen-ling, Fu-kou, Weishih, Hsi-hua, Chou-chia-k'ou, Lo-ho and Vicinities, 24 February to 3 March, 1947"(March 11, 1947), 4: UN S-0528-0544 A.R.-17a; UNRRA, "Survey Report on Yellow River Flooded Areas," 19; Xi et al. (1947): 31, 33–34; Zhu and He (1947): 110, 111; Han and Nan (1948): 18–20; Todd (1949): 54; Xi (1950): 103; Luo (1953): 242–243, 246, 247, 252–253; Xia (1953): 245; Huang and Wang (1954): 314–316; Wang (2003): 120; Xihua xian shizhi bianzuan weiyuanhui (1992): 106–107.

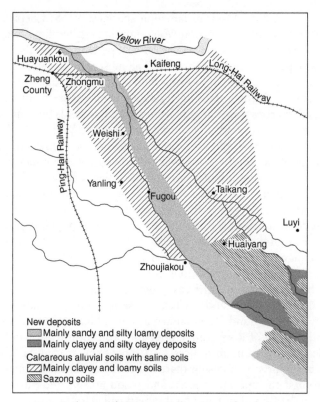

FIGURE 6.3 Soil map of Henan's Yellow River flooded area, 1947

and farmers' battle is against sand driven by the wind."[65] Dust storms near the breach at Huayuankou, as O. J. Todd recalled, sometimes grew so severe that workers had to "take cover behind the stacks of kaoliang stalks hauled in for dike revetment."[66] Three-quarters of the land in Zhongmu was "derelict owing to it being covered by drifting sand. Some could never be cultivated, but quite a lot could be used if some very hard work were put into it." Quality of arable lands in Zhongmu as a whole varied. Some were easy to cultivate, but some consisted of heavy, sticky clay that was not easy to farm. Deeply embedded roots filled unattended lands, making cultivation difficult.[67]

Soils tended to have an erosive quality, but with eastern Henan's level topography water erosion did not pose a serious problem. Given the depth of fertile

---

[65] Jean Liu, "Condition of the Flooded District of Chung-mou" (May 8, 1946): UN S-0528-0536 Folder 34. See also Fu (1947): 24–26; Ma (1947): 3; Zhu and He (1947): 107–108, 110.
[66] Todd (1949): 44.
[67] Liu, "Condition of the Flooded District of Chung-mou." See also Ma (1947): 3; Zhu and He (1947): 107–108, 110.

soil deposits, as UNRRA soil reclamation specialist W. S. Chepil explained, removal of surface soils via erosion would not damage fertility. "On the other hand," he noted, "wind erosion will be serious, particularly on the more sandy soils unless steps are taken to control it. The most serious damage from wind erosion is the cutting action of blowing sand and the consequent destruction of growing crops."[68] With virtually no vegetation left in dried streambeds after the wheat and other crops were harvested, erosion of fine sands by winds presented "a serious menace to good agricultural land nearby." These lands had low agricultural productivity and sometimes could not be cultivated. Streambed sands, susceptible to wind erosion when dry, were the most serious problem, though sandy soils caused similar difficulties in other areas as well.[69]

Shortages of energy intensified erosion, as people removed vegetation cover as quickly as it could grow. In Chepil's view, "The greatest handicap to permanent control of sands is the intense pressure of population for agricultural land. Every bit of vegetation that is grown is utilized either for food or fuel. Consequently, little organic matter is returned to the land, except in a digested form. Under such conditions, the land is denuded, and the soil, unless protected by some means, drifts easily with the wind."[70] With all vegetative materials needed for fuel and shelter, "these materials, including roots, are removed from the ground. The maintenance of a high content of soil organic matter and the use of a vegetative litter for protection from wind is almost impossible under the circumstances."[71] Chinese soil specialists echoed their foreign counterparts by advising that, "The way to fix sand dunes is first to strictly prohibit the cutting of grass and wood and secondarily to promote afforestation."[72] Chepil and other soil experts called for extensive tree planting to create windbreaks and protect against erosion. Planting trees held particular importance "in the areas adjoining the wandering courses followed by the swifter flowing flood waters where the soil has a high sand fraction."[73] Chepil favored planting willows because floods would not destroy them, but also recommended other trees that would have more value as timber.[74] Henan's farmers had practiced this system of wind erosion control "for many generations," he observed, so it was "definitely beyond the experimental stage."[75]

---

[68] Chepil, "Report of Survey of the Yellow River Flooded Area," 9. See also Xi et al. (1947): 35.
[69] An Han, H. K. Fu, and W. S. Chepil to Dr. P. C. Ma, "Recommended plan for soil conservation work in the Yellow River Flooded Area" (n.d.): UN S-1021 Box 55 File 4. See also Huang and Wang (1954): 327.
[70] Chepil (1949): 127.
[71] Ibid., 129. See also Fu (1947): 25–26.
[72] Zhu and He (1947): 115.
[73] Shirkey to West, "Recording Some Observations and Recommendations." See also Fu (1947): 24–26; Han, Fu, and Chepil to Ma, "Recommended plan for soil conservation work"; Xi et al. (1947): 35.
[74] Chepil, "Report of Survey of the Yellow River Flooded Area," 9.
[75] Chepil (1949): 128.

According to Chepil, lands in the flooded area tended to have too much moisture to grow summer crops. Sorghum grew well in wet soils, but beans and cotton did poorly. Winter wheat encountered few difficulties since farmers raised it in the dry season when waters receded.[76] Soils and sub-soils were porous, so drainage was not a pressing concern. Old stream channels would facilitate drainage as well. "The whole area, though remarkably level, has a slightly sloping topography and very few extensive depressions actually exist. Because of high soil porosity, tile drainage is unnecessary."[77] Yet during heavy summer rains drainage problems would become "particularly serious."[78]

Wind erosion threatened to grow more severe after waters receded. In dry farming areas such as Henan, as Chinese soil specialists pointed out, "after the Yellow River floodwaters are drained water sources will be lacking and irrigation problems will also occur. The Henan flooded area's sediments are relatively light and it is easy for the water to leach out. If there is dryness it will lead to wind erosion. Moreover, supplying sufficient water for dry farming will also turn into a serious problem in this area. Therefore, in the area returned to cultivation, using the Yellow River channel that was created this time as an irrigation channel will also be a good policy. Digging wells will also be a good method for resolving it."[79]

Henan's flooded region had one large saline area, covering approximately 1,200 acres (485.6 hectares) about 3.2 kilometers southwest of Fugou. Only backwaters from the floods inundated this area, which adjoined highlands near Fugou, so it had no silt deposits. Groundwater was one to three feet deep. Seepage from the Shuangji River made it even harder to leach out excess salt. Farmers used "the soil and the groundwater for extracting table salt, which is reported to be of poor quality." Deep drains were needed to lower the water table and remove excess salts. Soil was fairly permeable to water, so if the water table were lowered four or more feet rainfall could leach out the salt.[80] Other saline areas appeared on sandy soils in parts of Zhongmu, Weishi, and Xihua during the spring dry season. Though present only in limited territories, salinization damaged immature sprouts and impeded crop development, thereby decreasing sorghum, millet, and legume harvests on affected lands.[81]

Writing in 1947, UNRRA investigators warned that lack of organic matter posed "one of the limiting factors in producing good crops in this area. The weed and grass growth on much of the land has been beneficial in this respect

---

[76] Chepil, "Report of Survey of the Yellow River Flooded Area," 8.
[77] Ibid.
[78] W. S. Chepil, "What Have I Done in China?" (September 25, 1947): UN S-1021 Box 55 File 4.
[79] Xi et al. (1947): 34–35.
[80] UNRRA, "Survey Report on Yellow River Flooded Areas," 19; Xi et al. (1947): 30.
[81] Huang and Wang (1954): 316, 328.

until farmers can return to their normal use of compost." Cultivating legume crops promised to increase wheat production somewhat the following year.[82] Chepil, for his part, held an optimistic view of the soil's ability to recover fertility. Sediments basically consisted of the same soil types that existed before the war, but lacked "what little organic matter the original soil had." Judging from current crop conditions, sediments were not highly productive. But Chepil did not expect low productivity to last long.[83] Sediments seriously lacked nitrogen, but had the potential to regain fertility. Again, Chepil expected lack of nitrogen to be a temporary condition.

If conditions are anything like those in some other sub-humid regions of the world, there should be a gradual increase in nitrogen in the surface soil, even without addition of fertilizer or leguminous crops. This increase is the result of bacterial action, whereby nitrogen is transferred from the soil air and fixed in dead bacterial bodies from which it is then extracted by growing crops. The North China soils are highly productive after intensive growing of crops and virtually complete removal of every scrap of organic matter for thousands of years. During the whole course of history no nitrogenous fertilizers were brought in from outside regions, yet leaching away by floods must have been enormous. Few leguminous crops were grown to fix the nitrogen symbiotically, yet the nitrogen content in the soil must have remained reasonably high, judging by good crops that have and are being grown. All these conditions indicate that non-symbiotic fixation of nitrogen must be very high in this region.

Nevertheless, Chepil expected nitrogen fertilizers to be of great importance for the first few crops grown after land was drained. After this initial period, nitrogen fertilizers might not prove necessary.[84] Indeed, application of imported synthetic fertilizers helped compensate to some extent for lack of organic matter. During 1946–1947, UNRRA-CNRRA distributed 1,850 tons of ammonium nitrate and ammonium phosphate fertilizers, which were applied to over 20,730 hectares of land in Henan's flooded area.[85] Local farmers, for their part, expected that with farming and composting it would "take 10 to 20 years of good farming and addition of humus to bring the production of this rather sandy land up to good production."[86] Sustained human labor and investment were needed to rebuild soil fertility.

---

[82] UNRRA, "Survey Report on Yellow River Flooded Areas," 19.
[83] Chepil, "Report of Survey of the Yellow River Flooded Area," 7.
[84] Ibid., 7–8.
[85] Wan (1947b): 40. See also Wang Kejian (1947c): 8. In addition to synthetic fertilizer, CNRRA's Henan branch office also provided farmers with financial subsidies to purchase fertilizer. Han and Nan (1948): 103–105.
[86] Shirkey to West, "Recording Some Observations and Recommendations," 4. Shirkey later predicted that it would take eight to ten years "of good farming and addition of compost to bring the new land up to the productive capacity it previously had." The land produced legume crops well in the first year and "succeedingly better yields of cereal crops in rotation." Shirkey to Green, "Evaluation of the Report."

OBSTACLES TO AGRICULTURAL PRODUCTION

Regardless of soil quality, inadequate organic energy sources hampered all efforts to resume cultivation. First, there was an extraordinary shortage of seed. When harvests failed due to flood or drought, residents consumed seed reserves as food.[87] With seed unavailable, farmers could only plant small amounts of land. Large commercial centers in Henan had seed wheat, but most people did not have money or credit to purchase it.[88] UNRRA investigators claimed that in 1946 the Henan flood area required almost 4,600 tons of seed for land currently under cultivation.[89] To help restore production, UNRRA and CNRRA purchased seed from elsewhere in China to loan to farmers.[90] The first round of seed distribution came in fall 1946, when CNRRA's Henan branch office provided almost 473,250 kilograms of wheat seed to more than 20,200 households in Fugou, Xihua, and Huaiyang.[91]

War-induced flood and famine also led to heavy losses of animal power. Floods killed an estimated 220,000 draft animals and in 1942–1943 famine victims slaughtered or sold off thousands more.[92] By the Sino-Japanese War's end, villages with 100 households had fewer than ten draft animals, so cultivation mostly relied upon human labor power.[93] In Henan's flooded area, "Villagers who after the disaster kept cattle and other draft animals either sold them to exchange for food for humans, or had no way to obtain feed for them and all they could do was sell them." Draft animal losses came to 50–60 percent for Henan's flooded area as a whole, but reached around 90 percent in some locales.[94] In Fugou a single draft animal existed for every three or four families, giving them only half the number needed for farm production.[95] All over Henan, shortages of draft animals presented "the biggest hindrance towards getting spring planting in swing."[96] Henan as a whole had

---

[87] "Preliminary Report on Flooded Area Survey," Han and Nan (1948): 44.
[88] Chepil, "Report of Survey of the Yellow River Flooded Area," 7. See also Tian (1946): 11; Chen (1947): 5.
[89] Hamer, "A Study of the Yellow River Flooded Area," 9.
[90] "Preliminary Report on Flooded Area Survey," Wan (1947a): 8. See also Tian (1946): 11.
[91] In spring 1947, the office provided over 1,384,840 kilograms of seed for summer crops to 102,073 households in Zhongmu, Weishi, Yanling, Fugou, Xihua, Huaiyang, Shangqiu, and Shangshui counties. An additional 3,073,080 kilograms of wheat seed was distributed in fall 1947 to 193,645 households in those counties. Han and Nan (1948): 98, 99. Comparable figures on seed loans appear in Wan (1947b): 39.
[92] "Henan sheng zhanshi sunshi diaocha baogao," 15.
[93] Wang Kejian (1947b): 3.
[94] Chen (1947): 5.
[95] UNRRA, "Survey Report on Yellow River Flooded Areas," 5; Han and Nan (1948): 44.
[96] Community markets run by dealers carried out small-scale exchanges of animals. Prices ranged from 50,000 yuan for a "small and unserviceable donkey," to 150,000 yuan for a "large oxen in good condition," to 70,000–100,000 yuan for cows. UNRRA, "Honan weekly report of Office of the Economic and Financial Advisor" 2 (April 8, 1946): 3. UNRRA investigations stated that the Henan flooded area was in need of about 200,000 head, but

"greatly reduced numbers of animals," with shortfalls in some districts of 80 percent or more.[97] Prior to the war against Japan, according to one CNRRA survey, Henan had approximately 3,273,000 draft animals, which was an inadequate number. After 1945, the total number of livestock in Henan fell to 2,126,000 – a decline of nearly 1,147,000 animals. Due to postwar absence of livestock, workers only had the capacity to haul 300 tons of sorghum stalks and willow branches per day to Huayuankou for the breach closure project.[98] As CNRRA personnel put it, "Farmers' primary motive force for tilling, draft animals, are extremely scarce and farmers who have returned to cultivation do not have the power to plow and weed. As a result, many fields have turned into wasteland, which has a great influence on grain production."[99] Draft animals brought "fancy prices" and the average farmer could not afford to purchase the few that were available. Many draft animals had been driven out of the province because people could not afford to keep them. The farmers who had animals often sold them to get money to buy grain and pay tax levies. And in some parts of Henan, rinderpest epidemics further aggravated cattle shortages.[100]

Farmers were seldom able to plow their land in the usual manner. Instead, they prepared the land with hoes or digging hooks and sowed it with hand-pulled drills.[101] In areas planted to winter wheat in 1946, "The method was to use 3-run seeders, pulled by hand (generally five people pulling and one holding the seeder)." Land in the flooded area was "in the main bare," but a small proportion that was dry enough to plant had been seeded to winter wheat "in anticipation of reaping a harvest before the coming of the next summer flood." Most people lived on adjacent high ground and only went to their fields to till the soil and remove the harvest. Floodwaters often drowned crops, depriving people of food reserves.[102] Wartime floods washed away irrigation channels and sediments buried wells, jeopardizing the area's water supplies for irrigation as well as drinking.[103] With draft animals virtually nonexistent, human muscle power was the energy source that powered all farm work.[104] Residents tried to plant land that was no longer underwater by pulling seeders through muddy soil and putting in seed before the ground

the general postwar shortage of draft animals made it hard to find sources to replace those that had been lost. Hamer, "Study of the Yellow River Flooded Area," 7.

[97] D.K. Farris, "Report on General Conditions in Honan-Province, Dec. 24 1945," 6: UN S-0528-0071.
[98] Wang (2004): 129. See also Wang (1948): 6.
[99] Wan (1947a): 10. See also Xu (1983): 294.
[100] Farris, "Report on General Conditions in Honan-Province," 6.
[101] Chepil, "Report of Survey of the Yellow River Flooded Area," 3; UNRRA, "Survey Report on Yellow River Flooded Areas," 5; Han and Nan (1948): 44; Fugou xianzhi zong bianji shi (1986): 99.
[102] Chepil, "Report of Survey of the Yellow River Flooded Area," 3–4.
[103] Tian (1946): 11; Chen (1947): 5; Han and Nan (1948): 45.
[104] UNRRA, "Survey Report on Yellow River Flooded Areas," 5; Zuo (1947): 11; Han and Nan (1948): 44.

was dry. "People pulling" was common "since the shortage of animals – the almost non-existence of work-animal stock – meant that manpower had taken over the function of farm animals."[105]

Farm tool shortages existed throughout the area as well. Each village typically had fewer than five or six plows and harrows. On average, not even one hoe existed per household. Most people wielded only small metal shovels.[106] Fugou suffered acute scarcity, with fewer than eighty plows in the entire county and only one hoe for every five people. Farmers had plows and harrows for only half their draft animals.[107] As UNRRA reports advised, "Animals and implements are urgently needed in many areas, but people are willing to undergo the lack of these in preference to food, clothing, and seeds. Plows are not required unless animals are supplied with them – as the draft is too great to be pulled by hand. Some cultivating plows have been pulled by hand, but in the majority of cases, where no animals are available, the land was seeded directly without previous cultivation. Yields are expected to be low on this account."[108] Absence of livestock and tools – along with severe lack of human labor – made intensive cultivation impossible.[109]

To alleviate shortages, UNRRA agricultural specialists arranged to purchase farm animals from neighboring areas and supplied large numbers of farm tools. UNRRA-CNRRA cattle buyers had to bargain hard to avoid paying high livestock prices. Central pools under CNRRA-appointed directors loaned cattle to farmers, who returned them to the pool for care and feeding. Unfortunately, many of the farm tools that UNRRA imported did not fit local standards and had to be refashioned. For this reason, setting up blacksmith shops in villages and supplying them with materials for making tools proved more beneficial. Although efforts by UNRRA and CNRRA helped farmers resume cultivating some of their land, benefits were slow in coming. In formerly flooded areas in Henan that returned to cultivation by the end of 1946, agricultural production levels remained far below potential.[110] Fields had been planted up to the river, but crop yields were marginal.[111]

FUEL AND TIMBER SHORTAGES

Exploiting biomass energy stored in wild vegetation that colonized the flooded area's landscape gave residents access to badly needed income.

---

[105] "Preliminary Report on Flooded Area Survey."
[106] Wang Kejian (1947b): 3; Wang Kejian (1947c): 8.
[107] UNRRA, "Survey Report on Yellow River Flooded Areas," 5; Zuo (1947): 11; Han and Nan (1948): 44.
[108] Chepil, "Report of Survey of the Yellow River Flooded Area," 7.
[109] Hamer, "A Study of the Yellow River Flooded Area," 4; Song (1996): 153.
[110] Hamer, "A Study of the Yellow River Flooded Area," 4; Wan (1947a): 2; Song (1996): 153. In 1946, UNRRA provided 500,000 tools to the flooded area's inhabitants. See Tian (1946): 11.
[111] Johnson to Chamberlin, "Survey and Report on Administrative District 9."

Without work animals or farm implements, and with hardly any cash reserves, residents had to "resort to hauling firewood into Kaifeng in order to purchase food and build up a little capital for rehabilitating their land." Farmers who started to bring land back under cultivation had to "content themselves with clearing off knee-deep rushes and cat-tails that have overgrown the land, and with sowing individual seeds without plowing."[112] As another report described, "Most people do not have the ability to cultivate because they lack tools and animal power, and can only rely on fishing and cutting grass for their livelihood.... Since everyone cuts grass, the grass on the riverbank's sandy embankments has almost all been cut and gathered. As far as the eye can see in all directions, there is bare desert embellished with a few grass shanties in which three to five people reside."[113]

In Henan's flooded area, as UNRRA personnel reported, "As fast as the grass and straw grows in the area it is plucked, blade by blade, by men, women and children, bundled up and carried 20 to 30 miles on wheel barrows to be sold in the larger market towns outside the area."[114] Refugees who came back to Fugou in 1946 cleared reeds, willows, and other overgrowth. Some Fugou residents sold willow branches and grasses as fuel in Yanling, Xuchang, Huaiyang, and Taikang.[115] Others cut willows and grasses and sold them in Fugou and Kaifeng, "where they returned enough to support the refugees while the crops grew."[116] Some dug up old timbers and trees from beneath sediments, selling them in Fugou's county seat to get money to buy food.[117] Xihua residents dried and sold willow branches that were not needed for dike repairs as fuel, or dismantled houses and sold furniture for seed.[118]

Sizable markets existed for these energy sources. Due to coal shortages in Henan, the province was "rapidly being denuded of trees and scrub for fuel and even locomotives are being fired with wood."[119] When the Japanese occupied Fugou's county seat in 1944–1945, Japanese and collaborationist armies tore down a Confucian temple for wood, while local people looted and sold the cypress trees that grew within it.[120] After 1945, people cut whatever small trees and shrubs they could find to meet fuel needs. Flood refugees who flocked to dry areas in Zhongmu from other villages in the vicinity gathered

[112] UNRRA, "Honan weekly report of the Economic and Financial Advisor" 9 (May 28, 1946): 3–4. On fuel gathering, see Chen (1947): 5.
[113] Tian (1946): 10.
[114] Robert Hart to Walter West, "Report on Field Trip to Flooded Area, 16 to 26 March, 1947" (March 28, 1947): UN S-0528-0543, A.R. 8.
[115] Fugou xianzhi zong bianji shi (1986): 99; Bo (1989): 127–128.
[116] UNRRA, "Survey Report on Yellow River Flooded Areas," 5.
[117] Chepil, "Report of Survey of the Yellow River Flooded Area," 4.
[118] Han (1947): 18.
[119] "Monthly Report, March 1946, Section 11 – Intelligence," UN S-0528-0540. On railroads burning wood, see D. K. Ferris to E. Gale (December 10, 1945): UN S-0528-0071.
[120] Fugou xian zhengxie wenshi ziliao weiyuanhui (2004): 123.

The Beginnings of Post-Conflict Recovery 195

straw and brushwood to sell. Most children spent their time "gathering straw and sticks for fuel."[121]

Selling fuel held similar importance throughout the flooded area. In the words of a UNRRA representative, "At the present moment, instead of men being engaged in the cultivation of their land, they are gathering sticks from the willows which cover their land and bring them into Kaifeng by wheelbarrow, a distance of 30 miles. A complete operation of one journey takes approximately a week. 10–15 men make the journey each day." Fuel sold for 20 yuan per *jin* (1 *jin* = 500 grams) in the villages, but fetched 100 yuan per *jin* in Kaifeng. At these prices, fuel gathering could earn them approximately 14,000 yuan per week. Income from fuel gathering gave residents capital to purchase farming implements, seeds, animals, and other necessities.[122] People ate sorghum and sweet potatoes they were able to purchase by selling fuel.[123] It was vital for relief agencies to distribute food to returned refugees and their dependents, as CNRRA personnel put it, "so that people in the prime of their life can concentrate on dedicating their power to the work of resuming cultivation. Otherwise, if people in the prime of their life have to cut firewood every day to exchange for grain to support their families, how will they have the mental and physical power to fully engage in resuming cultivation?"[124]

Widespread shortages of building materials existed, with almost no bricks or timber available. Refugees who had returned home "have no way to make a living and many dig up bricks and wood from under the sediment and take them to Xuchang for sale. When construction materials are needed they are bought back from Xuchang." Relief personnel puzzled over how to end this "contradictory state of affairs."[125] Residents dug into sediment deposits and excavated roof timbers "by the hundred." In the southern part of Henan's flooded area, people took timbers to Zhoujiakou and then on to Louhe, where merchants purchased them at 60 yuan per *jin*. In the northern part of the flooded area timbers were often used as fuel. Wheelbarrow convoys exported tens of thousands of roofing tiles and burnt bricks. "Trees which have been buried by the silt are being excavated and chopped up for fuel – or coffins." All in all, UNRRA reports estimated that "at least 1,000 tons of building materials are being exported DAILY." It made little sense for relief agencies to import building materials when people were exporting them to earn their livelihood.[126]

---

[121] Liu, "Condition of the Flooded District."
[122] Robert Hart to Lucille L. Chamberlin, "Transport and Fuel Cooperative" (September 6, 1946): UN S-0528-0543 A.R. 8. See also "Monthly Report, September 1946, Land Reclamation in the Flooded Area."
[123] UNRRA, "Survey Report on Yellow River Flooded Areas," 6.
[124] Chen (1947): 5.
[125] Ma (1947): 2–3.
[126] Robert Hart to Flooded Area Committee, "Progress Report" (December 11, 1946): UN S-0528-0078. See also Shi (1947): 23.

TOWARD RECOVERY

Because reclaiming the abandoned land in Henan was "limited by human labor power and financial power," UNRRA-CNRRA devoted considerable effort to accomplishing this task.[127] In the few locales where UNRRA had set up tractor projects to assist with land reclamation, energy derived from fossil fuels powered recovery. At the bequest of the Nationalist regime and the Henan provincial government, in May 1946 UNRRA began to import tractors to plow land in the flooded area and return it to agricultural production. CNRRA's Henan branch office started a tractor station at Fanjia in the willow-and-weed area of Weishi, followed by another south of Fugou on the edge of the territory that remained flooded.

Land had to be cleared before it could be planted, but labor was insufficient. Tractors were brought in to fulfill this task until the necessary workforce was present. The first 57 tractors reached Henan's flooded area in 1946, and by February 1947 it had over 150 tractors divided into three teams. There were few residents at first, but after this tractor project got underway people started to come back. As they returned, villagers were encouraged to clear stumps so that the tractors could operate without obstruction. All in all, UNRRA shipped 264 tractors to the flooded area, with about 200 of them participating in reclamation activities. Tractors could plow four hectares per day, which saved a great deal of labor power. By the start of 1947, the tractors had already helped reclaim several thousand hectares of land, and the figure eventually reached far higher.[128]

Nevertheless, tractor teams operated on only a small portion of the flooded area's land. Lack of fossil fuels and qualified repair personnel hampered their effectiveness. Without adequate transport capacity available, it was impossible to obtain gasoline for tractors and they could not operate at full capacity.[129] As a result, land reclamation depended largely upon draft animal power. In October 1946, the CNRRA Henan branch office established a "cattle plowing station" in Fugou, buying 83 head of cattle for that purpose. In March 1947, after these livestock plowed over 1,030 hectares, CNRRA sold the animals to local farmers at their original price. In addition, the Henan branch office utilized work relief projects to assist people engaged in the preliminary work of land reclamation. These projects employed returned refugees in Xihua and elsewhere to reclaim over 2,570 hectares, while in Xihua, Weishi, Fugou, Zhongmu, and Huaiyang material assistance from CNRRA reportedly helped bring more than 66,660 hectares back under cultivation.[130]

---

[127] Wan (1947a): 9.
[128] Ma (1947): 1–2; Han and Nan (1948): 106–107; Barnett (1953): 20–21, 24, 26, 32–34, 44–45. See also Tian (1946): 11; Wan (1947a): 9–10; Wang Kejian (1947c): 3, 7; Shi (1947): 23; Ren (1991): 173–178; MHD: 227.
[129] Tucker (2005): 46–47.
[130] Ma (1947): 1–2; Han and Nan (1948): 106; Barnett (1953): 20–21, 24, 26, 32–34, 44–45. See also Tian (1946): 11; Wan (1947a): 9–10; Wang Kejian (1947c): 3, 7; Shi (1947): 23; MHD: 227.

Even with the energy subsidies provided by UNRRA-CNRRA, however, refugees only gradually trickled back to the flooded area and land reclamation proceeded at a slow pace. In spring 1946, for instance, a quarter of the land in Zhongmu – mostly the property of "wealthy men" – had been returned to cultivation. Landowners moved and took up residence a few kilometers away when floods occurred. They had returned to cultivate their land for the first time during the previous year, bringing animals and farming implements with them. The fortunate ones could gather their crops before the floodwaters returned and they had to leave. The rest of Zhongmu's populace lived in villages. Some had tools and animals; others borrowed them. All farmers had to race to bring in crops before floods devoured them.[131] In June 1946, it was reported that, "Labor is in short supply in the whole area at present, and all members of farm families are working long hours in the fields and on the threshing floors."[132]

Despite these obstacles, the rebuilding of agricultural landscapes gradually started to materialize. In some parts of the flooded area, recovery started even before the war against Japan had ended. With the Chinese Communist Party emerging as an influential force in Henan's flooded area after 1944, cadres aimed to mobilize the local populace via relief, mutual aid, and land reclamation schemes. As soon as floodwaters receded, the CCP's "military work teams" called on displaced people to come back and farm. To induce refugees to return, the CCP loaned them seed grain. In Odoric Wou's assessment, this seed loan program "greatly cemented" relations between the Communists and flood victims, strengthening the CCP and its collective defense movement.[133] According to Wou, from 1944–1945 the CCP mobilized farmers in Henan's flooded area to bring almost 670 hectares of land back into production.[134] Given their modest scale, however, these early recovery efforts made only a small dent in the huge amount of land that still lay waste.

In late 1945, people in Communist-controlled areas of Fugou built a 50 kilometer dike to protect farmland against floods. In addition to repairing a breach that occurred at Lütan in 1944, the local CCP leadership mobilized 3,000 people to construct a 15 kilometer dike in Weishi County that confined the Yellow River's waters to a fixed channel and enabled them to recover 3,330–4,000 hectares of land. By fall of 1945, residents cleared 20–30 percent of that area to plant wheat.[135] To further promote agricultural recovery, local

---

[131] Liu, "Condition of the Flooded District."
[132] John H. Shirkey to G.A. Fitch, "Crop and Agricultural Conditions noted enroute to Chengchow, Sinyang, Loshan, Loho, and Hsuchang, Yenling, Fukou, Wei-shih and Kaifeng, May 16 to May 30, '46" (June 4, 1946): UN S-0528-0544 AR-17a.
[133] Wou (1994): 248.
[134] Ibid., 249.
[135] UNRRA, "Survey Report on Yellow River Flooded Areas," 5; MHD: 187–188.

FIGURE 6.4 Post-conflict landscape in Henan's flooded area near Fugou
Source: Chinese National Relief and Rehabilitation Administration Photographs. Courtesy of Hoover Institution Archives.

FIGURE 6.5 Yellow River floodwaters and abandoned settlements
Source: Chinese National Relief and Rehabilitation Administration Photographs. Courtesy of Hoover Institution Archives.

CCP authorities in Fugou provided 50,000 kilograms of wheat seed and reduced taxes from two to three catties (*jin*) per *mu*.[136]

In 1946, larger numbers of displaced people began to return and reclaim land. But not all refugees benefited from CCP assistance. Many cut and sold willows in Fugou and Kaifeng, "where they returned enough to support the refugees while the crops grew." In fall 1946, farmers received 40,000 kilograms of seed from CNRRA, in addition to 20,000 kilograms from the local Communist government. Wheat was planted on 80–90 percent of the land, and in most areas it produced a good crop. Initially, human labor powered most of the planting, but after each harvest villagers were able to purchase additional livestock. Farmers had plows and harrows for only half of their animals, but managed to borrow them from other places. By fall 1946, wheat was planted on 66 percent of the land in Henan's flooded area. Willows and weeds had previously covered most of the landscape. But residents cleared all the willows except for a few left near new village sites.[137] The pace at which Henan's flooded area recovered production thus "exceeded all expectation."[138]

Most residents lived in shelters made of willows and grass, while others built better houses out of brick, thatch, and timber. Many dug up the remains of old villages to salvage bricks and roof frames for rebuilding homes. In addition to shortages of timber, "the main reason for delay in rebuilding houses is that all available labor has been devoted to clearing the land and transporting the willow branches to the towns to exchange for food." Thanks to the recent harvest, they expected to be able to rebuild their villages soon.[139] Farmers planted wheat in areas that had flooded in 1946 as soon as waters receded and land was sufficiently dry. "This resulted in a fringe of wheat bordering the flooded areas and also on high places" in Fugou County. Crops were still rather poor, "particularly if planted late on newly deposited silt."[140] By the end of 1946, even in Fugou – the most devastated county in the flooded area – approximately 70 percent of the refugees had returned and 90 percent of the land in the county was no longer underwater. Part of that landscape was already under cultivation, but reeds and other wild vegetation still covered much of it.[141] The first steps toward recovery had been taken, but much work still needed to be done.

CONCLUSION

World War II generated massive ecological dislocation in Henan, draining the energy surpluses needed for rehabilitation. Reconstructing war-ravaged

---

[136] UNRRA, "Survey Report on Yellow River Flooded Areas," 5.
[137] Ibid.
[138] Ibid.
[139] Ibid.
[140] Ibid.
[141] Fugou xian zhengxie wenshi ziliao weiyuanhui (2004): 120.

agricultural landscapes and restoring their productivity would require huge amounts of labor power. With the level of devastation that existed after 1945, however, displaced people did not dare venture back to the flooded area until they felt confident in their ability to wrest a livelihood from the land. Sediment deposition may not have caused soil conditions to deteriorate to the extent that some imagined. But returning farmers did not have the tools, seeds, or draft animals needed to reclaim land. Critical shortages of fuel and construction materials existed; infectious disease had assumed epidemic proportions. The head of CNRRA's Henan branch office had every reason to express his concern that, "localities and the people do not have the power to shoulder this great enterprise of restoration."[142]

Human inhabitation depended on the existence of an extensive "environmental infrastructure" that, as Kreike explains, people "grafted upon and shaped from and with local natural resources." But maintaining environmental infrastructure also required "continuous management and use" on the part of human communities.[143] Hydraulic networks, irrigation systems, villages, fields, and even productive soils could not exist without constant labor and investment. Yet most people were simply not willing or able to reside in a landscape that lacked such environmental infrastructure. Therein lay the problem. Remaking the ecological basis of viable rural communities was impossible without the presence of human actors. It took outside intervention by international relief agencies and the Chinese state to break out of this deadlock by priming the pump for recovery. The energy and resources channeled into Henan's flooded area by UNRRA-CNRRA, as well as reconstruction initiatives undertaken by local Communist authorities, kick-started the daunting task of repairing human-constructed agro-ecosystems. Gradually, rehabilitation made headway and populations trickled back. As seen in the following chapter, the huge inputs of energy provided by UNRRA-CNRRA and the labor of rural residents enabled the interrelated processes of repopulation and agro-ecological recovery to accelerate after spring 1947, when the Yellow River returned to its old course.

---

[142] Ma (1947): 3.
[143] Kreike (2006): 238–239.

7

Reconstruction and Revolution

The United Nations Relief and Rehabilitation Administration (UNRRA's) largest undertaking in China, launched in 1946, was to close the dike at Huayuankou and return the Yellow River to its pre-1938 course. This feat of hydraulic engineering involved building a large rock-fill dam and earthen dikes to stop water flowing through the breach and divert the river to its old bed. Setbacks came in June 1946, when high waters washed away part of the dike-repair structure. Thanks to energy inputs provided by transnational relief agencies, workers continued the re-diversion project unabated. The United States and other foreign countries offered a kind of "ghost acreage," defined as the hypothetical "tilled land that would be needed to supply, with given techniques, food of equivalent value to that brought from outside into the system." Transnational aid afforded an ecological windfall, serving as the source of energy flows that Henan's war-torn landscape could not provide.[1]

Closure work resumed in 1946 with up to 50,000 laborers fed 100,000 kilograms of flour per day, most of which was imported from the United States by UNRRA. Workers wielded picks, shovels, hoes, wheelbarrows, carrying poles, and willow baskets to excavate earth and dredge diversion channels.[2] Most laborers were disaster victims from areas near the work site, such as Zheng County, Zhongmu, and Guangwu. Due to transport difficulties, more distant counties in the flooded area could not send laborers.[3] In total, the Huayuankou closure project distributed almost 6,830 metric tons (or about 7,528 short tons) of flour, giving workers the energy required to counter the river's power.[4]

---

[1] This definition of "ghost acreage" comes from Jones (2002: 83). The concept has been masterfully utilized by Pomeranz (2001).
[2] Todd (1949): 49; Bao (2011): 132; MHD: 198.
[3] Han and Nan (1948): 79. Recollections of refugees who participated in the closure can be found in Wu (2004): 174.
[4] Wang (2004): 133. Bao (2011: 134–135) estimates that 3,312,500 kilograms of flour were distributed as work relief.

For the closure alone, UNRRA imported over 5,000 tons of flour, 1,000 pine pilings and 800,000 board-feet of lumber from Oregon, 2,300 rolls (300 tons) of iron wire mesh, and 43 tons of steel cable, not to mention pile drivers, bulldozers, trucks, barges, and other heavy equipment from the United States. From India came 2,243,000 jute sandbags; untold amounts of rope were imported from the Philippines. Not all energy inputs were of foreign origin. Nationalist authorities, for their part, procured 50,000 tons of willow branches, 1,000 tons of hemp for making rope, over 198,140 pilings and stakes, 20,000 tons of sorghum stalks, and more than 190 iron anchors. From quarries in other parts of Henan came around 200,000 cubic meters of rock. Because eastern Henan's hemp production fell dramatically due to war and flooding, trains and trucks brought more than 1,000 tons of hemp to the Huayuankou work site from Hankou, Shandong, and southern Henan.[5]

Despite these transnational subsidies, the military and political situation in China complicated re-diversion work. The Yellow River had by 1946 become the effective border between Nationalist- and Communist-controlled territories in the Civil War. Communist forces controlled territories north of the river and its pre-1938 bed, to which it would return after the closure. The Chinese Communist Party (CCP) demanded appropriations of grain and money to resettle 400,000 people who had built homes in the dry river bed and to strengthen dikes downstream. In December 1945, U.S. President Harry Truman appointed General George C. Marshall, former head of the Joint Chiefs of Staff and "architect of victory" for the United States and its allies in World War II, as his special envoy to China, charging him with brokering a cease fire between the two parties. Negotiations took place in mid-1946 among Marshall, the Nationalists, and the Communists regarding the re-diversion issue. Like the Marshall mission as a whole, however, these talks went nowhere. Nationalist representatives agreed to the CCP's resettlement terms, but never followed through. CCP leaders insisted that the closure and re-diversion could not take place until all compensation was received, and indicated their readiness to prevent it by force.[6]

The CCP had reason to suspect Nationalist intentions. In 1946, the region into which the river would be redirected had become the site of renewed fighting between Communist and Nationalist armies. As UNRRA personnel recalled, the river had once again "assumed strategic significance."[7] Re-diverting the river would benefit the Nationalists by severing links between CCP forces and their supply sources to the north and west of its pre-1938 course. For the second time in less than a decade, Nationalist leaders endeavored to utilize the river and

---

[5] UNRRA (1948a): 25; UNRRA (1948b): 259; Woodbridge (1950): 433; Wang (2004): 133. See also Han and Nan (1948): 75–77; Todd (1949): 45, 48, 51; MHD: 221.

[6] Woodbridge (1950): 256–258; Westad (2003): 169; Lary (2010): 187–188. For a detailed history, see MHS: 222–228, 232–242. For a chronology, see MHD: 195–221.

[7] Barnett (1953): 27–28.

its energy to advance their military objectives and augment their fading power. In the end, strategic factors determined the closure's timing. Nationalist military commanders took over dike repairs from civilian engineers, and in February 1947 they oversaw completion of the closure. Riverbed dwellers did not receive advance notice about the river's return, resulting in damage to lives and property. Some 500 villages were submerged and over 100,000 people were made homeless. This incensed the CCP, which filled its propaganda with denunciations of the Nationalists and UNRRA.[8]

Political contentiousness aside, on March 15, 1947 the closure was finally completed. The amount of work done – and energy expended – was considerable. Laborers spent over three million work days on the project, completing 3,013,900 cubic meters of earthworks and 566,060 cubic meters of revetments.[9] Aside from resources provided by UNRRA, most materials were procured locally. Militarized hydraulic engineering still taxed the flooded area's devastated environment, and the muscle power of its remaining human and livestock populations. Farmers spent days at a time hauling sorghum stalks and willow branches on slow-moving oxcarts over sandy and dilapidated roads to the worksite.[10] As a Chinese visitor to Huayuankou described it, "tens of thousands of workers, in the yellow sands and intense sun, unceasingly intensified their efforts to complete the closure, and human labor power and water power engaged in a large-scale decisive struggle. In the end, human labor could control all, and the insurmountable Yellow River has finally been conquered (*zhansheng*) by human labor power."[11]

Despite the cost, closing the breach yielded tangible benefits for Henan's rural populace. After the re-diversion, waters subsided in most of the flooded area, accelerating agro-ecological recovery. In 1946 and 1947, according to UNRRA, the agency distributed approximately 40,000 tons of food in Henan's flooded area. A portion supported the re-diversion, while the remainder went to direct relief (feeding centers, mobile kitchens, and raw food allotments to families) or work relief devoted to water conservancy, road building, reclamation, and tree planting.[12] UNRRA also provided 3,400

---

[8] Ibid. See also Westad (2003): 169; Wang (2004): 128–133, 225–254; Lary (2010): 187–188; MHS: 222–228, 232–242; MHD: 191–192, 195–221; Edgerton-Tarpley (2014): 463–464.
[9] Wang (2004): 133; MHD: 221; MHS: 241.
[10] According Han and Nan (1948: 69), local procurements consisted of 70 million kilograms of willow branches, 25 million kilograms of sorghum stalks, 240,000 wooden stakes, 23,000 kilograms of reeds, 750,000 kilograms of hemp cords, 705 iron anchors, 50,000 kilograms of lead wire, and 835,000 kilograms of grass rope, and 200,000 cubic meters of stone pieces. 515,000 kilograms of aluminum carbide (*huangliao*).
[11] Wu (1947): 47.
[12] UNRRA (1948a): 30; UNRRA (1948b): 144; Wang (2004): 136; MHD: 195. UNRRA imported over 94,500 long tons of food to Henan province as a whole. UNRRA (1948b): 139–140.

tons of clothing, 5,740 tons of seed, and 900 tons of chemical fertilizer to returning farmers.[13] The labor of returning refugees, with energy subsidies from UNRRA and the Chinese National Relief and Rehabilitation Administration (CNRRA), reconstructed agro-ecosystems and restored agricultural output to pre-1937 levels in a matter of years. But warfare's legacies were ambiguous. Although the most obvious damage proved fleeting, the war had enduring environmental effects.

This reconstruction of Henan's flooded area intersected with twentieth-century China's most significant political transformations. Rapidly changing conditions shaped geostrategic terrain on which the final stage of the Civil War between the Communists and Nationalists was fought. For the CCP, channeling energy to repair war-induced damage to human-sculpted landscapes overlapped with the revolutionary mobilization that would culminate in its seizure of power.

REFUGEE RETURN

Shifting the Yellow River to its pre-1938 course made possible influxes of labor needed to reconstruct environmental infrastructure. Following the closure, displaced people returned from western Henan and Shaanxi. The number of returnees increased daily and by March 1947 it had grown immense.[14] 1,000 people per day passed through Zhengzhou on their way back. Only lack of rail transport limited their movement. The Nationalist drive toward the CCP powerbase in Yan'an "called for all available rail transport for military operations." Transporting men and materials to wage war via railroads obstructed flows of labor power needed to rebuild the agricultural landscape. Many refugees accumulated in Xi'an, where transport bottlenecks assumed great proportions. Delays at railway junctions held refugees up for six days at a time.[15]

A difficult long-distance journey stood between return-migrants and their homes. With only a handful of reception centers set up by relief agencies, scores of refugees died en route from Xi'an to eastern Henan. People who endured the journey to Xuchang in cattle trucks or atop boxcars did not have any care provided for them. After arriving in Xuchang, refugees had to sleep out in the open. Before long, Xuchang's stationmaster agreed to set aside land near the train station to establish a refugee camp. Upon leaving Xuchang, refugees walked to the flooded area over 56 kilometers away. Most trekked at least 80 kilometers to reach their homes. UNRRA personnel observed that,

---

[13] Wang (2004): 136. See also UNRRA (1948a): 30; Han and Nan (1948): 103–104; MHS, 244–245.
[14] Barnett (1953): 28.
[15] Parenti to Newton Bowles, "Part I, Survey of Flooded Area Refugees," 3. See also Todd (1949): 51.

"There is no provision along this route for sleeping or feeding. People are completely exhausted making this last lap of their journey." Without rest camps, many elderly people died along the way.[16] Passing from Xuchang or Luohe into the flooded area, one saw "mostly women carrying children in their arms loitering on the road to their native villages. Those who walked carrying baskets on poles or pushed small carts with a few miscellaneous goods were the refugees who were in better circumstances."[17] As of July 1947, about 260,000 registered and 100,000 unregistered refugees made it back to Henan's flooded area, and numbers increased by the day.[18]

According to UNRRA relief officers, efforts to create a refugee aid organization in Henan since late 1945 – with registration offices, camps, distribution centers, and receiving stations to administer flows of refugees – became "bogged down ignominiously." The foremost problem was, "Indifference and outright contempt towards refugees." Local residents complained that clothing was too good for refugees or that they would not appreciate it. Police and soldiers threw stones at refugees, driving them out of their "miserable straw hovels." In numerous instances, "their 'unsightly' homes or their temporary shops erected in a noble effort to rise above mendicancy were destroyed, with naturally no compensation." High prices for lumber and other materials made it hard to build camps, as did the difficulty of obtaining land. Most places suitable for refugee camps made ideal sites for military drill grounds and were put to that use instead.[19] Poor supply systems, wartime damage to transport, and the monopoly that the military exerted over railroads hampered relief.[20] To remedy the situation, CNRRA's Henan branch office sponsored work relief to repair over 325 kilometers of roads.[21]

UNRRA-CNRRA opened a modest number of reception centers in spring 1947 to give water, food, and other supplies to returning refugees. Additional supplies were distributed when they arrived in their native villages.[22] Because refugees lacked currency, many exchanged carpets, cloth, and other goods distributed by UNRRA-CNRRA for cash, which caused relief materials to leave the area.[23] Flour received from UNRRA was "far better than that usually consumed by Chinese villagers, whose staple food was usually not

---

[16] Parenti to Bowles, "Part I, Survey of Flooded Area Refugees," 3.
[17] Shi (1947): 23.
[18] "Xingzong Henan fenshu shuzhang Ma Jie tan Huangfanqu fuxing gongzuo xianzhuang" (July 30, 1947): AH 272-1370. By the end of 1947, reception centers had assisted 318,610 refugees returning to Henan's flooded area. See Han and Nan (1948): 81.
[19] Parenti to Bowles, "Part I, Survey of Flooded Area Refugees," 3.
[20] Ibid., 4. See also Todd (1949):49, 51.
[21] Han and Nan (1948): 112-113; MHD: 196; Wang Kejian (1947c): 6, 10, 12; Xiong Benwen (1947c): 16; Shi (1947): 22; Chen (1947): 6.
[22] Wang Kejian (1947c): 5-6; Shi (1947): 23; Han and Nan (1948): 81-82, 85-86.
[23] Fugou zhengxie wenshi ziliao weiyuanhui (2004):127.

even poor-grade wheat flour, but cheaper, coarser grain such as millet." Most villagers opted not to consume UNRRA flour, selling it in cities, "where it was a normal article of consumption, and a much larger quantity of their customary food obtained in return. This became the usual practice."[24]

Large temples and buildings, "which were empty and in bad condition," were repaired and made suitable for refugees to live in temporarily. Lack of resources, particularly wood, ruled out more permanent accommodations. Fuel gathering by local residents made the situation worse. As UNRRA personnel described, "In 90% of the area there are no building materials to be found even for the construction of temporary dwellings. The grass and straw so essential for temporary dwellings has been gathered and sold for fuel, and the 300 catties [150 kilograms] which are necessary for the construction of a temporary house are impossible to find." Due to lack of biomass, the only alternative was to dig holes for refugees to live in and cover them with straw mats. Material shortages were so severe that relief agencies had to purchase straw for making mats from outside areas. Only 10 percent of Henan's flooded area had enough brick for building permanent dwellings. "In these areas, the people who have lived there for some time have accumulated stacks of grass and straw which they intend to sell during the course of the year." In those sections, people could construct permanent housing.[25] In most places, inadequate fuel supplies made brick and tile production impossible, so refugees constructed houses out of sun-dried brick.[26] CNRRA's branch office set up tent villages to give shelter to displaced people, but could not accommodate everyone.[27]

In this energy-starved environment, fuel was as important for human welfare as food. With refugees returning en masse after the closing of the breach in spring 1947, UNRRA voiced concerns about fuel scarcity. As one relief officer warned, "This condition is now worse than ever before. Something MUST BE DONE SOON about this matter. We have supplies of milk in the city [Xihua] but this cannot be prepared because we do not have the fuel. I just have no idea how the returning refugees are going to be fed if we cannot have a supply of fuel." Unless CNRRA trucks transported coal from Xuchang to alleviate shortages, relief officers worried that refugees would suffer dire consequences. The matter could not be put off because, "it will be a matter of life and death for many of the returning refugees."[28] Finding fuel sources presented challenges in Fugou as well.[29] A later UNRRA report described the "critical" fuel situation:

[24] Barnett (1953): 30.
[25] Hart to West, "Report on Field Trip to Flooded Area." On the lack of building materials see Zuo (1947): 11; Shi (1947): 23.
[26] Shirkey to Green, "Evaluation of the Report."
[27] Shi (1947): 23.
[28] Hart to West, "Report for Flooded Area Committee."
[29] Fugou xian zhengxie wenshi ziliao weiyuanhui (2004): 122.

Housing timbers, trees, grass, and anything that can serve as fuel has been taken out of the area by the people who have returned. In actual fact, our present Mass Feeding stations are burning housing timbers in order to cook food for the people. As fast as the grass and straw grows in the area it is plucked, blade by blade, by men, women and children, bundled up and carried 20 to 30 miles on wheel barrows to be sold in the larger market towns outside the area. This fuel issue is not something that can be sidestepped or put to one side as unimportant.

Cooking fuel needed to be imported, with UNRRA's feeding centers bringing it in by truck from Xuchang at considerable expense. To alleviate shortages, UNRRA took pains in 1947 to "ensure the planting of a large kaoliang [sorghum] crop which will in turn yield fuel, grain, housing materials, and a small amount of fodder. This, however, will not be harvested until September. In the meantime, an alternative source of supply is required."[30]

A UNRRA inspection tour, which visited 33 settlements in the flooded area during fall 1947, described the reestablishment of rural villages. Some villages that returned refugees inhabited had been partially destroyed. Others were new settlements, built atop silt that covered remains of old villages of the same name. "Although the new villages have nothing more in common with their namesake predecessors than identical coordinates of longitude and latitude, the former inhabitants have returned to the site which they somehow identify accurately, build a new village of the same name and rebuild what they call 'our land'." To foreign observers, this ability to identify abandoned village sites was "a demonstration of the Chinese affinity for the traditional soil – and the fact that the soil consists of yard upon yard of silt poured down from the upper reaches of the Yellow River does not seem to alter the fact that 'their home' is at that spot." Their judgment proved uncanny: "More than one skeptical observer who has raised a questioning eyebrow as a villager pointed to a nondescript spot on the barren land and announced 'That is our well', or 'That is our gate', has been stupefied to see the well or the gate appear in view as the grinning peasants ply their spades."

Nevertheless, most newly recovered areas had "pitifully poor" land. The 1947 bean crop's failure due to late planting and heavy rain made matters worse. Delays planting sorghum deprived people of building materials and fuel. Near Xihua, residents could dig up bricks or refurbish structures that had withstood floods thanks to their elevation. Most returned refugees lived "in primitive hovels, four feet high, five feet long, built entirely of straw and with a floor excavated a foot or so deep to increase living space."[31] A small number lived in tent villages. According to relief workers, refugees displayed "an excellent spirit of cooperation, industriousness, and good cheer – even though their bean harvest has failed,

---

[30] Hart to West, "Report on Field Trip to Flooded Area." See also Hart to West, "Report for Flooded Area Committee"; Xihua xian shizhi bianzuan weiyuanhei (1992): 118.
[31] Parenti to Bowles, "Part I, Survey of Flooded Area Refugees," 4.

their water supply is precarious, and what fuel they need must be provided by scratching the earth for grass roots."[32]

LAND RECLAMATION

Despite such dire conditions, agricultural rehabilitation yielded results. Wheat was planted on 66 percent of the Henan flooded area's land in 1946 and another 30 percent was planted with summer crops. Water levels fell slowly during winter, but after the gap at Huayuankou was closed in March 1947 they receded quickly. Dense grasses, cattails, and willows grew on land that dried in early winter; light grass covered land that dried later. Land that emerged following the closure had little or no vegetation. In April, some farmers planted sorghum. Most planted legumes in May, along with cotton, hemp, millet, and corn. Farmers typically did not prepare their land, relying solely on manual labor. Mung beans, sorghum, and millet were planted by seeder. Black beans were sown by hoeing holes every 1–1.5 square meters and planting a few beans in each. Another method was to plow furrows every 1.5 meters and plant beans at intervals along the rows. Such methods were easy on recently dried land, so farmers planted crops on most of the river's 1938–1947 bed. They could use these methods wherever grasses grew 30–50 centimeters high. Success in growing crops depended on whether there were "enough labor and hand tools to defeat the weeds by cultivating the land between the rows." In areas overgrown with cattails, such farming methods were not effective and plowing was essential.[33] Though the river had been rerouted to its pre-1938 course, dikes along smaller waterways needed rebuilding and strengthening. Dike repairs had to start in early spring to prepare for summer floods.[34]

Diverse energy sources powered recovery. UNRRA introduced elements of a fossil-fueled energy regime to Henan's agricultural sector, though only on a limited scale. Tractor teams set up by UNRRA at Liansi in Fugou operated on land with heavy weed and cattail growth. Yet draft animals and their muscle power held greater significance. According to UNRRA reports, "Some returning refugees have stock and others buy them on a promise to pay after the harvest. The price on such deals is fixed in grain and they have to pay double the price for immediate purchase. In addition, progressive farmers from outside the flooded area are bringing livestock and cropping flooded land as tenants." One such farmer, who reportedly owned 1.3 hectares of land south of the Sha River, brought a work team with him to Xihua and cultivated 6.6 hectares as a tenant.[35]

---

[32] Ibid., 5.
[33] UNRRA, "Survey Report on Yellow River Flooded Areas," 6. See also Han (1947):18.
[34] Hamer, "A Study of the Yellow River Flooded Area," 12; Shirkey to Green, "Evaluation of the Report."
[35] UNRRA, "Survey Report on Yellow River Flooded Areas," 6.

FIGURE 7.1 Displaced people returning to Henan's flooded area
Source: Chinese National Relief and Rehabilitation Administration Photographs. Courtesy of Hoover Institution Archives.

Newly returned refugees mainly inhabited lands planted with summer crops. They worked to remake the barren landscape into a viable agricultural environment, but energy shortages jeopardized recovery. "They are very poorly off for most necessities, and are making do with very primitive huts. Until November, they are faced with a long period of heavy work in cultivating their crops with insufficient tools and animals and they are in urgent need of food and assistance during this period." Some people had not moved back to their villages, but lived on high ground or in towns like Fugou's county seat, going to the surrounding countryside each day to till their fields. Villages located at higher elevations had many times the original number of people living in them due to flooding.[36] Other territories remained uncultivated because landlords had not returned to reach agreements with tenants. Lack of vegetation cover made sandy lands susceptible to dust storms. Some parts of what was recently the Yellow River's bed "were not planted because the silt was just sandy enough to blow." Crops failed in these places "because of physical abrasion cutting off the young plants rather than because of shortage of moisture through the soil being too sandy." However, most of these areas could be brought under cultivation after weed growth stopped the wind

[36] Ibid., 7.

FIGURE 7.2 Tent village set up by UNRRA-CNRRA for returning refugees
Source: Chinese National Relief and Rehabilitation Administration Photographs. Courtesy of Hoover Institution Archives.

erosion. Uncultivated lands were at first practically unpopulated, but by May 1947 refugees came back and started to reclaim them.[37]

In a short time, human labor and investment reconstructed agro-ecosystems throughout Henan's flooded area. Aerial surveys of Xihua, Fugou, Zhoujiakou, and Taikang conducted in early 1947 revealed "square after square of green" across the land, as crops grew in newly reclaimed fields. At that time, 70 percent of Henan's flooded area was under cultivation.[38] By the end of May 1947 – with three or four weeks of planting left – uncultivated land comprised only four percent. As UNRRA surveys put it, "The largest proportion of this land consisted of areas with thick weed and cattail growth that involved heavy work in cultivation." These lands had dried up during the previous autumn, but had not been planted with wheat because of their inaccessibility. Weeds covered them in the winter and spring. These areas were left until last, "and the easy land such as the dried up river bed was nearly all planted in the summer."[39] In early June 1947, even in locales

---

[37] Ibid.
[38] Han and Nan (1948): 18. See also Shi (1947): 23; Xihua xian shizhi bianzuan weiyuanhui (1992): 118.
[39] UNRRA, "Survey Report on Yellow River Flooded Areas in Honan, Anhwei and Kiangsu," 7.

FIGURE 7.3 Tractor team clearing land for cultivation
Source: Chinese National Relief and Rehabilitation Administration Photographs. Courtesy of Hoover Institution Archives.

adjacent to water courses in Fugou and Xihua – where land had a "higher than average sand fraction and a sparse population" – about 40 percent of the land was in crop. It was expected that 90 percent would be replanted by the following year "with little help from anyone."[40] At the end of summer 1947, cultivation had resumed in 80 percent of the entire flooded area.[41]

Tractor teams helped plow lands that remained uncultivated. The tractors, it was expected, could bring this wasteland back into production by the coming fall. No more than about 819 hectares remained underwater.[42] Farmers who returned in spring 1947, "were all extremely poor and lacked the power to cultivate."[43] Chinese reports thus held that farm machinery was more efficient than manual labor. Tractors could also plow deep or shallow as needed to turn over the soil evenly. By eliminating grass roots, mechanized farming would increase crop production per unit. "When necessary, they could even work day and night, which human labor power and draft animal power could not do."[44]

[40] Shirkey to Green, "Evaluation of the Report."
[41] Chen (1947): 2.
[42] UNRRA, "Survey Report on Yellow River Flooded Areas," 7.
[43] Wang and Jin (1949):133.
[44] Ibid., 134.

Inadequate transport facilities – and the military's monopoly over those available – limited tractors' effectiveness. In March 1947, UNRRA personnel complained that "a rather bad shortage of transportation on the part of CNRRA" delayed movement of machines and supplies. Obtaining fuel for farm machinery was always a headache: "You know, the same old story. No gasoline."[45] Nevertheless, tractor teams plowed and seeded a considerable portion of land that would have otherwise been fallow. When plowing commenced in spring 1947, only 40–50 tractors operated out of two bases in Henan's flooded area. By May 1947, there were more than 200 tractors, with four new bases set up in uncultivated parts of Xihua and Fugou, though not all were operational.[46] UNRRA predicted that the tractors already in Henan could "handle all the uncultivated land by the end of October at the very latest."[47] By late 1947, tractors had plowed most land near their bases. Willows, reeds, and grasses still grew on land east of the Jialu River in Taikang and Huaiyang. Xihua's county seat and a piece of land north of the Fugou county seat remained flooded due to poor drainage.[48] In all, over 260 tractors plowed and seeded over 113,310 hectares in Henan's flooded area, doing much to hasten recovery.[49]

Nevertheless, most farmers adhered to past practice and reclaimed land using their own muscle power. Along with providing material incentives to farmers who opened land for cultivation, UNRRA-CNRRA supported "land reclamation through human labor power" (*renli fuken*) as work relief, enabling farmers to reclaim nearly 26,670 hectares. In all, programs undertaken by UNRRA-CNRRA assisted farmers in bringing a total of 107,885 hectares under cultivation, or over 24 percent of the Henan flooded area's abandoned lands.[50] Even with the significant contributions made by relief agencies, human labor – that of returning refugees – was the most important energy source for reconstructing agro-ecosystems.

O. J. Todd noted that the tractors made it possible for returning refugees to plant at once. "But as more people came back to rebuild huts in the abandoned and flooded area of 1938, hoes were put to work in the usual way when plows were not available or animals too few to pull them. So the summer of 1947 saw much of the region which had been flooded by the Yellow River again under cultivation."[51] As a participant in the tractor program recalled,

---

[45] Tucker (2005): 49.
[46] UNRRA, "Survey Report on Yellow River Flooded Areas," 31–32; UNRRA (1948a): 32. See also Wang Kejian (1947c): 7; Han and Nan (1948):106; Fugou zhengxie wenshi ziliao weiyuanhui (2004): 128–131; Wang and Jin (1949): 133; Cui (1988): 188.
[47] UNRRA, "Survey Report on Yellow River Flooded Areas," 33.
[48] Wang Kejian (1947c): 2. See also Shi (1947): 23.
[49] UNRRA (1948a): 30. Han and Nan (1948: 107) estimated that tractors plowed, harrowed, seeded, and broke the sod on a total of over 101,400 hectares of land in Henan.
[50] Wan (1947b): 38–39; Wang Kejian (1947c): 6; Xiong Benwen (1947c): 18; Wang and Jin (1949): 133, 135.
[51] Todd (1949): 51, 54.

"Since farm equipment was inadequate, although the agricultural reclamation team plowed a lot of land, the machines planted only a small amount. Most land was planted by the farmers themselves. Most of the seeds like wheat and soybeans that they used were provided by the agricultural reclamation team, and farmers provided their own coarse grain seeds."[52] Farmers, many of whom subsisted on UNRRA flour and supplies, reportedly brought about 75 percent of Henan's flooded area back under cultivation.[53] As usual, most residents had to "use their own power to reclaim land."[54]

LOCUST CONTROL

Insects that obtained their food energy from the same grain plants that humans ate threatened to stifle this nascent recovery. In the early 1940s, as discussed in Chapters 3–5, locust infestations struck Henan on an annual basis. When the breach was closed in spring 1947, waters fell and left marshy wastelands in which locusts thrived. Unlike during the war against Japan, however, return of human populations, along with existence of relief agencies that provided resources and directed labor power, made it possible to enact locust control measures and prevent extensive crop damage. As soon as locusts appeared in Fugou, Xihua, and Huaiyang in May 1947, CNRRA's Henan branch office launched control efforts. Acting on the branch office's orders, eradication teams "adhered to the principle that controlling locusts is number one, using their full power to assist locust control personnel."[55] CNRRA oversaw eradication work, administered insecticides, and offered rewards to locals for killing locusts.

The worst infestations appeared in the easternmost part of Henan's flooded area. Since Communist forces controlled that territory, "local conditions were special" and CNRRA had limited ability to operate. In early June 1947, negotiations with "a certain side" (i.e. the CCP) enabled CNRRA personnel to enter the eastern flooded area and investigate locust conditions. With the large area affected, and because most of that section consisted of sparsely populated wasteland, neither spreading insecticide mixed with feed nor spraying it in liquid form were feasible. It was also impossible to mobilize people to exterminate locusts through the traditional strategy of driving them into ditches. Instead, CNRRA personnel opted to reward people with flour according to the number of locusts they collected.[56] By the end of June, these

---

[52] Cui (1988): 189.
[53] UNRRA (1948a): 30.
[54] Shi (1947): 23.
[55] SJZHFZ 93 (October 20, 1947): 1. See also SJZHFZ 73/74 (June 9, 1947): 2.
[56] Guo (1947): 2, 3. The same text by Guo appears in SJZHFZ 78/79 (July 14, 1947): 9–12. See also Wang Kejian (1947c): 8.

efforts "purged" (*suqing*) locusts in Nationalist-held parts of Xihua and Fugou, as well as the CCP-held eastern flooded area.[57]

Eradication strategies may have gotten rid of locusts, but they did not get rid of their eggs, which hatched later in summer. Locusts reappeared in mid-July and control work had to resume. This time, the swarms were particularly dense. Yet the infestation was limited to counties in the flooded area – Fugou, Xihua, Shangshui, and Huaiyang – and did not affect other places. Waters previously covered places where locusts emerged, but when floods subsided they turned into depopulated wasteland. These territories were overgrown with grasses or covered by sand and silt deposits. Returned refugees reclaimed some of this land, growing legumes and a little grain. In addition to unreclaimed lands along riverbanks, locusts struck bean and sorghum fields. As CNRRA reports stated, "The reason they appeared was because summer locust swarms had laid eggs in these areas. The amount of eggs and the severity with which locust nymphs appear have a close relationship. Based on local observations, on un-reclaimed lands and in places with little trace of humans, locust swarms laid lots of eggs and the autumn locusts were also rampant." Although some locusts appeared in reclaimed fields, they were not as numerous as in wastelands.[58]

Initially, the "special situation" in the flooded area and dearth of human population made it impossible to conduct comprehensive locust investigations.[59] Impediments to transport and communication also made it hard to mobilize people to drive locust swarms into ditches. That strategy was again dropped in favor of paying residents with flour to reward them for the number of locusts they killed. Chemical insecticides introduced to China by UNRRA – sodium fluoride in particular – supplemented eradication efforts.[60] Nature too lent its assistance. Heavy rain fell in late July and flooded low-lying areas, destroying locust eggs and nymphs, which decreased the infestation's severity.[61] Locust control continued into late August, when swarms were finally wiped out.[62] Unlike in previous years, human intervention combined with nature's rhythms to avert damage, and most crops went on growing.

REMAKING THE LAND

By fall 1947, people had cleared "much of the land, if not most, of what was overgrown with willows" and cultivated it.[63] In November, UNRRA

---

[57] SJZHFZ 93 (October 20, 1947): 1. See also Guo (1947): 3; Wang Kejian (1947c): 8.
[58] He (1947): 5. See also SJZHFZ 81/82 (August 4, 1947): 7; SJZHFZ 93 (October 20, 1947): 2; Wang Kejian (1947c): 8–9; Xihua xian shizhi bianzuan weiyuanhui (1992):118.
[59] He (1947): 7.
[60] Ibid, 6; Wang Kejian (1947c): 8; Han and Nan (1948): 111. See also UNRRA (1948a): 15.
[61] He (1947): 8.
[62] SJZHFZ 93 (October 20, 1947): 2–3; He (1947): 6–9; Wang Kejian (1947c): 8. See also Fugou xian zhengxie wenshi ziliao weiyuanhui (2004): 132.
[63] Chepil, "What Have I Done in China?"

representatives marveled at "the transformation in the flooded area within the last month and a half." Returned refugees were constructing makeshift grass huts by the thousands. "These grass huts are certainly not what one would call adequate, but they do protect the people from the weather, in most cases they seem to have quite a considerable stock of grass and willows for fuel and also seem to have a fair amount of clothing." Living conditions were "not as bad as one might expect." However, a critical time would come immediately prior to the wheat harvest in March and April, when there would "probably be considerable starvation" without outside assistance. Relief agencies stepped in to help ensure that people had adequate food supplies.

Inputs provided by UNRRA-CNRRA were considerable. From June to October 1947, the relief agencies distributed approximately 10,000 tons of food, as well as 1.25 million kilograms of bean, sorghum, and millet seed. Fall wheat seed purchases, totaling 10 billion yuan, supplied 3,000 tons of seed to the Henan flooded area's farmers. CNRRA acquired this seed from other regions of China and loaned it to farmers, who paid it back in kind after the harvest at low interest rates. UNRRA personnel reported that, "Thousands upon thousands of acres have been planted to wheat by the tractors and by the people themselves, and practically everywhere one can see wheat coming out of the ground. When inquiring of the people where the wheat seed came from, their reply was invariably that it came from CNRRA." Of the villages investigated, "not one had acquired seed from any other source."[64] In 1946 and 1947, the Henan branch office distributed over 3,563,360 kilograms of wheat seed, more than 1,368,590 kilograms of mixed grain seed, and 57,334 kilograms of vegetable seed, which farmers planted on over 91,960 hectares of land.[65] In addition, the office distributed over 202,740 tools to more than 101,370 households.[66] In winter 1947, in the words of a CNRRA report, "Now the wheat sprouts have already grown to over ten centimeters in height, the desolate flooded area has already turned into green fields, and it is predicted that next spring's wheat harvest will not be a problem."[67]

Irrigation presented even greater difficulties. When the Yellow River went back to its old course and floods subsided, water sources had disappeared. Before the Huayuankou breach was closed, the flooded area suffered from too much water. After the closure, water was scarce because sediments buried practically all wells.[68] To ensure water availability, CNRRA undertook work

---

[64] John C. Kassebaum to Harland Cleveland, "Confidential Personnel" (November 12, 1947): UN S-0528-0535. See also Barnett (1953): 32.
[65] Wang Kejian (1947c): 8. Comparable figures are given by Han and Nan (1948): 98–99.
[66] Barnett (1953): 39–40; Han and Nan (1948): 103–105. See also Wan (1947b): 41. Another source reports that UNRRA-CNRRA distributed 11,400 tons of food and 2,000 tons of other supplies in the flooded area. By July 1947, this assistance reportedly assisted 270,000 returning refugees. Shi (1947): 23. A figure of 18,727 tools is given in Wang (1947c): 8.
[67] Xiong Benwen (1947c): 18.
[68] Xiong Benwen (1947b): 18.

relief projects to dig approximately 1,600 new wells.[69] Siltation also made it necessary to dredge drainage channels, which UNRRA subsidized as another work relief project. With the channels cleared out in late 1947, waters flowing from western Henan's highlands passed relatively smoothly into the Huai River system, enabling farmers to plant late-summer and fall crops.[70]

In June 1947, UNRRA personnel observed that, "Trees are growing quickly and people are planting away. The people will produce crops and prevent soil erosion by wind. They are not much worried about wind erosion."[71] In places with sandy soils, the damage caused by wind erosion was a threat that called for active intervention. Nationalist authorities followed UNRRA experts' advice in 1947 and set about planting small-scale shelterbelts on about 14,000 acres (5,665 hectares) of land in Henan and Anhui.[72] Farmers supplied willow cuttings and planted them as work relief. For every *mu* (0.0666 hectares) of land planted with fifty willows, farmers got four catties – about two kilograms – of wheat as payment, with two catties given up front and two catties given upon completion. The wheat, badly needed for food and seed, motivated some farmers. But "there was also a genuine interest in establishing the shelterbelts for the much-needed protection of homes and fields."[73] Along with protecting soils, tree belts were expected to supply fuel and building materials.[74] UNRRA-initiated programs planted more than 3,804,900 trees on over 3,610 hectares of land, but made only a small step toward solving Henan's longstanding wind erosion problem.[75]

LAND TENURE

Even after land was reclaimed, figuring out who owned it was no easy task. With the landscape covered in silt, settling tenure claims could prove next to impossible. Land ownership was "in a chaotic state."[76] Sediment deposited by the Yellow River "left a difficult problem in the determination of landmarks, including particularly boundaries of farms."[77] In certain cases,

---

[69] Han and Nan (1948): 108–109. See also Chen (1947): 5; Wan (1947b): 38–39; Xiong Benwen (1947c): 18.

[70] Todd (1949): 54. Dredging along the Ying River in Xihua mobilized 500,000 workers, who were allocated 2,252 tons of grain as work relief. Han and Nan (1948): 73, 77.

[71] Shirkey to Green, "Evaluation of the Report."

[72] Chepil, "What Have I Done in China"; An, Fu, and Chepil to Ma, "Recommended plan for soil conservation work"; Fu (1947): 25–26; SJZHFZ 89 (September 1, 1947): 2; Chepil (1949): 129.

[73] Chepil (1949): 129. See also Fu (1947): 25–26.

[74] Chepil (1949): 127.

[75] Han and Nan (1948): 109–110. See also Wan (1947b): 40; Wang Kejian (1947c): 9; "Henan sheng di yi qu xingzheng ducha zhuanyuan jian baoan siling gongshu wu nian lai gongzuo jiyao."

[76] Hamer, "A Study of the Yellow River Flooded Area," 16A. See also Chen (1947): 5.

[77] Agriculture and Irrigation Sub-committee, "A Report of General Information and a Recommended Plan for Agricultural Rehabilitation in the Yellow River Flooded Area of

farmers possessed ownership credentials and could identify tracts based on existing landmarks. More commonly, records had been lost and landmarks were destroyed.[78] Henan's provincial government insisted that returning farmers provide title for all holdings. After conducting a land survey, Henan intended to let farmers keep land if titles existed and set aside the remainder as government land. Unsurprisingly, local residents were not pleased. The people, as UNRRA reports stated, "are very suspicious of these moves and they suspect that tractors and co-operatives are associated with them." It took much effort to allay their suspicions.[79]

Amicable settlement of land ownership claims was seen as "fundamental to successful reconstruction of the area." To that end, UNRRA urged cooperation among county, township, and mutual-security unit officials, and the National Land Administration. It was "equally essential to give the returning population confidence that their land will not be taken away from them for some form of government purpose which they do not understand." Households fell into two groups: those who retained land deeds and those who did not. To recognize property rights, UNRRA personnel advised establishing special sections in offices of county magistrates. "After the deeds and other kinds of contracts farmers send in have been examined and approved, some form of certificate might be sent to farmers to guarantee their title. In other cases reliance will have to be placed on the testimony of village elders and neighbours."[80]

Transfers of ownership made things even more complicated. Land speculation was rampant. Between 1938 and 1947, a large proportion of land in the flooded area changed hands due to distress sales. As UNRRA personnel noted, "The land became very cheap after it was flooded and the farmers became very poor and many were forced to sell. This condition has continued right up to the present time and transactions are still going on at very low prices because returning refugees are often unable to support themselves when they get back."[81] Faced with desperate circumstances, refugees had to

---

Honan, Anhwei and Kiangsu Provinces" (1946), 8: UN S-1021 Box 55 File 4. See also Tian (1946): 10; Han and Nan (1948): 46.

[78] Hamer, "A Study of the Yellow River Flooded Area," 16A. See also SJZHFZ 56 (February 3, 1947): 2; Chen (1947): 5. In July 1947, CNRRA stipulated that unclaimed land would be managed by counties and rented for profit. Within three years, original owners who provided evidence of property rights would have land returned to them. After three years, all land that was not returned would become "nationally-owned land" managed by the county governments. SJZHFZ 84 (August 18, 1947): 6.

[79] "Survey Report of Yellow River Flooded Areas," 25. See also SJZHFZ 84 (August 18, 1947): 6; Wang Kejian (1947c): 3.

[80] Agriculture and Irrigation Sub-committee, "A Report of General Information and a Recommended Plan for Agricultural Rehabilitation in the Yellow River Flooded Area of Honan, Anhwei and Kiangsu Provinces" (1946), 8: UN S-1021 Box 55 File 4. See also Han and Nan (1948): 46; SJZHFZ 56 (February 3, 1947): 2.

[81] UNRRA, "Survey Report on Yellow River Flooded Areas," 25. See also Chen (1947): 5; Ma (1947): 3; Han and Nan (1948): 46; Su (2009): 39–40.

sell land – often their last possession – at low prices. Land grabs ensued and people complained of speculators, usually government officials and army officers. A Nationalist Party branch secretary in Fugou reportedly purchased over 202 hectares. Rents were typically between 50–60 percent of the harvest. Opportunistic land dealings went hand in hand with high interest rates, as grain loans had to be paid back in double after six months.[82] In CCP-held areas, local cadres implemented land buy-backs for households who had been forced to sell during the floods and famine.[83]

As a result of wartime land speculation, UNRRA tractors often plowed "great tracts owned by single landlords. Thereafter they plant seed for him, and may even harvest for him. The effect is that not only do the wealthy, rather than the poor, benefit, but the tenants are not even needed on the farms, and for this year at least, the landlord can get along without them."[84] When tractors did the plowing, some landlords refused to give tenants their usual share of the harvest, so they had to move away.[85] For this reason, UNRRA worried that, "the ultimate benefit of tractors in China will go mainly to the big landlords, who will use them to replace the tenant farmers by hired labour." Officials and landlords wanted the tractors, but small farmers and tenants usually viewed them as part of a scheme to take their land.[86]

With wealthier, well-connected individuals buying large quantities of land from local residents, "a portion of the flooded area's improved conditions redounded to the benefit of those who had found a relatively cheap investment in land."[87] To remedy these inequities, CNRRA organized several dozen villages near tractor stations as "cooperative farms" to cultivate and harvest crops. The Liansi tractor station, for instance, encouraged villages to form cooperatives and bring in crops on land that it plowed. Villagers received payments based on the number of days worked weeding and harvesting. When harvests came in, 25 percent went to the landlord, 45 percent to the laborers, and 30 percent to management.[88] Landlords initially hesitated to participate in the cooperatives, but opted to join because, as a report on conditions in the flooded area put it, "they had so much land laying waste and for the time being they really did not have the power to cultivate all of it. Left with no other choice, they thought that being

---

[82] UNRRA, "Survey Report on Yellow River Flooded Areas," 25. See also Han and Nan (1948): 46; Tian (1946): 12.
[83] Wou (1994): 235, 347.
[84] Irving Barnett to Herbert Hummel, "Land Problems in the Flooded Area" (April 9, 1947): UN S-528-0358. See also Wang and Jin (1949): 135.
[85] UNRRA, "Survey Report on Yellow River Flooded Areas," 32.
[86] Ibid., 34. See also Barnett (1953): 50.
[87] Barnett (1953): 60.
[88] UNRRA, "Survey Report on Yellow River Flooded Areas," 32. See also Shi (1947): 23; Wang and Jin (1949): 135.

able to receive 20 percent of the harvest was better than leaving it lay there fallow."[89]

In the late 1940s, as during the Sino-Japanese War, female family members actively participated in agriculture. "Adult refugees formed adult teams, women formed women's teams, and children formed children's teams. They also hoed the land and cut grasses, working collectively in the fields."[90] In cooperatives, as UNRRA personnel observed, "The people divided their labor force into sections. Women and girls with some smaller boys worked in groups of from 50 to 200, weeding the beans and smaller growing crops which required tedious hard work. Men and larger boys hold [sic] the large Kaoliang [sorghum] fields in groups." After harvesting, cooperatives divided crops based on "work unit credits."[91] Cooperatives worked well in some villages, but sometimes "co-operatives which have every appearance of being run by the farmers, are simply a facade to enable a group of land owners to apply for relief supplies. In other cases they are set up by local government officials as a means of getting control of privately owned land."[92]

According to questionnaires distributed to county governments in 1947, land that was rented by tenants in Henan's flooded area came to only 7–10 percent. But information obtained via the questionnaires indicated that large numbers of farmers had miniscule holdings. Xihua, for instance, reported that about 32 percent of households owned a maximum of 10 *mu*, and another 25 percent owned 10–20 *mu*. Huaiyang reported that 33,935 families out of 70,000 owned less than 10 *mu*. If anything, these figures were "conservative" and landholdings were "exceedingly small."[93] Since wartime floods obliterated familiar landmarks like graves, UNRRA "suggested that a permanent improvement could be made in the efficiency of farm lay-out, by having farms cover a continuous land area instead of being scattered in small parcels." In reality, however, they also "recognized that this desirable principle cannot be followed in all cases."[94]

ECOLOGICAL CHANGE AND THE MILITARY SITUATION

The reconstruction of eastern Henan's environmental infrastructure took place amidst the Nationalist–Communist Civil War of 1946–1949. Nationalist leaders

---

[89] Shi (1947): 23.
[90] Ibid.
[91] John H Shirkey, "Honan Flooded Areas Tractor Program (The Work with the Villages, January 1947-September 1947)," UN S-1021 Box 55 File 4. See also Fugou zhengxie wenshi ziliao weiyuanhui (2004):131.
[92] UNRRA, "Survey Report on Yellow River Flooded Areas," 34.
[93] Ibid., 16A.
[94] Agriculture and Irrigation Sub-committee, "A Report of General Information and a Recommended Plan for Agricultural Rehabilitation in the Yellow River Flooded Area of Honan, Anhwei and Kiangsu Provinces," 8. See also Han and Nan (1948): 46.

tried to remilitarize the Yellow River to delink CCP armies from their supply sources, but the move had unintended consequences. As the director of CNRRA's Henan branch office explained, "Because local military power was weak, the eastern flooded area imperceptibly became CCP-controlled territory. After the breach closure, the river returned to its proper channel. Nationalist military power had not increased and the natural boundary line no longer existed."[95] Re-diverting the river to its pre-1938 course, according to UNRRA, caused a "sharp decrease in the size of the water barrier between the Nationalists and the Communists, [so] the Communists have had comparative freedom to go about this flooded area as they pleased."[96] When waters separated Nationalist territories to the west from Communist ones to the east, fighting rarely broke out. But with the barrier gone, armies began to vie for control and tensions mounted. Until 1947, the CCP showed little interest in holding this territory, "since the area has been thinly populated and generally impoverished." But once the flooded area received supplies and equipment in large quantities, and human populations returned, exerting direct military control assumed greater significance.[97]

In terms of UNRRA-led recovery efforts, the CCP had to be considered, "a) in determining whether the areas occupied by them should receive a share in the program and b) in carrying on a program of size in an area adjacent to constant visitations by guerilla troops." The Nationalist regime's "natural choice" was "to attempt a thorough clearing out of the Communists from this area, and then to have the program continue under military protection." But efforts to wipe out the Communist presence in the flooded area failed. In fall 1946, Nationalist leaders assured UNRRA that the CCP would be driven out in a month. Nationalist troops were transferred from Guizhou and Yunnan to Henan for that purpose. Contrary to expectations, however, the CCP only gained strength.[98] By March 1947, the situation in Henan's flooded area grew more tense than ever. The Nationalists made a concerted drive to eliminate all Communist forces, but utterly failed. The CCP launched a vigorous counterattack. As UNRRA personnel explained, "The Communist groups within the area are moving quickly in great numbers and are able at will to take any place and hold it while they procure whatever they may require. The Communists are exceedingly well organized and, apart from looting, which they carry on in a predetermined

---

[95] "Xingzong Henan fenshu shuzhang Ma Jie tan Huangfanqu fuxing gongzuo xianzhuang" (July 30, 1947): AH 272-1370.
[96] Irving Barnett to Herbert Hummel, "Communist Portions of the Flooded Area in Honan" (April 9, 1947): UN S-0528-035. See also Tian (1946): 12.
[97] Barnett to Hummel, "Communist Portions of the Flooded Area." See also Wang Kejian (1947c): 12, "Xingzong Henan fenshu shuzhang Ma Jie tan Huangfanqu fuxing gongzuo xianzhuang."
[98] Barnett to Hummel, "Communist Portions of the Flooded Area." See also UNRRA (1948a): 29.

manner from predetermined groups of the population including CNRRA and UNRRA employees, they are well disciplined."[99]

By spring 1947, the CCP controlled all territories east of the old river bed, with areas to the west in dispute. The Nationalists held only the northernmost strip of the flooded area from Weishi to Huayuankou, as well as the towns of Taikang and Huaiyang. The percentage of the Henan flooded area's territory controlled by each side reflected the CCP's surging influence:

Communist: 75%
Disputed: 20%
Nationalist: 5%

Previously, CCP territories had been "a guerilla area without any established organization." But in 1947 the Northern Henan Border Region organized Communist-held portions of the flooded area and established civilian administrations. CCP cadres carried out land reform and most villages organized Communist-led militia. Nationalist and Communist armies moved periodically through sections to the west of the river. But, as of summer 1947, little fighting had occurred. The Nationalists controlled Fugou, Weishi, and Zhoujiakou within their city walls, but the Communists had held each of these sites for a few days at a time. CCP armies moved in and out of Xihua, and the county's Nationalist administration withdrew. This fluid military situation led to chaos and instability. According to UNRRA reports, "In the western flooded area there is very little law and order except as administered by whichever army is there at the time." Nominal Nationalist administration still existed. When the Communists went away, *baojia* mutual-security unit personnel and police usually returned to larger villages. The CCP also appointed its own political commissar for areas west of the riverbed. Bandits took advantage of the divided situation to have their way in the region.[100]

Taxes imposed by military forces in Henan had been cause for anxiety since 1946, though the Nationalist regime supposedly waived the province's taxes for that year. Henan hosted three separate Nationalist armies, as well as guerilas, bandits, and Communist military forces. Together, this troop presence was "making heavy inroads upon the existing food stock." Without regard for the condition of the civilian population, militaries placed insistent pressures on grain supplies. The Nationalist army, in particular, earned a reputation for giving no monetary compensation for food it seized. At other times, armies reimbursed counties at a figure well below market prices. Places like Zhengzhou, which did not grow much wheat, had trouble meeting the demands. Grain prices were "sky-rocketing daily." As in the early 1940s, the

---

[99] Robert Hart to Walter West (March 28, 1947): UN S-0528-0543 A.R.8.
[100] UNRRA, "Survey Report on Yellow River Flooded Areas," 26. See also Han and Nan (1948): 37, 75–76; Barnett (1953): 38; "Xingzong Henan fenshu shuzhang Ma Jie tan Huangfanqu fuxing gongzuo xianzhuang."

local populace had to sell other commodities to purchase wheat in order to pay taxes in kind. Only food imports from outside Henan by the army and adjustment of payments given in exchange for grain kept this dearth from turning into another subsistence crisis. In some instances, troops beat villagers for failing to comply with their demands. As UNRRA reports stated, "The magistrates are powerless to do anything to help their people. One or two of the magistrates, disgusted with the state of affairs, have utilized local militia under their command to patrol their areas in order to avoid disorder." As before, the army's non-human members put added strain on scarce resources. In Zhengzhou, "the magistrate was compelled to order his machine-gun squad to surround his buildings in order to calm down one military officer who insisted on the payment of food for Army horses."[101]

Extraction of food for the military did not abate when the river returned to its pre-1938 course. In 1947, the Nationalist government's Administrative Yuan again announced that no taxes would be levied in the flooded area for that year. Yet this decision applied only to the land tax, which made up just a small fraction of total exactions. In actuality, local Nationalist officials were "continuing their policy of taxing up to the limit of what the people can bear." In Liansi, for instance, the local *baojia* mutual-security unit raised 6 million yuan in taxes to buy rifles following the wheat harvest. Discouraged CNRRA work team members complained that, "They are taking it out faster than we can bring it in."[102] Nationalist armies made a habit of seizing grain; sometimes even commandeering UNRRA-contributed flour.[103] Channeling energy to Nationalist military forces to fuel the Civil War against the Communists diverted that energy away from relief and recovery. Nationalist "military macroparasitism" continued to jeopardize its host society and the basis of its power.[104]

As during the Sino-Japanese War, Nationalist armies in the Civil War drafted large numbers of men as soldiers and laborers. Military conscription frequently left families without individuals who provided them with income.

---

[101] UNRRA personnel were especially concerned that residents would sell imported relief flour to buy wheat needed to pay taxes and that tax demands would impede the program of rehabilitation. Philip Chu to Robert Van Hyning, "Report of Observations made on a recent survey of 17 hsiens" (March 11, 1946): UN S-0528-0535. Another UNRRA source estimated that in May 1946 the food requirements for the 870,000 troops in Henan came to 30,000 tons a month or 360,000 tons a year, assuming each soldier got a daily ration of two catties per day. No figures were available for the amounts that armies procured locally by appropriation or purchase. George Dickey, "China Office UNRRA Office of the Financial Advisor, Food Resources – Honan" (April 21, 1946): UN S-0528-0091. See also Tian (1946): 12.

[102] UNRRA, "Survey Report on Yellow River Flooded Areas," 25. See also Han and Nan (1948): 46.

[103] Xiong Benwen (1947c): 20; Barnett (1953): 31; "Henan sheng di yi qu xingzheng ducha zhuanyuan jian baoan siling gongshu wu nian lai gongzuo jiyao."

[104] Barnett (1953): 65; "Henan sheng di yi qu xingzheng ducha zhuanyuan jian baoan siling gongshu wu nian lai gongzuo jiyao," 62.

UNRRA personnel noted that Nationalist methods of conscription "were unorganized and heartless." In many instances, conscription "appeared to be a matter of seizing any source of manpower and taking him off when he was needed and available." Fear of conscription raids "had a disheartening effect on returning refugees."[105] Patterns of military–civilian interaction that prevailed during World War II persisted into the Civil War period. "The relations between soldiers and farmers were traditionally bad. Soldiers felt free to abuse them in a most inhuman fashion – perhaps a reflection of the inhuman treatment which the soldiers themselves received and of their personal poverty and sometimes hunger. Since the flooded area was either a part of or near military zones, the situation in this regard became most difficult."[106] People in the flooded area found their land and farmed it, but needed "several years of respite from taxes and forced labor" to acquire funds and sufficient time to rebuild their homes.[107] Unsurprisingly, much of the local populace threw its support behind the Communists, as "tens of thousands" of rural residents were drafted into the CCP army, mostly to carry supplies. According to Odd Arne Westad, "This assistance did a great deal to help Communist forces quickly establish a foothold south of the Yellow River."[108]

The CCP proved more adept than the Nationalists at drawing people back to territories it controlled, and mobilizing their labor to reclaim land and restore agricultural production. Lower tax rates typically prevailed in Communist territories than in Nationalist-held sections. In the eastern part of the flooded area, the CCP enacted land reform alongside land reclamation campaigns. Since many landlords had fled, redistributing land proved relatively simple. Local cadres estimated the percentage of village residents who returned and divided available land accordingly, leaving a share for refugees who had not returned. Messages were then sent to the people who had not come back, telling them that land was waiting for them. After each family tilled its fields, villagers cooperatively farmed the remaining land. When refugees returned, they got land with a crop on it and divided the surplus. These land reform measures differed from those adopted in other Communist areas, "in that they are not making provision for any landlords."[109] A straightforward slogan informed CCP land policies in the

---

[105] Barnett (1953): 65; "Henan sheng di yi qu xingzheng ducha zhuanyuan jian baoan siling gongshu wu nian lai gongzuo jiyao," 38.
[106] Barnett (1953): 31
[107] Shirkey to Green, "Evaluation of the Report."
[108] Westad (2003): 170. Detailed accounts of military campaigns in eastern Henan can be found in Zhonggong Henan shengwei dangshi yanjiushi (2001): 321–359.
[109] UNRRA, "Survey Report on Yellow River Flooded Areas," 25. See also Han and Nan (1948): 46. Wou (1994: 353) notes that in 1947–1948 land reform movements redistributed 48,569 *mu* in the Sui-Qi-Tai border area, as well as 80,000 *mu* in Fugou and Tongxu counties.

flooded area: "whoever reclaims it is who plants it; whoever plants it is who harvests it." Returning farmers received seed, tools, and other supplies need for cultivation.[110] Tax rates ranged from 3 percent in the first year to 10 percent in subsequent years, and "extortionate interest rates" were not permitted.[111] These land policies did much to consolidate CCP military gains.

Although the Civil War proved far less devastating for Henan than World War II, it impeded recovery in several ways. The protracted military conflict against Japan had destroyed North China's transport infrastructure and UNRRA tried to assist in repairing it. However, "transport of troops was one of the major logistic problems for the Chinese Nationalist military and, again, their demands had priority." Military operations interfered with relief. Communist guerillas destroyed railroads, which prevented their use by the Nationalist military, but also impeded transport of relief and rehabilitation supplies. Troops on both sides commandeered materials, and protests from UNRRA-CNRRA rarely resulted in their return.[112]

CNRRA trucks operated on roads in the western part of the flooded area, where they frequently encountered Communist troops without taking fire. CNRRA teams working in Fugou and Xihua "established for themselves a measure of recognition as non-political and although they have minor troubles with both armies they are not seriously molested." UNRRA-CNRRA personnel did not visit areas to the south and east of Zhoujiakou and Huaiyang after floods subsided, since fighting made it unsafe to take in vehicles. Almost all supplies were directed toward territories disputed by the Communists and Nationalists. Winning hearts and minds was the obvious purpose: "A Nationalist army general admitted that his relations with the people in this area had improved after they had received CNRRA supplies." With most of Henan's flooded area under CCP control, Nationalist leaders hoped that these relief materials might bolster people's loyalty to the government and convince them of its interest in their welfare. Nationalist military forces also tried to keep supplies from entering CCP-held territories. Negotiations with Communist officials enabled UNRRA-CNRRA to send supplies east of the old riverbed. One truckload of shovels, one hundred bags of flour, and some bean seed made it to the CCP-held territories, but Nationalist armies captured four trucks carrying medical supplies to Communist areas.[113]

---

[110] Taikang xianzhi bianzuan weiyuanhui (1991): 96; Xihua xian shizhi bianzuan weiyuanhui (1992): 118–119.
[111] UNRRA, "Survey Report on Yellow River Flooded Areas," 25. See also Han and Nan (1948): 46. Other sources indicate that CCP authorities collected no taxes on newly reclaimed land for three years. Taikang xianzhi bianzuan weiyuanhui (1991): 96.
[112] Barnett (1953): 65. See also Tian (1946): 12; Todd (1949): 49, 50; UNRRA (1948a): 29.
[113] UNRRA, "Survey Report on Yellow River Flooded Areas," 26. See also Han and Nan (1948): 37, 75–76; Barnett (1953): 38; "Xingzong Henan fenshu shuzhang Ma Jie tan Huangfanqu fuxing gongzuo xianzhuang."

As the Civil War raged on, UNRRA-CNRRA personnel frequently had to cross military lines. Tractor projects that UNRRA had started in Communist territories in the eastern flooded area promised to improve relations between tractor teams and CCP armies in disputed areas to the west. Yet military conflict always loomed: "While the present situation makes it possible to continue distribution to the farmers, it must be remembered that serious fighting is likely to break out at any time. Furthermore the area west of the river where most work is being done is a disputed area, and it is unlikely that its present relative peacefulness will continue for long." Most of the recovery program was conducted in areas of shifting Nationalist–Communist control, with open hostilities in the vicinity. When armies clashed in locales where relief activities were taking place, programs stopped for a time, only to resume when temporary peace returned. No working agreements existed to allow CNRRA to operate in Communist-held areas. Settlements were reached between CNRRA work teams and CCP county officials, but none were confirmed by higher authorities.[114] In theory, UNRRA-CNRRA administered aid in Nationalist as well as Communist territories, assuming no discrimination for political reasons. In reality, despite almost continuous negotiations at one level or another, few supplies reached CCP-controlled areas. This politicization of relief generated resentment, especially when UNRRA-CNRRA sent shipments to areas as soon as Nationalist armies recaptured them from the CCP. Occasionally, Communist armies seized materials and gave them to the local populace. But when the Civil War's tide shifted decisively in the CCP's favor in the summer and fall of 1947, the Communists assumed a legitimate role in distributing relief supplies.[115]

A major Communist offensive struck south across the Yellow River in fall 1947 and penetrated deeply into Nationalist territory, occupying nearly all of Henan's flooded area. Even after the CCP gained control of this territory, UNRRA supplies poured in. As UNRRA personnel recalled, "The program at the end became one primarily of distribution of supplies to the returned refugees, with Communist cooperation and collaboration."[116] Tractors kept plowing until UNRRA's land reclamation program wrapped up in late 1947 on the eve of the agency's departure from China. By that time,

---

[114] UNRRA, "Survey Report on Yellow River Flooded Areas," 27. See also Wang Kejian (1947c): 11–12; Barnett (1953): 40; Cui (1988): 189; Xihua xian shizhi bianzuan weiyuanhui (1992): 118–119. All in all, CNRRA's Henan branch office sent 412,318 tons of food, 256,338 tons of old clothing, and 140,945 tons of medical supplies to the flooded area's CCP-held territories. Han and Nan (1948): 116–117.

[115] Barnett (1953): 28, 41, 63. In July 1947, UNRRA announced it would no longer transport materials into areas above 30 degrees north latitude, most of which had come under CCP control. More supplies made it to the Nationalist-controlled county seat in Fugou than to the CCP-held countryside. Fugou xian zhengxie wenshi ziliao weiyuanhui (2004): 122, 130.

[116] Barnett (1953): 41–42. See also Fugou xian zhengxie wenshi ziliao weiyuanhui (2004): 132; Westad (2003): 169–172.

95 percent of Henan's flooded area was under Communist control.[117] UNRRA personnel recognized that with CCP power ascendant, "what would become of this developmental project after the UNRRA's demise would be determined by them."[118] CNRRA tractors assisted the CCP by transporting materials, personnel, and wounded soldiers. In spring 1948, the Nationalists dissolved CNRRA's Henan branch office and, stating that "transporting materials to the flooded area is equivalent to assisting the enemy," stopped all supply shipments and dispersed its agricultural reclamation personnel. Nationalist military leaders made one last stab at suppressing Communist forces in 1948 during the Huaihai Campaign, which centered on the railroad junction at Xuzhou. But the Henan flooded area's landscape – covered by waterways, marshes, and swamps – impeded Nationalist mechanized equipment and left their forces susceptible to annihilation by outnumbered and outgunned but far more mobile Communist armies.[119] The CCP's capacity to flexibly adjust its strategies to the givens of this changed environment facilitated its ultimate victory in North China.

Once they had consolidated their power in eastern Henan, the Communists took over the UNRRA-CNRRA tractor teams.[120] However, conditions in eastern Henan prevented the CCP from taking advantage of this machinery. Repeated military engagements in Henan blocked transport routes, so by late 1947 sources of petroleum and spare parts did not exist. In spring 1948, lack of spare parts in the relatively isolated flooded area rendered one quarter of the tractors unusable "and over half stopped breathing because of lack of fuel." In June 1948, all farm machinery completely ceased operations, leaving it sitting idle and corroding.[121] As participants in the tractor team explained, "Our nation's lack of petroleum fuel is the greatest obstacle to the development of mechanized agriculture." Gasoline and diesel oil were all imported, so prices were prohibitively high. "If using [the tractors] is not as economical as human labor power and draft animal power cultivation, the farmers will not welcome them." Furthermore, "The farm machines that our nation currently has are all made in foreign nations and currently the amount of spare parts is inadequate. Moreover, they are all fragmentary and incomplete." A machine was useless if spare parts were unavailable. "Therefore, in the past the Henan flooded area's tractors had to use the 'suicide' method and disassembled usable parts from a few tractors that could not be repaired to supply replacements for repairing other, better

[117] UNRRA (1948a): 29.
[118] Barnett (1953): 40. See also Cui (1988): 189; Ye (1991): 173–174; Xihua xian shizhi bianzuan weiyuanhui (1992): 118.
[119] Fang (2011).
[120] Fugou xian zhengxie wenshi ziliao weiyuanhui (2004): 132; Xu and Li (2004): 298; Li and Liu (1952): 7.
[121] Wang and Jin (1949): 135. Shortages of fuel caused by war-related disruption of transport between Kaifeng and tractor bases are also mentioned in Ye (1991): 173.

tractors in order to try to maintain them." At the current rate, in three to five years all farm machinery in Henan would be lost.[122] Following the CCP's victory in 1949, return of peace and stability made it possible to import fuel and spare parts, thereby averting that outcome.

THE PEOPLE'S FLOODED AREA

For all intents and purposes, the first years of the People's Republic of China (PRC) witnessed continuation of reconstruction work that started in the aftermath of World War II. As UNRRA-CNRRA did before, the PRC allocated funds to restoring agricultural production and improving conditions in the flooded area. A local history narrated the story in heroic terms. PRC authorities "called on farmers to return to their villages to engage in production, stipulating that whoever reclaimed [land] was who would cultivate it, and for three years it would not be taxed. These policies greatly increased people's zeal for production. A large-scale war against nature opened up and a rejuvenation movement to reestablish homes in the flooded area vigorously arose." Under PRC leadership after 1949, "a great river control army of several tens of thousands of people was organized to control the Ying River, the Jialu River, and the Shuangji River, and drain standing waters in the area, assuring smooth progress in agricultural production. A tractor reclamation team was also founded to assist farmers with opening wasteland for cultivation. In one year it saw great results, receiving Premier Zhou Enlai's commendation, and rejuvenation work concluded."[123] None of this was new. The PRC inherited the legacy of postwar reconstruction, as well as the lingering problems that the war had created.

Land reform brought about unprecedented socio-economic transformation in Henan's flooded area, but these revolutionary policies had to grapple with issues derived from wartime ecological chaos. Floods wiped out farm boundaries, making it possible for the CCP to apply the "principle of complete equality." Yet CCP policies encouraging land reclamation enabled some households to amass far larger *de facto* holdings than others.[124] Directives issued by Henan's provincial government in 1951 captured the complicated land tenure patterns that prevailed in the flooded area during the late 1940s, as well as how the CCP adapted land reform measures in light of local conditions. Over the past few years, "reclamation by the laboring people" had enabled Henan's flooded area to gradually recover. But the level of disaster varied and some places recovered earlier than others. Since different areas had been liberated for different amounts of time, the CCP carried

---

[122] Wang and Jin (1949): 135.
[123] Xu and Li (2004): 299. See also Li and Liu (1952): 7; Huangfanqu nongchang zhi bianzuan weiyuanhui (1987): 7; Xihua xian shizhi bianzuan weiyuanhui (1992): 119, 164.
[124] Wou (1994): 353.

out a range of measures, "which also differ with the level of popular mobilization and changes in village class relationships." In general, areas broke down into three types.

In the first, disasters had been relatively light, recovery came about early, and land tenure relationships had largely returned to pre-flood conditions. "The landlord class and the rich peasants still possess large amounts of land, and they continue to maintain a feudally exploitative land system. The vast peasantry still has no land or a shortage of land, and is in urgent need of land." In such locales, cadres adhered to the PRC's basic land reform law.[125]

In the second type of area, redistribution gave land to the peasants and they were engaged in production. But in some villages "political control" by the landlord class had not been overthrown and unequal land distribution persisted. Some poor peasants and agricultural laborers had only small amounts of land or land of poor quality. Those who returned later had no land at all. Returning land to cultivation also complicated landholding patterns. Redistribution of land to one household and its reclamation by another often produced conflicting tenure claims. As the directive explained, "Some areas, after dividing land, also carried out the 'whoever reclaims it is who plants it and who harvests it' policy, and now land use conditions are unbalanced. Land needs to be properly adjusted to determine land rights ... In some areas (like Xihua), when emergency division of fields was carried out, land had still not been entirely reclaimed, population had still not entirely come back, and wastelands were redistributed. Later, to restore production and encourage reclamation, they also carried out the 'whoever reclaims it is who plants it and who harvests it' policy." Inconsistencies between land redistribution and land reclamation created confusion. People reclaimed wasteland that had been redistributed to others, or public wasteland that was not redistributed to anyone. Local authorities were charged with cleaning up the mess. If county governments had not already enacted measures to resolve these situations, they would be handled based on the following principles: "When taking back land planted by those who reclaimed it, considering the circumstances (based on the amount of labor power used when it was reclaimed and the amount of benefits already gained), part of this land is to be given to those who reclaimed it." Together with land originally distributed to them, lands possessed by households that reclaimed land could not exceed 150 percent of the average holding per person in the village. The remainder would be seized and redistributed.

The third type of locality had not yet redistributed any land. But after the floods they had carried out a "whoever reclaims it is who plants it and who harvests it" policy. As the directive stated, "In this type of area, class relations

---

[125] "Henan sheng Huangfanqu tudi gaige fang'an" (1951): 49. See also "Guanyu Huangfanqu tugai fang'an de ruogan shuoming he buchong guiding" (1951): 51–52; Xihua xian shizhi bianzuan weiyuanhui (1992): 141.

already underwent a great change. But politically in some villages the landlord class still occupies a predominant position, and economically they have also taken land out of the hands of those who reclaimed it. Moreover, since people from each class came back earlier and later, the labor power, production materials and living materials they possess differ along with other conditions, and the land that has been reclaimed differs in amount and quality." Some people possessed little land and those who came back later did not have any at all. In these places, local directives were to adhere to the land reform law, but could be adjusted "to solve the land problems of peasants who have no land or little land, determine land rights, and expand production."

Henan's provincial government also spelled out "substantive methods" for implementing these policies, which empowered local authorities in each village to confiscate and redistribute land to make holdings more equitable. Land that "the false Relief and Rehabilitation Administration" had reclaimed using machinery, or that landlords or wealthy peasants took possession of, would be confiscated and redistributed.[126] For land that peasant organizations such as mutual-aid teams, militias, children's associations, or women's associations had collectively reclaimed, "exhortative mobilization" would be undertaken to redistribute it. Generally speaking, if people reclaimed too much land, the amount exceeding 150 percent of the average holdings per person in the village would also be taken and redistributed through "exhortative mobilization."[127] If these methods proved unable to solve peasants' land problems, they could benefit from mutual aid, loans of money, grain, seed, farm tools, and draft animals, or simply relocate to areas that still had un-reclaimed land.[128]

In January 1951, the PRC's central government and Henan appropriated 92.882 square kilometers of land in southern Fugou and northern Xihua that had not been distributed to farmers to form the state-run Yellow River Flooded Area Farm (*Huangfanqu nongchang*). Part of the uncultivated territory taken over by the Flooded Area Farm consisted of sandy and saline-alkaline lands that needed additional rehabilitation work.[129] In terms of state practices and personnel, direct linkages existed between this state farm and pre-1949 relief and rehabilitation initiatives. The PRC gave all of the machinery that UNRRA had imported into Henan in the late 1940s to the Yellow River Farm, while CNRRA tractor team personnel stayed on and worked for the collective as well.[130] By the end of 1952, the Flooded Area Farm reclaimed

---

[126] "Henan sheng Huangfanqu tudi gaige fang'an" (1951): 50.
[127] Ibid.
[128] Ibid., 51.
[129] Xu and Li (2004): 299–301.
[130] Fugou xian zhengxie wenshi ziliao weiyuanhui (2004): 132; Xu and Li (2004): 299; Huangfanqu nongchang zhi bianzuan weiyunhui (1987): 7.

and planted over 3,730 hectares and produced 3.74 million kilograms of grain – 240 percent more than in the previous year.[131] News reports declared that, "This mechanized production not only increased work efficiency several-tenfold compared to farmers using human labor, draft animal power, and old-fashioned farm tools, but could also achieve deep plowing and fine harrowing to change the soil's physical properties, decrease insect damage, and retain moisture. For this reason, although fertilizer was not applied there was still an abundant harvest."[132]

Five years after World War II ended, and despite the instability caused by the Civil War in the late 1940s, the flooded area's agro-ecosystems returned to prewar levels of productivity. Inputs of labor and materials repaired the most obvious ecological deterioration caused by warfare. Human-engineered environmental infrastructure remolded war-ravaged landscapes. The virtually seamless continuity that existed with earlier agricultural rehabilitation programs goes a long way toward explaining how quickly this recovery was completed under the PRC. By the 1950s, the bulk of the Henan flooded area's population had returned. Agricultural production recovered as well. By 1952, cultivated land area in Fugou and Xihua counties, which suffered most heavily due to war-induced flooding, came to exceed prewar levels (See Table 7.1).[133]

In other counties, such as Yanling, population and cultivated area reached pre-1937 levels even more quickly.[134] By 1949, grain productivity per *mu* in Fugou (the only county for which data exist) exceeded prewar levels. Overall output likewise increased for soybeans, peanuts, and sesame, though productivity per unit wavered (See Table 7.2).[135]

Recovery that came to fruition under the PRC did not happen overnight. Work undertaken in the late 1940s set the stage. After nearly a decade of war-induced neglect, the labor of local residents, aided by energy subsidies contributed by UNRRA and CNRRA, brought the flooded area's environment back to something like its prewar condition and agricultural output returned to prewar levels.

Yet it must be emphasized that even after this post-conflict recovery, Henan's environment remained highly degraded. Humans transformed few

---

[131] Huangfanqu nongchang zhi bianzuan weiyuanhui (1987): 39. See also Li and Liu (1952): 7–8.
[132] Li and Liu (1952): 7.
[133] Tables from Zhang (2010): 37–38. See also Li and Liu (1952): 7–8; Fugou xian tudi guanliju (1999): 52–58.
[134] Yanling's cultivated area and population were both back to 1936 levels by 1951. Yanling xian tudi fangchan guanliju (1999): 68–71.
[135] Wheat (1949: 513,000 *mu*/41,510,000 *jin*; 1952: 706,000 *mu*/53,630,000 *jin*); maize (1949: 100 *mu*/10,000 *jin*; 1952: 500 *mu*; 44,000 *jin*); sorghum (1949: 83,000 *mu*/10,780,000 *jin*; 1952: 95,000 *mu*/15,700,000 *jin*); soybeans (1949: 117,000 *mu*/10,760,000 *jin*; 1952: 464,000 *mu*/30,890,000 *jin*); peanuts (1949: n.a./3,590,000 *jin*); 1952: n.a./6,540,000 *jin*); sesame (1949: 39,000 *mu*/ 2,160,000 *jin*; 62,000 *mu*/2,810,000 *jin*). Figures from Zhang (2010): 38.

TABLE 7.1 *Agricultural population and cultivated area in Fugou and Xihua counties*

County	Year	Agricultural population	Cultivated area (*mu*)	Cultivated area (*mu*) per capita
Fugou	1933	294,738	1,207,300	4.1
	1938	315,500	1,445,000	4.6
	1945	67,100	24,900	0.37
	1949	307,619	980,100	3.2
	1950	317,936	1,173,240.23	3.69
	1952	349,932	1,690,500	4.8
Xihua	1933	422,388	1,408,200	3.3
	1938	418,543	1,417,142	3.4
	1945	118,519	425,144	3.6
	1949	304,933	1,222,100	4.0
	1950	328,673	1,276,628.41	3.88
	1952	349,930	1,534,249	4.4

TABLE 7.2 *Agricultural productivity per unit of area in Fugou County* (jin/mu)

Year	Wheat	Maize	Sorghum	Soybeans	Peanuts	Sesame
1937	61	78	100	84	150	50
1945	23	26	36	15	–	–
1949	81	100	130	92	102	55
1952	76	88	165	66	87	45

landscapes in the world to the extent that they transformed the environment of the North China Plain. By the early twentieth century, few regions had existed in such a fragile ecological condition for as long. Flooding, drought, and famine had been persistent menaces for decades. Few landscapes needed such large investments of labor and resources to maintain some semblance of ecological equilibrium, however tenuous it may have been. For human residents, ecological instability made day-to-day survival a bitter struggle. None of this changed when the CCP assumed power in 1949. The Sino-Japanese War and its immediate aftermath, moreover, had discernible environmental effects. Over ten years of Yellow River floods silted up tributaries of the Huai River in eastern Henan and washed away hundreds of kilometers of dikes, leaving the area even more unstable and vulnerable to floods than before the war.[136]

At the same time, the environmental legacy of the Yellow River's wartime floods directly influenced agricultural productivity. In 1950, as soil conservation

[136] UNRRA (1948a): 29; Luo (1953): 243; Xia (1953): 245.

specialist Xi Chengfan related, "Farmers who fled gradually have returned to this land and in only three years' time they have already reclaimed almost all of the flooded area." That summer, "wheat was yellow and ripening, and one could hardly tell it was once a disaster area, but wheat growth had clear differences." Newly reclaimed wasteland's "productive power" was always lower than mature land, so in the first year of cultivation harvests were typically low. But the character of soils greatly affected wheat-growing conditions, "especially the influence of the arrangement of alluvial deposit levels (*chongji cengci pailie*)." With the general shortage of fertilizers in Henan's flooded area – another carryover from the war years – most land was unfertilized. For this reason, as Xi argued, the main factors that caused differences in productivity related to the soils.[137]

Soil structures that existed in the 1950s resulted from patterns of sediment deposition between 1938 and 1947, when the Yellow River flowed through eastern Henan. During the high-water season, the river's flow had accelerated. Fine particles did not settle, so normally only coarse particles were deposited, making the soil relatively sandy. Conversely, when flow volume decreased during dry season, fine particles were deposited and soil became relatively clayey. As a result, sediments deposited at different times of year formed alternating layers of clay and sandy soil. After the closing of the Huayuankou breach in 1947, the Yellow River's flow was cut off, water volume suddenly decreased, and floodwaters deposited almost all their sediments. For this reason, surface soils in several areas, such as Xihua, had a thick layer of extremely fine sand. Sediment deposition patterns affected land utilization because, as Xi put it, "These clayey soils, sandy soils, and alternating layers of clayey and sandy soil sediments directly influence agricultural production today."[138]

Soils that had the same type of sediments to a depth of one meter tended to be fertile, producing an average of 100 kilograms of wheat per *mu*. Soils with a mixture of clay and sandy soils were less widespread, but also had high productivity at around 100 kilograms per *mu*. In Xihua there were areas of sandy soil on which wheat did not grow well, producing only 50–75 kilograms per *mu*. Finer sands had even poorer wheat production, as did wind-eroded sands found along slightly inclined banks. The coarsest types of sands did not exist in particularly large quantities and were found only in a narrow area along what had been the river's main channel. These coarse sands generally remained uncultivated and their agricultural productivity was extremely low.

Most soils had complex sedimentation patterns, with different strata intermixing with one another. Differences in layering influenced land utilization and productivity. With heavy clays deposited over loamy sands, for

[137] Xi (1950): 103.
[138] Ibid.

example, cracks formed in the clay. Once it rained, water flowed out through the cracks, which decreased productivity. Farmers called this type of land "rain soaked hut" (*yulinpeng*), since water seeped through it like the thatched roof of a grass shanty. Xi advised that deep plowing could improve this type of land by mixing sandy soils and heavy clays together. When fine surface soils were deposited over heavy clays, by contrast, wheat production increased. When rainwater permeated this land, its clay layer retained larger amounts of water and kept it from seeping out. Wheat roots could grew easily in sandy surface soils, absorbing nutrients and water from the clay below. Because of its high fertility, farmers called this "hidden treasure land" (*mengjindi*).

Land with thin layers of new sediments deposited on ridges or slopes over alluvial deposits from earlier times had relatively high fertility as well. New alluvial deposits had lower productivity compared with older sediments, mostly because new sediments had not been fertilized or cultivated before. Older sediments possessed higher humus content and better soil structure. As Xi Chengfan concluded, "For this reason, new alluvial soils have to be cultivated for some time before their productivity can increase, so in utilizing them one must pay attention to increasing the surface soil's organic composition."[139]

On the Yellow River's 1938–1947 bed, an expanse of sandy land formed, stretching southeast from Huayuankou through portions of Zhongmu, Weishi, Fugou, and Xihua. These sediments' high sand composition made them susceptible to wind erosion, sometimes rendering agriculture nearly impossible. Blown by winds during the winter and spring dry seasons, sandstorms swept through the area and threatened crops growing in nearby fields. From 1950–1954, Henan took a cue from post-World War II reconstruction initiatives and planted large shelterbelts to fix the sands in attempt to address the problem.[140]

CONCLUSION

The period following the Yellow River's re-diversion to its pre-1938 course was marked by large-scale return of displaced people to Henan's flooded area. After 1947, repopulation made it possible to rebuild shattered environmental infrastructure. While carrying out agro-ecological recovery, returned refugees contended with a dearth of biomass energy. But influxes of human labor, combined with sizable material inputs provided by UNRRA-CNRRA,

---

[139] Ibid., 104.
[140] In addition to the 1938–1947 course of the Yellow River, Henan had four other stretches of sandy land located on the shifting river's previous beds. In Zhengzhou alone, sandy lands near the Huayuankou breach covered an area of 50,000 *mu*. Feng (1992): 2–5. See also Xihua xian shizhi bianzuan weiyuanhui (1992): 286.

afforded sufficient energy to achieve a rapid restoration of agricultural landscapes. On the other hand, although agricultural output returned to prewar levels by the early 1950s, war had transformed eastern Henan's environment in fundamental ways.

Based on his environmental history of World War II in Japan, William Tsutsui asserts "that the effects of warfare on the environment (be they favorable or detrimental) are often less lasting and less significant than we might imagine." War's environmental legacies "are complex, contingent, and often surprisingly transitory."[141] In the twentieth-century world as a whole, J. R. McNeill similarly finds that, "Combat had its impacts on the environment, occasionally acute but usually fleeting. More serious changes arose from the desperate business of preparing and mobilizing for industrial warfare."[142] In McNeill's view, "patient labor and the processes of nature" have usually hidden the scars of war and "assimilated into the surrounding countryside the sites of even the most ferocious battles – except where there has been conscious effort to preserve the battlefields as memorials." Dryland agriculture, as practiced in Henan and on the rest of the North China Plain, "recovered quickly from war, on average in about three years."[143]

These observations ring true for Henan's flooded area, at least to an extent. The rebuilding of agro-ecological systems and return of agricultural productivity to prewar levels indeed occurred in a rather short time. In line with McNeill's assertion, agricultural output in Henan's flooded area returned to pre-1937 levels about three years after full-fledged peace and stability returned in 1949. Human labor and investment remade landscapes of unparalleled devastation into environmental infrastructure. But in other respects, Henan's post-conflict experience makes it necessary to qualify conclusions about war's transitory environmental effects. Recovery did not result from nature's powers of regeneration alone. In conjunction with the labor of the rural populace, post-conflict ecological reconstruction garnered huge energy subsidies from transnational relief agencies. Without external inputs, human communities could not have remade war-torn landscapes into productive agro-ecosystems so quickly and the environmental scars of warfare would have lasted much longer. The PRC inherited the legacy of recovery measures undertaken before 1949 under the auspices of UNRRA-CNRRA. By the early 1950s, agricultural output returned to levels that prevailed before the Sino-Japanese War. But under the PRC – as before the Japanese military invasion of 1937 – Henan's environment consisted of an intensively managed landscape that provided only the most fragile and precarious underpinning for human existence.

War also produced changes that persisted after 1949. In certain fundamental ways, China's war against Japan left its mark on the landscape. At the

---

[141] Tsutsui (2003): 295.
[142] McNeill (2000): 347.
[143] Ibid., 345.

beginning of the 1950s, human population was lower and more wildlife inhabited the land, though the situation did not last long. More enduring were sediment deposition patterns created by wartime floods, which altered the distribution of productive and unproductive lands well into the 1950s, greatly influencing agricultural output levels. Some parts of the environment did not recover at all. Mature trees, of which there were few prior to 1937, scarcely existed thanks to wartime demand for biomass. The Yellow River's waters destroyed dikes and embankments, while its silt clogged the Huai River's tributaries and impeded their drainage, deteriorating water control infrastructure and leaving eastern Henan even more susceptible to flooding. Dike repairs made by UNRRA-CNRRA did little to resolve the problem. Recovery occurred on the most obvious levels, but less perceptible changes still lingered.

Conclusion

LOOKING BACKWARD

Through a history of the Sino-Japanese War of 1937–1945 and the Chinese Civil War of 1946–1949 in Henan's Yellow River flooded area, this book has sought to elaborate an analytical framework for the study of war and the environment. A conceptual focus on energy and energy flows, as I have proposed, holds potential to sharpen our understanding of ecological dimensions of World War II, as well as many other conflicts.

This exploration of World War II and its aftermath has employed the notion of metabolism to analyze processes by which military systems acquire energy and materials. Militaries, like living beings, need these inputs as a precondition for their existence. Whenever military forces expand their range of operations, the scope of their ecological footprint expands. As the scale of war and military preparation grows, they consume greater quantities of energy and release waste in greater amounts, reshaping environments in the process. Because intensively exploited agricultural landscapes and hydraulic systems like those that prevailed on the North China Plain also depended upon constant energy inputs for their maintenance, they proved especially vulnerable to war-induced disruption. War upset finely honed relationships with anthropogenic environments in Henan, triggering rapid and acute shocks. The military's insatiable appetite for energy drained labor and resources needed to maintain environmental infrastructure, making it impossible to recreate a viable human–ecological order until conflict came to an end. Warfare, in other words, rendered post-disaster recovery even more difficult than usual by monopolizing energy flows needed to pull things back together.

Multifaceted and multidirectional relationships played out between war, society, and environment. Armies in Henan intentionally disrupted hydraulic systems, after which they expended huge quantities of energy trying to manipulate rivers for strategic purposes. Warfare tore asunder agro-ecosystems and disrupted agricultural production, as Chinese and Japanese armies consumed increasing amounts of food energy to meet their metabolic demands. Military systems likewise extracted tremendous amounts of labor power from local societies in the form of soldiers and conscript labor, even as their actions caused death, displacement, and population loss. Due to precipitous war-induced population decline, local societies (or what remained of them) could not invest labor and resources needed to maintain agro-ecological systems from which they derived food and biomass. When hydraulic systems suffered disruption, flooding led to additional loss of labor and materials.

With military actors extracting increased amounts of energy in their efforts to manipulate waterways, maintaining militarized hydraulic systems placed greater burdens on devastated localities. At the same time, Henan's flooded area lost additional energy sources as refugees migrated west to Shaanxi, where their survival strategies generated further environmental change. After World War II ended in 1945, it took massive influxes of energy to draw human labor power back into eastern Henan's flooded area, making it possible to repair war-ravaged environmental infrastructure and restore agricultural landscapes to productivity. Waste that armies released into the environment has admittedly received little attention in the foregoing narrative. The only reason for that omission is that archival documents and other primary sources from wartime Henan and Shaanxi make little reference to the waste products that were byproducts of the military metabolism.

Given that military systems invariably depend on the environment and its resources, they cannot endure for long unless they reach some kind of balance with the ecological systems that they exploit. The short-term logic of military survival, however, often makes it impossible to attain this equilibrium. For the Nationalist regime, a desperate need to extract energy for the army and remold the hydraulic environment to meet its strategic priorities gave rise to socio-ecological disruptions that paved the way for its military collapse in North China. The Communist Party's military forces in Henan, during the 1940s at least, proved more capable of adapting to changed environmental conditions and improvising ways of capturing the energy needed to survive. To an extent, the contrast between the impact of the Chinese Nationalist and Communist militaries derived from their tactics. The Nationalist armies engaged in positional warfare, while the Communists relied primarily upon guerilla warfare, which gave them greater mobility and flexibility. Differing military-strategic choices necessitated by the war against the Japanese resulted in different ecological outcomes, which also carried political implications.

LOOKING OUTWARD

On a global scale, the period between the First and Second World Wars witnessed an acceleration of military industry that enabled states to mobilize greater resources and perpetrate unprecedented levels of destruction. In the 1930s and 1940s, militarized economies pursued energy and materials to fuel conflict with a sometimes reckless abandon. The world's forests felt the effects of this global pursuit of biomass. As Richard Tucker has shown, the limited labor force that was not already drafted into military service during World War II cut down trees as rapidly as possible. Energy-intensive, fossil-fueled harvesting machinery and transport networks were more developed than ever, making it possible to loot timber resources from every continent.[1]

In East Asia in particular, Japan's military expansion required attaining control of forests, as well as energy embodied in other forms. During the 1930s and 1940s, Japan's exploitation of natural resources at home and abroad accelerated as it prepared for and subsequently embarked upon the path of total war. As Ian J. Miller puts it, "Total mobilization required the subordination of all energies to the war effort. Short-term military needs took precedence over other claims on resources, both ideological and material." From the invasion of Manchuria in 1931 to Japan's unconditional surrender in 1945, the Japanese empire exploited and sacrificed natural resources in an "escalating frenzy of consumption" that encompassed all sectors of the economy.[2] Sticking to a pattern seen throughout Japan's empire during the war years, Japanese enterprises exploited coalmines in Manchuria with little concern for environmental consequences. Industrial development that got started in Manchuria under the Japanese ultimately paved the way for severe pollution in northeast China during the People's Republic of China (PRC) period.[3] On the Chinese side, wartime development of strategic industries in southwest China by the Nationalist regime from 1937–1945 surely led to similar consequences, but that wartime environmental history awaits comprehensive investigation.[4]

But not all energy needed to fight World War II came in the form of fossil fuels. Writing of Japan's wartime experience, Miller notes that, "To a surprising degree, given the standard depiction of the Second World War as a consummately modern and therefore mechanized conflict, trained domesticated animals were an important military technology."[5] This tendency was even more apparent in the "somatic energy regime" that characterized Henan in the 1930s and 1940s, where unbridled wartime pursuit of energy sources entailed extracting plant biomass as food and fuel, as well as exerting control over human and animal muscle power.

This book's focus on energy flows has also highlighted the significance of water in the history of warfare. Throughout World War II, Chinese and Japanese forces in Henan vied to manipulate the Yellow River and deploy its power against military adversaries. During the Chinese Civil War, Nationalist

---

[1] Tucker (2011), Tucker (2004). See also McNeill (2004): 399.
[2] Miller (2013): 95. See also Tsutsui (2003).
[3] Seow (2013).
[4] Kinzley (2012).
[5] Miller (2013): 96.

military forces yet again sought to unleash the river as a weapon against their Communist opponents. Although the scale of destruction caused by war-induced flooding in China was tremendous, it was not unique. Starting with the civil wars that shook the world during the 1850s and 1860s, through the two world wars of the first half of the twentieth century, and into post-1945 wars of decolonization and the Cold War, manipulation of surface waters has been an integral part of modern warfare.

During the American Civil War, as a part of operations along the Mississippi culminating in the Siege of Vicksburg in 1863, Union military leaders tried desperately to exert power over that river's course to eliminate dangers posed by its unpredictability and Confederate fortifications strung along its banks.[6] To manipulate strategic terrain and gain military advantage, as Lisa Brady shows, Union army engineers reshaped the river by constructing cutoffs and canals, thereby bypassing Confederate defenses.[7] Waters were an enemy for one army, but an ally for the other. When William Tecumseh Sherman's troops neared Savannah at the close of the Civil War in 1864–1865, Confederate forces in Georgia cut dikes, turning the landscape into a swampy marsh to impede Union armies. In the Carolinas, swamps and rivers swollen by heavy rain presented obstructions that left the Union forces practically immobilized.[8] As Brady concludes, "water – not rebel forces – posed the greatest challenge to Sherman's army."[9] Only after protracted battle against the waters of the American South was the Union Army finally able to conquer its Confederate adversary. In all likelihood, China's inland waterways held comparable significance during the Taiping Rebellion (1850–1864). But the environmental history of that conflict – the largest and most destructive civil war of the modern age – has not been written.[10]

Deliberate strategic floods figured just as prominently in the world wars of the twentieth century. When German armies invading Belgium moved to outflank their opponents shortly after the start of World War I, the flat and waterlogged landscape of Flanders presented serious obstacles. As in much of China, the environment of Flanders was governed by sophisticated human-constructed waterworks. For centuries, residents dug canals and ditches, constructed dikes, and built polders to reclaim land. In wartime, as William Storey explains, "these constructions were liable to be damaged, making it difficult for soldiers to move and dig." The waterworks of Flanders were an environmental challenge for German armies, but an opportunity for their opponents. To halt the German advance, Belgium's King Albert ordered the opening of locks along the heavily channeled Yser River in October 1914,

---

[6] Brady (2012): 27.
[7] Ibid., 31.
[8] Brady (2009): 54, 57, 59; Brady (2012): Chapter 4.
[9] Brady (2009): 58. See also Brady (2012): 112.
[10] The same goes for India's Sepoy Rebellion of 1857–1858.

inundating nearby countryside. By preventing German armies from moving southwest, much like Chiang Kai-shek's unleashing of the Yellow River against the Japanese, King Albert's "act of environmental warfare ensured that he preserved what was left of his country by submerging much of it."[11]

A few decades later, World War II featured repeated manipulation of surface waters for military purposes. For the first time, dams and hydraulic works became targets for aerial bombing. As part of "Operation Chastise" in May 1943, the British Royal Air Force bombed Germany's Eder, Möhne, and Sorpe dams, causing floods in the Ruhr Valley. In World War II's European theater, as in China, armies created strategic floods to impede enemies. The Dutch flooded the Gelderese Valley in 1940 to slow the German advance through the Netherlands. In 1944, when the war's tide turned against them, German armies deliberately flooded the Liri, Garigiliano, Rapido, Ay, and Ill rivers, as well as the Pontine Marshes to bog down Allied forces. By early 1945, German-created floods left more than 20 percent of western Holland's arable land under water and made it necessary to evacuate several thousand people.[12]

During the Korean War, the U.S. Air Force launched attacks on large dams in North Korea. The Suiho Dam on the Yalu River – second largest in the world at the time behind only the Hoover Dam – was bombed in May 1952, but never fully demolished. American bombers also hit the Toksan, Chasan, and Kuwonga dams in May 1953, causing inundations that destroyed newly planted rice crops. Shortly thereafter they attacked dams at Namsi and Taechon. When fifty-nine U.S. Air Force F-84 Thunderjets breached the Toksan Dam in May 1953, floods destroyed six miles of railroad, five bridges, two miles of highway, and five square miles of rice paddies. As Bruce Cumings writes, "The first breach at Toksan 'scooped clean' twenty-seven miles of river valley, and sent water rushing even into Pyongyang. After the war it took 200,000 man-days of labor to reconstruct the reservoir."[13]

Perhaps the most striking parallels with the militarization of waterways in Henan's flooded area are found in Vietnam during World War II and the First Indochina War of 1946–1954. As David Biggs describes in his history of the Mekong River Delta, Japanese military occupation during World War II led to degradation of intricate canal networks.[14] In the anti-colonial insurgency the Viet Minh waged against the French, colonial-era waterways further deteriorated due to war-induced neglect.[15] Military conflict severely disrupted the Mekong Delta's colonial water grid, as annual floods broke embankments.[16] As the First Indochina War escalated, combatants manipulated

---

[11] Storey (2010): 41.
[12] Kreamer (2012): 89. Examples from World War II are also discussed in Lary (2004): 157–158.
[13] Cumings (2010): 155.
[14] Biggs (2011): 129.
[15] Ibid., 130.
[16] Ibid., 134, 150.

Conclusion 241

hydraulic systems to gain strategic advantage. French counter-insurgency operations depended on navigable roads and waterways, as well as effective communication routes. By destroying bridges, roads, and small canals, the Viet Minh eliminated French military advantage by restricting them to vulnerable highways and a few large canals.[17] The riverine environment carried the utmost strategic importance. French forces deployed their firepower to destroy dams that Viet Minh militias had built to keep waters high. After each French assault, local laborers rebuilt barriers protecting Viet Minh bases. For the Viet Minh, "resisting a militarily superior enemy meant that guerillas not only fought to control waterways but became allies with the swamp as it encroached over roads and plantations."[18]

By allying "with the forces of tides, siltation, and plant succession," as Biggs puts it, "rebels by necessity embedded themselves in the landscape."[19] The Viet Minh gained strategic benefits from flooding and rapid sedimentation of canals.[20] By building barriers and becoming "friends" with natural forces, the Viet Minh contributed to regeneration of wetland conditions that existed before lands had been reclaimed as colonial plantations.[21] As Viet Minh forces manipulated the environment for military ends, abandoned lands in the Mekong Delta "reverted to swamp and, in some cases, young cajeput forest." The French and their Vietnamese allies labeled these lands "*terres mortes*" and criticized the Viet Minh's "scorched-earth tactics," yet taking advantage of this altered geostrategic terrain facilitated Viet Minh military survival.[22]

Analogous ecological changes occurred in Henan's Yellow River flooded area. Human labor had transformed North China's landscape for centuries and the intricate environmental infrastructure that existed in Henan, such as farms and hydraulic systems, needed constant labor and investment. Violent conflict, the river's strategic diversion, and the Henan famine of 1942–1943 eliminated energy sources needed to maintain anthropogenic landscapes, leading to acute ecological disruptions and the emergence of an environment that consisted largely of uncultivated wetlands and spontaneous vegetation. From a comparative perspective, the extreme vulnerability of North China's human-engineered environments to war-related disruption may not have been that different from places like Mississippi, Flanders, or southern Vietnam. The same goes for the willingness of military actors to capitalize on that vulnerability for strategic ends. Nevertheless, transformations caused by deployment of the Yellow River as a weapon and the energy that Chinese

---

[17] Ibid., 132, 139.
[18] Ibid., 132.
[19] Ibid.
[20] Ibid., 135.
[21] Ibid., 139.
[22] Ibid., 134.

and Japanese forces invested in channeling and manipulating the river appear remarkable for their sheer size. Water has taken on similar military functions in other places and times. But the environmental changes derived from the Yellow River's militarization in the 1930s and 1940s were unparalleled in terms of their scale and duration.

LOOKING FORWARD

Between 1946 and the dawn of the 1950s, massive transnational energy subsidies contributed by the United Nations Relief and Rehabilitation Administration (UNRRA) and the Chinese National Relief and Rehabilitation Administration (CNRRA) made it possible for returning refugees to rebuild eastern Henan's devastated environmental infrastructure. Human actors promptly remade the flooded area's war-ravaged landscapes into productive agro-ecosystems. Though war-induced flood and famine had thoroughly altered Henan's environment, by 1952 inputs of labor and material resources brought agricultural output back to prewar levels.

To be sure, the landscape was not fully repaired. The same environmental problems (pervasive fuel shortages, hydraulic instability, salinization, etc.) that existed in eastern Henan before the war against Japan in the 1930s existed in the early years of the PRC. Whatever post-conflict recovery that did take place, moreover, would not last for long. By the end of the 1950s, the drive launched by Mao Zedong and other PRC leaders to remold China's environment to achieve self-reliant economic growth through agricultural collectivization and rapid industrialization caused further environmental damage and human suffering. As with the breaking of the Yellow River dikes in 1938 and the famine of 1942–1943, national objectives severely distorted energy flows. Strengthening the nation remained the absolute priority, regardless of the devastating ecological consequences.

With the Great Leap Forward (1958–1961), Mao and his supporters endeavored to make China into an industrial nation on a par with the world's major powers. But their campaign to revolutionize China's economy ended in a catastrophic famine that took approximately 30 million lives. During the Great Leap Forward, Mao urged the development of industry and agriculture through mass mobilization of rural labor. The campaign, in essence, mobilized energy sources from the country's vast rural sector to pursue modernization and socialist development. Peasants joined communes and consolidated landholdings, endeavoring to raise agricultural yields while also initiating local industries like backyard steel furnaces. As always, however, energy devoted to one purpose was rendered unavailable for others. People who had to work at steel production or other Great Leap projects could not farm. Agricultural yields fell sharply from 1959 to 1961, straining food supplies. Based on wildly exaggerated production figures, state procurements took most grain that was produced. Mass starvation resulted.

As the PRC state mobilized rural labor power to achieve breakthroughs in agriculture and industry, it simultaneously deprived rural residents of food energy in order to feed urban populations and fuel economic development. At a basic level, the Great Leap famine happened because the PRC's leaders decided to fuel the metabolism of China's cities and its industrial sector instead of making energy available to the rural populace. Urban party members, industrial workers, and the military received food rations from the state; rural dwellers did not enjoy such entitlements. Instead, people in the countryside were left to starve without adequate supplies of food.[23] State extraction and lack of effective relief created what was likely the largest famine in world history. Building a Communist utopia in China and attaining the longstanding goals of national wealth and power justified unlimited sacrifice.

The Great Leap famine struck Henan more severely than most other parts of China.[24] From 1958 to 1961, the province suffered an estimated famine-related death toll of 2–3 million. At the Great Leap Forward's outset, Henan stood as the campaign's nationwide model. The radical faction in control of the provincial government implemented the Great Leap's policies with gusto.[25] Breakneck steel production destroyed the meager trees and other vegetation that the landscape had left. Frank Dikötter asserts that eastern Henan lost 80 percent of its shelter forests during the Great Leap, while in areas around Kaifeng some 27,000 hectares were lost to sandstorms.[26]

It is worth emphasizing that baselines mattered here as well. Henan, like the other regions severely affected by the famine in 1959–1960, had been "infamously famine prone in the past."[27] Chronic ecological problems and resource scarcity, which only intensified during World War II and the Chinese Civil War, partly explain this grave misfortune. As Ó Gráda notes, Henan and the other regions hit hardest by the Great Leap were "economically very backward, even by Chinese standards in the 1950s. Given their poor track record, it is hardly likely that they would have escaped severe and repeated harvest shortfalls without significant loss of life."[28] One should add that over a decade of incessant warfare had accentuated pre-existing environmental problems, leaving Henan even more susceptible to disaster.

Despite obvious differences in scale and political motivation, parallels existed between the famine experience in Henan during 1942–1943 and catastrophes that struck after the Great Leap. Following the drought that some

---

[23] Perdue (2010): 114–115
[24] Yang (1996): 38); Lillian M. Li (2007): 359; Ó Gráda (2008): 17; Dikötter (2010): 23, 34, 332–333; Wemheuer (2010): 185; Yang (2012): 41–46.
[25] The worst horrors occurred during the Xinyang Incident, a horrific episode of mass starvation in which cadres used terror and humiliation to make farmers hand over grain. Dikötter (2010): 116–117, 197, 306; Wemheuer (2010): 178,
[26] Dikötter (2010): 177.
[27] Ó Gráda (2008): 11.
[28] Ibid., 13.

parts of Henan experienced in 1959, local leaders exaggerated output and handed over grain procurements to the state accordingly, leaving rural people without food.[29] As in the famine of 1942–1943, local authorities inflated harvest yields and appropriated grain regardless of cost to villagers. In each instance, state procurements privileged the energy needs of strategically important groups (the army in 1942–1943; urban dwellers in 1959–1961) at the expense of rural people. Again, the state failed to transport grain across administrative boundaries promptly enough to relieve stricken areas. Although authorities attempt to block migration, from 1959 to 1960 significant numbers of Henan residents took to the roads and fled.[30]

At least to some degree, the Great Leap disaster in Henan was deeper than it might have otherwise been if not for changes that occurred from 1938 to1947. Despite surprisingly rapid post-conflict reconstruction of environmental infrastructure, the counties of Henan's flooded area remained mired in a precarious set of ecological circumstances. War aggravated fuel shortages and persistent hydraulic instability. Salinization and sandstorms – though certainly nothing new – plagued parts of eastern Henan throughout the first decade of the PRC.[31] The Yellow River, as unruly as ever, experienced flood crests in the 1950s that ranked among the highest of the twentieth century. In July 1958, the river's flow reached 21,000 cubic meters per second at Huayuankou, well above the normal crests of 5,000–8,000 cubic meters per second. According to Charles Greer, the 1958 high waters, "in which the levees were breached in five places," approximated the huge floods that occurred in 1933 (23,000 cubic meters per second at Huayuankou) during which the dikes broke in more than fifty places.[32]

During the Great Leap, utopian faith in the human ability to triumph over nature and achieve large-scale environmental transformation led to disaster. For Mao and other PRC leaders, nature was little more than another enemy to conquer.[33] In Perdue's estimation, Mao "refused to accept constraints of nature, believing that human labor could overcome all obstacles. His 'war against nature' indeed saw production as a military operation in which mobilizing all available human resources could accomplish miracles." Mass mobilization was understood as the weapon for gaining victory over environmental constraints.[34] Farmers and workers were organized into quasi-military units and mobilized to enter into combat against the environment, forming platoons, battalions, and regiments. The war against nature became

---

[29] Yang (2012): 76. Information from weather stations in China during the Great Leap is available from: http://www.famine.unimelb.edu.au/weather_stations.php (accessed May 26, 2013).
[30] Lillian M. Li (2007): 359; Ó Gráda (2008): 17; Dikötter (2010): 233, 253; Wemheuer (2010): 184.
[31] Dikötter (2010): 183.
[32] Greer (1979): 80.
[33] Shapiro (2001).
[34] Perdue (2010): 115.

Mao's "central reason for modernizing China's economy as quickly as possible, but his efforts ended in disaster because he disregarded environmental constraints."[35]

Militarized hydraulic engineering initiatives were central to the Great Leap in Henan, where poorly conceived projects grappled with environmental conditions bequeathed by the Sino-Japanese War of 1937–1945. Mass mobilization of human labor along military lines was supposed to reorder hydraulic systems that had fallen into disarray. However, human labor proved no more capable of harnessing rivers during the Great Leap than it had during World War II. As Yang Jisheng writes, "In November 1959, 130,000 laborers embarked on the Huayuankou turnkey project on the Yellow River near Zhengzhou, and although it was completed in the early 1960s, the dam had to be blown up because of design flaws. Many other canal projects also failed to achieve the desired results, while impractical irrigation targets drew large amounts of water from the Yellow River, resulting in serious secondary salinization of cropland."[36]

Between 1938 and 1947, the Yellow River's floodwaters destroyed dike systems along the Huai River's tributaries and deposited sediments that clogged and obstructed their drainage. To remake the hydraulic environment, a "large-scale canal excavation project" on Henan's eastern plain was launched in 1958–1959 to connect the Hai, Huai, Han, and Yellow rivers.[37] The "chaotic directives" that characterized this and other water conservancy efforts during the Great Leap helped pave the way for catastrophe. In Yang's words, "Villagers deployed to irrigation projects labored on full stomachs [for the] first two months, but from October 1958 on into 1960 they went hungry. Cadres resorted to violence, threat, and humiliation, and countless irrigation workers died of starvation or physical abuse."[38] When men went away to engage in the projects, in another parallel with the war, women took over in the fields, resulting in what Hershatter terms "feminization of agriculture."[39]

Management of hydraulic engineering projects during the late 1950s bore the mark of a coercive "work style of war" that, as Ralph Thaxton contends, Japanese invasion and Civil War had fostered among Henan's Chinese Communist Party (CCP) cadres.[40] In waging their war against the Yellow River and other waterways, local leaders simply worked people to death. As Thaxton characterizes it, "the imprint of war fostered a tendency to suspend critical thinking, to portray all sacrifice, no matter how rational or irrational,

---

[35] Ibid., 117.
[36] Yang (2012): 73. See also Dikötter (2010): 183–184.
[37] Yang (2012): 73.
[38] Ibid.
[39] Hershatter (2011): chapter 9.
[40] Thaxton (2008): 83–88, 327–331. On militarized regimentation see also Dikötter (2010): 48.

as necessary for holding together the ascendant national community being crafted by Mao."[41] Water control and irrigation projects launched during the Great Leap closely resembled the highly coercive militarized hydraulic engineering efforts that prevailed during the Sino-Japanese War of 1937–1945, when army commanders took over dike maintenance and directed armies of civilian laborers.

From this perspective, World War II and the Chinese Civil War fit into a longer-term history of militarization in modern China that spanned from the 1850s to the 1970s. Throughout the late nineteenth and twentieth centuries, according to Hans van de Ven, "leading conceptions about China's future and how to reach that future were influenced by the military and military ways of thinking."[42] Modern Chinese leaders of all political stripes consistently promoted military regimentation, mobilization, and struggle as ideals for emulation and employed military organization to achieve their goals. This process of militarization also infused human interactions with China's environment.

Language that equates efforts to control nature with warfare implies "the existence of immediate and serious threat, with a need for quick and forceful action, increased government intervention and authority, decreased individual autonomy, and mobilization of large resources."[43] But the interplay between war and environment goes beyond mere rhetorical strategy. Military conflict and preparation for war generate vast environmental changes, while military technology and organization have enhanced people's ability to transform the environment and extract its wealth. The conquest of nature, as David Blackbourn observes with reference to modern Germany, not only stands as the "moral equivalent of war" but has also emerged as the "the by-product, even the hand-maiden of war."[44]

In China, environmental changes linked to military conflict and war preparation predated the conflict with Japan and persisted long after 1945. The drive to control and exploit the environment for military ends and along militarized lines reached unprecedented levels of urgency during World War II, profoundly altering human relations with nature. This tendency to employ militarized organizational structures to alter the environment carried profound implications for how people in China manipulated nature and its energies.

---

[41] Ibid., 84.
[42] van de Ven (1997): 373. See also Mitter (2005): 537; Szonyi (2008).
[43] Tucker and Russell (2004): 8.
[44] Blackbourn (2006): 6.

Glossary of Chinese Characters

Anhui	安徽
bailu cun	白鷺村
Baimagou	白馬溝
Baitan	白潭
bangjia zhi you	邦家之憂
bao	保
Baoji	寶雞
baojia	保甲
baozhang	保長
Beigang	北崗
Beijing	北京
Beiping	北平
bili	筆力
bingli	兵力
caili	財力
canyiyuan	參議員
Cao Wenzhang	曹文章
Caohu	草狐
Caoli	曹里
Chang'an	長安
Changsha	長沙
Chen Ruzhen	陳汝珍
Cheng Qian	程潛
Chiang Kai-shek (Jiang Jieshi)	蔣介石
chongji cengci pailie	沖積層次排列
Chongqing	重慶
chuli	畜力
Ci River	茨河
Ciyuan	辭源
cong li shi sheng	從力執聲

Dagongbao	大公報
daizhen renshu	待振人數
Daolinggang	道陵崗
daoyin	道尹
Dazhu	大朱
Dean	德安
di banzi	地班子
Di Fengzhu	翟鳳翥
difang liliang	地方力量
Duan Yucai	段玉裁
ermai	二麥
Fanjia	樊家
fenduan baogan	分段包乾
Feng Zhaoxue	馮兆學
fenshatu	粉沙土
fen shuishi	分水勢
Fugou	扶溝
Gansu	甘肅
Gao Zhaolin	高照臨
Gaoxian	高賢
gongxundui	工巡隊
gongzhen	工振
Guacun	瓜村
Guangwu	廣武
Guanzhong	關中
Guizhou	貴州
Guo Chengzhang	郭成章
Guo River	渦河
guofang tianxian	國防天險
guomai	國脈
guomin bingtuan	國民兵團
Haizhou	海州
Han	漢
Han River	漢江
Hankou	漢口
Hansiying	韓寺營
He Chengpu	何成璞
He Yaozu	賀耀組
He Zhuguo	何柱國
hefang ji guofang, zhihe ji weiguo	河防即國防, 治河即衛國
heli	合力
Henan	河南
Hexi	河西

Glossary of Chinese Characters

Hong River	洪河
Hongze Lake	洪澤湖
Hu Minying	胡民英
Huai River	淮河
Huaihai	淮海
Huaiyang	淮陽
huang	荒
Huang Yanli	黃炎離
Huang zai hui	黃災會
Huangfanqu	黃泛區
Huangfanqu nongchang	黃泛區農場
Huanghe	黃河
Huanghe shuili weiyuanhui Henan xiufangchu	黃河水利委員會河南修防處
Huanglongshan	黃龍山
huangyang	黃羊
Huayin	華陰
Huayuankou	花園口
Hubei	湖北
huiguire	回歸熱
Huiji River	惠濟河
huoluan	霍亂
Ichigō	一号
Ji Luhuan	計路環
Jialu River	賈魯河
Jiang Dingwen	蔣鼎文
Jiang Xiuying	姜秀英
Jiangcun	江村
Jiangsu	江蘇
Jieshou	界首
jiewan quzhi	截彎取直
Jin	金
Jin Mancang	靳滿倉
jinli zhi suoneng	盡力之所能
Jingshui	京水
Jin-Pu	津浦
jiuzai wuli	救災無力
jungongba	軍工壩
junshi guanli	軍事管理
junshi hegong cailiao	軍事河工材料
junzheng liliang	軍政力量
Kaifeng	開封
kangpi bingzi	糠皮餅子

Kang-Ri zhanzheng	抗日戰爭
Kani Kenhei	可兒廉平
Keshan	克山
laoli	勞力
li	力
Li Hezhi	李合志
Li Peiji	李培基
Li Xiangtang	李相唐
lianbao	連保
Liansi	練寺
Liao	遼
liliang	力量
liqi	力氣
Liu Dongmin	劉東敏
Liu Huan	劉煥
Liu Huo	劉貨
liushi	流勢
lizhan	力戰
Long-Hai	隴海
Long-Hai tielu tebie dangbu	隴海鐵路特別黨部
Lu Bingyin	盧丙寅
Lugouqiao	盧溝橋
Luohe	漯河
Luoyang	洛陽
Lushan	魯山
Lütan	呂潭
Luyi	鹿邑
mali	馬力
Manchukuo	滿洲國
Mao Guangde	毛廣德
Mao Zedong	毛澤東
mazha dui	螞蚱隊
mengjindi	蒙金地
Mi County	密縣
Ming	明
mingong fangxundui	民工防汛隊
minli	民力
minnian	民埝
minqi	民氣
Nanjing	南京
Nanmin mousheng zhidao	難民謀生指導
Nanyang	南陽
nengyuan	能源

nisha	泥沙
Panzhuang	潘莊
Ping-Han	平漢
Pingxin	平新
Poxie	坡謝
Pukou	浦口
Qi County	杞縣
qiangliang	搶糧
Qiao Guanghou	喬廣厚
Qing	清
Qu Chuanhe	曲傳和
quanli	權力
renli	人力
renli fuken	人力復墾
renli shengtian	人力勝天
Rongcun	榮村
Sha River	沙河
Shaan-Gan-Ning	陝甘寧
Shaanxi	陝西
Shaanxi sheng zhenhui	陝西省振會
shahua	沙化
Shandong	山東
Shangcai	上蔡
Shanghai	上海
Shangshui	商水
Shanxi	山西
shanzhu	山主
Shao Heniu	邵河妞
Shaying River	沙潁河
shengchanli	生產力
shengwu chengwu	生物成物
Shenqiu	沈丘
shi	勢
Shi Andong	史安棟
shi shi jiu kong	十室九空
shigong weili	施工爲力
shili	實力
Shilipu	十里舖
shoushi	手勢
Shuangji River	雙洎河
Shuidong duli tuan	水東獨立團
shuijianbao	水煎包
Shuipoji	水坡集

shuishi	水勢
Shuitai	水台
Shuo wen jie zi	說文解字
Sichuan	四川
Song	宋
Suiping	遂平
suqing	肅清
Su-Lu-Yu-Wan	蘇魯豫皖
Taierzhuang	台兒莊
Taikang	太康
Tang Enbo	湯恩伯
tanpai	攤派
Tao Lüdun	陶履敦
Tianjin	天津
Tongbai Mountains	桐柏山
Tongguan	潼關
tongxianghui	同鄉會
Tongxu	通許
tudi miao	土地廟
Wang Heting	王鶴亭
Wang Ruiying	王瑞英
Wang shi	王氏
Wangpan	王盤
Wei Lihuang	衛立煌
Wei River	渭河
Weichuan	洧川
weiran henggen	巍然橫亙
Weishi	尉氏
Wuhan	武漢
wuli	物力
Xi Chengfan	席承藩
Xi'an	西安
xian	縣
xiangbao	鄉保
Xiangcheng	項城
Xianyang	咸陽
Xiaoen	小恩
xiaohao minli	消耗民力
Xiaoyaozhen	逍遙鎮
Xihua	西華
Xing Youjie	邢幼杰
xingzheng ducha zhuanyuan	行政督察專員
Xinjiang	新疆

Xinxiang	新鄉
Xinzheng	新鄭
Xiong Xianyu	熊先煜
Xiulan	秀蘭
Xu Fuling	徐福齡
Xu Guangdao	許光道
Xuchang	許昌
Xunmukou	遜母口
Xuzhou	徐州
Yan'an	延安
Yang Yifeng	楊一峯
Yangzi River	揚子江
Yanling	鄢陵
yi Huang zhi di	以黃治敵
Ying River	穎河
yixiang gui	異鄉鬼
Yu Benyi	喻本義
yu juesuan zhidu	預決算制度
Yu zai diyi shourongsuo	豫災第一收容所
Yu zai jiuji weiyuanhui	豫災救濟委員會
yuandongli	原動力
yulinpeng	雨淋棚
Yunnan	雲南
yuni zhi di	淤泥之地
zaimin	災民
Zhang Dingfan	張定璠
Zhang Fang	張方
Zhang Guangsi	張光嗣
Zhang Hanying	張含英
Zhang Weiya	張維亞
Zhang Zhizhong	張治中
Zhangtie	張鐵
zhansheng	戰勝
Zhanyang	占楊
Zhao Xiuchun	趙岫春
Zhaokou	趙口
Zhaolan	趙蘭
Zhecheng	柘城
Zhejiang	浙江
Zheng County	鄭縣
zhenggou	徵購
zhengli senlin	整理森林
zhengliang	徵糧

zhengshi	徵實
Zhengzhou	鄭州
Zhongmu	中牟
Zhou Enlai	周恩來
Zhoujiakou	周家口
Zhu Guoheng	朱國衡
zhuangnian nanü	壯年男女
zhuli	主力
Zhuxianzhen	朱仙鎮
zili gengsheng zhi jihua	自力更生之計劃
zishi	姿勢
zuli jiyu biaozhun	租力給予標準

Archives

Academia Historica

Chen Bulei, "Guanyu Henan junliang wenti zhi jingguo qingxing yu chuli banfa" [On Henan's military grain problems and methods for dealing with them]. October 26, 1942: 001000004790A.
"Henan sheng zhengfu kuaiyou daidian" [Express mail in lieu of telegram from Henan provincial government]. July 1943: 001000004791A.
"Jiang Dingwen dian" [Telegram from Jiang Dingwen]. February 22, 1943: 001000004791A.
"Jiuji ru Shaan Yu ji nanmin shenchahui zhaiyao" [Excerpts from examination meeting on relief for Henan refugees entering Shaanxi]. December 17, 1943: 271 2984.
"Junliang gaishan yijian" [Ideas for improving military grain]. September 1942: 001000004790A.
"Junzhengbu daidian" [Express mail in lieu of telegram from Ministry of Military Affairs]. June 14, 1943: 001000004791A.
"Junzhengbuzhang He Yingqin qiancheng" [Strip petition from Minister of Military Affairs He Yingqian]. February 11, 1943: 001000004791A.
Liangshibu canshiting, "Jiuji jianyi" [Relief proposals]. May 1947: 212 1368.
Petition from Li Peiji to Chiang Kai-shek. September 7, 1942: 001000004790A.
Petition from Zhang Zhizhong and Zhang Dingfan. September 9, 1942: 001000004790A.
"Shaanxi sheng zhengfu kuaiyou daidian" [Express mail in lieu of telegram from Shaanxi provincial government]. July 1943: 062 673.
"Xingzhengyuan daidian" [Express mail in lieu of telegram from Administrative Yuan]. October 5, 1942: 001000004790A.
"Xinzhengyuan daidian" [Express mail in lieu of telegram from Administrative Yuan]. December 25, 1942: 001000004791A.
"Xingzhengyuan mishuchu gonghan" [Document for consultation from secretariat of the Administrative Yuan]. December 25, 1943: 271 2984.
"Xingzhengyuanzhang Jiang Zhongzheng xunling gao" [Draft instructions from head of Administrative Yuan, Jiang Zhongzheng {Chiang Kai-shek}]. June 28, 1943: 062 673.

"Xingzong Henan fenshu shuzhang Ma Jie tan Huangfanqu fuxing gongzuo xianzhuang" [CNRRA Henan branch office director Ma Jie on the current condition of recovery work in the Yellow River flooded area]. July 30, 1947: 272 1370.

"Yu jing ge jun bojie junliang jiuzai ji jieshi zhuzhen shuliang" [Amount of military grain loaned to relieve disaster and amount obtained by abstaining from food to assist with relief from armies in Henan]. July 9, 1943: 001000004791A.

"Zhang Ji and Zhang Lisheng dian" [Telegram from Zhang Ji and Zhang Lisheng]. October 21, 1942: 001000004790A.

Henan Provincial Archives

"1939 nian Henan sheng ge xian shuizai sunshi diaocha tongji biao" [Table of investigation statistics on flood disaster losses in Henan province during 1939]. 1940: AB6-591.

"Guomindang Henan sheng dangbu guanyu dangzheng jiguan qianyi, Huang zai jiuji gao minzhong shu, biaoyu" [Proclamation from Nationalist party Henan province party branch to the masses regarding party and government organs carrying out Yellow River disaster relief, with charts]. July 1938: M2-27-753.

"Guomindang Henan sheng dangbu tepai Qu Yingguang deng banli fuji shiyi" [Nationalist party Henan province party branch specially deputes Qu Yingguang and others to administer relief]. August 15, 1938: M2-25-686.

"Henan sheng Shangcai xian Pingxin xiang xiang gongsuo cheng" [Petition from Henan province's Shangcai County and Pingxin township offices]. October 1942: M02-25-692.

"Henan sheng zhengfu daidian" [Express mail in lieu of telegram from Henan provincial government]. November 1944: M08-50-1469.

"Henan sheng zhengfu jiuzai zong baogao" [Henan provincial government disaster relief report]. December 1943: AB6-588.

"Henan sheng Zheng xian, Zhongmu, Weishi deng xian guanyu Huang zai jizhen gongzuo baogao" [Work report on Yellow River flood relief from Zheng County, Zhongmu, and Weishi counties]. 1938: M8-08-0194.

"Zhongguo guomindang Henan sheng zhixing weiyuanhui xunling xingzutuan zi 68 hao" [Chinese Nationalist party Henan province executive committee directive, organization category, number 68]. August 9, 1943: M2-25-690.

"Zhongguo guomindang wei juxing Huang zai jiuji juankuan yiri yundong gao dangyuan minzhong shu" [Message from the Chinese Nationalist party to party members and the masses on carrying out a one-day donation movement to relieve the Yellow River disaster]. July 1938: M2-25-690.

Hoover Institution Archives

Chiang Kai-shek Diary. June 3, 1938.

Farm Credit Division of the Farmers Bank of China. "Land Reclamation in War-time China: A Memorandum for the U.S. Technical Experts to China." October 1942: Walter C. Lowdermilk Papers, Box 9.

"Henan sheng sanshiyi nian mai shou ji xiaofei shuliang tongji biao" [Statistical tables on the amount of Henan province's 1942 wheat harvest and consumption]. July 1942: KMT Project, TE 29 6.2.

Walter C. Lowdermilk. "Preliminary Report to the Executive Yuan, Government of China on Findings of a Survey of a Portion of the Northwest for a Program of Soil Water and Forest Conservation." November 26, 1943: Walter C. Lowdermilk Papers, Box 4.

Wang Bingjun, "Wei baogao shi ju bao Henan sheng Zheng xian, Zhongmu, Guangwu san xian zaiqing" [Report on disaster conditions in Henan province's Zheng County, Zhongmu, and Guangwu counties]. July 28, 1942: KMT Project TE 20, Reel 13, File 534.

"Wei Huang zai canzhong jiuji wei zhou ni qing zhi bo ju kuan chedi jiuji an" [Request to allocate large amounts of funds to provide comprehensive relief for the terrible Yellow River disaster]. October 24, 1939: KMT Project 003, Reel 45, File 389.

Wei Lihuang et al. "Beixiu Huang di zenggu guofang yi li kangzhan er wei minsheng an" [Shore up the Yellow River dikes in order to benefit the War of Resistance and support the people's livelihood]. July 1940: KMT Project, 003 Reel 64, File 658.

"Zhuan'an baogao: Huangfan digong qingxing" [Special report: Yellow River flood dike defense work situation]. July 27, 1941: KMT Project, 003 Reel 212, File 1717.

Institute of Modern History Archives, Academia Sinica

"Henan sheng zhenwu baogao" [Henan province relief report]. 1944: 20–00–03 9–1.

"Huanglongshan kenqu guanliju shicha baogao" [Inspection report on Huanglongshan reclamation area management bureau]. June 1943: 20–26 60–12.

"Huanglongshan kenqu nanmin shourong jiuji qingxing ji muqian kenmin gaikuang shicha baogao" [Inspection report on Huanglongshan reclamation area refugee reception and relief situation and the current general situation of settlers]. 1943: 20–26 60–12.

"Nonglinbu Shaanxi Huanglongshan kenqu guanliju daidian" [Express mail in lieu of telegram from Ministry of Agriculture and Forestry Shaanxi Huanglongshan reclamation area management bureau]. February 15, 1942: 20–26 31–8.

"Nonglinbu Shaanxi Huanglongshan kenqu guanliju saner niandu gongzuo jihuashu caoan" [Ministry of Agriculture and Forestry Shaanxi Huanglongshan reclamation area management bureau 1943 draft work plan]. 1943: 20–26 60–12.

"Shaanxi sheng Huanglongshan kenqu senlin shicha baogao" [Inspection report on the Huanglongshan reclamation area's forests]. 1943: 20–26 60–12.

Shaanxi Provincial Archives

"Di san qu xingzheng ducha zhuanyuan gongshu bugao" [Proclamation from the third special area special administrative supervisor]. June 15, 1943: 9–2–815.

"Ju zhanqu jun fengji di wu xunchatuan jianyi gaishan jiuji lai Shaan nanmin banfa dengqing dianyang zunzhao" [Telegraph containing methods suggested by the warzone military conduct and discipline fifth inspection group for improving relief for refugees coming to Shaanxi]. April 2, 1943: 64–1–280.

"Junshi weiyuanhui Xi'an banshiting kuaiyou daidian" [Express mail in lieu of telegram from the Military Affairs Commission Xi'an office]. February 26, 1943: 9–2–800.

"Li Shanji cheng" [Petition from Li Shanji]. December 28, 1942: 9–2–800.

"Long-Hai tielu tebie dangbu nanmin fuwudui canjia sanmin zhuyi qingniantuan Shaanxi zhibu Yu zai fangwen gongzuo baogao" [Work report on Long-Hai special party branch refugee service team participating in Three Principles of the People Youth Corp Shaanxi branch Henan famine inquiry]. June 1943: 9-2-823.

"Long-Hai tielu yunshu Yu sheng nanmin renshu zongbiao, sanshiyi nian ba yue – sanshier nian liu yue [Table of numbers of Henan province refugees transported by the Long-Hai railroad, August 1942-June 1943]. July 1943: 9-2-823.

"Nanmin mousheng zhidao" [Refugee livelihood guide]. February 1942: 9-2-819.

"Nonglinbu Huanglongshan kenqu gaikuangshu" [General situation of the Ministry of Agriculture and Forestry Huanglongshan reclamation area]. December 31, 1941: 9-2-823.

"Shaanxi sheng Huanglongshan kenqu banshichu gongzuo baogaoshu" [Shaanxi province Huanglongshan reclamation area office work report]. September 30, 1939: 7-1-2.

"Shaanxi sheng di san qu xingzheng ducha zhuanyuan jian baoan siling gongshu daidian" [Express mail in lieu of telegram from Shaanxi province third special area administrative supervisor and military garrison command office]. November 30, 1942: 9-2-800.

"Shaanxi sheng di san qu xingzheng ducha zhuanyuan jian baoan siling gongshu daidian" [Express mail in lieu of telegram from Shaanxi province third special area administrative supervisor and military garrison command office]. February 3, 1943: 9-2-722.

"Shaanxi sheng di san qu xingzheng ducha zhuanyuan jian baoan siling gongshu dai dian" [Express mail in lieu of telegram from Shaanxi province third special area administrative supervisor and military garrison command office]. February 10, 1943: 9-2-800.

"Shaanxi sheng di san qu xingzheng ducha zhuanyuan jian baoan siling gongshu daidian," [Express mail in lieu of telegram from Shaanxi province third special area administrative supervisor and military garrison command office]. March 22, 1943: 9-2-808.

"Shaanxi sheng minzhenting daidian/qianhan" [Express mail in lieu of telegram/letter from Shaanxi province department of civil affairs]. November 24, 1942: 9-2-805.

"Wei jiuji Henan nanmin bao quan qu bao jiao renyuan ji quanti minzhong shu" [Message on relieving Henan refugees to the whole area's mutual-security and educational personnel and the masses]. December 21, 1942: 9-2-800.

"Yichuan xian jiuji nanmin huiyi jilu" [Record of Yichuan county refugee relief meeting]. January 28, 1943: 9-2-722.

"Yu zai jiujihui Xi'an shi fenhui han" [Letter from Henan famine relief association Xi'an city branch association]. November 14, 1942: 9-2-805.

Zhou Changyun, "Huanglongshan zhi turang" [Huanglongshan's soils]. 1938: 9-5-285.

United Nations Archives and Records Management Section

Agriculture and Irrigation Sub-committee. "A Report of General Information and a Recommended Plan for Agricultural Rehabilitation in the Yellow River Flooded Area of Honan, Anhwei and Kiangsu Provinces." 1946: S-1021 Box 55 File 4.

An Han, H.K. Fu, and W.S. Chepil to Dr. P.C. Ma. "Recommended plan for soil conservation work in the Yellow River Flooded Area." n.d.: S-1021 Box 55 File 4.

Barnett, Irving to Herbert Hummel. "Land Problems in the Flooded Area." April 9, 1947: S-528–0358.

Barnett, Iriving to Herbert Hummel. "Communist Portions of the Flooded Area in Honan." April 9, 1947: S-0528–035.

Chepil, W.S. "Report of Survey of the Yellow River Flooded Area of Honan." November 11, 1946: S-528–0357 AR17a.

Chepil, W.S. "What Have I Done in China?" September 25, 1947: S-1021 Box 55 File 4.

Chu, Philip to Robert Van Hyning. "Report of Observations made on a recent survey of 17 hsiens." March 11, 1946: S-0528–0535.

Dickey, George to Will B. Rose. May 16, 1946: S-0528–0091.

Dickey, George. "China Office United Nations Relief and Rehabilitation Administration Office of the Financial Advisor, Food Resources – Honan." April 21, 1946: UN S-0528–0091.

Farris, D.K. "Report on General Conditions in Honan-Province, Dec. 24 1945": UN S-0528–0071.

Farris, D.K. to E. Gale. December 10, 1945: S-0528–0071.

Hamer, Burlin B. "A Study of the Yellow River Flooded Area in Honan Province by Regional Office, C.N.R.R.A. and Regional Office, U.N.R.R.A." December 1946: S1021 Box 58 File 6.

Hanson, Perry O. "A History of UNRRA's Program Along the Yellow River, Chapter I. – Background": S-1021 Box 55 File 3.

Hart, Robert to Flooded Area Committee. "Progress Report." December 11, 1946: S-0528–0078.

Hart, Robert to Walter West. "Report for Flooded Area Committee, Field Trip. 16/3/47 – Report No. 3" (March 18, 1947): S-0528–0544 AR-17a.

Hart, Robert to Walter West. "Report on Field Trip to Flooded Area, 16 to 26 March, 1947." March 28, 1947: S-0528–0543, A.R. 8 Flooded Area, General.

"Health. Honan Regional Office Month of October, 1946": S-0528–0540.

Johnson, Harold to Lucile Chamberlin. "Survey and Report on Administrative District 9, South Honan." June 1946: S1021 Box 58 File 7.

Kassebaum, John C. to Harland Cleveland. "Confidential Personnel." November 12, 1947: S-0528–0535.

Liu, Jean. "Condition of the Flooded District of Chung-mou." May 8, 1946: S-0528–0536 Folder 34.

"Memorandum from Mildred Bonnell to R. Van Hyning dated 3 April, 1946, Hsi Hua," attached to "UNRRA History – Honan Region": S1021 Box 58 File 7.

"Monthly Report, March 1946, Section 7 – Welfare Attachment (2)": S-0528–0540.

"Monthly Report, March 1946, Section 11 – Intelligence": S-0528–0540.

"Notes on Information from Dick Hillis, H.I.R.C. Regarding Conditions in parts of the Flooded Area, Honan, March, '46." March 1946: S-0528–0543 A.R. 8.

"Outline of Plan for Rehabilitation of Yellow River Flooded Area." 1946: S-1021 Box 55 File 4.

Parenti, A.J. to Newton Bowles. "Part I, Survey of Flooded Area Refugees as basis for estimating post-UNRRA food requirements." September 7, 1947: S-0528–0543 A.R. 8B.

Parenti, A.J. to Newton Bowles. "Honan Flooded Area Survey, Part II: Shensi and Northwest." October 1947: S-1021 Box 55 File 4.
"Preliminary Report on Flooded Area – Oct. 17–26." November 11, 1946: S-0528–0541 A.R. 8.
"Recording Some Observations and Recommendations Made During a Trip to Chengchow, Hsu-chang, Yen-ling, Fu-kou, Weishih, Hsi-hua, Chou-chia-k'ou, Lo-ho and Vicinities, 24 February to 3 March." March 11, 1947: S-0528–0544 A.R. 17a.
"Report and Recommendations on Joint Flooded Area Survey of Fukow Hsien by Representatives of CNRRA, Provincial Government, Hsien Governments & UNRRA 10 August to 10 September 1946": S-0528–324.
"Survey Through Honan Province – Mildred Bonnell, 12 Dec. 1945," attached to "UNRRA History – Honan Region": S1021 Box 58 File 7.
Shirkey, John H. to G.A. Fitch. "Crop and Agricultural Conditions noted enroute to Chengchow, Sinyang, Loshan, Loho, and Hsuchang, Yenling, Fukou, Wei-shih and Kaifeng, May 16 to May 30, '46." June 4, 1946: S-0528–0544 AR-17a.
Shirkey, John H. to William J. Green. "Evaluation of the Report prepared by Professor A.A. Stone and Professor H.F. McCaulley." June 2, 1946: S-528–0356.
Shirkey, John H. "Honan Flooded Areas Tractor Program (The Work with the Villages, January 1947-September 1947)": S-1021 Box 55 File 4.
Shirkey, John H. to Walter West. "Recording Some Observations and Recommendations Made During a trip to Chengchow, Hsu-chang, Yen-ling, Fu-kou, Weishih, Hsi-hua, Chou-chia-k'ou, Lo-ho and Vicinities, 24 February to 3 March, 1947." March 11, 1947: S-0528–0544 AR 17a.
UNRRA. "Survey Report on Yellow River Flooded Areas in Honan, Anhwei and Kiangsu." July 4, 1947: S-0528–0070.
"UNRRA History – Honan Region. Health Section": S1021 Box 58 File 7.
West, Walter. "Report from Flooded Area Committee. Field Trip 16th March. Report No. 4." March 19, 1947: S-0528–0544 A.R. 17a.

Wake Forest University Archives

Murray, Katie. "God Working in Chengchow, Honan: Interior China Baptist Mission, 1936–1950." August 14, 1970: Katie M. Murray Papers. Box 2, Folder 161.

Yellow River Conservancy Commission Archives, Zhengzhou

"Chakan Huaiyang zaimin qingqiu xiuzhu xin di luxian baogao shu" [Report on survey of new dike course repairs requested by Huaiyang disaster vicitims]. August 1940: MG4.1–51.
"Chakan Taikang Huaiyang jingnei Huangfan qingxing baogaoshu" [Report on survey of Yellow River flood conditions in Taikang and Huaiyang counties]. December 31, 1941: MG 4.1–135.
"Fangfan xindi Weishi duan qiangxian dukou huiyi jilu" [Record of meeting on emergency repairs and dike closures to the new flood defense dike Weishi section]. August 10, 1940: MG4.1–177.

"Fangfan xindi Weishi duan qiangdu linshi gongcheng weiyuanhui zhiling" [Directive from the new flood defense dike Weishi section emergency closure provisional engineering committee]. September 21, 1940: MG4.2-71.

"Henan sheng Xihua xian zhengfu cheng" [Petition from Henan province, Xihua county government]. November 11, 1943: MG4.1-340.

"Huaiyang xian zaimin daibiao ni qing bo kuan zhu di" [Huaiyang county disaster victim representatives request allocations of funds to reinforce dikes]. March 1940.: MG4.1-51.

"Huanghe shuili weiyuanhui ji Xihua xian dang zheng jiguan shishen zuotanhui" [Discussion meeting between the Yellow River Conservancy Commission and local elites from Xihua county's party and government organs]. May 25, 1943: MG4.1-218.

"Huanghe shuili weiyuanhui Yu sheng hefang tegong linshi gongchengchu gongzuo baogao" [Work report from Yellow River Conservancy Commission Henan province river defense special project provisional engineering office]. May 21, 1940: MG.1-134.

"Huangfanqu yan Huang kuishui ge xian beizai baogao" [Disaster reports on inundated counties in the Yellow River flooded area]. August 1938: MG4.3.3-6.

"Li Jingtang cheng" [Petition from Li Jingtang]. December 17, 1939: MG.4.1-8.

"Nan yi duan zong duanzhang Yan Kai cheng" [Petition from first southern dike section section-head Yan Kai]. n.d.: YRCC MG2.2-277

"Nan yi duan zong duanzhang Yan Kai cheng" [Petition from first southern dike section section-head Yan Kai]. January 19, 1940: YRCC MG2.2-277.

"Quan Xianmiao cheng" [Petition from Quan Xianmiao]. January 19, 1940: MG2.2-277.

"Shin Kōga karyū ibban kaikyo chōsa hōkokusho" [Investigation report on general situation in the lower reaches of the new Yellow River]. September 24, 1943: MG 10-140.

"Taikō shin Kōga chihō chōsa hōkoku" [Investigation report on new Yellow River dike defenses in Taikang]. August 1939: MG10.29.

"Wang Qiuhang qiancheng" [Strip petition from Wang Qiuhang]. January 15, 1940: MG2.2-277.

"Yu Wan Huangfanqu chakantuan baogao" [Report of the Henan and Anhui flooded area survey delegation]. 1941: MG4.1-124.

"Zheng xian zhengfu bugao" [Zheng county government proclamation]. 1940: MG4.1-43.

"Zhi Huanghe shuili weiyuanhui xiudu hefang zaishi yuangong ci" [Message to Yellow River Conservancy Commission work personnel engaged in repairs, closures, and river defense]. November 1943: MG4.1-298.

Zhengzhou Municipal Archives

"Henan sheng sanshiqi nian bian xiaji fangyi jihua" [Henan province 1948 summer epidemic prevention plan]. 1948: 6-1-7 10.

"Henan sheng di er qu xingzheng ducha zhuanyuan jian baoan siling gongshu dai dian Zheng Erjian zi di 1769 hao" [Express mail in lieu of telegram from Henan province second special area administrative supervisor and military garrison command office, Zheng Erjian category, number 1769]. December 1945: 6-1-13 18.

"Henan sheng di yi qu xingzheng ducha zhuanyuan jian baoan siling gongshu wu nian lai gongzuo jiyao" [Work record of the Henan province first special area administrative supervisor and military garrison command office over the past five years]. July 1, 1947: 6-1-37.

Bibliography

"1938 nian Huanghe juedi shiliao yi zu" [A selection of historical materials on the 1938 Yellow River breach] 1997. *Minguo dang'an* [Republican archives] 3 (August), 11–17.

Bao Mengyin 2011. "Kangzhan shengli hou guomin zhengfu Huanghe dukou zhong de gongzhen" [Work relief during the Nationalist government's breach closure after victory in the War of Resistance]. *Minguo dang'an* [Republican archives] 3 (August), 128–136.

Barnett, Irving 1953. *UNRRA Aid to Redevelopment of Yellow River Flooded Area in Honan, China.* Haverford, PA: Haverford College.

Beck, Melinda A. and Levander, Orville A. 2000. "Host Nutritional Status and Its Effect on a Viral Pathogen." *The Journal of Infectious Diseases* 182, Supplement 1: S93–96.

Belden, Jack 1943. *Still Time to Die.* New York: Harper.

Bennett, Judith 2009. *Natives and Exotics: World War II and the Environment in the Southern Pacific.* Honolulu: University of Hawaii Press.

Bi Chunfu 1995. *Kangzhan jianghe juekou mishi* [Secret history of river breaches in the War of Resistance]. Taibei: Wenhai jinhui.

Biggs, David 2011. *Quagmire: Nation-Building and Nature in the Mekong Delta.* Seattle: University of Washington Press.

Black, Richard 1998. *Refugees, Environment and Development.* Harlow: Longman.

Blackbourn, David 2006. *The Conquest of Nature: Water, Landscape, and the Making of Modern Germany.* New York: Norton.

Bo Haitao 1989. "Huanghe lei" [The Yellow River's tears]. *Fugou wenshi ziliao* [Fugou literary and historical materials] 1, 119–128.

Bose, Sugata 1990. "Starvation amidst Plenty: The Making of Famine in Bengal, Honan, and Tonkin, 1942–45." *Modern Asian Studies* 24:4 (October), 699–727.

Brady, Lisa M. 2009. "Devouring the Land: Sherman's 1864–65 Campaigns." In Charles E. Closmann, ed. *War and the Environment: Military Destruction in the Modern Age.* College Station: Texas A&M University Press.

Brady, Lisa M. 2012. *War upon the Land: Military Strategy and the Transformation of Southern Landscapes during the American Civil War.* Athens: University of Georgia Press.

Brönnimann, Stefan et al. 2004. "Extreme Climate of the Global Troposphere and Stratosphere in 1940–1942 Related to El Niño." *Nature* 431 (October 21), 971–974.

Brook, Timothy 2005. *Collaboration: Japanese Agents and Local Elites in Wartime China*. Cambridge: Harvard University Press.

Burke III, Edmund 2009. "The Big Story: Human History, Energy Regimes, and the Environment." In Edmund Burke III and Kenneth Pomeranz, eds. *The Environment and World History*. Berkeley: University of California Press.

Chang, Kia-Ngau 1958. *Inflationary Spiral: The Experience in China, 1939–1950*. Cambridge: MIT Press.

Chen Chuanhai 1986. *Rijun huo Yu ziliao xuanbian* [Selected materials on calamities caused by the Japanese army in Henan]. Zhengzhou: Henan renmin chubanshe.

Chen Hongyou 1947. "Yu Wan Su san sheng Huangfanqu fuxing fangzhen chuyi" [Tentative suggestions on plans for revival of the Yellow River flooded area in Henan, Anhui, and Jiangsu provinces] *Zhong nong yuekan* [China farmers monthly] 8:9, 1–8.

Chen Yunping and Chen Ying 2009. "Kangzhan da houfang nanmin yiken dui shengtai huanjing de yingxiang" [The effects of refugee land reclamation on the ecological environment of the great rear areas in the War of Resistance] *Xinan daxue xuebao: shehui kexue ban* [Journal of Southwestern University: social science edition] 35:5 (September), 182–187.

Cheng Youwei et al. 2007. *Huanghe zhong xia you diqu shuili shi* [History of water control in the middle and lower Yellow River basin region]. Zhengzhou: Henan renmin chubanshe.

Chepil, W. S. 1949. "Wind Erosion Control with Shelterbelts in North China." *Agronomy Journal* 41:3 (March), 127–129.

China Office, UNRRA, Office of the Economic and Financial Advisor 1946. "Honan CNRRA – UNRRA Food Report."

Christensen, Erleen J. 2005. *In War and Famine: Missionaries in China's Honan Province in the 1940s*. Montreal: McGill Queen's University Press.

Christian, David 2005. *Maps of Time: An Introduction to Big History*. Berkeley: University of California Press.

Closmann, Charles E., ed. 2009. *War and the Environment: Military Destruction in the Modern Age*. College Station: Texas A & M University Press.

Coble, Parks M. 2003. *Chinese Capitalists in Japan's New Order: The Occupied Lower Yangzi, 1937–1945*. Berkeley: University of California Press.

Cronon, William 1992. "A Place for Stories: Nature, History, and Narrative." *Journal of American History* 78:4 (March), 1347–1376.

Cui Fude 1992. "Han, huang, bing zai mudu ji" [Eyewitness record of drought, locust, and military disasters]. *Yanling wenshi ziliao* [Yanling literary and historical materials] 4, 62–68.

Cui Yuhua 1988. "Yi Huangfanqu nongkendui he nongken xuexiao" [Recollections of the Yellow River flooded area agricultural reclamation team and the agricultural reclamation school]. *Henan wenshi ziliao* [Henan literary and historical materials] 27, 186–192.

Cumings, Bruce 2010. *The Korean War: A History*. New York: Modern Library.

"Dagongbao de baodao" [Report from *Dagongbao*] (June 28, 1938). *Zhengzhou wenshi ziliao* [Zhengzhou literary and historical materials] 2 (1986), 26–29.

Davis, Mike 2001. *Late Victorian Holocausts: El Niño Famines and the Making of the Third World*. New York: Verso.

Des Forges, Roger V. 2004. *Cultural Centrality and Political Change in Chinese History: Northeast Henan in the Fall of the Ming*. Stanford: Stanford University Press.

Dikötter, Frank 2010. *Mao's Great Famine: The History of China's Most Devastating Catastrophe*. New York: Walker and Company.

Dodgen, Randall A. 2001. *Controlling the Dragon: Confucian Engineers and the Yellow River in Late Imperial China*. Honolulu: University of Hawaii Press.

Drea, Edward J. and van de Ven, Hans 2010. "An Overview of Major Campaigns during the Sino-Japanese War." In Mark Peattie, Edward J. Drea, and Hans van de Ven, eds. *The Battle for China: Essays on the Military History of the Sino-Japanese War of 1937–1945*, 27–47. Stanford: Stanford University Press.

Duan Yucai 1815. "Shuo wen jie zi zhu" [Commentary on Explaining Single Component Graphs and Analyzing Compound Characters]. http://www.esgweb.net/html/swjz/imgbook/index2.htm

Dutch, Steven I. 2009. "The Largest Act of Environmental Warfare in History." *Environmental & Engineering Geoscience* 15:4 (November), 287–297.

Eastman, Lloyd E. 1980. "Facets of an Ambivalent Relationship: Smuggling, Puppets, and Atrocities during the War, 1937–1945." In Akira Iriye, ed. *The Chinese and the Japanese: Essays in Political and Cultural Interactions*, 275–303. Princeton: Princeton University Press.

Eastman, Lloyd E. 1984. *Seeds of Destruction: Nationalist China in War and Revolution, 1937–1949*. Stanford: Stanford University Press.

Eastman, Lloyd E. 1986. "Nationalist China during the Sino-Japanese War, 1937–1945." In Mary B. Rankin, John K. Fairbank, and Albert Feuerwerker, eds. *The Cambridge History of China, Vol. 13: Republican China, 192–1949, Part 2*. Cambridge: Cambridge University Press.

Edgerton-Tarpley, Kathryn 2008. *Tears from Iron: Cultural Responses to Famine in Nineteenth-Century China*. Berkeley: University of California Press.

Edgerton-Tarpley, Kathryn 2014. "From 'Nourish the People' to 'Sacrifice for the Nation': Changing Responses to Disaster in Late Imperial and Modern China." *The Journal of Asian Studies* 73:2, 447–469.

Elvin, Mark 1993. "Three Thousand Years of Unsustainable Growth: China's Environment from Archaic Times to the Present." *East Asian History* 6, 7–46.

Elvin, Mark 2004. *Retreat of the Elephants: An Environmental History of China*. New Haven: Yale University Press.

Evenden, Matthew 2011. "Aluminum, Commodity Chains, and the Environmental History of the Second World War." *Environmental History* 16:1 (April), 69–93.

Fang Ce 1942. "Ben sheng feichang shiqi banli jiuji shiye zhi genggai" [The broad outlines of relief administration in this province during the period of emergency]. *Henan zhengzhi* [Henan politics] 1:4 (March), 10–12.

Fang Wanpeng 2011. "Lun Huang Huai pingyuan shui huanjing dui Huaihai zhanyi de yingxiang – cong 1938 nian Huayuankou juedi tanqi" [On the influence of the Yellow River and Huai River plain's water on the battle of Huaihai – a discussion starting from the 1938 Huayuankou breach] *Junshi lishi yanjiu* [Military history research] 2 http://sino-eh.com/ThesesHTML/Thesis_698.shtml.

Feng Yufan 1991. "Tianyuan yanmo yibing liuxing" [The countryside flooded and diseases rampant]. *Zhongmu wenshi ziliao* [Zhongmu literary and historical materials] 4, 36–37.

Feng Zhongli 1992. "Cong fengsha cheng dao lüman Zhengzhou de huigu" [Looking back on the change from a sandstorm city to verdant Zhengzhou]. *Zhengzhou wenshi ziliao* [Zhengzhou literary and historical materials] 11, 1–26.

Fiege, Mark 2004. "Gettysburg and the Organic Nature of the American Civil War." In Richard P. Tucker and Edmund Russell, eds. *Natural Enemy, Natural Ally: Toward an Environmental History of War*. Corvallis: Oregon State University Press.

Fischer-Kowalski, Marina and Haberl, Helmut 2007. *Socioecological Transitions and Global Change: Trajectories of Social Metabolism and Land Use*. Northampton: Edward Elgar Publishing.

Flath, James and Smith, Norman 2011. *Beyond Suffering: Recounting War in Modern China*. Vancouver: University of British Columbia Press.

Fu Huanguang 1947. "Henan Huangfanqu fuxing zhi shuguang (Zhongmu tongxun)" [The dawn of restoration in Henan's Yellow River flooded area (bulletin from Zhongmu)]. *Jing-Han zhoukan* [Jing-Han weekly] 1:46, 24–26.

Fugou xianzhi zong bianji shi 1986. *Fugou xianzhi* [Fugou county gazetteer]. Zhengzhou: Henan remin chubanshc.

Fugou xian tudi guanliju 1999. *Zhoukou diqu tudi zhi: Fugou juan* [Zhoukou area land gazetteer: Fugou section]. Zhengzhou: Zhongzhou guji chubanshe, 1999.

Fugou xian zhengxie wenshi ziliao weiyuanhui 2004. "Erzhan hou Zhongguo 'xingzong' zai Fugou de jiuji huodong" [The relief work of China's 'CNRRA' in Fugou after World War II]. *Zhoukou wenshi ziliao xuanji* [Zhoukou literary and historical materials collection] 1:3, 120–132.

Garnaut, Anthony 2013. "A Quantitative Description of the Henan Famine of 1942." *Modern Asian Studies* 47: 6 (May), 1–39.

Greenough, Paul R. 1982. *Prosperity and Misery in Modern Bengal: The Famine of 1943–1944*. Oxford: Oxford University Press.

Greer, Charles 1979. *Water Management in the Yellow River Basin of China*. Austin: University of Texas Press.

Guan Jianchu 1991. "Huiyi woxian yijiusisan nian de da jihuang" [Recalling our county's great 1943 famine] *Fugou xian wenshi ziliao* [Fugou county literary and historical materials] 2, 111–116.

"Guanyu Huangfanqu tugai fang'an de ruogan shuoming yu buchong guiding" [Several explanations and supplementary regulations on land reform plans in the Yellow River flooded area] (March 23, 1951). *Henan sheng renmin zhengfu gongbao* [Henan province people's government gazette] 4 (May 1, 1951), 51–52.

Guo Erpu 1947. "Henan fanqu xia huang fangzhi gongzuo" [Summer locust defense work in Henan's flooded area] *Shanhou jiuji zongshu Henan fenshu zhoubao* [Weekly report of CNRRA's Henan branch office] 93 (October 20), 2–4.

Guo Jianxuan 1940. "Kaizhan Shaan sheng kenhuang yundong" [Launching Shaanxi province's land reclamation movement] *Xibei yanjiu* [Northwest research] 2: 13, 6–8.

Han Fahai and Han Zhangyu 1991. "Hanzhai cun de bianqian" [The vicissitudes of Hanzhai village] *Zhongmu wenshi ziliao* [Zhongmu literary and historical materials] 4, 59–61.

Han Qingxiang 1947. "Di si gongzuodui de guoqu xianzai he jianglai" [The past, present, and future of the fourth work team]. *Shanhou jiuji zongshu Henan fenshu zhoubao* [Weekly report of CNRRA's Henan branch office] 81/82 (August 4), 18–22.

Han Qitong and Nan Zhongwan 1948. *Huangfanqu de sunhai yu shanhou jiuji* [The Yellow River flooded area's damage and rehabilitation and relief]. Shanghai: Xingzhengyuan shanhou jiuji zongshu.

Han Zhaoqing 2010. *Huangmo shuixi sanjiaozhou – Zhongguo huanjingshi de quyu yanjiu* [Desert, rivers, lakes, deltas: Studies in China's regional environmental History]. Shanghai: Shanghai keji wenxian chubanshe.

Hao Zhixin et al. 2008. "Precipitation Cycles in the Middle and Lower Reaches of the Yellow River (1736–2000)." *Journal of Geographical Science* 18 (2008): 17–25.

Hara Takeshi 2010. "The Ichigō Offensive." In Mark Peattie, Edward J. Drea, and Hans van de Ven, eds. *The Battle for China: Essays on the Military History of the Sino-Japanese War of 1937–1945*. Stanford: Stanford University Press.

"He Chengpu jianyi chen taoxun juedi" [He Chengpu's recommendation to take advantage of the summer highwaters to breach the dikes] (May 5, 1938). *Zhengzhou wenshi ziliao* [Zhengzhou literary and historical materials] 2 (1986), 4.

He Zhong 1940. "Huanglongshan kenqu gaikuang" [General situation of the Huanglongshan reclamation area]. *Xibei yanjiu* [Northwest research] 2:11–12, 15–16.

He Ziping 1947. "Henan fanqu qiu huang fangzhi gongzuo" [Autumn locust protection work in Henan's flooded area]. *Shanhou jiuji zongshu Henan fenshu zhoubao* [Weekly report of CNRRA's Henan branch office] 93 (October 20), 4–9.

Henan nongqing 1942 [Henan agricultural conditions] 1:4/5 (December).

Henan sheng difangshizhi bianzuan weiyuanhui 1990. *Henan dili zhi* [Henan geographical gazetteer]. Zhengzhou: Henan renmin chubanshe.

"Henan sheng Huangfanqu tudi gaige fang'an" [Henan province Yellow River flooded area land reform plan] (March 23, 1951). *Henan sheng renmin zhengfu gongbao* [Henan province people's government gazette] 4 (May 1, 1951), 49–51.

Henan sheng minzhengting 1941. *Henan sheng minzheng gongzuo baogao* [Henan province civil affairs report]. n.p.: Henan sheng zhengfu.

"Henan sheng zhanshi sunshi diaocha baogao" [Henan province war damage investigation report] (December 15, 1945) 1990. *Minguo dang'an* [Republican archives] 4 (December), 13–18.

Henan sheng zhengfu 1938. *Deng xian kenhuang jihua* [Deng county land reclamation plan] n.p.

Henan sheng zhengfu 1941. *Henan sheng zhengfu ershijiu niandu xingzheng zong baogao* [Henan provincial government 1940 administrative report] n.p.: Henan sheng zhengfu mishuchu.

"Henan sheng zhengfu bennian jiuzai jihua" [Henan provincial government relief plan for this year] 1943. *Henan dangwu* [Henan party affairs] 3: 5, 69–70.

Henan shuiliting shui han zaihai zhuanzhuo bianji weiyuanhui 1998. *Henan shui han zaihai*. [Henan flood and drought disasters] Zhengzhou: Henan shuili chubanshe.

Hershatter, Gail 2007. *Women in China's Long Twentieth Century*. Berkeley: University of California Press.

Hershatter, Gail 2011. *Gender of Memory: Rural Women and China's Collective Past*. Berkeley: University of California Press.

Huang, Philip C. 1985. *The Peasant Economy and Social Change in North China*. Stanford: Stanford University Press.

Huang Xiaokui and Wang Anqiu 1954. "Huangfanqu turang dili" [The Yellow River flooded area's soil geography]. *Dili xuebao* [Geography Journal] 20:3 (September), 313–331.

Huang Zhenglin 2005. *Shaan-Gan-Ning bianqu de shehui jingji shi* [Social and economic history of the Shaan-Gan-Ning border area]. Beijing: Renmin chubanshe.

Huang Zhenglin 2006. *Shaan-Gan-Ning bianqu xiangcun de jingji yu shehui* [Economy and society of villages in the Shaan-Gan-Ning border area]. Beijing: Renmin chubanshe.

Huangfanqu nongchangzhi bianzuan weiyuanhui 1987. *Huangfanqu nongchangzhi* [Yellow River flooded area farm gazetteer]. Zhengzhou: Henan renmin chubanshe.

Huanghe shuili weiyuanhui 2004. *Minguo Huanghe dashiji* [Chronology of the Yellow River during the Republican period]. Zhengzhou: Huanghe shuili chubanshe.

Huanglong xian difangzhi bianzuan weiyuanhui 1995. *Huanglong xianzhi* [Huanglong county gazetteer]. Xi'an: Shaanxi renmin chubanshe.

Jacobsen, Karen 1997. "Refugees' Environmental Impact: The Effect of Patterns of Settlement." *Journal of Refugee Studies* 10:1 (March), 19–36.

Jarman, Robert L. ed. 2001. *China: Political Reports, 1911–1960. Volume 7: 1942–1945*. London: Archive Editions.

Jin Pusen 2001. "To Feed a Country at War: China's Supply and Consumption of Grain during the War of Resistance." Translated by Larry N. Shyu. In David P. Barrett and Larry N. Shyu, eds. *China in the Anti-Japanese War, 1937–1945: Politics, Culture, and Society*. New York: Peter Lang.

Jin Tianshun 1990. "Duanzhuang cun shuihuan shi" [History of flood disasters in Duanzhuang village]. *Weishi wenshi ziliao* [Weishi literary and historical materials] 5, 74–76.

"Jiuzai yu fangyi" [Disaster relief and disease prevention] 1943. *Yanling zhoubao* [Yanling weekly] (May 10), 2.

Jones, Eric 2002. *The European Miracle: Environments, Economies and Geopolitics in the History of Europe and Asia*. Third Edition. Cambridge: Cambridge University Press.

Kibreab, Gaim 1997. "Environmental Causes and Impact of Refugee Movements: A Critique of the Current Debate." *Disasters* 21:1, 20–38.

Kinzley, Judd 2012. "Crisis and the Development of China's Southwestern Periphery: The Transformation of Panzhihua, 1936–1969." *Modern China* 38:5 (September), 559–584.

Kreamer, D. K. 2012. "The Past, Present, and Future of Water Conflict and International Security." *Journal of Contemporary Water Research & Education* 149 (December), 87–95.

Kreike, Emmanuel 2004a. *Recreating Eden: Land Use, Environment, and Society in Southern Angola and Northern Namibia*. Portsmouth: Heinemann.

Kreike, Emmanuel 2004b. "War and the Environmental Effects of Displacement in Southern Africa (1970s–1990s)" In William G. Moseley and B. IkubolajehLogan, eds. *African Environment and Development: Rhetoric, Programs, Realities.* Burlington, VT: Ashgate, 2004.

Kreike, Emmanuel 2006. "Architects of Nature: Environmental Infrastructure and the Nature-Culture Dichotomy." PhD dissertation, Wageningen University.

Kreike, Emmanuel 2013. *Environmental Infrastructure in African History: Examining the Myth of Natural Resource Management in Namibia.* Cambridge: Cambridge University Press.

Laakkonen, Simo 2004. "War, an Ecological Alternative to Peace?: Indirect Impacts of World War II on the Finnish Environment." In Richard P. Tucker and Edmund Russell, eds. *Natural Enemy, Natural Ally: Toward an Environmental History of Warfare.* Corvallis: Oregon State University Press.

Lamouroux, Christian 1998. "From the Yellow River to the Huai: New Representations of a River Network and the Hydraulic Crisis of 1128." In Mark Elvin and Ts'ui-jung Liu, eds. *Sediments of Time: Environment and Society in Chinese History.* Cambridge: Cambridge University Press.

Lary, Diana 1985. *Warlord Soldiers: Chinese Common Soldiers, 1911–1937.* Cambridge: Cambridge University Press.

Lary, Diana 2001. "Drowned Earth: The Strategic Breaching of the Yellow River Dyke, 1938." *War in History* 8:2 (April), 191–207.

Lary, Diana 2004. "The Waters Covered the Earth: China's War-Induced Natural Disasters." In Mark Selden and Alvin So, eds. *War and State Terrorism: The United States, Japan, and the Asia-Pacific in the Long Twentieth Century.* Lanham, MD: Rowan and Littlefield.

Lary, Diana 2010. *The Chinese People at War: Human Suffering and Social Transformation, 1937–1945.* Cambridge: Cambridge University Press.

Lary, Diana and Stephen R. MacKinnon, eds. 2001. *Scars of War: The Impact of War on Modern China.* Vancouver: University of British Columbia Press.

Latour, Bruno 2005. *Reassembling the Social: An Introduction to Actor-Network Theory.* Oxford: Oxford University Press.

Lee, Jame Z. and Wang Feng 1999. *One Quarter of Humanity: Malthusian Mythology and Chinese Realities, 1700–2000.* Cambridge: Harvard University Press.

Lei Yu and Lou Yunhai 1991. "Huanghe juekou hou de Xingjie cun" [Xingjie village after the Yellow River breach]. *Zhongmu wenshi ziliao* [Zhongmu literary and historical materials] 4, 56–57.

Li Chungui and Liu Peiliang 1952. "Guoying Huangfanqu nongchang chuangzao le xiaomai de da mianji gaoe chanliang" [The Yellow River flooded area state farm creates high levels of wheat production over a large area] *Renmin zhoubao* [People's weekly] 10, 7.

Li Haishan 2003. "Xihua xian de 'shi nian Huangshui'" [Xihua county's "ten-year Yellow River flood"] *Zhoukou wenshi ziliao xuanji* [Zhoukou literary and historical materials collection] 1: 2, 113–116.

Li Jingrong 1942. "Jiuzai wenti de shangque" [A discussion of disaster relief problems]. *Henan zhengzhi* [Henan politics] 1:10 (October), 35–37.

Li, Lillian M. 2007. *Fighting Famine in North China: State, Market, and Environmental Decline, 1690s–1990s.* Stanford: Stanford University Press.

Li Lixia and Wang Jianjun 2006. "Kangzhan shiqi ru Shaan yimin qunti de renkouxue fenxi" [Demographic analysis of migrant groups entering Shaanxi during the

period of the War of Resistance]. *Xibei renkou* [Northwest population] 3:3 (May), 5–8.
Li Wenhai et al. 1993. *Jindai Zhongguo zaihuang jinian xubian* [Continued chronological record of disasters in modern China]. Changsha: Hunan jiaoyu chubanshe.
Li Wenhai et al. 1994. *Zhongguo jindai shi da zaihuang* [Modern China's ten great disasters]. Shanghai: Shanghai renmin chubanshe.
Li Yanhong 2007. "1941–1947 nian Yudong Huangfanqu de huangzai" [Locust disasters in eastern Henan's Yellow River flooded area, 1941–1947]. *Fangzai keji xueyuan xuebao* [Journal of the Institute of Disaster-Prevention Science and Technology] 9:1 (March), 25–28.
Li Yubao 1991. "Guoxin zhuang canzao Huangshui hai" [Guoxin village meets with the Yellow River flood disaster] *Zhongmu wenshi ziliao* [Zhongmu literary and historical materials] 4, 68–71.
Lin Ruiwu 1996. "Huangfanqu nanmin Liu Dongmin de beican zaoyu" [Yellow River flooded area refugee Liu Dongming's miserable experience] *Lushan wenshi ziliao* [Lushan literary and historical materials] 12: 143–144.
Ling Daoyang and Xu Weijian 1943. *Shicha Xibei jiuji gongzuo baogao ji jianyi* [Work report and recommendations on relief work in the Northwest]. n.p.: Meiguo yuan Hua jiuji lianhehui.
Liu Canruo 1947. "Xiansheng, gei wo xiang ge banfa ba" [Sir, think of a way for me] *Shanhou jiuji zongshu Henan fenshu zhoubao* [Weekly report of CNRRA's Henan branch office] 38 (August 11), 7–8.
Liu Jingrun 1990. "Fanqu canshi shilu"[Veritable record of the flooded area disaster] *Weishi wenshi ziliao* [Weishi literary and historical materials] 5: 57–66.
Liu Jingwen 1991. "Huangshui weikun xiancheng de qianqian houhou" [The whole story of the Yellow River's floodwaters surrounding the county seat] *Zhongmu wenshi ziliao* [Zhongmu literary and historical materials] 4, 3–10.
Liu Keming and Mao Wenxue 1991. "Duo zai duo nan de Zhanyang cun" [Disaster-stricken Zhanyang village]. *Zhongmu wenshi ziliao* [Zhongmu literary and historical materials] 4, 47–52.
Liu, Lydia H. 1995. *Translingual Practice: Literature, National Culture, and Translated Modernity-China, 1900–1937*. Stanford: Stanford University Press.
Liu Minglai and Dang Taihe 2001. "Huanglongshan cishenglin zai Shaanxi shengtai huanjing jianshe zhong de zuoyong" [The function of Huanglongshan's secondary growth forests in Shaanxi's environmental reconstruction]. *Shaanxi linye keji* [Shaanxi forestry technology] 3 (March), 32–34.
Liu Zaishi and Qi Honghao 1988. "Huanglong xian difangbing shi" [History of local disease in Huanglong County]. *Huanglong xian wenshi ziliao* [Huanglong literary and historical materials] 2, 177–181.
"Liu Zhongyuan deng jiang dian" [Telegram from Liu Zhongyuan, et al.] (June 3, 1938). *Zhengzhou wenshi ziliao* [Zhengzhou literary and historical materials] 2 (1986), 4.
Lowdermilk, Walter C. 1944. "Hwang Lung Shan, Where China's History Is Written in the Land." *Soil Conservation* (March), 3–7.
Lu Erkui et al. 1997. *Ciyuan zhengxiubian hedingben* [Source of words, revised and expanded combined edition]. Shanghai: Shangwu yinshuguan, 1939. Second reprint edition. Zhengzhou: Zhongzhou guji chubanshe.

Lu Hejian 2005. "Kangzhan shiqi xibu nongken shiye de fazhan" [The development of agricultural reclamation in the west during the period of the War of Resistance]. *Minguo dang'an* [Republican archives] 2 (May), 87–92.

Lu Shaokun 1990. "Huayuankou juedi yu Weishi renmin de zainan" [The Huayuankou dike breach and Weishi people's disaster] *Weishi wenshi ziliao* [Weishi literary and historical materials] 5, 53–56.

Lu Yuwen 1942. "Tianfu gai zheng shiwu hou Henan sheng liangshi chuyun ji zhenggou" [Grain transport and compulsory purchase in Henan province after the change to collecting the land tax in kind]. *Henan zhengzhi* [Henan politics] 1:7, 33–39.

Luo Laixing 1953. "1938–1947 nianjian de Huanghe nan fan" [The Yellow River's southern flood from 1938–1947]. *Dili xuebao* [Geography journal] 19:2 (December), 234–244.

Ma Jie 1947. "Huanghe fanqu xianzhuang yu shanhou jihua" [The Yellow River flooded area's current conditions and rehabilitation plans]. *Shanhou jiuji zongshu Henan fenshu zhoubao* [Weekly report of CNRRA's Henan branch office] 55 (January 27), 1–4.

Ma Jinxiang 1993. "Nanmin yu zaitong" [Refugees and child disaster victims]. *Lushan wenshi ziliao* [Lushan literary and historical materials] 9, 100–101.

Ma Lingfu 1989. "Kangzhan ba nian Xi'an shenghuo de linzhao" [Fragments of life in Xi'an during the eight years of the War of Resistance]. *Xi'an wenshi ziliao* [Xi'an literary and historical materials] 23, 1–30.

Ma Yonghe, Xu Guangdao, and Zhou Xueshi 1991. "Huanghe hen" [The Yellow River's hatred] *Zhongmu wenshi ziliao* [Zhongmu literary and historical materials] 4, 45–46.

MacKinnon, Stephen R. 2001. "Refugee Flight at the Outset of the Anti-Japanese War." In Diana Lary and Stephen R. MacKinnon, eds. *Scars of War: The Impact of Warfare on Modern China*. Vancouver: UBC Press.

MacKinnon, Stephen R. 2008. *Wuhan, 1938: War, Refugees, and the Making of Modern China*. Berkeley: University of California Press.

MacKinnon, Stephen R. 2010. "The Defense of the Central Yangtze." In Mark Peattie, Edward J. Drea, and Han van de Ven, eds. *The Battle for China: Essays on the Military History of the Sino-Japanese War of 1937–1945*. Stanford: Stanford University Press.

MacKinnon, Stephen R. Diana Lary, and Ezra F. Vogel, eds. 2007. *China at War: Regions of China, 1937–1945*. Stanford: Stanford University Press.

Mao Guangde 1991. "Xianyang taonan" [Fleeing disaster in Xianyang] *Zhongmu wenshi ziliao* [Zhongmu literary and historical materials] 4, 74–76.

Marks, Robert B. 2002. *The Origins of the Modern World: A Global and Ecological Narrative*. Lanham, MD: Rowman and Littlefield.

Marks, Robert B. 2012. *China: Its Environment and History*. Lanham, MD: Rowman and Littlefied.

Marten, Gerald G. 2001. *Human Ecology: Basic Concepts for Sustainable Development*. London and Sterling, VA: Earthscan Publications.

Martinez-Alier, Joan 1987. *Ecological Economics: Energy, Environment and Society*. New York: Blackwell.

Martinez-Alier, Joan. 2007. "Marxism, Social Metabolism, and International Trade." In Alf Hornborg, J.R. McNeill, and Juan Martinez-Alier, eds. *Rethinking

Environmental History: World-System History and Global Environmental Change. Lanham, MD: AltaMira Press.
McNeill, J. R. 1998. "China's Environmental History in World Perspective." In Mark Elvin and Ts'ui-jung Liu, eds. *Sediments of Time: Environment and Society in Chinese History*. Cambridge: Cambridge University Press.
McNeill, J. R. 2001. *Something New Under the Sun: An Environmental History of the Twentieth-Century World*. New York: Norton.
McNeill, J. R. 2004. "Woods and Warfare in World History." *Environmental History* 9:3 (July), 388–410.
McNeill, J. R. and Corinna R. Unger, eds. 2010. *Environmental Histories of the Cold War*. Cambridge: Cambridge University Press.
McNeill, J. R. and Verena Winiwarter, eds. 2006. *Soils and Societies: Perspectives from Environmental History*. London: Whitehorse Press.
McNeill, William H. 1977. *Plagues and Peoples*. Paperback edition. New York: Anchor.
Mei Sangyu 1992. *Huayuankou juedi qianhou* [Before and after the Huayuankou breach]. Beijing: Zhongguo guangbo dianshi chubanshe.
Mei Sangyu 2009. *Xuezhan yu honghuo: 1938 Huanghe Huayuankou juedi jishi* [Bloody battle and flood disaster: Record of the 1938 Yellow River breach at Huayuankou]. Beijing: Zhongguo chengshi chubanshe.
Meng Shiheng 1941. "Henan junmai wenti ji qi gaishan jianyi" [Henan's military grain problem and suggestions for resolving it]. *Changcheng* [Great wall] 1:2 (October), 11–17.
Miller, Ian J. 2013. *The Nature of the Beasts: Empire and Exhibition at the Tokyo Imperial Zoo*. Berkeley: University of California Press.
"Minguo ershiqi nian Huanghe juekou zaiqing diaocha biao" [1938 Yellow River breach investigation table] (1938). *Henan sheng jianshe yuekan* [Henan province reconstruction monthly] (September), 144.
Minguo Huanghe shi xiezuo zu 2010. *Minguo Huanghe shi* [History of the Yellow River in the Republican period]. Zhengzhou: Huanghe shuili chubanshe.
Mitchell, Timothy 2002. *The Rule of Experts: Egypt, Techno-Politics, Modernity*. Berkeley: University of California Press.
Mitter, Rana 2005. "Modernity, Internationalization, and War in the History of Modern China." *The Historical Journal* 48:2 (June), 523–543.
Mitter, Rana 2013a. *China's War with Japan, 1937–1945: The Struggle for Survival*. London: Allen Lane.
Mitter, Rana 2013b. "Imperialism, Transnationalism, and the Reconstruction of Postwar China: UNRRA in China, 1944–7." *Past and Present*, Supplement 8, 51–69.
Mitter, Rana and Aaron W. Moore, eds. 2011. "China in World War II, 1937–1945: Experience, Memory, and Legacy." *Modern Asian Studies* 45: Special Issue 2 (March), 225–290.
Mitter, Rana and Schneider, Helen M. 2012. "Introduction: Relief and Rehabilitation in Wartime China." *European Journal of East Asian Studies* 11:2, 179–186.
Muscolino, Micah S. 2010 "Refugees, Land Reclamation, and Militarized Landscapes in Wartime China: Huanglongshan, Shaanxi, 1937–45." *The Journal of Asian Studies* 69:2 (May):453–478.
Myers, Norman 1997. "Environmental Refugees." *Population and Environment* 19:2, 167–182.

Myers, Norman 2002. "Environmental Refugees: A Growing Phenomenon of the 21st Century." *Philosophical Transactions of the Royal Society of London B* 357 (May), 609–613.
Nordstrom, Carolyn 1997. *A Different Kind of War Story*. Philadelphia: University of Pennsylvania Press.
Ó Gráda, Cormac 2008. "The Ripple that Drowns?: Twentieth-Century Famines in China and India as Economic History." *The Economic History Review* 61: Supplement 1 (August), 5–37.
Ó Gráda, Cormac 2009. *Famine: A Short History*. Princeton: Princeton University Press.
Pearson, Chris 2009. *Scarred Landscapes: War and Nature in Vichy France*. New York: Palgrave Macmillan.
Pearson, Chris, Peter A. Coates, and Tim Cole, eds. 2010. *Militarized Landscapes: From Gettysburg to Salisbury Plain*. London: Continuum.
Peattie, Mark, Edward Drea, and Hans van de Ven, eds. 2010. *The Battle for China: Essays on the Military History of the Sino-Japanese War of 1937–1945*. Stanford: Stanford University Press.
Peck, Graham 1967. *Two Kinds of Time: Life in Provincial China during the Crucial Years 1940–1941*. Second revised edition. Boston: Houghton Mifflin.
Pei Qian 1942. "Jiuzai fang'an" [Disaster relief plan]. *Henan zhengzhi* [Henan politics] 1:10 (October), 44–55.
Peng Ruogang 1942. "Henan sheng tianfu gai zheng shiwu zhi jingguo" [The process of Henan province changing to collection of the land tax in kind]. In Qin Xiaoyi, ed. 1988–1989. *Kangzhan jianguo shiliao, Tianfu zhengshi* [Historical materials on national reconstruction during the War of Resistance, land tax collection in kind], *Geming wenxian* [Documents on the Revolution], vol. 116. Taibei: Zhongyang wenwu hongyin she.
Perdue, Peter C. 2005. *China Marches West: The Qing Conquest of Central Eurasia*. Cambridge: Harvard University Press.
Perdue, Peter C. 2010. "Is There a Chinese View of Technology and Nature?" In Martin Reuss and Stephen H. Cutcliffe, eds. *The Illusory Boundary: Environment and Technology in History*. Charlottesville: University of Virginia Press.
Perry, Elizabeth J. 1983. *Rebels and Revolutionaries in North China, 1845–1945*. Stanford: Stanford University Press.
Pietz, David 2002. *Engineering the State: The Huai River and Reconstruction in Nationalist China, 1927–1937*. New York: Routledge.
Pietz, David, and Giordano, Mark 2009. "Managing the Yellow River: Continuity and Change." In François Molle and Philippus Wester, eds. *River Basin Trajectories: Societies, Environments, and Development*. Wallingford: CAB International.
Pimentel, David and Pimentel, Marcia H. 2007. *Food, Energy, and Society*. Third Edition. Boca Raton: CRC Press.
Pomeranz, Kenneth 1993. *The Making of a Hinterland: State, Society, and Economy in Inland North China, 1853–1937*. Berkeley: University of California Press.
Pomeranz, Kenneth 2001. *The Great Divergence: China, Europe, and the Making of the Modern World Economy*. Princeton: Princeton University Press.
Pomeranz, Kenneth 2009. "The Transformation of China's Environment, 1500–2000." In Edmund Burke III and Kenneth Pomeranz, eds. *The Environment and World History*. Berkeley: University of California Press.

Qin Xiaoyi, ed. 1988–1989. *Kangzhan jianguo shiliao, Tianfu zhengshi* [Historical materials on national reconstruction during the War of Resistance, land tax collection in kind], *Geming wenxian* [Documents on the Revolution], vol. 116. Taibei: Zhongyang wenwu hongyin she.

Qinfeng zhaopianguan, ed. 2008. *Kangzhan Zhongguo guoji tongxun zhaopian* [Photographs of China during the War of Resistance from international news bulletins]. Guilin: Guangxi shifan daxue chubanshe.

Qu Changgen 2003. *Gongzui qianqiu: Huayuankou shijian yanjiu* [Merits and wrongdoings for a thousand years: Research on the Huayuankou incident]. Lanzhou: Lanzhou daxue chubanshe.

Qu Changgen 2007. "Kangzhan qijian guomin zhengfu zai Huangfanqu de ziyuan zonghe yu guojia diaodu – yi Yudong diqu wei li" [The Nationalist government's resource synthesis and national management in the Yellow River flooded area during the War of Resistance – eastern Henan as an example]. *Junshi lishi yanjiu* [Military history research] 1 (March), 57–63.

Rawski, Thomas C. and Lillian M. Li, eds. 1992. *Chinese History in Economic Perspective*. Berkeley: University of California Press.

Ren Fuli 1991. "Nongye jiqi kenhuangdui zai Huangfanqu" [The agricultural machinery land reclamation team in the Yellow River flooded area]. *Fugou wenshi ziliao* 2, 173–178.

Ren Fuli 1996. "Gaishu Huangshui zai wo xian fanlan gundong gaidao qingkuang" [General discussion of situation of the Yellow River flooding, rolling, and changing course in our county]. *Fugou xian wenshi ziliao* [Fugou county literary and historical materials] 3, 116–153.

Rogaski, Ruth 2002. "Nature, Annihilation, and Modernity: China's Korean War Germ-Warfare Experience Reconsidered." *The Journal of Asian Studies* 61:2 (May), 381–415.

Russell, Edmund 2010. "Afterword: Militarized Landscapes." In Chris Pearson, Peter Coates, and Tim Cole, eds. *Militarized Landscapes: From Gettysburg to Salisbury Plain*. London: Continuum.

Sawyer, Ralph 2004. *Fire and Water: The Art of Incendiary and Aquatic Warfare in China*. Boulder, CO: Westview.

Schoppa, R. Keith 2011. *In a Sea of Bitterness: Refugees during the Sino-Japanese War*. Cambridge: Harvard University Press.

Sen, Amartya 1981. *Poverty and Famines: An Essay on Entitlement and Deprivation*. Oxford: Oxford University Press.

Sen, Amartya 2000. "Wars and Famines: On Divisions and Incentives." *Peace Economics, Peace Science and Public Policy* 6:2 (Spring), 10–26.

Seow, Victor 2013. "Carbon Technocracy: Energy, Expertise, and Economy in Japan and Manchuria." Paper presented at Asia and the New Energy History workshop, Harvard University, February 22.

Service, John S. 1974. "The Famine in Honan Province." In Joseph W. Esherick, ed. *Lost Chance in China: The World War II Dispatches of John S. Service*. New York: Random House.

Shaan-Gan-Ning bianqu caizheng jingji shi bianxiezu 1981. *Kang Ri zhanzheng shiqi Shaan-Gan-Ning bianqu caizheng jingji shiliao zhaibian, di er bian, nongye* [Excerpts from materials on the fiscal and economic history of the Shaan-Gan-

Ning base area during the Anti-Japanese War of Resistance period, volume 2, agriculture]. Xi'an : Shaanxi renmin chubanshe.
Shaanxi sheng difangzhi bianzuan weiyuanhui 1994. *Shaanxi shengzhi: Nongmu zhi* [Shaanxi provincial gazetteer: agriculture and animal husbandry gazetteer]. Xi'an: Shaanxi renmin chubanshe.
Shaanxi sheng difangzhi bianzuan weiyuanhui 2000. *Shaanxi shengzhi: Dili zhi* [Shaanxi provincial gazetteer: geography gazetteer]. Xi'an: Shaanxi renmin chubanshe.
Shaanxi shifan daxue dili xi Yan'an diqu dili zhi bianxie zu 1983. *Shaanxi sheng Yan'an diqu dili zhi* [Shaanxi province Yan'an area geography gazetteer]. Xi'an: Shaanxi renmin chubanshe.
Shapiro, Judith 2001. *Mao's War against Nature: Politics and the Environment in Revolutionary China*. Cambridge: Cambridge University Press.
Shi Jinghan 1947. "Huangfanqu de zaiqing he xinsheng" [The Yellow River flooded area's disaster conditions and new life]. *Guancha* [Observation] 3:3 (April 13), 22–23.
Shu Xincheng et al. 1940. *Cihai [bingzhong]* [Sea of words (third edition)]. Shanghai: Zhonghua shuju.
Smil, Vaclav 1994. *Energy in World History*. Boulder, CO: Westview.
Smil, Vaclav 2008. *Energy in Nature and Society: General Energetics of Complex Systems*. Cambridge: MIT Press.
Song Hongfei 1996. "Ba nian Huangshui shui suo ji" [Record of eight years trapped by the Yellow River floodwaters]. *Fugou xian wenshi ziliao* [Fugou county literary and historical materials] 3, 150–153.
Song Zhixin, ed. 2005. *1942: Henan da jihuang* [1942: the great Henan famine]. Wuhan: Hubei renmin chubanshe.
Stein, Guenther 1945. *The Challenge of Red China*. New York: McGraw Hill.
Storey, William K. 2010. *The First World War: A Concise Global History*. Lanham: Rowan and Littlefield.
Su Xinliu 2004. *Minguo shiqi Henan shui han zaihai yu xiangcun shehui* [Flood and drought disasters and village society in Henan during the Republican period]. Zhengzhou: Huanghe shuili chubanshe.
Su Xinliu 2009. "1942 nian Henan da hanzai dui diquan yidong de yingxiang" [The influence of the 1942 Henan drought on changes in landholding rights] *Nandu xuetan* [Nandu academic forum] 29:4 (July), 39–40.
Sugimoto Hisashi 1939. "Kanan chihō ringyō gaikan to sono no kensetsuteki ringyō seisaku kō" [An investigation of the forestry system and foreign policy in Henan]. *Nihon ringakkai zashi* [Japan forestry association magazine] 11:8, 46–53.
Sun Yankui 1993. *Ku'nan de renliu: Kangzhan shiqi de nanmin* [Stream of hardship: refugees during the War of Resistance]. Guilin: Guangxi shifan daxue chubanshe.
Szonyi, Michael 2008. *Cold War Island: Quemoy on the Front Line*. New York: Cambridge University Press.
Taikang xianzhi bianzuan weiyuanhui 1991. *Taikang xianzhi* [Taikang county gazetteer]. Zhengzhou: Zhongzhou guji chubanshe.
Tan Jian'an, ed. 1996. *Huanjing shengming yuansu yu Keshan bing shengtai huaxue dili yanjiu* [Research on environmental and life elements and Keshan disease's ecological and chemical geography] Beijing: Zhongguo yiyao keji chubanshe.

Tan Shuangcheng 1991. "Taohuang ji" [Record of fleeing famine]. *Zhongmu wenshi ziliao* [Zhongmu literary and historical materials] 4, 77–79.
Thaxton Jr., Ralph A. 1997. *Salt of the Earth: The Political Origins of Peasant Revolution in China*. Berkeley: University of California Press.
Thaxton Jr., Ralph A. 2008. *Catastrophe and Contention in Rural China: Mao's Great Leap Forward and the Origins of Righteous Resistance in Da Fo Village*. Cambridge: Cambridge University Press.
The Times (London).
Thomas, Julia Adeney 2009. "The Exquisite Corpses of Nature and History: The Case of the Korean DMZ." *The Asia-Pacific Journal* 43:3 (October 26). http://japanfocus.org/-Julia_Adeney-Thomas/3242#sthash.2shsZp11.dpuf.
Tian Leting 2000. "Jiu Zhongguo de Fugou shangye" [Commerce in Fugou in old China]. *Fugou xian wenshi ziliao* [Fugou county literary and historical materials] 4, 75–88.
Tian Lin 1946. "Huayuankou helong hou Huangfanqu de xingjian wenti" [The problem of the reconstruction of the Yellow River flooded area after the Huayuankou closure]. *Pinglun bao* [Commentary] 11 (April 16), 10–12.
Tian Yunsheng 1991. "Huanghe shui li du tongnian" [A childhood spent in the Yellow River's waters]. *Zhongmu wenshi ziliao* [Zhongmu literary and historical materials] 4, 72–73.
Tobe Ryōichi 2010. "The Japanese Eleventh Army in Central China." In Mark Peattie, Edward J. Drea, and Hans van de Ven, eds. *The Battle for China: Essays on the Military History of the Sino-Japanese War of 1937–1945*. Stanford: Stanford University Press.
Todd, O. J. 1949. "The Yellow River Reharnessed." *Geographical Journal* 39:1, 38–56.
Tsutsui, William M. 2003. "Landscapes in the Dark Valley: Toward an Environmental History of Wartime Japan," *Environmental History* 8:2 (April), 294–311.
Tucker, Richard P. 2004. "The World War and the Globalization of Timber Cutting." In Richard P. Tucker and Edmund Russell, eds. *Natural Enemy, Natural Ally: Toward and Environmental History of War*. Corvallis: Oregon State University Press.
Tucker, Richard P. 2011. "War and the Environment." *World History Connected* 8:2 (June) http://worldhistoryconnected.press.illinois.edu/8.2/forum_tucker.html.
Tucker, Richard P. and Edmund Russell, eds. 2004. *Natural Enemy, Natural Ally: Toward an Environmental History of War*. Corvallis: Oregon State University Press.
Tucker, Roy S. 2005. *Tractors and Chopsticks: My Work with the UNRRA Project in China, 1946 to 1947*. Lincoln: iUniverse.
UNRRA 1946–1947. "Honan Weekly Report of Office of the Economic and Financial Advisor."
UNRRA 1948a. *Agricultural Rehabilitation in China*. Opertional analysis papers, no. 52. Washington, DC: UNRRA.
UNRRA 1948b *UNRRA in China, 1945–1947*. Operational analysis papers, no 53. Washington, DC: UNRRA.
van de Ven, Hans 1997. "The Military in the Republic." *The China Quarterly* 150 (July), 352–374.
van de Ven, Hans 2003. *War and Nationalism in China, 1925–1945*. New York: RoutledgeCurzon.

van de Ven, Hans 2010. "The Sino-Japanese War in History." In Mark Peattie, Edward J. Drea, and Hans van de Ven, eds. *The Battle for China: Essays on the Military History of the Sino-Japanese War of 1937–1945*. Stanford: Stanford University Press.
Vermeer, Eduard B. 1988. *Economic Development in Provincial China: The Central Shaanxi since 1930*. Cambridge: Cambridge University Press.
Wadley, Reed L. 2007. "Slashed and Burned: War, Environment, and Resource Insecurity in West Borneo during the Late Nineteenth and Early Twentieth Centuries." *Journal of the Royal Anthropological Institute* 13:1 (March), 109–128.
Waldron, Arthur N. 2003. *From War to Nationalism: China's Turning Point, 1924–1925*. Cambridge: Cambridge University Press.
Walker, Brett L. 2010. *Toxic Archipelago: A History of Industrial Disease in Japan*. Seattle: University of Washington Press.
Wampler, Ernest 1945. *China Suffers; or, My Six Years of Work during the Incident*. Elgin, IL: Brethren Publishing House.
Wan Jin 1947a. "Yi nian lai zhi nongye shanjiu yewu" [Agricultural rehabilitation and relief over the past year]. *Shanhou jiuji zongshu Henan fenshu zhoubao* [Weekly report of CNRRA's Henan branch office] 51 (January 1), 8–13.
Wan Jin 1947b. "Liang nian lai Henan nonggongye zhi jiuji yu shanhou" [Agricultural and industrial relief and rehabilitation in Henan over the past two years]. *Shanhou jiuji zongshu Henan fenshu zhoubao* [Weekly report of CNRRA's Henan branch office] 100 (December 31), 37–43.
Wang Boou 1947. "Heirebing zhi liuxing ji fangzhi" [The prevalence and prevention of kala-azar disease] *Shanhou jiuji zongshu Henan fenshu zhoubao* [Weekly report of CNRRA's Henan branch office] 66 (April 14), 25–28.
Wang Dechun 2004. *Lianheguo shanhou jiuji zongshu yu Zhongguo (1945–1947)* [UNRRA and China (1945–1947)]. Beijing: Renmin chubanshe.
Wang Guanglin 1943. "Jiuzai baogao: Henan sheng diyi xingzhengqu jiuzai gongzuo gaishu" [Relief report: brief account of disaster relief work in Henan province's first administrative area] *Henan zhengzhi* [Henan politics] 2:1/2 (February), 70–76.
Wang Heping 2003. "Qiangu qihuo renjian jienan – zhuiji jiaxiang Huangshui zhi huan" [An unparalled calamity and human disaster – remembering our village's Yellow River disaster]. *Zhoukou wenshi ziliao xuanji* [Zhoukou literary and historical materials selections] 1:2, 117–121.
Wang Jinsheng and Jin Yinghong 1949. "Nongken jiqi zai Henan Huangfanqu de gongji yu zhanwang" [Achievements and prospects for agricultural reclamation machinery in Henan's Yellow River flooded area]. *Kexue shijie* [Science world] 18: 3–4(November/December), 133–135.
Wang Kejian 1947a. "Huangfanqu renmin shenghuo de yiban" [General life of the people in the Yellow River flooded area]. *Shanhou jiuji zongshu Henan fenshu zhoubao* [Weekly report of CNRRA's Henan branch office] 65 (April 7), 3–6.
Wang Kejian 1947b. "Henan fanqu xianzhuang" [Current conditions in Henan's flooded area]. *Shanhou jiuji zongshu Henan fenshu zhoubao* [Weekly report of CNRRA's Henan branch office] 83 (August 11), 2–3.
Wang Kejian 1947c. "Henan Huangfanqu gongzuo teshu" [Special account of work in Henan's Yellow River flooded area]. *Shanhou jiuji zongshu Henan fenshu zhoubao* [Weekly report of CNRRA's Henan branch office] 100 (December 31), 1–12.

Wang Qisheng 2010. "The Battle of Hunan and the Chinese Military's Response to Operation Ichigō." In Mark Peattie, Edward J. Drea, and Hans van de Ven, eds. *The Battle for China: Essay on the Military History of the Sino-Japanese War of 1937–1945*. Stanford: Stanford University Press.

Wang Wanchun 1948. "Gaijin Henan chumu shiye zhi shangque" [Comments on improving Henan's animal husbandry industry]. *Henan nongxun* [Henan agriculture report] 2:3 (March), 6.

Wang Xiaoqiu 1990. "Shui man Hutuo cun ji" [Record of floodwaters inundating Hutuo village]. *Weishi wenshi ziliao* [Weishi literary and history materials] 5, 67–68.

Wang Yuanlin 2005. *Jing Luo liuyu ziran huanjing bianqian yanjiu* [Research on changes in the natural environment of the Jing-Luo basin]. Beijing: Zhonghua shuju.

Watson, John T., Michelle Gayer and Marie A. Connolly 2007. "Epidemics after Natural Disasters." *Emerging Infectious Diseases Journal* 13:1 (January), 1–5.

Weisz, Helga 2007."Combining Social Metabolism and Input-Output Analyses to Account for Ecologically Unequal Trade." In Alf Hornborg, John Robert McNeill, and Juan Martínez-Alier, eds. *Rethinking Environmental History: World-System History and Global Environmental Change*. Lanham, MD: AltaMira Press.

Weller, Robert P. 2006. *Discovering Nature: Globalization and Environmental Culture in China and Taiwan*. Cambridge: Cambridge University Press.

Wemheuer, Felix 2010. "Dealing with Responsibility for the Great Leap Famine in the People's Republic of China." *The China Quarterly* 201 (March), 176–194.

Wen Fang, ed. 2004 *Tianzai renhuo – tianhuo* [Natural disasters and human calamities – natural calamities]. Beijing: Zhongguo wenshi chubanshe.

Wen Yan 2006. "Shi lun kang Ri zhanzheng dui Xibei diqu zaihuang zhi yingxiang" [Tentative discussion of the Anti-Japanense War of Resistance's effect on disasters in the northwest region] *Gansu shehui kexue* [Gansu social science] 2 (March), 82–84.

Westad, Arne Odd 2003. *Decisive Encounters: The Chinese Civil War, 1946–1950*. Stanford: Stanford University Press.

White, Richard 1995. *Organic Machine: The Remaking of the Columbia River*. New York: Hill and Wang.

White, Theodore H. 1978. *In Search of History: A Personal Journey*. New York: HarperCollins.

White, Theodore H. and Jacoby, Annalee 1980. *Thunder Out of China*. 1946. Reprint edition. New York: Da Capo Press.

Wilkinson, Endymion 2012. *Chinese History: A New Manual*. Cambridge: Harvard University Asia Center.

Wojniak, Edward J. 1957. *Atomic Apostle, Thomas M. Megan, S.V.D*. Techny, IL: Divine Word Publications.

Woodbridge, George 1950. *UNRRA: The History of the United Nations Relief and Rehabilitation Administration*, Volume II. New York: Columbia University Press.

World Health Organization 2004. *Vitamin and Mineral Requirements and Human Health*. Geneva: World Health Organization and Food and Agriculture Organization of the United Nations.

Wou, Odoric Y.K. 1994. *Mobilizing the Masses: Building Revolution in Henan*. Stanford: Stanford University Press.

Wou, Odoric Y.K. 2007 "Food Shortage and Japanese Grain Extraction in Henan." In Stephen R. MacKinnon, Diana Lary, and Ezra Vogel, eds. *China at War: Regions of China, 1937–1945*. Stanford: Stanford University Press.
Wrigley, E. A. 1990. *Continuity, Chance, and Change: The Character of the Industrial Revolution in England*. Cambridge: Cambridge University Press.
Wu Shukuan 2004. "Taohuang jishi" [True record of fleeing famine]. *Fugou xian wenshi ziliao* [Fugou county literary and historical materials] 7, 172–176.
Wu Tianbao 1947. "Renli yu shuili de juedou – canguan Huayuankou Huanghe dukou helong jishi" [Struggle between human labor power and water power – a true record of a visit to the Huayuankou Yellow River breach closure]. *Yinhang tongxun* [Banking bulletin] 43, 47–48.
Wu Zhixuan 1944. "Luochuan zhi dizheng yu nongye" [Land policy and agriculture in Luochuan] *Shaan hang huikan* [Bank of Shaanxi journal] 8: 4, 25–38.
Xi Chengfan 1950. "Huangfanqu chongjitu de cengci pailie yu turang shengchanli de guanxi" [The structural arrangement of the Yellow River flooded area's alluvial soils and its relationship with soil productivity] *Zhongguo turang xuehui huizhi* [China soil study association bulletin] 1:2 (December), 103–106.
Xi Chengfan, Cheng Borong, and Zeng Shaoshun 1947. "Huangfanqu turang yu fugeng" [The Yellow River flooded area's soils and the recovery of cultivation] *Turang jikan* [Soil quarterly] 6:2 (June), 29–37.
Xia Kairu 1953. "Yudong Jialuhe liuyu Huangfan chenji [Yellow River flood sedimentation in eastern Henan's Jialu river basin." *Dili xuebao* [Geography journal] 19:2 (December), 245–253.
Xia Mingfang 2000a. "Kangzhan shiqi Zhongguo de zaihuang yu renkou qianyi" [Disasters and population movement in China during the War of Resistance period]. *Kang Ri zhanzheng yanjiu* [Research on the Anti-Japanese War of Resistance] 2, 59–78.
Xia Mingfang 2000b. *Minguo shiqi ziran zaihai yu xiangcun shehui* [Natural disasters and village society during the Republican period]. Beijing: Zhonghua shuju.
Xia, Yiming 2000. "Keshan Disease." In Kenneth F. Kiple and Kriemhild Coneè Ornelas, eds. *The Cambridge World History of Food*, Volume I. Cambridge: Cambridge University Press.
Xie Tonglan 2002. "Huangfan qijian de Poxie" [Poxie during the Yellow River flood]. *Fugou xian wenshi ziliao* [Fugou county literary and historical materials] 5, 99–104.
Xie Yanzhi et al. 1942. *Taikang xuxiu xianzhi* [Continued and revised Taikang county gazetteer].
Xihua xian shizhi bianzuan weiyuanhui 1992. *Xihua xianzhi* [Xihua county gazetteer]. Zhengzhou: Zhongzhou guji chubanshe.
Xing Hansan 1986. *Ri wei tongzhi Henan jianwen lu*. [Record of things seen and heard during Japanese rule in Henan]. Zhengzhou: Henan daxue chubanshe, 1986.
Xing Junji 1996. *Huanghe da juekou* [The great Yellow River breach]. Beijing: Jiefangjun chubanshe, Xinhua shudian.
Xiong Benwen 1947a. "Yi nian lai zhi zhenwu gongzuo" [Relief work over the last year]. *Shanhou jiuji zongshu Henan fenshu zhoubao* [Weekly report of CNRRA's Henan branch office] 51 (January 1, 1947), 14–18.
Xiong Benwen 1947b. "Fanqu shicha guilai" [Returning from an observation trip to the flooded area]. *Shanhou jiuji zongshu Henan fenshu zhoubao* [Weekly report of CNRRA's Henan branch office] 73/74 (June 9), 17–19.

Xiong Benwen 1947c. "Liang nian lai de zhenji yewu yu guan'gan" [Impressions of relief work over the past two years]. *Shanhou jiuji zongshu Henan fenshu zhoubao* [Weekly report of CNRRA's Henan branch office] 100 (December 31), 13–20.

Xiong Xiangyao 1947. "Gongzuo zai Xihua" [Work in Xihua]. *Shanhou jiuji zongshu Henan fenshu zhoubao* [Weekly report of CNRRA's Henan branch office] 67 (April 21), 2–6.

Xu Daofu 1983. *Zhongguo jindai nongye shengchan ji maoyi tongji ziliao* [Statistical materials on agricultural production and trade in modern China]. Shanghai: Shanghai renmin chubanshe.

Xu Fuling 1991. "Kangzhan shiqi Henan sheng Huanghe fanghong" [Yellow River flood defense in Henan province during the period of the War of Resistance]. *Henan wenshi ziliao* [Henan literary and historical materials] 37, 24–30.

Xu Guiyun and Li Yu 2004. "Huangfanqu nongchang zai Fugou fenchang fenbu qingkuang" [Situation of the distribution of the Yellow River flooded area farm's branches in Fugou]. *Fugou xian wenshi ziliao* [Fugou county literary and historical materials] 7, 298–301.

Xu Kan 1997. "Kangzhan shiqi liangzheng jiyao" [Summary of grain policy during the War of Resistance]. In Zhang Bofeng and Zhuang Jianping, eds. *Kang Ri zhanzheng* [Anti-Japanese War of Resistance], *vol. 5: Guomin zhengfu yu da houfang jingji* [The Nationalist government and the economy in the great rear areas]. Chengdu: Sichuan daxue chubanshe.

Xu Shen 121 CE. *Shuo wen jie zi* [Explaining Single Component Graphs and Analyzing Compound Characters]. http://ctext.org/shuo-wen-jie-zi/li-bu9.

Xu Shouqian 1991. "Wo dui Huanghe juekou de huiyi" [My recollections of the Yellow River breach]. *Zhongmu wenshi ziliao* [Zhongmu literary and historical materials] 4, 22–26.

Xu Youli and Zhu Lanlan 2005. "Luelun Huayuankou juedi yu fanqu shengtai huanjing de ehua" [Brief discussion of the Huayuankou breach and environmental degradation in the flooded area]. *Kang Ri zhanzheng yanjiu* [Research on the Anti-Japanese War of Resistance] 2 (June), 147–165.

"Yan min kunku xianzhuang zhongzhong" 1943 [The current difficulties and hardships of Yanling's people]. *Yanling zhoubao* [Yanling weekly] (July 5), 2.

Yang, Dali 1996. *Calamity and Reform in China: State, Rural Society, and Institutional Change since the Great Leap Forward*. Stanford: Stanford University Press.

Yang Hongjuan and Hou Yongjian 2005. "Qingdai Huanglong shandi kenzhi zhengce de xiaoying" [The effects of hilly-land reclamation policy in Huanglong during the Qing period] *Zhongguo lishi dili luncong* [Collected essays on Chinese historical geography] 1 (February), 125–131.

Yang Jisheng 2012. *Tombstone: The Great Chinese Famine, 1958–1962*. Translated by Stacy Mosher and Jian Guo, edited by Edward Friedman, introduction by Roderick MacFarquhar. New York: Farrar, Strauss, and Giroux.

Yang Quesu 2005a. "Guanyu 'Henan haojie' de hua" [On the 'the great Henan disaster']. In Song Zhixin, ed. *1942: Henan da jihuang* [1942: The Great Henan famine]. Wuhan: Hubei renmin chubanshe.

Yang Quesu 2005b. "Yi minguo sanshi niandai chu de yi chang da zainan" [Remembering a great disaster in the early 1940s]. *Xuchang wenshi ziliao* [Xuchang literary and historical materials] 19: 52–62.

Yang Quesu 2005c. "Yi minguo sanshi niandai de yi ci haojie" [Remembering a great disaster in Henan during the 1940s]. In Song Zhixin, ed. *1942: Henan da jihuang* [1942: The Great Henan famine]. Wuhan: Hubei renmin chubanshe.
Yang Xinshan 1991. "Lianheguo shanhou jiuji zongshu ji Zhongguo xingzhengyuan shanhou jiuji zongshu zai Fugou de gongzuo" [UNRRA and CNRRA's work in Fugou]. *Fugou xian weshi ziliao* [Fugou county literary and historical materials] 2, 161–172.
Yanling xian tudi fangchan guanliju 1999. *Xuchang shi tudizhi: Yanling juan* [Xuchang municipality land gazetteer: Yanling section]. Zhengzhou: Zhongzhou guji chubanshe.
Yao Guangyu 1941. "Ruhe zengjia zhanshi nonglin shengchan" [How to increase wartime agricultural and forestry production]. *Yu nong yuekan* [Henan agriculture monthly] 1:1, 1–6.
Yao Guangyu 1942. "Zhanshi nongye laoli wenti" [Wartime agricultural labor problems]. *Yu nong yuekan* [Henan agriculture monthly] 2:1/2, 1–5.
Ye Xiangyu 1991."Dui Huangfanqu kenhuang shenghuo de huigu" [Looking back on life reclaiming wasteland in the Yellow River flooded area]. *Zhoukou wenshi ziliao* [Zhoukou literary and historical materials] 8, 170–174.
"Yijiusisan nian Shuidong dulituan yijiusisan nian gongzuo baogao" [1943 Rivereast independent regiment 1943 work report] 1985. In Sui-Qi-Tai dangshi bianxiezu, ed. *Sui-Qi-Tai diqu shiliao xuan (zhong)* [Selection of historical materials on the Sui Qi Tai area, volume 2]. Zhengzhou: Henan renmin chubanshe.
Young, Arthur N. 1965. *China's Wartime Finance and Inflation, 1937–1945.* Cambridge: Harvard University Press.
Yue Qianhou 2008. *Zhanshi Rijun dui Shanxi shehui shengtai zhi pohuai* [The Japanese army's damage to Shanxi's social ecology during wartime]. Beijing: Shehui kexue wenxian chubanshe.
Zhang Bofeng and Zhuang Jianping, ed. 1997. *Kang Ri zhanzheng* [The Anti-Japanese War of Resistance], vol. 5. Chongqing: Sichuan daxue chubanshe.
"Zhang Fang guanyu Huanghe juekou beizai nanmin ying guangchou yiken ti'an" (1940) [Zhang Fang's proposal that refugees stricken by Yellow River flood should be resettled on a large scale to reclaim land].*Zhengzhou wenshi ziliao* [Zhengzhou literary and historical materials] 2 (1986), 42–45.
Zhang Genfu 2004. "Zhanhuo, ziran zaihai yu nanmin qianyi – Kangzhan shiqi Anhui sheng gean yanjiu [Military calamity, natural disaster, and refugee migration – a case study of Anhui province during the War of Resistance period]. *Minguo dang'an* [Republican archives] 4 (November), 105–111.
Zhang Genfu 2006. *Kangzhan shiqi de renkou qianyi – Jianlun dui Xibei kaifa de yingxiang* [Population movement during the War of Resistance – with a discussion of its influence on the development of the northwest]. Beijing: Guangming ribao chubanshe.
Zhang Huiquan 1947. "Yi nian lai yi weisheng yewu" [Disease and hygiene affairs over the past year]. *Shanhou jiuji zongshu Henan fenshu zhoubao* [Weekly report of CNRRA's Henan branch office] 51 (January 1), 19–22.
Zhang Jinxing 1987. "Huiyi Xi'an beiguan Henan nanmin shourongsuo" [Recollections of the Henan refugee reception center at Xi'an's north gate] *Henan wenshi ziliao* [Henan literary and historical materials] 23, 173–174.

Zhang, Ling 2009. "Changing With the Yellow River: An Environmental History of Hebei, 1048–1128," *Harvard Journal of Asiatic Studies* 69:1 (June), 1–36.

Zhang, Ling 2011. "Ponds, Paddies and Frontier Defence: Environmental and Economic Changes in Northern Hebei in Northern Song China (960–1127)." *The Medieval History Journal* 14:1 (April), 21–43.

Zhang Xianwen 1997. *Zhongguo kang Ri zhanzheng shi, 1931–1945* [History of the Anti-Japanese War of Resistance, 1931–1945] Nanjing: Nanjing daxue chubanshe.

Zhang, Xin 2000. *Social Transformation in Modern China: The State and Local Elites in Henan, 1900–1937*. Cambridge: Cambridge University Press.

Zhang Xishun 2007. "1938–1952 nianjian Huangfanqu de nongcun jingji yanbian qushi – yi Fugou, Xihua xian wei gean yanjiu" [Trends in the evolution of the rural economy of the Yellow River flooded area, 1938–1952 – a case study of Fugou and Xihua counties]. *Xuchang xueyuan xuebao* [Journal of Xuchang University] 26:3 (May), 110–113.

Zhang Xishun 2010. "Shilun minguo shiqi Huangfanqu nongcun shehui jingji fazhan tedian ji chengyin" [Tentative discussion of the special characteristics of social and economic development in the Yellow River flooded area during the Republican period and the causes of their formation]. *Pingdingshan xueyuan xuebao* [Journal of Pingdingshan University] 25:6 (December), 37–41.

Zhang Yihe 2008. *Zhongguo huangzai shi* [History of China's locust disasters]. Hefei: Anhui renmin chubanshe.

Zhang Zhibin and Dianmo Li 1999. "A Possible Relationship between Outbreaks of the Oriental Migratory Locust (*Locusta migratoria manilensis* Meyen) in China and the El Niño episodes." *Ecological Research* 14, 267–270.

Zhang Zhongli 1994. "Huangfanqu nanmin" [Yellow River flooded area refugees]. *Lushan wenshi ziliao* [Lushan literary and historical materials] 10, 133–134.

Zhang Zhonglu 2005. "1942 nian Henan da zai de huiyi" [Reminiscences of the great Henan famine of 1942]. In Song Zhixin, ed. *1942: Henan da jihuang* [1942: The great Henan famine]. Wuhan: Hubei renmin chubanshe.

Zhao Boyan 1985. "Kang Ri zhangzheng shiqi Henan nongcun jingji gaikuang" [General situation of Henan's rural economy during the Anti-Japanese War of Resistance period]. In Henan sheng difang shizhi bianzuan weiyuanhui, ed. *Kang Ri zhanzheng shiqi de Henan – Jinian kang Ri zhanzheng shengli sishi zhounian* [Henan in the Anti-Japanese War of Resistance period – commemorating the fortieth anniversary of the Anti-Japanese War of Resistance]. Zhengzhou: Henan sheng difang shizhi xiehui.

Zhe Fu 1942. "Huangfan jishi" [Record of the Yellow River flood] *Yi zhan yuekan* [First warzone monthly] 1:4 (September), 43–44.

Zhonggong Henan shengwei dangshi yanjiushi 2001. *Yu-Wan-Su bianqu geming shi* [History of revolution in the Henan-Anhui-Jiangsu border area]. Zhengzhou: Henan renmin chubanshe.

Zhongguo dier lishi dang'anguan, ed. 1991. *Zhonghua minguo shi dang'an ziliao huibian* [Compendium of archival materials on the history of the Republic of China]. 5:3:3, vol. 8. Nanjing: Jiangsu guji chubanshe.

Zhongyang diaocha tongjiju tezhong jingji diaochachu 1944. "Liu nian lai Huangfanqu zhi zousi" [Smuggling in the Yellow River flooded area over the past six years] *Diwei jingji cankao ziliao* [Reference materials on the enemy economy] 68.

Zhu Dejun 1986. "Huanglongshan, wo huainian ni! Huiyi feng fu ming jinru Huanglongshan kenqu zhi xing" [Huanglongshan, I cherish your memory! Recollections of receiving my father's orders and travelling into the Huanglongshan reclamation area]. *Huanglong xian wenshi ziliao* [Huanglong county literary and historical materials] 1, 215–229.

Zhu Hanguo and Wang Yinhuan 2001. "Minguo shiqi Huabei nongmin de li cun yu shehui biandong" [North China farmers leaving their villages and social change during the Republican period]. *Shixue yuekan* [History monthly] 1, 134–142.

Zhu Huisen, Jian Shenghuang, and Hou Kunhong, eds. 1990. *Liangzheng shiliao* [Historical sources on grain policy] v. 5, *Tianfu zhengshi* [Land tax collection in kind]. Taibei: Guoshiguan, 1990.

Zhu Xianmo and He Jinhai 1947. "Henan Zhongmu fanqu zhi turang ji qi liyong" [Soils in the flooded area of Zhongmu, Henan and their utilization] *Turang jikan* [Soil quarterly] 6:4 (December), 107–118.

Zuo Zhou 1947. "Wo jiandao de fanqu" [The flooded area that I saw]. *Shanhou jiuji zongshu Henan fenshu zhoubao* [Weekly report of CNRRA's Henan branch office] 85/86 (September 1), 11–13.

Index

Administrative Yuan, 51, 131, 135, 222
advanced organic economy, 11, 16
agriculture, armed forces dependent upon, 7–8, and climate, 90, 92–93, 117–118, and dike construction, 33, 50, 52, 125, 136, 141, disruption by warfare, 17–18, 19, 89, 100, 172, 236, female participation in, 142, 154–155, 170, 219, 245, and Great Leap Forward, 242–243, in Henan, 13–14, 93, land reclamation, 20, 60, 81–86, 165–166, 177, and livestock, 112–113, 148, and military grain transport, 97, postwar obstacles to, 191–193, 197, 204, recovery of, 20, 196–197, 208–209, 213, 227–235, 237, sedimentation and, 184–185, 232–233, as solar-energy system, 11, 134, and wartime floods, 12, 57, 90–92, 120, 128, 134
agro-ecosystems, and energy, 18–19, 100, 175, 234, 236–237, and militaries, 90, 100, 116, post-conflict recovery, 20, 172, 200, 210, 230, 234, and refugee flight, 85, 169, 175, 212, 233, UNRRA-CNRRA reconstruction of, 172–173, 200, 203–204, 234, 242, vulnerability of, 3–4, 17–18, war-induced disruption of, 19, 23, 58, 69, 169
American Civil War, 239
Anhui, dikes in, 35, 46, 52, 121, 135, floods in, 2, 29–30, refugees, 4, 31, relief grain from, 109, sediment deposition in, 184, shelterbelts in, 216
animals, as energy source, 6, 10, 11–12, and militaries, 5, 238, wildlife in flooded area, 66, 85, 178, 235, wildlife in Huanglongshan, 84, 86 (see also specific types of animals)

Baimagou, 53
Baitan, 43, 138

bandits, in flooded area, 66, 221, as guerillas, 143, in Huanglongshan, 82, 84, and Nationalist military collapse, 114, as threat to refugees, 145, 154
Baoji, 17, 79, 158, 161
baselines, for war's ecological impact, 18, 85–86, 243
Beijing, 1, 23, 38, 46
Beiping, see Beijing
Belden, Jack, 56
Belgium, 238–239
Bengal, 2
Biggs, David, 240–241
biomass, for dike repairs, 48, global demand in world wars, 238, scarcity in Henan flooded area, 159, 206, 233, 235, 237, shortage in North China, 77, 86, 159, sold as fuel, 60, 75–77, 86, 193, and trophic pyramids, 8
birds, 66, 178
Blackbourn, David, 246
Boserup, Ester, 170
Brady, Lisa, 239
Brook, Timothy, 38
Burke III, Edmund 6

Cao Wenzhang, 152–153
Caoli, 66
Chang'an, 159
Changsha, 53
Cheng Qian, 25, 27, 34
Chen Ruzhen, 133
Chepil, W.S., 188
Chiang Kai-shek, and breaking of Yellow River dikes, 1, 22, 25–26, 240, and Henan famine, 89, 106, and militarized water control, 34, 41–42
Chinese Civil War, ecological dimensions, 3, 204, 236, and epidemic disease, 180–181,

183–184, expanding Communist influence, 177, 220–221, 225–226, 230, flooded area's role in, 219–220, 225–226, and Huayuankou closure, 202, 238–239, impediment to recovery, 221–223, 224–225, inflation during, 96, and militarization, 245–246
Chinese Communist Party (CCP), in Chinese Civil War, 3, 177–178, 197–204, 218–230, 239, competition for food, 90, 114–119, and militarization, 245, and refugees in Shaanxi, 84, 162, 166, 171, during Sino-Japanese War, 1–2, 38–39, 66, 125, 197, 237
Chinese National Relief and Rehabilitation Administration (CNRRA), health and medical work by, 180–184, and postwar construction, 173, 175, 190–200, 204, 206, 212, 215–218, 230, 233–235, and Huayuankou breach closure, 173, locust control, 213–214, and refugee relief, 174, 205–206, 242, relations with Communists, 224–226, 229
cholera, 63, 145, 160, 179, 181, 182
Chongqing, 27, 34, 106
Christian, David, 118
Ci River, 16, 29
Ciyuan, 10, 12
climate, of Henan, 13, and famine, 90–95, 117, 118
collaborators, grain seizure by, 114–116, and hydraulic engineering, 38–39, 43–46, 51, 125–128, 141, shelterbelts planted by, 76, and smuggling, 73
collective defense, 116–117, 197, 221–222
commerce, 16, 70, 72–75, 113, 179, 191
commodity chains, 8–9
complex systems, 6–7, 19
compulsory purchases, 95–100, 105–108, 112, 139
conscription, and gender, 152–155, 170, Henan as site of, 70, 99–100, 112, for military, 19, 50, 64, 134, 162, 222–223, of labor, 39–40, 47, 51, 54, 97–98, 100, 121, 125, 131, 237
cooperatives, 218–219, 213
Cronon, William, 20
Cumings, Bruce, 240

Dagongbao, 80
Daolinggang, 121, 122, 130, 132, 151
deforestation, in Henan, 13, 76, 148, 170, of Loess Plateau, 14, 81, in North China, 18–19, in Shaanxi, 143, 163–166, 170–171
dikes, in late imperial China, 14–15, 19, 57, deterioration in war, 55–56, 65, 140, 231, 235, 244–245, and disaster control, 2, 32–33, 42–43, 60–62, 64, 71–72, local cost of constructing, 128–135, 136–139, and military conflict in world history, 239–241, and militarized water control, 34–37, 41–43, 46–55, 65, 78, 120–125, 136, 141, 246, Nationalist army's breaching of, 1, 3, 22, 25–32, 57, 60, 117, 239, 242, refugees living atop, 61, 75, 179–180, refugees working on, 151, 155, 177, 180, Huayuankou closure, 187, 201–204, in occupied territories, 37–40, 43–46, 51, 125–128, postwar reconstruction of, 175, 197, 208, 231, strategic breaching in Chinese history, 17, 22, willow trees planted on, 75–76
Dikötter, Frank, 243
disease, and famine, 117, 145, in flooded area, 63–64, 78, 180–184, 200, in Huanglongshan, 82, 168–169
dogs, 148–149, 151
drought, and climate in Henan, 13, 231, and Henan famine, 88, 92–95, 100–102, 110, 115, 138
Duan Yucai, 10
dysentery, 63, 145, 181

Eastman, Lloyd, 88
El Niño Southern Oscillation (ENSO), 2, 90, 92–95
energy, and agro-ecosystems, 17–19, 169, 172, 175, 241, biomass, 60, 75, 85, 193–194, 206, and complex structures, 6–7, for Communist forces, 114, 117, 119, conversion of, 6, definition of, 6, and disease, 180–181, and Great Leap Forward, 242–244, and famine, 88–90, 94–95, 101–103, 117–119, 142, and global history of World War II, 237–238, for human survival, 12, 19–20, 59, 206, and hydraulic engineering, 22–23, 26, 33, 50, 57–58, 120–128, 134–141, and land reclamation, 81, 86, and locusts, 94–95, 213, and military systems, 5–9, 12–13, 57, 118, 236–237, for Nationalist army, 95–102, 106–108, 112–114, 222, and post-conflict recovery, 20, 172, 192, 199, 202, 204, 208, 212, 230, and power, 21–22, and railroads,

56, regimes, 11, 12, 16, 196, 208, of rivers, 5, 12, 21–23, 28, 56, and social metabolism, 4–5, 7, subsidies from UNRRA-CNRRA, 173, 191, 200, 201–203, 233–234, 235, 242, translating, 9–11, 12

epidemics, see disease

environmental infrastructure, concept of, 18, 200, war's impact on, 19, 59, 69, 89, 172, 236, 241, reconstruction of, 233–234, 237, 242, 244, Yellow River as, 23

erosion, in Huanglongshan, 81–82, 143, 164–165, 167, 170–171, in North China, 19, 77, in Shaanxi, 166, of sandy land by winds, 185, 188–189, 209–210, 216, 233, by water, 184, 187–188

Evenden, Matthew, 8–9

famine, and conscription, 99, and Great Leap Forward, 242–244, and gender, 155, in Henan (1942–1943), 2–4, 87–95, 101–119, 134–139, 143–149, 191, and migration, 17, 69, 153, 155–159, 169–170, in North China (1876–1879), 93, 118, in Republican period, 19, 231, and war, 87–88, 89

family, see households

Fanjia, 196

farming, see agriculture

Feng Zhaoxue, 60

fertilizer, 82, 185, 190, 204

Fifteenth Group Army, 36, 121

First War Zone Command, 25, 27, 34–37, 51, 54, 99

Flanders, 238–239

floods, and Henan's geography and environment, 13–16, and migration to Shaanxi, 17, of Yellow River (1938–1947), 1–4, 23–68, 71–79, 90–91, 120–141, 172–177, during 1950s, 239–241, 244, and environmental crisis in North China, 19, 59

fodder, and Henan famine, 102, 107–108, 137, seizure by armies, 67, 97, 100, 137, 143

food, for civilian laborers, 47, 52, 54–55, 127, for Communist forces, 114–117, during Great Leap Forward, 242–244, for Henan's civilian populace, 93, for Huanglongshan settlers, 82–83, 166, 168, inability to transport, 105, 108, 110, and land reclamation, 81, 83, livestock consumed as, 112–113, 148, for militaries, 2, 5, 12, 19, 89–90, 118, 143, 237–238, for Nationalist army, 88, 90, 95–102, 107–108, 111, 113, 221–222, prices, 102–105, and refugee populations, 61–62, 70, 77, 91–92, 143–146, 150–158, 162, 170, 174, from UNRRA-CNRRA, 172–173, 195, 203–209, 215–216, 225, violent competition for, 90, 118, war and famine, 87–89, 117–118

food chains, 7–8

Forman, Harrison, 156

fuel, for militaries, 5, 11–12, 237–238, fossil, 16, 196, 208, 238, for dike repairs, 134, gathering by refugees, 60, 75–77, 85, 86, 144, 149, 165, 193–195, 206, needed by disaster victims, 61, 75, prices, 103, refugee pressure on, 170, scarcity in Henan flooded area, 77, 181, 188, 195, 200, 206–208, 242, 244, seizure by armies, 97, 137, shortages in North China, 19, 76–77, 142–143, for tractors, 212, 226–227

Fugou, 4, dikes in, 33–35, 43–44, 52, 55, 71, 121–123, 134–136, 176, floods in, 29–33, 65–66, 121, 124, 138–140, 175–179, 196, locusts, 94, 213–214, malaria, 183, military activities in, 27, 221, 224–225, nutritional survey, 182, reconstruction and recovery in, 191–194, 196–199, 206–212, 229–231, refugees, 62–65, 72–75, 143–145, 149, 152–154, 160–161, 177, smuggling in, 73–74, soils, 189, 233

Gansu, 17, 109, 161

Gao Zhaolin, 129

Gaoxian, 44, 45

Garnaut, Anthony, 93

gasoline, 196, 212, 226

gender, 42, 149–155, 170

Germany, 239, 240, 246

ghost acreage, 201

Great Leap Forward, 242–245

Greer, Charles, 244

Guangwu, 35, 52, 67, 201

guerillas, Communist, 116, 125, 220–221, 224, 237, and dike construction, 38, 40, in Henan flooded area, 66, 116, 143, warfare and environment, 117, 237, 241, and smuggling, 72–74

Guo River, 16, 30, 43, 51, 54, 56, 114

Guo Chengzhang, 45

Haizhou, 73

Han Dynasty, 10, 18–19

Hankou, 2, 72, 149, 202

Hansiying, 52, 138

He Chengpu, 25
He Yaozu, 34
He Zhuguo, 36, 122, 135
hemp, 48, 100, 159, 164, 202, 203, 208
Henan, disease in, 63–64, 145, 180–184, famine, 2, 87–90, 93–113, 115–119, 144–149, fuel shortages in, 75–77, 193–195, 206–208, geography and environment, 13–21, 92–93, 166, 242, Great Leap Forward in, 242–245, Japanese occupied areas, 38–40, 43–46, 51, 125–128, land tenure in, 216–219, 227–229, locusts in, 94–95, 213–214, military operations in, 24–27, 53–54, 113–114, 219–227, 237, post-conflict recovery in, 20, 172–173, 191–193, 196–204, 208–216, 230–231, 234–235, 242, refugees, 4, 59–71, 77–81, 85–86, 142–164, 167–174, 204–206, 237, smuggling in, 72–74, soils, 184–190, 232–233, war's ecological impact in, 3, 12, 236, 241, wartime hydraulic engineering in, 32–57, 120–141, 236–237, 238, Yellow River floods in, 1–2, 22–23, 28–32, 41, 56, 90–92, 120–123, 130–141, 175–180
Henan Disaster Relief Committee, 158
Henan Repair and Defense Office, 34, 36, 43, 47, 51, 54, 133
Hershatter, Gail, 143, 245
Hong River, 124
Hongze Lake, 30
households, disaster's effects on, 70, 137, 142, 145–155
horses, 107–108, 112, 113, 114, 222
housing, destruction by armies, 74, 194, destruction by floods, 60–61, 64, 70, 91, 122, 136–138, 145, 149, 178, for refugees, 124, 158, 162–163, 165, 174, 179–181, rebuilding of, 150, 199, 206, timbers used as fuel, 75, 137, 194, 207
Hu Minying, 130
Huai River, 1931 floods, 57, and Yellow River, 15–17, 29–30, 56, 173, 231, 235, 245
Huai River Conservancy Commission, 121
Huaihai Campaign, 226
Huaiyang, 4, Communist presence in, 177, 221, floods in, 29, 42, 51, 53, 65, 122, dikes in, 35, 42–43, 51–52, landholdings, 219, locusts in, 94, 213–214, postwar land reclamation in, 212, refugees, 75, 194, UNRRA-CNRRA in, 191, 196, 224
Huang Yanli, 133

Huanglongshan, 17, 81–86, 163–170
Huayin, 158
Huayuankou, dike breach, 26–29, 34–37, 40, 42, 60–61, 77, dike closure, 173, 192, 201–203, 208, 215, 232, and floods during 1950s, 244, sedimentation, 184–187, 233, turnkey project, 245
Hubei, 88, 109
hydraulic systems, energy demands of, 7, 12, 18–19, 57, 85, 120, 135, 169, 200, 236–237, labor and materials for, 22, 39–40, 47–55, 78–79, 125–139, 170, 200–203, vulnerability of, 3, 90–94, 122–124, 144, 237, 242, 244, militarized, 22–23, 34–39, 46–47, 56–58, 121, 128–135, 140–141, 245–246, and warfare in global history, 240–242

Ichigō Offensive, 56, 113–114, 116, 119, 140
inflation, 96, 102–103, 129
insecticides, 213–214
irrigation, 165, 189, 192, 200, 215–216, 245–246

Japan, control of railroads, 108, environment during World War II, 234, 238, grain expropriation by army, 89–90, 99, 110, 115–116, Ichigō Offensive, 113–114, 116, 140, military competition for energy, 11–12, 23, military invasion of China, 1–3, 17, 19, 23–31, 34–35, 41–42, 51, 53–56, 67, 79–80, 84, 95–97, planting of shelterbelts, 76–77, smuggling, 72–74, 78, and translation of Western terms, 10, wartime hydraulic engineering, 22, 37–40, 43–46, 52, 120, 125–129, 141
Ji Luhuan, 126
Jialu River, 16, dikes, 42, 124, 131–132, 135, 140, 237, flooding, 29, 32, 42, 55, 65, 124, 139–140, sedimentation, 56, 178, 184, 186, transport, 16, 73
Jiang Dingwen, 108, 111, 113
Jiang Xiuying, 152–153
Jiangcun, 43, 51, 52, 74
Jiangsu, 2, 30, 31, 73, 121, 182, 184
Jieshou, 52, 73
Jin Mancang, 61
Jin-Pu Railway, 24, 25, 30
Jingshui, 37, 40, 41, 55, 65

Kaifeng, dikes in, 35, 37, 43, 44, 45, 65, 73, disease in, 182, floods in, 29, fuel selling in,

194–195, 199, Japanese occupation of, 25, 40, 72, 73, sandstorms in, 76, 243
kala-azar, 182
Kani Kenhei, 44–45
Keshan disease, 168–169
Korea, 175, 240
Kreike, Emmanuel, 18, 200

labor, for agricultural production, 89, 91, 97, 111–112, 125, 148, and anthropogenic landscapes, 18, 19, 26, 69, 85, 169, 170–171, 236–237, 241, conscription by military, 98, 99–101, 112, 154, 222–223, 237, as energy/power, 12, 21–22, 59, of females, 142, 154–155, 170, for Huayuankou breach closure, 173, 201, 203, for hydraulic engineering, 21–23, 32–33, 35–37, 39–55, 57–58, 64, 78, 120–141, 151, for land reclamation, 60, 81, 86, 166, 168, 177, 196–199, 208, 210, 212, for locust control, 94, 213, mobilization in Great Leap Forward, 242–243, 245, for post-conflict recovery, 20, 175, 190, 191, 193, 200, 204, 230–231, 233–234, 237, 242, of refugees, 69–71, 75, 80, 83, 144, 147, 150, 154, 156, 160–161, 164–165
land reclamation, in Gansu, 161, in Henan flooded area, 128, 175, 177, 196–200, 203, 208–214, 223–229, 232, in Huanglongshan, 60, 82–85, 143, 163–169, and wartime economy, 20, 81, 84–85, Zhang Fang and, 80, 158.
land reform, 221, 223, 227–229
land tenure, 105, 168, 216–219, 227–229
Lary, Diana, 31, 89
Li Hezhi, 147, 148
Li, Lillian, 19, 88
Li Peiji, 91, 125, 135
Liansi, 208, 218, 222
Liu Dongmin, 152–153
Liu Huan, 150–151
livestock, as energy source, 9, 11, 97, 172, 203, destruction in floods, 2, 33, 61, 65, 71, 137, for land reclamation, 82, 83, 196, 208–210, loss during famine, 112–113, 137, 148, requisitioning of, 97, 98, 100, 101, 112, 136, 139, sale to meet tax quotas, 105, shortages of, 78, 109, 111, 138, 178, 185, 191–193, 200
locusts, and Henan famine, 90, 94–95, 111, 115, 118, 143, in Henan flooded area, 136–139, 149, 213–214

Long-Hai Railway, destruction of, 72, 79, 96, and geography of Henan, 16–17, and grain transport difficulties, 96, 108, refugee migration along, 79, 83, 157, 158, 181, strategic importance of, 16, 24–25, 35, 28, 113
Walter C. Lowdermilk, 166
Lower Yangzi, 23
Lu Bingyin, 48
Lu-Su-Wan-Yu Border Area Headquarters, 36
Luohe, floods in, 121, 122, prices in, 103, refugees, 62, 144, 149, 205
Luoyang, grain prices in, 103, 104, refugees, 79, 80, 150, 156, and smuggling, 73, strategic significance of, 73, 113
Lushan, 74, 75, 144, 152–153
Lütan, 72, 132, 134, 197
Luyi, 4, 51, 62, 78, 127

macroparasitism, 118–119, 140, 180, 222
malaria, 63, 179, 183–184
malfeasance, in dike repairs, 78, 127, 129, 133, 139, in tax collection, 97, 101
Malthus, Thomas, 170
Manchuria, 1, 126, 238
Mao Guangde, 79–80
Mao Zedong, 20, 242, 244–245, 246
Marco Polo Bridge Incident, 1, 23
Marks, Robert, 18
Marshall, George C., 202
McNeill, J.R, 11, 234
McNeill, William, 118, 180
Mekong River, 240–241
metabolism, concept of 4–7, 95, 243, human, 120, 142, 175, of militaries, 7–9, 59, 89–90, 116, 236–237
Mi County, 74, 113, 129, 136
militaries, and energy, 4–13, 17–20, 89–90, 236–237
militarization, and environment, 3, 5–9, 17, 246, of hydraulic systems, 34, 57–58, 120–121, 125, 140–141, 203, 237, 245, of Yellow River, 36, 220, 240, 242
Military Affairs Commission, 34, 43, 51, 54, 135
Miller, Ian J., 238
Ministry of Economics, 83
missionaries, 105, 111, 112, 147, 155, relief work by, 62, 93, 109, 110, 158
Mississippi River, 239
mules, 108, 112–113, 148

muscle power, 10–11, 85, 124, 203, 208, 212, 238, scarcity of, 109, 112, 192
Muslim Rebellion, 82
mutual-security units, and conscription, 39, 47, 70, 149, 151, and dike repairs, 48–49, and land ownership claims, 217, livestock protection by, 125, and refugee relief, 63, 152, 162, tax collection by, 100–101, 143, 162, 222

Nanjing, 1, 23, 24
Nanyang, 41, 103
People's Political Council, 98, 129
National Relief Commission, 83
Nationalist government, and breaking of Yellow River dikes, 1–2, 17, 22–28, 31–32, 56–60, Civil War against Communists, 3, 177–178, 180–184, 202–204, 219–221, 224–226, 238–239, conflict with Japan, 1, 23–24, 113–114, famine relief, 106–107, 108, 110–112, 158, 162–163, flood relief, 62–63, 77–79, grain taxes and compulsory purchases, 95–99, 106–107, 118, 143, 221–222, and inflation, 96, 102–103, military conscription, 70, 99–100, 222–223, and post-conflict recovery, 173, 175, 196, 202, 216, refugee resettlement by, 60, 80–84, 86, 163–167, responsibility for Henan famine, 88–90, 119, scorched-earth tactics, 31–32, in southwest China, 238, wartime hydraulic engineering, 34–37, 41–43, 46–56, 65, 78, 120–123, 128–141
Nationalist Party, 46, 158, 218, Long-Hai Railway branch, 145, 157, Xihua branch, 128–129
native-place associations, 160
New Yellow River Dike Repair Commission, 39
nitrogen, 82, 190
North China Plain, as advanced organic economy, 11, 16, anthropogenic environments, 236, and disasters, 59, environmental degradation, 18–19, 86, 231, geography of, 17, locusts, 94, migration, 68
Northern Henan Border Region, 221
nutrition, 63, 107, 145, 160, 167–169, 181–182

Ó Gráda, Cormac, 87, 243
Operation Chastise, 240
oxen, 97, 112–113, 148, 190

Peck, Graham, 155
People's Republic of China, 227–233, 238, 242–245
Perdue, Peter, 118, 244
Perry, Elizabeth, 119
Ping-Han Railway, destruction of 72, 96, and disease, 181, and geography of Henan, 16, and grain transport, 96, 108, strategic importance of, 16, 24–25
Pingxin, 100
population, affected by floods, 66, of Communist-held territories, 177, and environment, 13, 18, 77, 170–171, of Henan refugees in Shaanxi, 79, 157, 161, 173–174, in Huanglongshan, 167, 169, loss due to famine, 87, 112, 137, 144, 156, loss due to floods, 31, 138, 144, recovery of, 230–231, of refugees from Henan, 4, 31, 157, sample from flooded area, 153–154, wartime loss of, 18–19, 173–174, 237
position-power (*shi*), 12
power (*li*), 9–12, 21–22
Poxie, 35, 55, 72–74, 138–139
predation, 118–119, 180
provisional levies, 78–79, 97–98, 139, 152

Qi County, 38, 43, 44
Qiao Guanghou, 32–33
Qing Dynasty, 10, 57, 67, 81–82, 84, 118, 168
Qinghai-Tibetan Plateau, 21
Qu Chuanhe, 125

rabbits, 66, 177
railroads, construction in Henan, 16, 17, 72, destruction, 30, 53, 58, 79, 96, 108, and disease, 181, needed for relief, 109, 205, 224; and refugee migration, 79, 83, 157–158, 204, strategic importance of, 2, 16–17, 24–28, 35, 40, 56, 113, 226
reconstruction and recovery, of agricultural landscapes, 20, 172, 203, 208, 210–213, 227, 229–231, 233–234, 244, Communist role in, 197–199, 223–224, energy subsidies for, 172, 175, 201, 234, 237, 242, labor required for, 112, 174–175, 199–200, 204, 212, loss of energy for, 19, 57–59, 169, 180, 222, 236, obstacles to, 177, 191–193, 200, 224, 246, UNRRA-CNRRA role in, 172–173, 196, 200, 201–206, 208–216, 220, 242
refugees, and disease, 180–184, and environment, 7, 60, 85–86, 143, 169–171,

237, famine, 143–147, 151–152, 155, in Henan, 4, 31, migration to Shaanxi, 7, 79, 143, 155–163, 174, resettlement and land reclamation, 20, 60, 80–85, 86–87, 143, 163–169, return of, 173–174, 180, 194–197, 199, 204–210, 212, 215, 223, 242, survival strategies, 59–60, 68–78, 85, 142, Yellow River flood, 31, 60–68, 90–91, 149–150, 152–154

relapsing fever, 145, 181

relief, famine, 88, 105–113, 118, flood, 33, 57–58, 61–63, 77, 86, 127, 138, in Japanese occupied territories, 45–46, 127, and land reclamation, 80–81, 83, 86, 163–169, in Shaanxi, 79, 80, 158–163, from UNRRA-CNRRA, 172–173, 195, 203–206, 215–216, 222, 224–225, in wartime China, 158, work projects as, 35, 43–44, 47, 52, 80, 121, 151, 196, 212, 216

Republican period, 19, 68

River East Independent Regiment, 38, 115

Rongcun, 121–124, 135–139

Rogaski, Ruth, 2

Russell, Edmund, 7–8, 88

salinization, due to floods, 15, 186, 189, 229, 242, 244, 245, and salt production, 74–75, 78, 189

sand, deposited by Yellow River, 15, 138, 173, 244, and soils in Henan flooded area, 184–190, 211, 216, 229, 232–233, storms, 15, 76, 179, 186–187, 209, 233, 243

Schoppa, Keith, 31

sedimentation, buries farmland, 64–65, 71, 90, 138, 178–179, 207, covers irrigation channels and wells, 192, 215–216, and deforestation, 19, 165, due to wartime floods, 30–31, on Henan plain, 14–15, 16, and hydraulic systems, 23, 57, and post-1949 hydraulic instability, 231, 235, 245, and soils in flooded area, 184–190, 200, 209, 232–233, 235, and Yellow River's wartime shifts, 37–38, 42, 51, 55–56, 120–122, 131–132, 175, 184

seed, during famine, 105, 110, shortages of, 65, 78, 191, 193–195, 200, loans by Communists, 197, 199, 224, 229, loans in Huanglongshan, 72, from UNRRA-CNRRA, 191, 199, 204, 213, 215, 224

Service, John S., 98, 110

Sha River, 16, 42, and Yellow River floods, 29, 51–53, 65, 124, 131, 139, dikes, 42–43, 51, 53, 135, 140, sedimentation, 56, 184, 186, transport, 72, 73

Shaan-Gan-Ning Border Area, 84, 162, 166

Shaanxi, geography and environment of, 14, 17, land reclamation in, 80–86, 143, 163–171, refugee migration to, 60, 79–80, 143–147, 150, 155–163, 173–174, 204, 237, relief grain shipments from, 88, 108–110

Shaanxi Provincial Relief Commission, 162

Shandong, 15, 26, 121, 202

Shangcai, 100

Shanghai, 23, 74

Shangshui, 35, 191, 214

Shanxi, 3, 14, 17

Shao Heniu, 75, 80

Shaying River, 16

Shenqiu, 35, 65

Sherman, William Tecumseh, 239

Shi Andong, 47

Shilipu, 46, 47

Shuangji River, 16, 189, 227, dikes, 33, 135, 136, 140, and Yellow River floods, 46, 65, 124, 140, sedimentation, 56, 124

Shuipoji, 74

Shuo wen jie zi, 10, 12

silt, see sedimentation

Sino-Japanese War (1937–1945), background of, 1, 27, Communists during, 90, 177, environmental impact of, 3, 19, 82, 86, 172, 231, 236, 245–246, and energy, 9, and Henan refugees, 79, 153, Henan's role in, 17, 56, loss of draft animals in, 191, and military grain, 98, scorched-earth tactics, 31, and Yellow River, 22, 69–60, 141

smallpox, 182

smuggling, 60, 72–74, 78, 92

soil, in Henan, 15, 77, in Huanglongshan, 71–72, 143, 164–170, postwar conditions in flooded area, 184–190, 209, 216, 230–233, saline, 75, 78, 184

somatic energy regime, 11, 238

Song Dynasty, 15, 19, 63, 68, 74

Special Are Administrative Supervisors, 36, 53, 130, in Shaanxi, 163–164, in Zhengzhou, 47, 60

Su-Lu-Yu-Wan Border Area General Command, 121

Suiping, 152

Taierzhuang, 24

Taikang: 4, 221, Communist bases in, 115–116, 177, dikes, 37–39, 43–44, 54, 64,

126–127, floods, 31, 42–43, 45, 51, 78, 122, 178, military activities in, 27, 41, 73, reconstruction, 210, 212, refugees, 62, 65, 194
Taiping Rebellion, 239
Tang Enbo, 73, 101, 113, 121, 133, 135
Tao Lüdun, 47
taxes, collection in kind, 95–99, exemption for refugees, 83, and famine, 88, 93, 101–102, 105–107, 137, 143, and hydraulic engineering costs, 134, 139, levied during Civil War, 221–223, reduced by Communists, 199, 224, 227
Thaxton, Ralph, 245
thermodynamics, 6–7
Third Group Army, 41, 54
Thomas, Julia Adeney, 175
Tianjin, 23, 24, 73
Todd, O.J., 173, 187, 212
Toksan Dam, 240
Tongbai Mountains, 15–16
Tongxu, 38, 39, 43, 44, 126, 223
tools, loans by Communists, 224, 229, lost during war, 71, 105, 169, 174, shortages of, 65, 168, 193–194, 200, 208–209, UNRRA-CNRRA distribution of, 194, 215
tractors, 196, 208, 211–212, 215, 217–218, 225–227, 229
trees, cut during World War II, 238, damaged in Henan famine, 147–148, 156, 178, for dike repairs, 32, 44, 55, 75, as fuel, 76, 98, 194–195, 207, and land reclamation, 81–82, 86, 163, 165, scarcity in flooded area, 235, scarcity in Shaanxi, 159, shelterbelts, 188, 216, 233, to strengthen dikes, 129, 132–133
trophic pyramids, 7–8
Truman, Harry, 202
Tsutsui, William, 234
Tucker, Richard, 88, 238
typhus, 63, 160, 181

United States, 34, 201, 202, 239, 240
United Nations Relief and Rehabilitation Administration (UNRRA), in China, 172–173, and flooded area's reconstruction, 173, 180, 190–193, 200, 203–204, 212–216, 233–235, 242, health and medical work, 182–184, and Huayuankou breach closure, 173, 201–203, refugee assistance from, 195, 205–206, 207, 215, relations with Communists, 220–221, 224–226, 229, tractor teams, 196, 208, 211–212, 218, 225, 226–227, 229–230

van de Ven, Hans, 90, 246
Vicksburg, 239
Viet Minh, 240–241
Vietnam, 240–241

Brett Walker, Brett, 88
Wampler, Ernest, 110
Wang Heting, 131–133
Wang Ruiying, 150–152
Wangpan, 41, 43, 51, 54, 122
war and the environment, conceptualization, 4–9, 12–13, 18–20, 236–237, 247, and famine, 87–89, 117–119, historiography of, 2–3, in modern world, 234, 237–242
wastes, 5, 7, 63, 179, 236, 237
wasteland, and domesticated environments, 18, in flooded area, 66, 78, 136–137, 192, 211–214, 227–228, 232, in Huanglongshan, 82–86, 143, 163–166, 169, 171
Water Conservancy Commission, 131, 133
Wei Lihuang, 54
Wei River, 13, 17, 29, 81
Weichuan, 46, 136
Weishi, 4, Communist presence in, 177, 197, death and displacement rate, 31, dikes in, 35, 52, 121–122, 125, floods in, 29, 46, 51, 55, 65, 77, 122, 132, 136, 175–176, hydraulic engineering demands in, 47–50, 124, 134, 136–137, 139–140, locusts, 94, 137, military operations in, 27, 221, postwar reconstruction in, 191, 196, refugees, 61–62, 64, 71, 145–147, 150–152, 160, sedimentation and soils in, 178, 184, 186–187, 189, 233, smuggling in, 74
Weishi Section Emergency Closure Provisional Project Commission, 48
Westad, Odd Arne, 223
White, Richard, 21–22
White, Theodore, 88, 105
wildlife, see animals
women, and agricultural labor, 69, 143, 154–155, 170, 219, 246, in flooded area, 54, 64, 78, 153–154, 155, fuel gathering by, 142–143, 194, 207, refugees, 70–71, 142–143, 145–147, 149–152, 169–170, 205, salt smuggling by, 74–75, 78
wood, cutting in Huanglongshan, 85, 165–166, for dike repairs, 48–49, 55, 136–137, 203, for military, 67, 97, 100,

102, 194, refugee selling of, 75–76, 131, 149, 165, 194–195, for shelter, 159, 206
work, see labor
Wou, Odoric, 16, 89, 99, 116, 197
World War I, 238–239
World War II, aluminum commodity chains in, 8–9, and energy, 11, 48, 236–237, and environment in Henan, 2–5, 19–20, 85, 140, 169, 172, environmental legacy in PRC, 245–246, and global environment, 237–240, and Japan's environment, 234, 238, and Yellow River, 22–23, 238. see also Sino-Japanese War (1937–1945)
work relief, and dikes, 35, 43–44, 47, 52, 121, 182, and UNRRA-CNRRA, 196, 201, 203, 205, 212, 216
Wuhan, 24–27

Xi Chengfan, 232–233
Xi'an, refugees in, 17, 79–80, 150, 156–162, 174, 204, and smuggling, 73, in Sino-Japanese War, 41, 84
Xiangcheng, 35, 65
Xianyang, 79–80
Xiaoyaozhen, 135
Xihua, 4, Communists in, 177, 221, 224, 228, dikes in, 35, 52, disease in, 63, 182, displacement rate, 31, floods in, 29, 65, 122, 124, 138–139, 175–176, 212, famine in, 138–139, fuel shortages in, 206, household survey, 153, landholdings in, 219, locusts, 94, 213–214, postwar landscape, 178–179, postwar reconstruction in, 196, 208, 210, 212, 216, recovery of agriculture in, 230–231, refugees, 70–72, 144, 150, 152, 160, sedimentation and soils in, 178, 184–185, 189, 211, 232–233, seed loans in, 191, shortage of building materials in, 207, wartime hydraulic engineering demands in, 128–133, 136, 139, and Yellow River Flooded Area Farm, 229
Xing Youjie, 38–40, 44–45, 125–127
Xinjiang, 118
Xinxiang, 40
Xinzheng, 74, 113, 136
Xiong Xianyu, 27
Xu Fuling, 36, 50, 55
Xu Guangdao, 71
Xuchang, disease in, 145, floods, 122, fuel shipments from, 206–207, prices in, 103, refugees in, 62, 64–65, 150, 194–195, 204–205, smuggling, 73

Xunmukou, 51
Xuzhou, 24–27, 43, 72, 226

Yan'an, 84, 204
Yang Jisheng, 245
Yang Yifeng, 47.
Yangzi River, 23, 27, 57, 72, 106
Yanling, 4, dikes in, 71, disease in, 145, famine in, 112, 137–138, 144, floods in, 46, 64, 65, 122, 124, 137, 138–139, 140, locusts, 94, military operations in, 27, postwar recovery in, 191, 230, refugees, 64, 74, 75, 155, 160, 161, 194, wartime hydraulic engineering burden, 48–50, 125, 136, 139–140
Yellow River, as actor in World War II, 4, 5, 22, 141, in Chinese Civil War, 219–220, 235, course changes, 15, 16, dikes broken in 1938, 1–3, 17, 22, 25–29, 31–32, 56–58, 60, energy of, 12, 21–22, as environmental infrastructure, 23, flooded territory in Henan, 4, 174–177, floods in 1950s, 244, in Great Leap Forward, 245, and Henan's geography and environment, 13–17, and Huai River, 15–16, hydraulic systems, 23, 57, and locusts, 94, and militarized hydraulic engineering, 34–58, 65, 120–136, 139–142, 151, 238, 241–242, re-diversion of, 172–173, 201–204, 215, 233, and salinization, 74, seasonal floods, 14, sedimentation, 14, 15, 19, 56, 71, 178, 184–190, 209, 216, 231–235, and smuggling, 72–73, strategic diversions in imperial China, 22, wartime flooding of, 29–33, 55–56, 61–62, 65–66, 77–78, 90–92, 122–124, 136–141, 144–145, 149–150, 173–174
Yellow River Conservancy Commission, 32–37, 41–43, 47–53, 77, 121, 128, 131–135, 173
Yellow River Disaster Relief Commission, 33
Yellow River Flooded Area Farm, 229–230
Ying River, 16, dikes, 44, 135, 140, floods, 44, 65, 124, 139, 140, post-1949 control of, 227, sedimentation, 44, 178, 216
Yser River, 238–239
Yu Benyi, 126, 128
Yunnan, 184, 220

Zhang Dingfan, 106
Zhang Fang, 80–81, 158
Zhang Guangsi, 155
Zhang Hanying, 121, 128–129, 133
Zhang Weiya, 130, 133

Zhang Zhizhong, 106
Zhanyang, 66
Zhao Xiuchun, 128
Zhaokou, 26, 27, 29, 40
Zhaolan, 80
Zhecheng, 127
Zhejiang, 158
Zheng County, 4, dikes in, 35, 37, 76, 136, 201, floods in, 55, 61
Zhengzhou, disease in, 181–182, grain prices in, 103–104, 221, in Great Leap Forward, 245, during Henan famine, 156, and Huayuankou breach, 17, 26, Japanese occupation of, 53–54, 99, 113, and railroads, 2, 16, refugees, 62, 65, 69–70, 204, sand deposition in, 233, smuggling, 73, strategic importance of, 24–25, 27, 37
Zhongmu, 4, attempt to break dikes in, 26, dike construction in, 35, 140, disease in, 63–64, dredging in, 54, floods in, 29, 55, 61, 65, 77, 140, military operations in, 27, 53–54, 66–67, postwar reconstruction in, 191, 196, 197, refugees, 31, 71, 79, 194–195, sand deposition in, 185–187, 189, 233, and smuggling, 73, 74
Zhou Enlai, 227
Zhoujiakou, in Civil War, 221, 224, dikes in, 42, 43, 51, 135, 140, floods in, 29, 124, 140, inflation in, 103, and postwar reconstruction, 210, refugees, 62, 65, 75, 179–180, 195, sedimentation in, 186, and smuggling, 73
Zhu Guoheng, 130, 131
Zhuxianzhen, 43

Other Books in the Series (*continued from page iii*)

Nancy J. Jacobs, *Environment, Power, and Injustice: A South African History*

Adam Rome, *The Bulldozer in the Countryside: Suburban Sprawl and the Rise of American Environmentalism*

Judith Shapiro, *Mao's War Against Nature: Politics and the Environment in Revolutionary China*

Edmund Russell, *War and Nature: Fighting Humans and Insects with Chemicals from World War I to Silent Spring*

Andrew Isenberg, *The Destruction of the Bison: An Environmental History*

Thomas Dunlap, *Nature and the English Diaspora*

Robert B. Marks, *Tigers, Rice, Silk, and Silt: Environment and Economy in Late Imperial South China*

Mark Elvin and Tsui'jung Liu, *Sediments of Time: Environment and Society in Chinese History*

Richard H. Grove, *Green Imperialism: Colonial Expansion, Tropical Island Edens and the Origins of Environmentalism, 1600–1860*

Elinor G. K. Melville, *A Plague of Sheep: Environmental Consequences of the Conquest of Mexico*

J. R. McNeill, *The Mountains of the Mediterranean World: An Environmental History*

Theodore Steinberg, *Nature Incorporated: Industrialization and the Waters of New England*

Timothy Silver, *A New Face on the Countryside: Indians, Colonists, and Slaves in the South Atlantic Forests, 1500–1800*

Michael Williams, *Americans and Their Forests: A Historical Geography*

Donald Worster, *The Ends of the Earth: Perspectives on Modern Environmental History*

Samuel P. Hays, *Beauty, Health, and Permanence: Environmental Politics in the United States, 1955–1985*

Warren Dean, *Brazil and the Struggle for Rubber: A Study in Environmental History*

Robert Harms, *Games Against Nature: An Eco-Cultural History of the Nunu of Equatorial Africa*

Arthur F. McEvoy, *The Fisherman's Problem: Ecology and Law in the California Fisheries, 1850–1980*

Alfred W. Crosby, *Ecological Imperialism: The Biological Expansion of Europe, 900–1900*, Second Edition

Kenneth F. Kiple, *The Caribbean Slave: A Biological History*

Donald Worster, *Nature's Economy: A History of Ecological Ideas*, Second Edition

Lightning Source UK Ltd.
Milton Keynes UK
UKHW012020160820
368305UK00001B/28